SPORTSMEN UNITED

THE STORY OF THE
TENNESSEE CONSERVATION LEAGUE

On the cover:

THE TENNESSEE CONSERVATION LEAGUE FIFTIETH ANNIVERSARY QUILT

blank	TCL logo 1946-1968	Industrial Conservationist	Conservationist of the Year	bald eagle	blank
Partners in Flight	Tennessee Valley Sportsmen's Club	Youth Conservationist	tree	TCL headquarters	Lou Williams Founders Award
quilt star	blank	Birds and Biodiversity	Wildlife Conservationist	blank	purple iris
Water Conservationist	Air Conservationist	NatureLink	Land Conservationist	black bear	Governor's Dove Hunt
TCL Presidents 1946–1969	blank	Forest Conservationist	Eagle Volunteer	blank	tree
TCL Presidents 1970–1996	TCL logo 1969–1993	Hunter Educator	purple iris	Legislative Conservationist	Conservation Communicator
blank	Conservation Pledge	TCL logo 1994—	TWRA logo	tulip poplar leaf	blank

THE TENNESSEE CONSERVATION LEAGUE HISTORY PROJECT
WAS MADE POSSIBLE BY THE GENEROUS SUPPORT OF

BRIDGESTONE / FIRESTONE, INC.
CRACKER BARREL OLD COUNTRY STORE FOUNDATION
WALLER LANSDEN DORTCH & DAVIS

SPORTSMEN UNITED

THE STORY OF THE
TENNESSEE CONSERVATION LEAGUE

MARGE DAVIS, PH.D.

Benchtop Books
Mt. Juliet, Tennessee
1997

Printed in the United States of America.

LC 96—79647   ISBN 0—9654561—8—8 (pbk.)

For ordering information, use the form at the back of this book, or contact:
Bench Top Books
45 Burris Court
Mt. Juliet, Tennessee 37122-2001
Phone: (615) 758-8647

The TCL History Project is sponsored by the Tennessee Conservation League,
a not-for-profit membership organization. For more information, use the form
at the back of this book, or contact:
Tennessee Conservation League
300 Orlando Avenue
Nashville, Tennessee 37209-3200 .
Phone: (615) 353-1133

A portion of the proceeds from the sale of this book goes to support the work
and programs of the Tennessee Conservation League.

Sportsmen United: The Story of the Tennessee Conservation League.

Includes bibliographical references and index.
ISBN 0—9654561—8—8 (pbk.)
Suggested cataloguing data:
1. Conservation of natural resources—Tennessee—History.   I. Title.
2. Environmental protection—Tennessee—History.
3. Wildlife management—Tennessee—History.
4. Conservationists—Tennessee.

Library of Congress Catalog Card Number: 96—79647

CONTENTS

ILLUSTRATIONS

ERRATA

In reviewing *Sportsmen United: The Story of the Tennessee Conservation League*, I have found a number of errors. (Sorry about that!) Most are minor typographical blunders, but some are more substantive:

page	para	line	amend to read:
18	3	5	... recently hired chief of the U.S. Bureau ...
24	2	7	... (established officially in 1929).
26	5	6	... to head the Bureau of Biological Survey ...
32	5	5	... founded Ducks Unlimited in 1937.
57	1	4	... Howell Buntin was once again director ...
80	3	6	... would not come until 1957.
126	7	4	... designed for the League's 1969 annual meeting ...
128	4	1	... a fee increase to five dollars in 1966.
146	3	6	... finally got its own magazine in 1977.
297	13	1	... 1937 ... Ducks Unlimited is founded.
307	23	1	... 1977 ... TWRA starts publishing *Tennessee Wildlife*.

Should you find other significant errors not included here, I would be grateful to learn of them. (Perhaps someday there'll be a second printing.)

Marge Davis
BENCH TOP BOOKS
45 Burris Court
Mt. Juliet, TN 37122-2001
(615) 758-8647   fax (615) 754-0966

Foreword

By Gary T. Myers
Executive Director, Tennessee Wildlife Resources Agency

A half-century is a long time. The events of fifty years, taken together, come to define a person—or, in the case of the Tennessee Conservation League, an entire organization.

From the beginning, the Conservation League wanted to be more than just a hunting and fishing club. It did not matter that most of its members *were* hunters and fishermen. They were also naturalists, hikers, campers, amateur biologists, bird watchers and of course, citizen lobbyists. They understood politics, were not afraid of people in high places; and they spent countless hours in committee rooms and legislative offices when they might just as easily have been casting for trout on the Tellico.

Of course, it was largely because of the League that there *was* a Tellico wildlife management area, or that there were any trout in it. Karl Steinmetz, the Knoxville attorney who wrote the bill creating the Game and Fish Commission in 1949, also wrote the agreement creating the Tellico Wildlife Management Area in 1936. Steinmetz used to carry trout fingerlings to the river in his backpack. Later, it would be his TCL colleagues trying to keep a tourist road out of the area, or fighting to save old-growth pine trees for red-cockaded woodpeckers, or lobbying to protect its free-flowing streams.

And that was just one section of the state. The League also joined the fight to save wetlands in West Tennessee, the fight to save open space in Middle Tennessee and the campaign to build sewage treatment plants in every town and city across the state. It praised those who helped protect the environment and it opposed those who would destroy it. To expand its reach, it teamed up with government agencies, businesses and like-minded citizen groups, and it organized seminars and task forces. TCL members served on committees and regulatory boards; a great many of them also served on the Game and Fish Commission (now TWRA). When the Commission faltered, TCL helped put it back on course. When it was threatened, they were the ones who rallied to save it.

Yet even such a long and memorable history as the League's was in danger of being forgotten. Documents had been lost or misplaced, chronologies were getting fuzzy and important happenings were unrecorded or mis-recorded.

And then there were the many little things that might not make history books, but they also influenced outcomes. My experience had been that nothing of significance is accomplished by a single person—it takes lots of people each doing what needs to be done for good things to happen.

That, I think, is what the League has always done best. It has given concerned citizens a forum to put their concerns into concrete action. We all care about the environment, the wildlife and clean water. But how does one person make an impact? Since 1946, TCL has been the collective voice of men and women who loved the natural resources of this state and could not bear to see them wasted.

My only hope is that, after fifty years of progress, the conservationists of Tennessee don't let down their guard. It would be easy to do. Things are probably better now than they have ever been, in terms of wildlife and water quality and everything else. But the founders of TCL understood the need for constant vigilance.

Fifty years is a milestone, but the journey is not over. There are always new challenges, always new threats. And it will be the average unnamed TCL member down in the trenches, fighting the battles and hopefully winning the war. Sure, it takes someone out front like Karl Steinmetz, Lou Williams, Herman Baggenstoss or Lucius Burch to get things rolling. Their contributions are significant. But they would have accomplished little by themselves. All the individual members of TCL had a hand in building this conservation history, their accomplishments are significant, and this is their story, too.

Author's Preface

My grandmother would be happy that I wrote this book. She was one of the great Maine woodswomen of the early century, always eager for the start of deer season, ice-fishing at subzero temperatures, hiking for miles in search of wild fiddleheads. My favorite photo of her (see page xvi) shows a young woman in high leather hunting boots, standing on the shore of some remote northern lake with an enormous fish in each hand. Salmon? Trout? I really have no idea. Fishing and hunting were never my thing. The few times I went fishing with Grammy rank among the most boring experiences of my life.

Writing this book, however, has not been boring. On the contrary, it has given me a new respect for my grandmother and those like her—the sportsmen and sportswomen of the early century, who took a passionate interest in their natural surroundings and worked to protect them. For many of us younger environmentalists, this comes as a bit of a shock. We assume that nobody gave much thought to resource protection before 1970. We think that Earth Day was the turning point for America's environment, and we were the ones who started it.

What I now realize is that we are merely the latest wave of recruits in a battle that has been waging for more than a century. Its first soldiers were the hunters and fishermen.

I first learned about TCL in 1984, when I took a part-time job with the Tennessee Environmental Council (which, incidentally, was created by the League in 1969). At the time, the Council was operating out of the League's offices on West End Avenue. That's how I got to know Tony Campbell, Sue Garner and Alan Polk. It was great fun working around these three (plus, they let Mayo Taylor and me use their envelope-stuffing machine). They always seemed to have a hundred projects going on at once, from organizing those Youth Conservation Summits to researching coon hunting in East Tennessee. Yet even then, I don't think I fully grasped the extraordinary breadth of their activity.

So I was delighted when, just over a year ago, TCL's board of directors asked me to write a new history of the League for its upcoming fiftieth anniversary in 1996. (TCL founder Lou Williams had published a twenty-five-year history in 1971.) I had written about conservation matters before. In fact, TCL had named me its Conservation Communicator of the Year for 1987. Still, it was clear that I would need the help of more seasoned veterans.

Tony Campbell, TCL's executive director for almost a quarter of a century, agreed to serve on the Editorial Advisors Board; so did Dr. Ruth Neff, the first director of the Tennessee Environmental Council and later an environmental policy analyst for the state. Nashville physician Dr. Greer Ricketson had served six years on the Game and Fish Commission, a term as president of the League and twenty years on the board of the National Wildlife Federation, TCL's parent organization in Washington, D.C. Dr. Edward Thackston, chairman of the environmental engineering department at Vanderbilt University, had been environmental policy advisor to Governor Winfield Dunn in the early 1970s. He had also been a director of the League since 1974, including two terms as president.

The chairman of this excellent team was Mike Pearigen, a former deputy attorney general for Tennessee and now a partner in the Nashville law firm of Waller Lansden Dortch & Davis, where he specializes in environmental law. It was Mike who proposed this book, Mike who secured the necessary funding and Mike who recommended me to write it.

For that I'm grateful—though at first I wasn't so sure. Assembling the data of a half-century is a daunting task in any case, harder still if some of the archives are missing. The League has kept excellent records since 1972, when it opened a full-time office, but only a few odd scraps survived from the early years. I put out a frantic appeal for help from members' private collections. Frankly, if Herman Baggenstoss and Doc Jernigan hadn't been such packrats, this history, at least the first half of it, would have been scanty indeed.

Obviously, original documents are crucial to tell a story that has not been told before. Apart from Lou Williams' 1971 history and a few general studies of American conservation, published books were of little use to me except as background. Most of the information in these pages comes from the minutes of League board meetings, official (and sometimes unofficial) correspondence, proceedings of annual meetings, newspaper clippings and of course, the League's own *Tennessee Out-of-Doors.*

I relied heavily on back issues of *The Tennessee Conservationist* and *Tennessee Wildlife* (the 1930s version), as well as its modern incarnation published since 1975 by the Tennessee Wildlife Resources Agency. The wildlife agency's annual reports were priceless, especially those from the 1950s and 1960s, when they actually divulged stuff like who had been hired and who had been fired. I also spent a good deal of time in the State Archives, the microfilm room at Vanderbilt and the Vanderbilt law library, where I spent days huddled in the stacks, surrounded by two centuries of Tennessee Public and Private Acts.

Most of these sources are listed, collectively if not individually, in the bibliography. However, with the blessing of the Editorial Advisors Committee, I decided against using footnotes. This is an informal history, not a scholarly one, and most casual readers find footnotes intrusive and unnecessary.

But scholarly or not, I have tried to give this book a measure of accuracy and detail that will make it a useful reference not only for members of the League but for all Tennesseans with a stake in resource conservation and an interest in the outdoors. The text has been scrutinized by many eyes besides mine, and I have double-checked as much of the information as possible. Nonetheless, it is ultimately my work, and I am responsible for its shortcomings.

Marge Davis
March 1997

Acknowledgments

Many good folks—and some very patient ones—deserve thanks for their contributions to this book. First, I must thank the Editorial Advisors Committee, Dr. Ruth Neff, Dr. Greer Ricketson, Dr. Edward Thackston, Tony Campbell and chairman Mike Pearigen. They helped define the shape of this book in the beginning, guided it through the months of research and writing, and gave it careful readings at the end. I particularly wish to thank Ed Thackston, who devoted countless hours to reading, advising, and rereading; and also to Mike Pearigen. As founder of the book project, Mike bore much of the anxiety for seeing it completed.

I'm also grateful to Gary Myers, executive director of the Tennessee Wildlife Resources Agency, who provided an eloquent foreword, shared some wonderful anecdotes and set me straight on a number of points. I'm grateful to all of the wildlife professionals at TWRA, especially Ron Fox, David McKinney, Bob Hatcher, Larry Marcum and Bill Reeves. Dave Woodward, chief of Information and Education, let me reproduce as many photographs as I wished. TWRA receptionist Paulette Fuqua loaned me a truly priceless resource, nearly fifty years of the agency's annual reports.

Several individuals provided irreplaceable archival materials. Mrs. Mary Elizabeth Baggenstoss of Tracy City gave me several boxes of records that Herman had saved from his long years with the sportsmen's groups, including a complete set of *Tennessee Wildlife* magazines from the 1930s and the minutes of the very first meeting of the Conservation League in 1946. Mary Elizabeth has generously donated these materials to TCL's permanent collection, finally restoring some of the written history that has been missing for many years.

Outdoor writer Joe Halburnt of Maryville, probably the only surviving member of the fifteen incorporators of the League, shared a wealth of memories, as well as his personal copy of the first *Tennessee Valley Sportsman*. (I am grateful to Mrs. Mae Evans, Mr. Halburnt's assistant at the short-lived magazine, for putting me in touch with her former boss.) Thanks, also, to V. H. "Doc" Jernigan of Manchester, who shared several old photographs and documents as well as his extensive file of clippings from the 1960s. Owen Schroeder, outdoor writer for the *Leaf Chronicle* and a former president of the Tennessee Outdoor Writers Association, gave me a copy of the TOWA history compiled by Doc Jernigan.

Several of the League's affiliates trusted me with photos dating back many decades. I am indebted to Bob McConnell and Loyd Ezell of the Highland Sportsman Club, Mr. H. C. Hardy of the Nashville Sportsman's Club; and Bob Burns and Marvin Johnson of the Tennessee Valley

Sportsmen's Club for granting me such generous access to their collections. The League itself has a massive collection of photographs, including many given to the League by its affiliates. I have credited these donors as accurately as possible, but in some cases I could only credit "TCL file photo." I apologize for any unintended slights or oversights.

Several publications allowed me to reproduce, without charge, photographs that had appeared in their pages over the last half-century. Thanks particularly to Tom Stanford, picture editor at *The Tennessean*; Lee Anderson, publisher and editor of the *Chattanooga Free Press*; Henry Stokes of the Memphis *Commercial Appeal*; Louise Zepp, editor of *The Tennessee Conservationist*; Turner Hutchison, *Nashville Banner* photographer and outdoor writer; Joseph H. Bailey, *National Geographic Society* photographer; and Ron Smith, managing editor of *The Chattanooga Times*, whose photographer (known to posterity only as "staff") captured the historic image of twelve founders assembled at the Read House on that winter afternoon in 1946.

Buford Wilson of Waverly, whose grandfather Robert A. Wilson took over "Fins, Furs and Feathers" in the *Nashville Banner* in 1912, let me borrow several precious archival materials, as well as hundreds of fragile, yellowed clippings hoarded by his grandfather more than half a century ago.

Many individuals helped by granting interviews, answering questions and pointing me to further resources: J. Clark Akers, III, of the National Ecological Foundation; Mack Prichard of the Tennessee Department of Environment and Conservation; Bill Griswold and Ray Norris of the Tennessee Scenic Rivers Association; Chattanooga historian Dr. James Livingood; Cecil Branstetter, past League president and a founder of the Tennessee Environmental Council; Sheila Shay of the Environmental Action Fund, Sierra Club, Audubon Society and just about every other environmental organization in Tennessee; Paul Somers, formerly a botanist with the Tennessee Natural Heritage Program, now with Massachusetts' environmental agency; Sam Pearsall of the North Carolina office of The Nature Conservancy; Gina Latendresse of the American Pearl Company; Carolyn Waldron of the National Wildlife Federation; Nathaniel Winston, Jr., son of League founder Nat T. Winston; Sam Venable, Jr., of *The Knoxville News-Sentinel*; Dodd Galbreath, director of the Tennessee Environmental Policy Office; Hart Applegate of the Tennessee Division of Forestry; C. Ron Culberson of Tennessee's Division of Air Quality Control; Dan Eagar of the Division of Water Pollution Control; Larry Bowers, formerly with the same agency, now with Wheland Foundry; Don Anderson of TVA; Manley Fuller of the Florida Wildlife Federation; and Mark Reefe of the International Association of Fish and Wildlife Agencies. Thanks also to the three men who headed Tennessee's first environmental agencies: Harold Hodges of the Division of Air Pollution Control, Tom Tiesler of the Solid Waste Management Division and S. Leary Jones, director of Tennessee's original water quality agency, the 1945 Stream Pollution Control Board.

Fish and wildlife agencies around the country were most helpful as I tried to put Tennessee's conservation history into a national context. Pennsylvania's Bruce Whitman, for instance, sent a complimentary copy of *Pennsylvania Game Commission 1895-1995*. I got valuable historical background also from Arkansas' Stephen Wilson, Michigan's George Burgoyne, Jr., North Dakota's Harold Umber, Charles Sledd of Virginia, Lynn Garrison of

Kentucky, Bill Phippen of Montana, Ken Moum of South Dakota, Bob McDowell of New Jersey, Terry Mansfield of California, Diane Ronayne of Idaho, Ron George of Texas, Iowa's Allen Farris, Corky Pugh of Alabama, Al Langston of Wyoming, Michael Budzik of Ohio, James Cardoza of Massachusetts, Nels Rodefeld of Oklahoma, Richard Hamilton of North Carolina, John Crenshaw of New Mexico and W. Brock Conrad, Jr., of South Carolina.

In addition to Ed Thackston and Mike Pearigen, several members of the TCL board and conservation policy board helped by providing documents, data, interviews and other background. Thanks especially to Larry M. Richardson, Mitchell Parks, Bill Miller, Dick Urban, Rosemary MacGregor, Mark Benko and Judge Lee Asbury. It goes without saying that the staff at TCL have been uniformly helpful, especially Ann Murray and Sue Garner.

But the bottom line is that without the support of the three Nashville-based underwriters, this book would not have happened at all. Whatever they may think of the final product, Tennessee's conservationists should be grateful to Bridgestone / Firestone, Inc., the Cracker Barrel Old Country Store Foundation and the law firm of Waller Lansden Dortch & Davis for subsidizing an unprecedented conservation research project.

My final and best thanks go to my husband, Paul Davis, director of the Tennessee Division of Water Pollution Control. His practical wisdom and technical knowledge made this project much easier. His patience, humor and constant encouragement made it possible.

SPORTSMEN VS. SPORTSWOMEN: A WORD ABOUT USAGE

When women may belong as well as men, how does one properly refer to the people who make up the nation's sporting clubs? Are they, in spite of increasing numbers of women, still to be called sports*men*? Sportsmen-women? Sports*persons*? Fifty years ago, when the Tennessee Conservation League was founded (by a roomful of men), this question would never have come up. But it is an issue today.

In general, I use the term "sportsmen" and "sportsmen's clubs" to refer generically to America's organized hunters and anglers. It is a convenient and familiar shorthand, and means no disrespect to the growing numbers of women who are taking to the fields and streams. If there were a more inclusive term that was just as efficient, I would use it. Unfortunately, language doesn't always keep up with changes in society.

My grandmother, Alice Knapp,
somewhere in the Maine woods,
circa 1925.

INTRODUCTION

THE POWER OF SPORTSMEN'S CLUBS

[T]he organized sportsmen [of Tennessee] can have anything of
a rightful nature they see fit to ask for in unity, and in a perfect spirit
of harmony. Ten thousand men as members of the Federation
... can easily control one hundred thousand votes.

—Matt G. Thomas, in *Organization News of the*
Tennessee Federation of Sportsmen, June 1936

THE ROAD TO THE READ HOUSE

Ten years after Matt Thomas tried to calculate the power of Tennessee's unified sportsmen, they were about to offer renewed proof of it.

On February 12, 1946, in a room of Chattanooga's new Read House, fifty-three men from around the state had gathered to build a new organization on the ashes of the old one. They called themselves the Tennessee Conservation League, to signify a broadened agenda, but in fact they had the same central objective as before—namely, to restore the state's wildlife by removing the state's wildlife agency from political control.

Within twenty-four hours of the meeting, every major newspaper in the state had heard of the new group and its agenda. Within a few months, several dozen chapters had signed up, representing several thousand members. Within a year, club leaders were drafting a law to spell out their proposed reforms; within two years they had secured the full support of the governor-elect.

Finally, on February 25, 1949, just three years after its founding, the Tennessee Conservation League saw its model fish and game law pass both houses of the Legislature with overwhelming majorities. At the League's third annual meeting in Knoxville in April, the program bore the headline *VICTORY*. It referred, of course, to the success of the model law. But if the sportsmen-conservationists of Tennessee had mastered the art of the well-organized offense, they had also learned the value of a good defense. Already their program had been broadsided by opponents in the House, and further assaults were guaranteed. To relax their grip now would, they knew, be as good as throwing away the new program altogether.

They were right to be vigilant. Within a few years, the commission form of wildlife administration came dangerously close to repeal. But its supporters were ready. The model law survived the 1953 skirmish relatively unscathed, as it has survived every challenge since.

Victory, therefore, came by degrees. Though passing the model law was certainly significant, the acid test of the League's power would lie in defending it. That the law is still intact after almost fifty years is remarkable. That the League itself is still intact may be even more so.

THE STRONG SURVIVE

Like any volunteer organization, sportsmen's clubs were often plagued by lack of money, lack of committed volunteers and even sometimes a lack of focus. As one writer of the period noted, many clubs seemed to wither away almost as soon as they were formed. J. N. "Ding" Darling, the great sportsman-cartoonist who founded the National Wildlife Federation, often taunted sportsmen for their lack of staying power. Even the Tennessee Federation of Sportsmen, the group Matt Thomas had such high hopes for in 1936, was all but dead by the end of the decade.

Some clubs, however, not only survived but flourished. Their leaders had the right combination of vision, experience, enthusiasm and something like business acumen to keep the club always vital, always moving forward. If the club stalled—as indeed the League has done several times over the last fifty years—they had the good grace to look within for the causes, and correct them. They did not make the mistake, as the Tennessee Federation of Sportsmen may have done, of vesting too much responsibility in a single individual. The best clubs nurtured their supporters and did not readily antagonize their opponents. They developed a strong political presence without becoming politicized themselves. They picked their battles carefully, and fought them with facts. Through it all, they kept their focus squarely on what mattered most—the wise use of resources.

The Tennessee Conservation League seemed to understand all these things instinctively. Almost from the moment of its forming, it was considered the most powerful conservation organization in the state. The Tennessee Ornithological Society, founded in 1915 by several of Middle Tennessee's leading naturalists and sportsmen, was much older and certainly effective, but its interests were narrower, nor was it overtly political.

Of course, things were different fifty years ago. Today the field is much more crowded, and many of the newer environmental organizations have built strong programs and reputations of their own. Still, by any appropriate measure, TCL continues to lead the pack. It continues to have enviable access to lawmakers, regulatory agencies and community leaders. It is still solicited for its opinions on wildlife management and habitat protection issues, even as it forges new ground in the environmental issues of the next century, especially land-use planning and global diversity. It is attracting a broader range of supporters than ever before, not just hunters and fishermen but social conservationists, folks whose chief concern is preserving not just wildlife but life itself.

And though the numbers of hunters and anglers who now belong to the League have dropped from what they were forty, thirty, even ten years ago, they still wield the sort of collective force that Matt Thomas envisioned back in 1936.

THE OUTDOOR WRITERS ISSUE A CALL TO ARMS

Yet that strength should be understood in context. Unique as it may be in Tennessee, the League is a cog in a much larger wheel, a nationwide network of sportsmen and sportsmen's clubs that originated more than a century ago, drawn together not so much by their mutual pleasure in the outdoors as by their growing sense that those pleasures were in jeopardy.

"Most sportsmen's clubs were formed initially because people who liked to hunt and fish were concerned about something that threatened their interests," wrote Chuck Griffith in a 1981 article for the National Wildlife Federation. "A single issue often [was] the catalyst needed to put such an organization together." The very first conservation group in the country—the New York Sportmen's Club, formed in 1844—was organized at least in part to preserve fishing in and around New York City, a sport even then showing signs of exhaustion.

By the 1870s, the single galvanizing issue that brought these sportsmen together—if such a complex of causes and effects can be called a *single* issue—was the steady, unchecked decline of wildlife on a continent that had at one time been legendary for its immense supplies of large and small game, waterfowl, fish and birds. Market hunting and poaching accounted for much of the loss, but so did sport hunting and game fishing. Moreover, as the industrial age gathered steam, the early conservationists became aware of a new threat: the loss of habitat. Logging, drainage projects, industrial waste, municipal sewage, dams, farming and urban development—the nation was on the move, but its economic progress was doing serious damage to the national ecosystem.

Nowhere were these complaints so persistently expressed as in the outdoor media that emerged around this time. The first of the national periodicals, *American Sportsman*, appeared in 1871; *Forest and Stream* debuted two years later. *Field and Stream* came out in 1874, *American Angler* in 1881. Dedicated to the principles of good sportsmanship and intelligent wildlife management, these magazines resonated deeply with America's sportsmen. Writers like George Bird Grinnell and Charles Halleck not only put into words the sportsman's vague fears about the disappearing fish and game. More important, they explained the reasons for their disappearance and convinced readers they could do something about it.

Whether the outdoor journalists merely tapped into a movement that was already brewing, or whether their editorials touched it off, by the winter of 1874-1875 America's sportsmen had coalesced into nearly a hundred sportsmen's organizations all over the country, ten or twelve state associations and one national association. We know that at least one of the earliest clubs was in Tennessee. Chattanooga's McRae Club was founded by Z. Cartter Patten, Sr., and several of his friends in 1865.

So enthusiastic was this so-called "club movement," according to George F. Reiger in *American Sportsmen and the Origins of Conservation*, that when *Forest and Stream* editor Charles Halleck published the *American Club List and Sportsman's Glossary* in 1878, the numbers of sportsmen's clubs and fishing associations had more than tripled, to 342 nationwide. By century's end, the fledgling community of sportsmen-conservationists included such legendary organizations as the original Audubon Society, founded by George Bird Grinnell in New York in 1886, and the Boone and Crockett Club, founded by Teddy Roosevelt and some of his cronies in 1887.

Though still a young man in 1887, Roosevelt was even then (and always with the guidance of his friend George Grinnell) developing the perceptions and values that would eventually make him the most important president in America's environmental history. By the time he got to the White House in 1901, and for the two terms that he stayed there, Roosevelt never wavered from his early commitment to scientific wildlife management, manifested in everything from his establishment of a national wildlife refuge system to his belief in the "wise use" of natural resources.

RALLYING THE RICH AND POWERFUL

That men of the stature of a Theodore Roosevelt or a Dr. Grinnell or even a Z. Cartter Patten should be involved in the club movement was crucial to its success, but it was no accident. The early sportsmen's movement was largely a phenomenon of the upper classes, organized by highly educated, articulate, well-connected and well-heeled men. When Teddy Roosevelt invited a select few of his sportsmen friends to dinner in Manhattan to propose the Boone and Crockett Club, the group included John J. Pierrepont, Rutherford Stuyvesant, J. West Roosevelt and five others—all thoroughly patrician. Another of Roosevelt's inner circle was the powerful Tennessee jurist Jacob McGavock Dickinson, secretary of war under President Taft and one of the first presidents of the Izaak Walton League of America.

The state organizations tended to be equally weighted with men of stature. Tennessee's Robert Love Taylor, a U.S. Senator as well as two-term governor, was a prominent member of the Tennessee Game and Fish Protective Association, the first statewide conservation group in Tennessee. Judge Marshall Morgan, later an honorary member of the Tennessee Outdoor Writers Association, began writing what was reportedly the nation's first outdoor column, "Fins, Furs, Feathers and Other Comment," in the *Nashville Banner* in 1906. Lawyers, doctors, businessmen, bankers, professors, industrialists, engineers, journalists and philanthropists dominated the ranks of Tennessee's organized sportsmen from the first.

Apparently there was even a bit of snobbery among the hunting elite. Though the vast majority of early hunters and fishermen in this country were average fellows who took to the field mainly to feed their families, there seems to have been a certain class consciousness. As early as 1771, for instance, the New Jersey Legislature passed a law condemning hunting by the "great numbers of idle and disorderly persons [who] made a practice of hunting on the waste and unimproved lands in this colony, whereby their families are neglected, and the public is prejudiced by the loss of their labor." The only ones allowed to hunt on these "unimproved lands" were the citizens who were qualified to vote—that is, men who already owned estates of their own.

If the New Jersey statute sounds rather stuffy, it had its precedent in early English law, which restricted hunting to the ruling classes, forbade commoners to carry arms and imposed harsh penalties (including death) on poachers. Though Americans rejected the notion that outdoor sport was a privilege *conferred* by social class, they nevertheless seemed to accept that it could *imply* class. That attitude got a boost in the late 1830s, when a wellborn Englishman named William Herbert moved to America and began writing essays on hunting and fishing under the pseudonym "Frank Forester." Readers were fascinated by his descriptions of such quintessentially British sports as grouse shooting and fly-fishing, just as they were charmed by his insistence on fair play and sporting etiquette. Suddenly field sports began to acquire an almost aristocratic respectability, proof alike of a man's talent and character.

"THE STYLE, THE DASH, THE HANDSOME WAY" OF THE SPORTSMAN

According to the system of ethics espoused by Forester and his followers, the ideal sportsman "had to have a knowledge of the quarry and its habitat; a familiarity with the rods, guns, or dogs necessary to its pursuit; a skill to cast or shoot with precision and coolness that often takes years to acquire; and most of all, a 'social sense' of the do's and don'ts involved." These "do's and don'ts" made up what was generally called the sportsman's code, an unwritten but powerful system of honorable behavior. As defined by one of the magazines of the period, genuine sportsmanship lay not in "the mere killing" or the certainty of killing, nor in the monetary value of the things killed, but rather in "the vigor, science, and manhood displayed . . ., in the true spirit, the style, the dash, the handsome way of doing what is to be done, and above all, in the unalterable *love of fair play*."

Such flattering associations probably did as much for the rapid growth of the clubs as their commitment to outdoor sport. It was a badge of honor, a mark of quality, to belong to a leading sportsmen's club, and in fact, some became as exclusive (and expensive) as today's country clubs. Almost all the great Adirondacks clubs, for instance, required that new members be sponsored and approved by existing members. Once voted in, members had to abide by strict rules of conduct regarding everything from marital status to dinner dress. Such exclusivity may seem silly today, but in fact it was one of the reasons the clubs were so successful. Men who were leaders in their workplaces and communities soon became leaders in the conservation movement.

They all, in their respective ways, applied their professional resources to the needs of their clubs. The lawyers drafted by-laws; the industrialists provided capital; the academics wrote policy; the politicians introduced bills; the journalists wrote articles. As for the businessmen, they helped create a management standard that has characterized the best sportsmen's clubs ever since: the notion, in short, that a successful club can and should be run very much like a successful business, with multiple levels of leadership, ongoing product development, short-term and long-range planning, rigorous bookkeeping and aggressive marketing. A 1927 expansion plan for the Izaak Walton League called for "[a]n administrative organization ... comparable with the executive business organization of any large corporation with numerous branch houses." The duties of this organization, the plan continued, should include "aggressive national publicity[,] sales methods, development, inspiration and promotion."

If members' professional acumen was useful in managing the club, it was no less so in getting the conservation message before the lawmakers. These were men of standing, men who understood the political process and knew how to use it to their advantage. Already accustomed to having the ear of their elected representatives in professional matters, they expected to have it in matters of leisure also. And to a remarkable degree they did.

As Dr. Durwood Allen of Purdue University would later put it, "Sportsmen can talk to the President of the United States ..., to the secretaries of Interior and Agriculture and to their Senators and Congressmen. They can talk to the governor, the legislator, the commissioner and to the field man who is doing a fine job on some particular problem. They can go over anybody's head and get facts where they choose without apology—the sportsman can do these things impossible for the administrator, biologist and public relations man."

HEALTHFUL, MANLY AND INVIGORATING: THE VIRTUES OF SPORT

But there was another reason America's sportsmen had such political clout: the almost mythic popularity of hunting and fishing. By the beginning of this century, and especially in rural states such as Tennessee, hunting and fishing were as common, and almost as sacrosanct, as sandlot baseball. Indeed, by some accounts, outdoor sport was one of the virtues that made America great. "Americans are pioneer people," suggested an executive for E. I. DuPont de Nemours, the gunpowder manufacturer, in 1927. "The ability to think and act quickly and independently is a distinctly American pioneer trait. ... [developed] especially [in] hunting, fishing and camping." The most famous sportsmen's club in the nation, the Boone and Crockett Club, was named for two of Tennessee's legendary pioneer huntsmen.

In many states, and certainly in Tennessee, state legislators and chief executives tended to be sportsmen themselves, and represented districts where sport was a vital part of life. Until *Baker v. Carr* (one man, one vote) reapportioned political power after 1962, rural interests ruled Tennessee politics well into this century. Even if an individual legislator were not personally fond of fishing or gunning, he understood that many of his constituents were. He also understood that for many of these families, hunting and fishing were more than just pleasant diversions; they helped put food on the dinner table, whether directly, in the form of fresh venison or fish fillets, or indirectly, through such corollary enterprises as bait shops or cabin rentals. For these folks, good hunting and healthy fishing must have seemed an inalienable *right*, up there with life, liberty and the pursuit of happiness.

Indeed, judging by some of the prose of the period, outdoor sport in those days bore almost a religious aura. Robert (R. A.) Wilson of Nashville, who took over Judge Morgan's "Fins, Furs and Feathers" column in 1912, tried repeatedly, and in terms more of poetry than sport, to convey the profound joy he found in fishing. "The spirit of spring broods over a regenerated world," he rhapsodized in 1922. "[T]he winding stream, singing merrily on its way to the river, insistently calls the angler. ... To [him] no music is sweeter than the song of the reel." Wilson referred frequently to the Biblical adventurer "Cush, son of Nimrod," thereby invoking not only the ancient associations of hunting but the endorsement of Scripture itself.

Outdoor sport was considered a singularly wholesome, uplifting, even a highly moral pastime. Fishing, wrote Washington Irving, produced "a gentleness of spirit, and a pure serenity of mind." Hunting, wrote George Perkins Marsh in *Man and Nature*, produced "healthful and invigorating" effects, including "hardy physical habits," "quickness of eye, hand, and general movement" and "dexterity in the arts of pursuit and destruction." Hunting gave a man courage, self-reliance and a "half-military spirit"—all "elements of prosperity and strength in the bodily and mental constitution of a people."

That outdoor sport restored one's physical as well as mental and moral well-being was a frequent conceit. In *Adventures in the Wilderness*, an 1869 account of hunting and fishing in New York's Adirondacks, the Reverend William H. H. Murray told of a feeble and dying man from the city who found his cure in the woods: "[The] healing properties of the balsam and pine, which were his bed by day and night, began to exert their power," wrote Murray. "Their pungent and healing odors penetrated his diseased and irritated lungs. The second day out his cough was less sharp and painful. At the end of the first week he could walk by leaning on the paddle. The second week he needed no support. The third week the cough ceased entirely."

The notion that wilderness purified the soul was a basic tenet of romanticism; and in fact, sport was heavily romanticized in the nineteenth century. *Home From the Woods: The Successful Sportsmen*, an 1867 lithograph by Currier and Ives, depicts two sturdy huntsmen entering the front hall of their handsome home, carrying their bulging game bags and followed by their loyal hunting dogs. While the womenfolk admire the catch, a well-mannered groom leads away their horses. The not-so-subtle message, of course, was that hunting was somehow linked to prosperity, virility and domestic comfort.

For even though vast portions of the United States were still utterly remote and unsettled well into the present century, Americans as early as 1867 felt they were living in an age increasingly dominated by industry and development. The simple, primitive pleasures of hunting and fishing must have seemed a comforting antidote to that perceived growth.

SPORTSMEN UNITED

It is easy to understand, then, why the sportsmen of the twentieth century were so aggrieved by the pending loss of such security and well-being. The loss of good fishing and hunting were assaults on America itself. It did not matter that hunting and fishing were no longer matters of literal survival. To sportsmen, they were matters of spiritual survival, the preservation of what one writer called the "heritage" of fifteen million Americans. "Unless we learn to give as well as take," said an executive at E. I. DuPont de Nemours, "it [is] possible that even within our own lives we shall be deprived of all pleasures afield and astream."

This was the call to arms that echoed throughout the first half of the twentieth century. By 1946, it had called fifty-three men to Chattanooga from every part of Tennessee.

CHAPTER 1

AMERICA'S CONSERVATION CRISIS

*The disquieting fact is that though game protection in the
United States is now more than two hundred years old,
it has not protected the game.*

—George D. Pratt, New York
commissioner of conservation, around 1934

IN THE BEGINNING, ABUNDANCE

Considering the vast numbers of mammals, fish, waterfowl and bird life that inhabited this continent around, say, the time of the first British settlements, the remnants that survived into the twentieth century seem almost inconceivably minuscule. Bison herds that had once exceeded fifty million had all but disappeared by the end of the 1800s. The white-tailed deer herd, once estimated at 35 million nationwide, numbered as few as 300,000 by 1900. While many deer had ended up on pioneers' dinner tables, many more had been killed for trade by Indians and white men alike. In the mid-eighteenth century in South Carolina, for instance, traders shipped 160,000 buckskins to England in a single year.

Tennessee had been a particularly rich hunting ground. In 1714, a French trader named Charleville built a trading post on the site of a natural salt lick at what is now Castalian Springs, just east of Nashville on Lick Creek. His principal trade was buffalo tongues and tallow, which he bought from local hunters and shipped down to New Orleans. The property soon grew so thick with buffalo bones that they made a grisly kind of carpet. As a later visitor recalled, "One could walk for several hundred yards around the Lick and in the Lick on buffalow skuls and bones and the whole flat around the Lick was bleached with buffalows bone, and they found out the cause of the canes growing up so suddenly a few miles around the Lick which was in consequence of so many buffalows being killed."

In his famous 1780 voyage up the Cumberland River, Nashville settler John Donelson described killing many buffalo along the riverbanks, as well as along the Stones River near his home at Clover Bottom. John Haywood, a member of the party, described the scene as he stood on a bluff overlooking what is now Nashville: "Nothing was presented to the eye but one large plain of woods and cane, frequented by buffaloes, elk, deer, wolves, foxes, panthers and other animals suited to the climate." Buffalo were widespread in East Tennessee also, noted in Hamblen County, for instance, in 1761, and throughout what is now the Cherokee National Forest. Though buffalo were all but extirpated in Tennessee by the late nineteenth century, sightings were recorded on the Tellico River as late as 1872.

The state's deer herd at the time of white settlement was certainly in the millions; one report told of ten thousand deer quarters being traded in a single season from a single area in the Cumberland Mountains. In 1788, the governor's salary in the State of Franklin (the 1784 settlement that preceded the formal statehood of Tennessee) was set at one thousand deer skins per annum; the chief justice received half that many. Small game species were so plentiful that lesser administrators were paid in pelts of otter, beaver, mink or raccoon. The treasurer's salary, for instance, was fixed at 480 otter skins; justices received one muskrat skin each time they signed a warrant, while the constable got a mink pelt for serving it. By 1900, most of these furbearers had been decimated by the market trade, though otter were still common at Reelfoot Lake as late as 1896.

Reelfoot was even more of a hunter's paradise then than it is now. Davy Crockett supposedly killed 105 bears around the lake in a single winter; "a hog could not live [at Reelfoot] for the bears," said a reporter in 1848. A Carroll County man named R. S. Cole recounted that during his annual fall excursion to the lake in 1848, "[w]e hunted in Dyer County on Mill Creek and killed two deer then crossed at the head of Obion Lake and went to Stones Ferry on Reelfoot Lake and camped on the Blue Bank Bayou at Crocketts pasture and killed 12 deer and 22 turkeys and possums." During the same trip, one of his party "got a shot at a panther but did not kill it"; on another outing Cole recorded killing a "catamount"—probably a cougar. Cougar (variously known as panther, puma or mountain lion) were present in Tennessee if not numerous. According to naturalist Albert Ganier, early settlers claimed to have lost small children to cougars, and it is certain they lost livestock to them. Early reports placed the big cats on the Tellico River in 1762, in Davidson and Smith Counties in 1780, and in Shelby and Lauderdale Counties as late as 1896. In 1928, Ganier said, they were all gone except for possibly a half dozen in the Smokies. One was reported near Johnson City in 1929, another on Roan Mountain in 1937.

Grey wolves were first recorded in Johnson County in 1673. In 1795, John Lipscomb saw two buffalo bulls pursued by a wolf, while settlers in Nashville were so harassed by the animals that they built pens to catch them. In 1839 the General Assembly offered a bounty of up to ten dollars for wolves killed in Morgan County. A female with pups was reported killed in Wayne County in 1917; another account placed a grey wolf in Cumberland County in 1919.

Elk were abundant throughout the state, noted in East Tennessee by 1673, near Nashville in 1779 and at French Lick as late as 1859. Davy Crockett referred to elk in Obion and Dyer Counties in 1834. And though one report claimed the last one around Reelfoot was killed in 1849, at least one more was recorded in Obion County at the end of the Civil War.

Waterfowl must have been numerous beyond counting, because in 1905, when the declining duck population forced Tennessee's legislators to limit the daily bag, they set the limit at fifty ducks per hunter, *per day.* Wild turkey, upland game birds and small game were everywhere: grouse, rabbit, quail, groundhog, squirrel. John Donelson wrote of killing a swan, "which was very delicious"; robins and other songbirds were likewise considered delicacies. Fisher and porcupine were rare, according to records, but there were probably some red fox, and certainly there were grey. It was a land of more than plenty.

THE SCOURGE OF MARKET HUNTING

It is hard to imagine that such abundance could ever be depleted, but it was. By the end of the nineteenth century, the nation's wildlife stocks had reached crisis levels. While legitimate sportsmen were responsible for a fair share of the carnage, and poachers for still more, the single most devastating threat to wildlife was the commercial trade in fish and game.

Furbearers were at particular risk in an economy based on goods rather than cash. In the State of Franklin, for instance, a "good, clean beaver skin" was worth six shillings, twice the value of a gallon of brandy; otter skins brought five to six shillings; raccoon and fox, one shilling and three pence each. It was the same story all over the country. According to a manifest from the Dutch West India Company, a single ship left the Hudson River Valley in 1626 loaded with the pelts of 675 otters, minks and muskrats, and 7,246 beaver skins. Beaver were probably saved from extinction only by the shift in European fashion from beaver-felt to silk hats in the mid-1800s.

The commercial slaughter of waterfowl, game birds and songbirds was, if possible, even more bloody. By 1900, wild turkeys that were once known to gather into "veritable armies" every fall had become rare or extinct in every state except Pennsylvania. On a single summer day in 1863, hunters on Massachusetts' Nantucket Island shot more than seven thousand golden plovers and Eskimo curlews, quitting only when they ran out of gunpowder and shot. In 1871, shooters converging on a flock of passenger pigeons in south-central Wisconsin wiped out a single nesting flock estimated at 136 million birds, leaving behind a "rancid wasteland" of decaying and mutilated bodies.

The extent of the country's passenger pigeon flock at its height was almost unimaginable, an estimated nine *billion* birds as late as 1850. In Tennessee, flocks of pigeons blackened the sky and blotted out the sun. In Michigan, a single colony was alleged to have been twenty-eight miles long and four miles wide.

Although the greatest threat to the pigeons may have been the loggers who clear-cut the beech and hickory forests where they spent their summers, market hunting hastened their extinction. With no laws to stop them, and with wholesale pigeon prices as high as fifteen to twenty-five cents per dozen, the market pigeoners trapped entire flocks in enormous pigeoners' nets, lured there by decoy "stool pigeons," so-called because they were made to flutter mechanically on raised platforms called stools. In spite of eleventh-hour efforts to save her, the last passenger pigeon, a female named Martha, died at the Cincinnati Zoological Gardens on September 1, 1914.

THE LAW OF SUPPLY AND DEMAND

But as greedy as the profit hunters may have been, they were, after all, merely supplying a demand. In the nineteenth century and even into the twentieth, wild game and fish were staples not only in the average American diet but on the bills of fare of the finest restaurants. Consider the staggering variety of game dishes offered by Nashville's famous Maxwell House Hotel on Christmas Day, 1879: leg of Cumberland Mountain black bear, Tennessee opossum, Kentucky raccoon, roasted quail, saddle of Minnesota venison, canvasback and redhead ducks, blue-wing and wood ducks, roasted wild turkey, wild goose, young prairie chickens, broiled pheasants, roasted mallard duck, legs of young rabbits, boned wild boar's head and buffalo tongue.

According to outdoor writer Marshall Morgan, a visitor to downtown Nashville at the turn of the century could still buy a broiled quail dinner for twenty-five cents. In fact, it was a picture of quail hanging by their necks in a Cherry Street (now Fourth Avenue) restaurant that triggered the 1911 law prohibiting the sale of bobwhite and robins—including those "served under any fictitious name."

Nor were edible species the only ones at risk. The catalyst behind the New York Audubon Society in 1886 (the "original" Audubon Society; the national association didn't form until 1905) was the grotesque Victorian practice of decorating women's hats with whole birds or bird parts, including songbirds and waterfowl. Such showy species as the peacock and snowy egret were in particular danger. In an editorial in the February 11, 1886, edition of *Forest and Stream* announcing his idea for a bird protection society, George Bird Grinnell decried the gruesome trade:

> Statistics are as yet wanting to show the proportions to which this traffic has grown in North America, but we know that it reaches well into the hundreds of thousands. Some figures published in *Forest and Stream* of August 4, 1884, showed that in a three-months' trip a single taxidermist collected bird skins to the number of 11,018, which, including specimens too badly mutilated for preservation, and skins spoiled in the making, would perhaps represent a destruction of 15,000 birds. This same person states that he handles annually about 30,000 bird skins, almost all of which are used for millinery purposes.

Grinnell's plea—and the resulting millinery boycott by hundreds of New York society matrons—led to state and federal bans on the sale of nongame birds or bird parts. The Tennessee General Assembly banned the practice in 1903.

The methods used to take wild prey were varied, ingenious and often cruel. A 1917 promotional catalogue issued by E. I. DuPont's sporting powders division described the various methods of hunting the Canada goose: "On the Maine coast it is hunted amid the drifting ice with a gunning float partly disguised by a piece of ice on the bow. . . . From Maryland south a water-tight box is often used. . . . In the corn belt geese are shot from pits dug in the fields." The same booklet recommended brant hunters load up their guns during "severe easterly storms" when the birds would be "exhausted by their battle with the elements." Fishermen were equally inventive, dynamiting rivers, placing seines across the mouths of streams and building homemade fish traps, crude wooden contraptions shaped like a giant funnel with no exit.

THE SPORTSMEN SPEAK OUT

So badly, indeed, had the nation's wildlife been depleted by the turn of the century that many observers took it as a matter of course that hunting and fishing would never recover. In their view, it was only a matter of time before increasing demand outstripped dwindling supplies. In 1906, geologist W. J. McGee (the man credited with first using the term *conservation* to describe natural resource protection) defined wildlife management as "the use of the natural resources for the greatest good of the greatest number for the longest time." Restrictions would delay, but could not prevent, the mass extinctions McGee and others felt were inevitable.

Fortunately, not everyone was so fatalistic. Many sportsmen, and the small but growing ranks of trained game and fish personnel in both state and federal governments, believed that wildlife *could* be not only restored but infinitely sustained. First, they said, states had a responsibility to protect game and fish, and they must do so rigorously. By the early 1900s every state in the union had some manner of wildlife code, including penalties for violators. Tennessee's first law, for instance, passed in 1833, made it illegal to kill fish by poisoning the streams.

On March 26, 1870, Tennessee gave itself formal permission to protect wildlife when the thirty-sixth General Assembly approved the revised Constitution of 1870, the one still in use today. According to Article XI, Section 13,

the General Assembly shall have power to enact laws for the protection and preservation of game and fish, within the state, and such laws may be enacted for and applied and enforced in particular counties or geographical districts, designated by the General Assembly.

The lawmakers lost no time putting their new Constitutional privilege to work. When the thirty-sixth General Assembly convened again two months later, in June 1870, lawmakers passed the first in a long line of private (local) wildlife acts. One act banned the use of any fishing device except hook-and-line or trot line in twelve Middle Tennessee counties; another banned deer hunting with dogs in Benton and Humphreys; and a third set a closed season on deer, game birds and songbirds in Shelby, Rutherford and Fayette counties, thus creating the first closed season in the state's history. In the coming years, lawmakers would use the powers of Section 13 to ban the export of game, outlaw the hunting of songbirds, establish statewide closed seasons on wild turkey and deer, set fines for violators, require market and sporting licenses and a host of other strong and much-needed wildlife regulations.

But regulating the individual [sportsman] and market hunter was only a small step, said the conservationists. The time had come to stop the commercial trade in fish and game altogether. Few Americans still depended on wild game for food, they argued; and where such dishes as elk, grouse or wild duck were still served in restaurants, the prices were so high as to make them a luxury. As George Reiger has documented, the appeal to ban market hunting was spearheaded by the outdoor journals, especially *Forest and Stream*, which ran this front-page editorial in 1894:

> For four centuries … we have been killing and marketing game, destroying it as rapidly and as thoroughly as we knew how, and making no provision toward replacing the supply. The result of such a course is that for the most part the game has been blotted out from wide areas, and today, after four hundred years of wanton wastefulness, we are just beginning to ask one another how we may preserve the little that remains, for ourselves and our children.
>
> … [T]he markets are answerable for a larger proportion of game destruction than any other agency or all other agencies combined. … The work of the sportsman, who hunts for the sake of hunting, has had an effect so trivial, that in comparison with that of the market hunter it need not be taken into consideration. The game paucity of to-day is due to the skin hunter, the meat killer, [and] the market shooter. …
>
> Well, then, why not recognize this, and direct our efforts, in line with such a recognition, toward the utter abolition of the sale of game? Why should we not adopt as a plank in the sportsman's platform a declaration to this end—*That the sale of game should be forbidden at all seasons?*

Once again, *Forest and Stream* proved prophetic. In 1896, the U.S. Supreme Court ruled, in *Geer v. Connecticut*, that states have a right to claim ownership of all wildlife living within their borders. By upholding states' jurisdiction over resident wildlife, this important precedent made it possible for them to outlaw market hunting and fishing. Over the next ten years, almost every state would declare its game and fish to be public property. Tennessee passed its first such law in 1903, stating that "the wild game within this state belongs to the people in their collective capacity. It is not the subject of private ownership." In 1907, the General Assembly stipulated the same thing for fish.

Since individuals could not sell something that did not belong to them without permission, there was an end to the great majority of market hunting, though there were exceptions—the trapping and selling of animal furs, for example—and exemptions—fishermen would continue to sell crappie and other game fish from Reelfoot Lake almost uninterrupted. Still, as Lou Williams points out in *Tennessee's Conservation Revolution* (1971), the 1903 statute was perhaps the most significant of any conservation bill passed in the state before or since, because it provided the legal basis for virtually every other protective act that followed.

"UTTER CHAOS": THE PRIVATE WILDLIFE ACT

However, important as the 1903 law was, Tennessee had undermined it thirty-three years earlier when it sanctioned the private wildlife act. The 1870 Constitution, remember, provided that wildlife laws "may be enacted for and applied and enforced in particular counties or geographical districts, designated by the General Assembly."

Private acts were not necessarily bad things, at least not at first. All three of the private acts passed in June 1870, for instance, had placed reasonable restrictions on hunting and fishing in their respective counties. In the 1800s, in a state with virtually no protective laws for wildlife, and certainly no central agency in charge of its welfare, the private act was sometimes the only recourse a concerned sportsman or thoughtful community had.

But far more often, the private act was used not to create restrictions but to weasel out of them. Within a year, the three acts passed in 1870 were already unraveling—at the request of the very counties that had asked for them in the first place. The ban on dog-hunting in Humphreys and Benton counties was repealed; six of the twelve counties in the 1870 fish law decided they wanted their names taken off the list. In 1873, Stewart County became number seven.

The unfortunate precedent had been set. As J. Charles Poe, commissioner of Conservation under Prentice Cooper, said in 1942, the repeals and exemptions unleashed "[u]tter chaos." (Prentice Cooper was one of only two governors to take a strong stand against private wildlife acts. In fact, both Cooper and Governor Malcolm Patterson banned them, Cooper in 1939, Patterson in 1907.) Often laws were passed in one session only to be overturned the next. A March 1875 law banning profit hunting for ducks at Reelfoot Lake, for instance, was repealed in March 1877. In 1899, the General Assembly passed forty-three private wildlife acts in one session, a record.

By the time Tennessee passed the first general (statewide) wildlife law in 1875, the counties had no intention of taking it seriously. That law, which banned seines or fish traps near the mouths of streams (among various other restrictions), was supposed to apply to all ninety-five counties, but forty counties were specifically listed as exempt, along with "all counties in East Tennessee" not already on the list.

Bad as this was, it soon got worse.

The state's first general game law, an act regulating deer and quail hunting, was passed in 1889; *sixty-five* counties were listed as exempt. When the 1905 Legislature set a bag limit on ducks and closed the deer season for two years (a ban that would not be lifted until 1919), thirty-two counties claimed immunity. "Every effort to establish a sound statewide wildlife conservation program was thwarted by local exemptions." said Commissioner Poe.

By the time Tennessee hired its first state game warden, Joseph Acklen, in 1903, private acts had become the scourge of the state's struggling wildlife program. They were, said Colonel Acklen, "wholly ineffective, [tending] only to confuse and not to enlighten. ... A law that is good enough for one county should be good enough for all the State." Yet political forces being what they were, and selfish interests being what *they* were, the private act was firmly entrenched.

THE BIG STICK: FEDERAL INTERVENTION

Private acts were not peculiar to Tennessee, however; far from it. In Texas in 1883, for instance, 130 counties claimed exemption from every single game law in the state! State laws had other limitations, too. For one thing, adjacent states often had differing statutes, tempting hunters in more regulated states to sell their kills in states where the laws weren't so strict.

(For years, fishermen from Missouri and Arkansas laundered their crappie through the Reelfoot market, since Tennessee was the only state still allowing trade in game fish.) Where good laws did exist, they were often poorly enforced or ignored entirely. Third, state ownership laws did not in general apply to migratory wildfowl, since ducks, geese and many insect-eating songbirds regularly crossed state boundaries in their annual migrations. Said James Trefethen in *Crusade for Wildlife*, "The result was a grim competition to see which state could kill the greatest number before the migrating flocks passed from the range of its hunters' guns."

To most conservationists, it was clear that some sort of uniform control was needed that would override the differences of individual states. Such regulation would have to be federally mandated, they said, for voluntary compliance would probably not work. In 1866, the American Ornithologists' Union had written a model law for any state wishing to use it to protect their nongame birds. The trouble was, only five states took advantage of it.

John F. Lacey, an Iowa Congressman as well as a prominent member of the Boone and Crockett Club, was one of the first to see that federal intervention was necessary to resolve the weaknesses and inconsistencies in state laws. Lacey, author of the historic 1894 Yellowstone Park Protection Act granting federal immunity to all natural resources in the nation's first true national park, now offered a bill making it illegal to transport illegally-killed game across state lines. Despite the reluctance of some states to recognize what they considered an infringement of their rights, the Lacey Act passed easily on May 25, 1900, and the country had its first federal wildlife management law.

Robert A. (R. A.) Wilson wrote the weekly "Fins, Furs and Feathers" in the Nashville Banner *from 1912 until about 1939. Begun in 1906, the popular Sunday feature was said to be the first outdoor column in the country. Courtesy of Buford Wilson.*

WEEKS-MCLEAN: PROTECTION FOR WATERFOWL

Government control over migratory waterfowl was much harder to come by, however. Unlike the Lacey Act, which affirmed state ownership of wildlife, the proposed migratory bird acts required that states cede custody of waterfowl to the federal government. As Dian Olson Belanger notes in her excellent history of the International Association of Fish and Wildlife Agencies (IAFWA), many states flatly refused to make such a concession. When the first migratory bird act was introduced in Congress in 1904, it did not even make it out of committee. Similar attempts failed in 1906 and 1908. Gradually, however, the opposition was being won over. The ducks were still disappearing, only now it wasn't just the hunters, ornithologists and wildlife biologists complaining. Now they were joined by the businesses that sold guns, ammunition and gunpowder. Realizing that fewer birds meant fewer sales, a coalition of firearms manufacturers organized in 1911 as the American Game Protective Association (forerunner of the American Wildlife Institute).

Supporters were ready to try again. In 1912, Senator George McLean of Connecticut and Congressman John Weeks of Massachusetts—both Republicans, as so many of the early conservationists were—introduced a new migratory bird bill. Besides placing all migratory game and insectivorous birds "within the custody and protection of the government of the United States," Weeks-McLean placed strict limits on market hunting and spring shooting. In what was probably the first large-scale partnership between conservationists and industry, the American Game Protective Association lobbied hard for the bill, and on March 4, 1913, President William Howard Taft signed the Weeks-McLean Migratory Bird Act. (During the same session, Congress also banned the importation of songbird parts.)

Weeks-McLean was welcomed as a significant victory by Tennessee's Colonel Acklen. In 1913, Acklen was the third president of the eleven-year-old National Association of Game and Fish Wardens and Commissioners (the original name of the IAFWA). Acklen predicted that the law would prove a vital step in restoring the nation's wildlife. There was more potency "in the little finger" of the strong arm of the federal government, he declared, "than [in] the entire body of any state."

Acklen's optimism—and his metaphor—were echoed by R. A. Wilson, now writing the weekly "Fins, Furs and Feathers" column for the *Nashville Banner*. "[W]hile it is too early to determine whether [Weeks-McLean] will meet the expectations of its friends," Wilson wrote, "one thing is certain, and that is that the law will be obeyed as no state law is. ... "[Uncle Sam's] hand is heavy, and ... it falls surely." According to Wilson, there was a class of men in Tennessee, "usually ignorant and illiterate," who "hold the game laws of the state in contempt, shooting and fishing in and out of season, according to their own sweet will, and trapping, netting and dynamiting as the spirit moves them. ... [T]hey have learned that the state laws, as a rule, are laxly enforced, and that they have nothing to fear from the state."

Unfortunately, Weeks-McLean was not an immediate antidote. The law was immediately challenged as unconstitutional and a violation of states' rights. To deflect that challenge and establish the constitutional authority to protect the birds, Senator McLean proposed a compact between the United States and Canada, calling for uniform hunting regulations for all birds that crossed annually between the two countries. In August 1916, Canada and the United

States jointly approved the Migratory Bird Treaty. However, the challenge to Weeks-McLean was not dropped until 1918, when Woodrow Wilson signed the Migratory Bird Treaty Act authorizing the United States to comply with the 1916 treaty. But then the Treaty Act itself was challenged. It was not until 1920—sixteen years after the effort first began—that the U.S. Supreme Court finally upheld the power of the federal government to regulate migratory birds. (When a similar treaty with Mexico was signed in 1936, the process went much more smoothly.)

Over the next twenty years, other federal protections would follow: the Migratory Bird Conservation Act of 1929 (authorizing waterfowl refuges); the Migratory Bird Hunting Stamp Act of 1934 (more familiarly known as the Duck Stamp Act); and the seminal 1937 Federal Aid to Wildlife Restoration Act, otherwise known as Pittman-Robertson, or P-R. The latter two were revenue-producing bills, and it is hard to say which has done more good, for they both came at a time when wildlife programs needed far more financing than either Congress or the states were inclined to give them. In fact, the Duck Stamp Act was written specifically to fund the waterfowl refuges authorized by the 1929 Migratory Bird Conservation Act.

TWO MAJOR WILDLIFE MEASURES: DUCK STAMPS AND PITTMAN-ROBERTSON

By combining wetlands protection with collectible art, the Duck Stamp Act quickly proved one of the most remarkable conservation laws ever to come out of Washington. The first Duck Stamp, a black-and-white etching of a pair of mallards coming in for a water landing, was designed by Pulitzer Prize-winning cartoonist Jay Norwood "Ding" Darling. At the time, Darling was the recently hired first chief of the U.S. Bureau of Biological Survey (forerunner of the U.S. Fish and Wildlife Service), on leave from his job as the popular political cartoonist for the *Des Moines Register*. Darling was an avid hunter and tireless activist who would soon leave government service to start the General (later National) Wildlife Federation.

Darling's stamp went on sale August 14, 1934. Twelve months later, it had raised $635,001—at one dollar per stamp—for buying and maintaining waterfowl refuges. Though hunters were required by law to attach a stamp to their regular hunting license, many stamps never saw active duty. Instead, they went directly into collectors' albums, where today they may be worth thousands of dollars. While the inspiration for a duck stamp should probably go to Pennsylvania's legendary game commissioner Seth Gordon, who had suggested a supplementary duck hunting license as early as 1931, the credit for making the license into a peculiarly American *objet d'art* lies entirely with Darling.

For several years Darling and other well-known wildlife artists took turns designing the annual Duck Stamp, but in 1949 the U.S. Fish and Wildlife Service turned the design process into a national competition. Today, thousands compete for the honor of Duck Stamp artist; the die proofs become part of the permanent collection in the Smithsonian's Hall of Philately. And although the winner gets no cash prize nor any share of stamp receipts, sales of the winning print typically net the artist well over a million dollars.

Compared to the flashy public profile of the Duck Stamps, the wildlife bill introduced in 1937 by Senator Key Pittman of Nevada and Representative A. Willis Robertson of Virginia may have seemed a rather pedestrian way to make money for wildlife restoration. It simply

The first Duck Stamp, featuring Ding Darling's pen-and-ink drawing of mallards, generated $635,001 for habitat protection—at $1 a stamp. Courtesy of the U.S. Fish and Wildlife Service.

appropriated a soon-to-expire federal excise tax on certain sporting equipment. Sportsmen were already paying a 10-percent tax on guns and ammunition. Under the new arrangement (said to have been suggested by Ding Darling), this money would be returned to them in the form of a stronger state wildlife program. (The tax has since been expanded to include archery gear and handguns; on the latter the tax is 11 percent.) The monies collected under Pittman-Robertson were to be divided among the states according to a formula based on land area and numbers of licenses sold. The state wildlife agency could use it for whatever wildlife restoration projects it needed most: buying lands, reintroducing species and so on.

Pedestrian it may have been, but the Pittman-Robertson Federal Aid to Wildlife Restoration Act would do more for wildlife than any other federal act in history, not even excepting its 1950 clone, the Dingell-Johnson Federal Aid to Sport Fish Restoration Act. Dingell-Johnson funds came from a 10-percent tax on fishing tackle; its 1984 expansion added a 3-percent tax on boats and trolling motors (and changed the name of the fund to Wallop-Breaux).

In return for these infusions, the government asked two things. The state's wildlife agency had to put up 25 percent of the costs; and second, the state's legislature had to pass a bill promising that hunting and fishing revenues would be earmarked for the exclusive use of the wildlife agency.

States could hardly afford not to comply. Tennessee passed its enabling law in 1939; later that year it got its first P-R distribution of some forty thousand dollars. Since then, states have shared in a massive pot totalling nearly three billion dollars; Tennessee's share alone has been more than fifty million dollars, used for everything from acquisition of wildlife management areas (including Catoosa and Cheatham) to development (such as the Hiwassee waterfowl refuge) to research (including aquatic weed studies at Reelfoot). From Dingell-Johnson (or Wallop-Breaux), Tennessee has reaped roughly thirty million dollars. The annual rebate to Tennessee from motors and fishing tackle now exceeds that from the sale of guns and ammunition, which is why a portion of Wallop-Breaux funds go to the boating section of the wildlife agency.

The true value of these federal subsidies to the nation's wildlife and fisheries programs cannot be calculated in mere dollars, however. Not only was such funding politically unassailable, since it came from the hunters and fishermen themselves. It also put those funds precisely where they would do the most good, and at a time when they were most needed. For as vital as federal supports were, wildlife management was always—and still is—primarily a state matter.

REFINING THE STATE GAME AND FISH PROGRAMS

From the start—indeed, even while they were still colonies of the British empire—individual states (sometimes individual townships) took upon themselves the responsibility for managing and controlling the local wildlife. Until Congress passed the Lacey Act in 1900, most states neither wanted nor would have tolerated federal intervention. Citing the "forest jurisdiction" principle of English wildlife law, they declared that they alone had inherited the right to regulate wildlife. Whatever laws were needed, they wrote themselves; whatever policing they required, they provided themselves; whatever bureaucracies were called for, they created themselves.

One result of this parochial outlook was that there was no system to speak of, no long-term strategy; it was the brushfire method of game management. Thus when the Massachusetts Bay Colony noticed wolves threatening its deer herds in 1630, it passed a bounty on the predators. When Portsmouth, Rhode Island, noticed its herds declining around 1646, it closed the deer season for six months. Pennsylvania's first package of hunting regulations included, among other things, a fine of five shillings for shooting birds "in the open streets of Philadelphia" as well as a law effectively denying hunting rights to the poor.

With little policy and almost no science to back them up, the results of these early laws were mostly haphazard, often misguided and occasionally disastrous: consider Ohio's sneering refusal to protect passenger pigeons in 1857: "The passenger pigeon needs no protection." But gradually, as the states moved together into the twentieth century, as they compared notes about similar problems and workable solutions, a sort of order emerged, a rough agreement of principles and practices that would eventually be refined and codified into the science of wildlife management.

The first step in this refinement process was the creation of official game and fish agencies in every state. Though every state had wildlife laws by 1900, and many states had state game wardens or protectors, very few states ran their game and fish programs within the framework of a dedicated agency. In 1776 Daniel Boone was put in charge of the "game committee" at Boonesborough, the first permanent settlement in what is now Kentucky, but the commonwealth itself did not form a fish and game department until 1912. Tennessee hired a state game warden in 1903 and put him in charge of a new Department of Game, Fish and Forestry in 1905. However, forestry was not separated from fish and game until 1915, when a reorganization bill created the Tennessee Game and Fish Department and made Forestry a division of the Office of Geological Survey.

The Commonwealth of Pennsylvania may have been the first state to establish a formal wildlife agency when it created the Pennsylvania Fish Commission in 1866; the Pennsylvania Game Commission followed in 1895. (Pennsylvania is the only state that never did combine game and fish functions under one roof; both still exist as freestanding agencies.) Maine may have been the first state to consolidate its game and fish sections; the Maine Department of Inland Fisheries and Game was founded in 1880. Massachusetts created a game and fish department in 1886, New Jersey in 1892, Rhode Island and New Hampshire and Connecticut and New York all formed agencies around the same time. It was no coincidence that most of the early wildlife agencies were in the northern states: this was the fastest-developing region in the nation and consequently the first to feel the need for regulation. Nevertheless, by the turn of the century, wildlife agencies were everywhere: Idaho in 1903, Alabama and Texas in 1907, North and South Dakota in 1909, California in 1909, Virginia in 1916. By 1920, there wasn't a state without a formal administration for both game and fish.

The second step in refining wildlife management in this country was the formation, in 1902, of a small but dedicated coalition of state game and fish commissioners. (A similar group, the Wildlife Society, was founded in 1937 as an association for all fish and wildlife professionals.) At first, the commissioners called themselves the National Association of Game and Fish Wardens and Commissioners. When Canada joined in 1917, they became the International Association of Game, Fish and Conservation Commissioners. Finally, in 1977, as more states changed their emphasis from "game" to "wildlife," they became simply the International Association of Fish and Wildlife Agencies.

Over the years, IAFWA presidents would include some of the most familiar names in conservation: Seth Gordon of Pennsylvania, T. Gilbert Pearson of New York, John Gottschalk of Virginia, Ira Gabrielson of Virginia, I. T. "Ping" Bode of Missouri, Robert Jantzen of Arizona, Elliott Barker of New Mexico. (Gary Myers became Tennessee's second IAFWA president in 1985; Joseph Acklen had been the first.) The IAFWA had a hand in nearly all the major pieces of early wildlife legislation in this country, including Weeks-McLean, the Migratory Bird Conservation Act, the Duck Stamp Act and Pittman-Robertson. Though the group met fitfully at first, and though it represented fewer than half the existing states as late as 1920, the IAFWA (and its regional subgroups) was from the beginning the most important organized body of wildlife management professionals in the country, at a time when scientific wildlife management was still an emerging discipline.

MANAGING THE NATION'S FORESTS

The notion that wildlife needed careful, systematic management was not, after all, universally accepted. Though the so-called "wise use" of resources had long been promoted by such leading conservationists as George Bird Grinnell and Roosevelt's chief forester Gifford

Pinchot, not everyone agreed that wildlife should be managed in the first place. John Muir, the Scottish-born eccentric who founded the Sierra Club in 1895, was the best known of what were commonly called the "preservationists." Muir argued that wildlife and wild lands alike should be left undisturbed, appreciated purely for their scenic, spiritual and educational values. He called hunting "the murder sport" and condemned it as needless brutality. In an interesting flight of anthropomorphism, he once compared hunting to another kind of resource consumption: lumbering. "Any fool can destroy trees," he wrote. "[The trees] cannot run away; and if they could, they would still be destroyed—chased and hunted down as long as fun or a dollar could be got out of their bark hides, branching horns, or magnificent bole backbones."

Earnest as Muir's convictions were, they were never taken very seriously by the mainstream conservationists. Trees were the very resource on which the principles of scientific management had been most thoroughly and successfully demonstrated. No less than its wildlife, America had plundered its forests for most of the last century, clearing and burning thousands of acres of virgin hardwood and old-growth pine with little thought for the next generations. Again, it was sportsmen who raised the alarm. Lumbermen were "the curse and scourge of the wilderness," said the mid-century outdoorsman William Murray. The mountains were "shorn of trees," the "hills and shores littered with rotten wood," the streams and trout pools "choked with saw-dust, and filled with slabs and logs."

Faced with growing clamor about the crisis in the forests, Congress in 1876 created an Office of Forestry in the Department of Agriculture (the Division of Forestry after 1881) and appropriated two thousand dollars for a study of forest management methods. It was a small allotment, but that it was made at all was significant. By the 1880s, a number of America's forests were being successfully restored according to methods developed in western Europe, especially Germany, where the science of silviculture was already far advanced. In 1892, the wealthy outdoorsman George Vanderbilt invited Gifford Pinchot to design a European-style management plan for the forests around Biltmore House, his mountain estate in Asheville, North Carolina. When Pinchot left Biltmore in 1905 to head the newly-formed U.S. Forest Service, he was succeeded by a German forester named Karl Schenck. Schenck would soon establish the nation's first school of forestry in a small building on the Biltmore grounds.

THE LEARNING CURVE TOWARD WILDLIFE MANAGEMENT

The success of sustainable forestry had heartened many of America's sportsmen, who saw in it not only the saving of a vital habitat for wildlife, but also a principle—managed growth and controlled harvests—that could perhaps be applied to all natural resources, including wildlife. The wildlife professionals agreed. However, with so few precedents to guide them, they could not, at least at first, agree how to go about it.

The clearest proof of their collective inexperience was the miserably failed promise of game farms and fish hatcheries. Hailed with great enthusiasm in the teens and 1920s, these programs were often abandoned with equal fervor in the 1930s, as mortality outpaced births and costs vastly exceeded returns. Restoration, the propagation managers learned, was not a matter of simple arithmetic.

"Except in 'barren' waters," wrote John Gottschalk, an IAFWA leader who went on to become director of the U.S. Fish and Wildlife Service, "restocking ... produced few results." Eventually it occurred to fish biologists that "there was much more to restoring fish populations than planting hatchery-reared fish." Missing from the equation, of course, was the factor of carrying capacity. If, for whatever reason—lack of food, lack of cover, pollution, competing species—the stream habitat would support no more than, say, ten fish, then they could add a thousand fish and it would do no good. In fact, the overcrowding would only stunt or kill the ten that had survived.

Similar results occurred with vulnerable game species. Tennessee's experience with bobwhite quail in the 1930s was unfortunate but typical. Despite the disappointing results from similar programs in other states, in 1935 Tennessee built the vast hatcheries at Rutledge known as the Buffalo Springs game farm, specifically to raise quail as well as a few other game birds, including wild turkey. By 1937, the hatchery had reared 11,410 quail chicks and released 10,000 of them. Within a few years, however, the program had been scrapped. As the agency ruefully explained in 1942, although "[r]eleasing pen-reared stock is the most obvious way of putting more birds in the fields, is therefore much in demand by the public, and has been tried by every State ... it is economically unfeasible. The cost of releasing a quail chick is only 30¢ but mortality is so high that every one which finds its way into the hunter's bag costs $33."

Attempts to establish non-native species could also be precarious. Though a few exotic species fared well in appropriate habitats (notably the "Russian," or European, wild boar, rumored to have escaped into the Smokies from a North Carolina estate during a forest fire around 1910), others quickly dominated the native species. Native black bass, for instance, were displaced by German brown trout. Other exotics did not survive at all. The first efforts to introduce Pacific salmon in the Great Lakes, for instance, merely resulted in a lot of dead salmon, while five dozen reindeer brought to Michigan from Norway in the 1920s all succumbed to a parasite.

Yet regrettable (and expensive) as these and other mistakes were, they were all part of a necessary learning process. The compensation was that, once a mistake was made, it need not be repeated. In Tennessee, for instance, the Game and Fish Commission in the early 1950s undertook a brief experimental program to propagate Coturnix quail, a species that did just fine in its native India and Afghanistan but fared miserably in Tennessee. This time, however, the state cut its losses early. The Coturnix was "not adaptable" to farm game management in the Southeast, acknowledged the commission in a 1959 progress report. "Enough information has been gained from the dozen States which have seriously attempted to establish Coturnix quail to know that the project is doomed."

The Pennsylvania Game Commission had realized the futility of most pen-rearing programs even earlier. That state, one of the most progressive in the country, had concluded as early as 1905 that "efforts to raise in captivity our native game birds ... had not yet met with any success." After considering the alternatives, the commissioners turned "with renewed conviction to the preserve idea, by which [their] native birds and game could multiply without assistance from man, other than the systematic extermination of vermin and the absolute protection afforded by a perpetual closed season."

THE CONCEPT OF GAME PRESERVES—TENNESSEE AND ELSEWHERE

Of course, the idea of game preserves was not altogether new. The federal government had endorsed the refuge concept when it passed the 1894 law protecting Yellowstone from marauding tourists and greedy sportsmen. In 1892, President Benjamin Harrison had proclaimed a national salmon reserve on Alaska's Afognak Island. Theodore Roosevelt created a bird sanctuary on Florida's Pelican Island in 1903, and by the time he left office in 1909, he had established fifty-two more refuges, the makings of the National Wildlife Refuge System (established officially . The creation in 1916 of the National Park Service, followed by the National Conference on State Parks in 1921 and the establishment of national and state forests, all helped the cause of refuges generally, for parks and forests were often treated as game preserves and many were open to fishing if not hunting.

Nonetheless, it took a while for states to grasp the fact that habitat management was the key to wildlife management. As basic as this concept seems now, it was revolutionary then, and it soon made Pennsylvania the leading game state in the country. Pennsylvania's success was inspiring: between 1913 and 1925, twenty-four states set up game management refuges of some sort.

Tennessee began in 1923 by passing a bill authorizing private land holdings of five thousand acres or more to be designated state game preserves for a period of three years. The state could stock the areas if it wished, or take animals from the property to stock other preserves; the landowner agreed to ban hunting during the period. The Reelfoot Lake Park and Fish and Game Preserve was established in 1909 (and deeded to the state in 1925), but with its cabins, clubhouse and heavy tourism, it was probably more tourist park than nature preserve. The Buffalo Springs game farm and quail hatchery was built at Rutledge in the mid-1930s, and according to *The WPA Guide to Tennessee*, a 1939 history and tour guide compiled by the Federal Writers' Project of the Works Projects Administration, there was at least one other state preserve in the late 1930s. It was at Idaho Springs, near Dunbar Cave outside Clarksville. However, it must have been a small affair, because it is not mentioned in Game and Fish accounting for 1937-38.

By the late 1930s, it had become state policy to set aside a portion of state forests as game preserves. There were eight or nine state forests by then, the first, a small tract of tax-delinquent land in Madison County, having been donated to Tennessee in 1927. Pickett, Morgan and Bledsoe followed in 1933, Grundy and Stewart in 1935, Lewis and Franklin-Marion in 1936, Scott in 1940.

THE SPORTSMEN'S PRIVATE PRESERVES

However, the local heroes of the game preserve movement were the sportsmen themselves, for they had been operating their own private game reserves since at least the 1870s. The first in the nation, according to George Reiger, was the twelve thousand-acre Blooming Grove Park in Pennsylvania, founded in 1871. Six years later the Bisby Club leased nine thousand acres of wilderness in the Adirondacks. In Tennessee in the early 1900s, a wealthy patrician named Hobart Ames established a private quail sanctuary in Grand Junction, where for years he presided over the National Field Dog Trials. In 1917, Nashville-area sportsmen established a small game preserve at Glendale Park, and around 1935 a Nashville club leased the rights to hunt and fish at Radnor Lake. For years Radnor had been maintained as a waterfowl sanctuary by the Nashville Terminals, with fishing restricted to railroad employees. Apparently the fishing privilege was abused, however, and L & N Railroad officials decided to turn the sanctuary over to the sportsmen.

In 1938, Edward Meeman, editor of the *Memphis Press-Scimitar* and soon-to-be president of the Tennessee Wildlife Federation, established the state's first private forest reserve next to Shelby Forest at Millington (now the Meeman-Shelby Forest State Recreational Area). "I intend to make this place an example of man's living in harmony with nature," explained Meeman, who also helped create the Great Smoky Mountains National Park. "I intend to invite many Clubs and individuals to use these quiet nature trails. ... Artificial planting will be limited to an area close to the house [now the Meeman Museum]—the chief gardening interest will be in restoring and preserving nature's garden—the fields and woods."

Though most of these private refuges were *not* closed to fishing and hunting (except, that is, by non-members), the owners took care to maintain the wildlife populations at healthy levels, often by increasing food supplies or enhancing stream cover. Reiger notes, "Because each association enforced its own rules, in addition to state laws, game stocks were preserved; where game already had been reduced before the creation of the club, artificial propagation often filled the void. Nongame species also benefitted by having their habitat guarded against 'improvements.' In many areas the only substantial acreage remaining in an undeveloped state was the land controlled by sportsmen's clubs."

In certain respects these private holdings resembled the exclusive hunting grounds of the old English nobility. Therefore, it was probably natural that some local folks objected. At any rate, when a group of Tennessee sportsmen developed a 2,500-acre private preserve along the Duck River in Maury County in the early 1920s, some disgruntled residents complained. R. A. Wilson, however, had no sympathy for the whiners. "In this democratic country, where all men are supposed to have equal privileges, the withdrawal of large areas from public shooting is resented with the usual bunk talk of the 'classes against the masses,' but those who oppose these preserves and sanctuaries are the very men who have made them necessary. ... [T]he only hope of saving the game and fish and making the sport of hunting and fishing worth while, lies in the creation of many and well distributed preserves, which will be safe from the invasion of those who take game and fish in and out of season in any way that brings the best results."

Besides, as Wilson pointed out, because the Maury County sportsmen planned to stock their preserve with both game and fish, the abundance of wildlife would eventually spill beyond the preserve boundaries, where they would become fair game to all. Thus everyone— "even the man who is careless in his observance of the laws"—would reap some benefit.

MASTERING THE ART OF GAME MANAGEMENT

When they were well managed, with proper habitat, adequate food supplies and limited predation, the nation's game preserves did precisely what Wilson said the Maury County refuge would do: strengthen resident stocks and populate the neighboring lands.

However, the very successes of the reserves created a shortage of competent, trained professionals to manage them. Though the nation had plenty of college programs in forestry, zoology and the like, only a handful specialized in wildlife management before 1932. Most game managers, if they got professional training at all, got it in one of these tangential fields, then adapted it as well as they could to the needs of game and fish. The University of Michigan, for instance, offered wildlife management training as early as 1927, but it was considered a branch of forestry. The dean himself admitted that "[t]here was little background of educational or practical experience" in his field, and "the literature on the subject was decidedly meagre."

Others gathered information piecemeal from a welter of sources: the handful of books on natural history, outdoor sport and game laws; the annual proceedings of the International Association of Game, Fish and Conservation Commissioners; back issues of magazines like *Forest and Stream*; reports of the Biological Survey, and so on. Many game personnel got no specialized training at all. As for the front line of game wardens, many of them never even finished high school.

Education was the obvious next step. The country needed professional wildlife training schools where emerging theories could be taught, new ones researched, methods analyzed, techniques applied and findings published. Such schools could develop standards for the industry and offer certification for wildlife personnel.

For some time, Ding Darling—along with fellow Iowan Aldo Leopold—had long been calling for better training opportunities for game and fish personnel. In 1932, Darling convinced the Iowa Fish and Game Department and Iowa State College (now Iowa State University) to help him set up a wildlife management course at the college. But that wasn't the end of Darling's ambitions for wildlife education. When Franklin Roosevelt asked him, early in 1934, to head the new Bureau of Biological Survey, he accepted, even though the President was a Democrat and Darling an outspoken Republican. Darling stayed with the Biological Survey barely two years. But before he left, in 1935, he launched the Cooperative Wildlife Research Unit program, a graduate-level program in wildlife management modeled after his Iowa State prototype.

At first there were just nine of these research units nationwide, based at widely-scattered land-grant colleges around the country, including Virginia, Texas, Maine and Utah. (Today there are units in almost every state, including the fisheries unit at Tennessee Technological University in Cookeville.) The schools did original research, conducted demonstration projects and offered extension services. They also stimulated other academic institutions, both private and public, to design wildlife programs of their own. In 1937 they helped organize a membership organization for wildlife and resource-management professionals called the Wildlife Society.

But equally important, when Pittman-Robertson funds began flowing into state wildlife agencies in 1939, the wildlife research units supplied the suddenly burgeoning demand for qualified wildlife administrators.

THE BIG GOVERNMENT PROGRAMS OF THE '30S

At about the same time that Ding Darling was bringing formal wildlife training to the United States, other government initiatives were underway that would prove, in their way, no less important to conservation and conservation training. Three of these were founded in a single year: the Civilian Conservation Corps (CCC), the Soil Conservation Service (SCS) and the Tennessee Valley Authority (TVA), all authorized in 1933. The Works Progress Administration (later called the Works Projects Administration) followed in 1935. Though none of these agencies was uniformly friendly to conservation interests (the CCC, for instance, drained dozens of wetlands in what R. A. Wilson called an "ill-advised program of sanitation"), their potential for good was enormous.

The CCC in Tennessee, for instance, fought forest fires, built lookout towers, built erosion check dams, planted thousands of acres of trees, built lakes, surveyed public lands and designed park structures of astonishing beauty and strength, including the arched bridge at Cumberland Mountain State Park, made of local Crab Orchard stone. It was CCC "boys," along with crews from the WPA, who built the Buffalo Springs game farm in 1935, and they who impounded the half-dozen Game and Fish lakes built between 1938 and 1940. It was the CCC who developed the first state forests, including the one in Grundy County supervised by Herman Baggenstoss. And it was the CCC who began restoring the denuded Copper Basin in southeast Tennessee just before World War II put an end to the Corps altogether.

The focus of the Soil Conservation Service was narrower than that of the CCC or the WPA, but because its principal audience was farmers, its impact was equally far-reaching. By explaining to landowners the physics of soil erosion and developing methods to prevent it, the SCS (called, briefly, the Soil Erosion Service) was also protecting watersheds, forests and other habitat. By getting farmers to take part in small farm-game management projects (such as stocking bass and bream in Tennessee farm ponds), the agency not only increased wildlife populations, it shored up the vital but often strained relationship between farmers and sportsmen.

As for the Tennessee Valley Authority, it was clear from the start that the huge agency would be a major force in conservation in the Tennessee Valley, affecting everything from wildlife and fisheries management to pollution control and recreational land use. Within a year after its founding, the TVA structure included a Wildlife Unit, staffed by some of the best wildlife scientists then available. In 1938 it began a fourteen-year study of the fishery in the recently-impounded Norris Reservoir, headed by fisheries biologist Reuben William Eschmeyer, later the executive vice president of the Sport Fishing Institute in Washington. In Tennessee, Eschmeyer became best known as the man responsible for year-round fishing in TVA lakes. Eschmeyer (who won the second Z. Cartter Patten Award for his discovery) had concluded that it was neither necessary nor even advisable to close large lakes to fishing during the spawning season. Like forests, said Eschmeyer, fisheries were healthier when they were harvested aggressively and regularly, and spring was the best season for culling oversized or undesirable fish.

TVA also launched waterfowl programs, deer programs and small game programs; it developed dozens of wildlife management areas and waterfowl refuges; it built boat ramps and picnic areas; and beginning in 1937, it deeded thousands of acres to Tennessee for its emerging state park system. Harrison Island Park, a TVA demonstration area on Chickamauga Reservoir, was leased to the state for a dollar in June 1938, opening officially as Harrison Bay State Park in 1942. In September 1938, TVA leased an additional 350 acres on the south shore of Harrison Bay for Booker T. Washington State Park—touted by the Parks Division as the first "Negro State Park" in the nation.

In addition, TVA sponsored recreation-demonstration projects such as the ones at Norris and Big Ridge and later, of course, at Land Between the Lakes. But perhaps TVA's most significant contribution to the emerging science of resource conservation was its broad, region-wide perspective, its ability to see the Tennessee Valley as, in President Franklin D. Roosevelt's words, one of the country's "great natural territorial units." At a time when neighboring states often had differing and even contradictory laws for their natural resources, TVA was compelled by its structure to overlook political boundaries in preference of natural ones imposed by watersheds, soil types and topography.

A TIME OF TRANSITION

Given the extraordinary activity in wildlife-related matters in the 1930s, the decade should have been a heyday for conservation, and viewed from the larger perspective of the entire twentieth century, it was. After two hundred-plus years of abuse and exploitation, the nation was now poised to reclaim its once-proud natural heritage. Yet despite the flurry of new programs, emerging professionalism, unprecedented funding, acres of refuges and new understanding of management techniques, several factors converged in the late 1920s and early 1930s to make this very period one of the worst for wildlife in recent history.

First, there was the severe and prolonged drought of the early 1930s—the Dustbowl years. By 1934 wildlife photographer Arthur Newton Pack, president of the American Nature Association, was calling the drought "the most severe on record. ... Testimony of observers of all kinds, shooters, and non-shooters, indicates a decided and increasingly alarming decline [of waterfowl]. Whether the evidence be tabulated by numbers or percentages of observers, by species, or by lines of flight, it points to an appalling wastage of this beautiful and useful resource." Hunters themselves were urging a closed season until the birds could recover. "But," concluded Pack, "instead of being accorded freedom from shooting, the harassed birds faced an open season that promised to be the most disastrous in the history of North American wild-fowling."

Development, poor farming practices and other human activity only made things worse. The Soil Conservation Service had not yet taught farmers the folly of plowing straight down a hillside or tilling next to a stream. In the wetlands of West Tennessee as in the entire Mississippi River basin, thousands of acres of prime duck habitat were being drained and filled for farming and flood control. Much of this work was subsidized by the state itself. In 1909, the Legislature had passed a law authorizing levee and drainage districts "for the purpose of the draining and reclamation of the wet and swamp lands and lands subject to overflow"— precisely the sort of lands waterfowl require.

Another factor in the wildlife crisis of the '30s was the exploding popularity of outdoor sport. From 1926 to 1936, hunting and fishing license sales quadrupled nationwide; in 1936, Tennessee issued 59,000 licenses. (By 1946 that number would quadruple again.) There were several reasons for this dramatic growth. Americans had more leisure time than ever before; they also had what one observer called "good roads with fast cars." Since World War I there had also been an "enormous increase" in the efficiency of arms and ammunition as well as in fishing tackle and lures. At the same time, there were more places to hunt and fish. A 1936 management agreement between the state of Tennessee and the U.S. Forest Service had opened up vast lands in the Cherokee to managed hunts. The first Tellico wild boar hunt took place (with great national fanfare) that autumn.

The late 1920s and 1930s also marked the birth of a national ethic for parks and recreation lands. Tennessee's State Park and Forestry Commission was convened in 1925, the same year a joint legislative committee began studying the feasibility of creating a state or national park in the Great Smokies. (Ed Meeman was one of the citizens lobbying hardest for a national park.) The Great Smoky Mountains National Park opened in 1931, followed six years later by the Appalachian Trail. The first TVA lake was open by 1936, Tennessee's first state lake by 1938, its first state park the same year. Most state parks and forests allowed fishing; some were open to hunting. Even when state parks were officially declared wildlife preserves in 1958, most continued to allow fishing, and hunting was still allowed in state forests.

THE SPORTSMEN START TO ORGANIZE

With so many more sportsmen and women taking to the field, the demand for game and fish soon outstripped the supply. By the 1930s, tens of thousands of sportsmen nationwide were no longer content merely to gripe about the sorry state of fishing and hunting. They understood that there was little the government could do to control droughts or the huge influx of new license holders. But they did believe there was something human ingenuity could do to manage the resources better. A few states were already applying scientific principles to their game and fish programs, and the results were promising. The problem in many states was that political alliances, not scientific training, determined who ran the wildlife agency. The sportsmen began to organize.

A similar movement had occurred before, around the turn of the century, when states were just setting up their fish and game administrations. Numerous conservation leagues had formed to lobby for stricter wildlife laws in their respective states: Tennessee's Game and Fish Protective Association, for instance, had organized in 1905. This group appealed for, and eventually won, a comprehensive fish law, a ban on dynamiting streams and, in 1907, a repeal of local wildlife laws. The Michigan Sportsmen's Association, in existence since 1875, had managed to ban market hunting as early as 1881; it also helped form Michigan's first game warden department. Several other sportsmen's groups formed around this time: the League of Ohio Sportsmen in 1908, the Southern Idaho Fish and Game Association in 1909, the New Mexico Game Protective Association in 1914.

But the first wave of sportsmen's clubs had died down by this time. For the next decade or two the conservation movement was quiet if not altogether stagnant.

By the late 1920s, however, sportsmen were again raising the alarm. "That wild life is slowly, but steadily, vanishing from the Atlantic to the Pacific Coast is a cold fact," editorialized R. A. Wilson, "and not the lamentation of a chronic Jeremiah. . . . This condition leads to the inevitable conclusion that, if the game and fish of this country are [to be] saved and increased, it must be done through a closer tie-up between the Game and Fish Department, the sportsmen and the farmers."

The Izaak Walton League of America was the first national group to organize. Founded in Chicago in 1922, its leaders were some of the most powerful men in the country; Theodore Roosevelt himself was an ardent supporter. "If we are to accomplish the great ends in conservation and outdoor recreation for which we are all disinterestedly striving," the former president wrote in 1927 to the group's president, Tennessee native son Jacob M. Dickinson, "we must have coordination of effort."

The Izaak Walton League established a number of influential state affiliates, especially in the upper Midwest. In other states, however, including Tennessee, it failed to develop a statewide presence. Nonetheless, Tennessee had several local chapters. Men who would later be leaders in the Tennessee Conservation League were leaders in their local branches of the Izaak Walton League, including "Peck" Peckinpaugh in Chattanooga, Karl Steinmetz in Knoxville and Nash Buckingham in Memphis.

Dr. S. John House, the second president of the Tennessee Federation of Sportsmen in 1937, was the first president of Nashville's Davy Crockett Chapter of the Izaak Walton League. Organized around 1928, it was one of most active conservation groups in Tennessee. When the Buffalo Springs quail hatchery was built, for instance, the Davy Crockett chapter helped stock it, encouraging "the boys and girls on the farms to gather eggs" from the nests before their daddies plowed. The Nashville chapter also helped establish the state's first fish hatchery at Springfield, building a series of rearing pools in the early 1930s and stocking them with fry from the federal hatchery at Erwin. A photograph in the May 25, 1932, *Nashville Banner* shows members of the chapter posing in front of a large truck parked in front of the *Banner*'s offices. Inside were five thousand, week-old brown trout in ten-gallon cans, their tops iced to keep the fish cool during the drive.

ALL CREATURES GREAT AND SMALL: SPORTSMEN AND NONGAME

Though the main focus of the sportsmen's movement was game species, they occasionally worked on behalf of nongame, especially birds. Nashville's Albert F. Ganier, for instance, though apparently an occasional fisherman, was far better known for his work in ornithology. Ganier and four friends founded the Tennessee Ornithological Society in 1915, today the oldest conservation group in the state. As the group's curator, Ganier catalogued 2,300 bird and mammal skins; in 1930 he founded and for many years edited *The Migrant*. A Mississippi native with a degree in civil engineering, Ganier spent his entire career with the Nashville railroads; it was largely thanks to him that naturalists and fishermen were allowed to enjoy Radnor Lake.

R. A. Wilson was one of the first members of TOS. His regular columns in the Sunday *Banner* were as passionate about mockingbirds, snakes and goldfish as they were about white-tailed deer and rainbow trout. "Soon the young birds in our gardens will be coming from their nests to test their wings in unfamiliar surroundings," he wrote in 1936, "and it will be a period of more or less tragedy because it is the harvest season for the prowling cat. ... The robins, perhaps, suffer more than other urban-bred birds, and their distress over the murder of their nestlings is pathetic and unpleasant to remember."

Wilson was delighted by the idea of "hunting with a camera"; in fact, like many of his generation, he stopped hunting altogether in his later years. "There comes a time in the life of most men of advanced years when they lose the lust of killing," he wrote in 1935 at the age of seventy-nine, "and this is especially true in the case of deer whose mild and reproachful eyes, when in the throes of death, will return to plague the hunter." In 1936 he referred to the duck hunting season as the *dies irae* for waterfowl. "Years ago we killed [ten ducks] in two shots," he wrote a bit sadly. "We were proud of it then; we are ashamed of it now."

THE NATIONAL CLUB MOVEMENT

Yet Wilson did not condemn hunting or hunters. On the contrary, he often praised the power and commitment of organized sportsmen, and threw the full weight of his weekly column behind Tennessee's newest group, the Tennessee Federation of Sportsmen.

Founded in April 1934, the Tennessee Federation of Sportsmen was among the earliest groups to organize during this second wave of club activity. The New Jersey Federation of Sportsmen's Clubs was founded the following year; so was the League of Kentucky Sportsmen and the North Dakota Wildlife Association. The Arkansas Wildlife Federation, the Georgia Wildlife Federation and the Idaho Wildlife Federation all formed in 1936, the Alabama Wildlife Federation in 1937. By the end of the decade there was a central sportsmen's organization in every state.

It's no coincidence that after 1936 most of these groups called themselves Wildlife Federations (in 1937 the Tennessee Federation of Sportsmen renamed itself the Tennessee Wildlife Federation). They were all affiliates of the National Wildlife Federation (known briefly as the General Wildlife Federation), the newest and most aggressive national conservation group. Proposed by Ding Darling in 1935 and consecrated by ballot during the first North American Wildlife Conference in February 1936, the Federation sought to coalesce the power of all the nation's sporting and conservation clubs into one enormous force.

The 1936 North American Wildlife Conference, called by President Franklin D. Roosevelt and presided over by the American Wildlife Institute, drew nearly fifteen hundred delegates from all forty-eight states to the Mayflower Hotel in Washington, D.C. Herman Baggenstoss was probably, thought not certainly, one of the delegates from Tennessee.

As chairman of the general session on February 5, Darling explained his plan. "This body here gathered together should devote itself to an organization which will first, unite on a comprehensive program of common aims and second, use the agencies which our Government provides to see that the program is carried forward. Specify your objects and use the pressure of your great numbers where it will do the most good—on your elected officials."

By the end of the day the delegates had endorsed the Federation and elected Darling its first president. Darling would serve in that role for the next three years, attracting thousands of new members as well as chapters in almost every state. In 1938 he instituted the tradition now known as National Wildlife Week, an annual event whose honorary chairmen have included Bing Crosby, Lorne Greene, Dick Van Dyke, Loretta Lynn and for many years Walt Disney. (Actually, President Roosevelt proclaimed the first National Wildlife Restoration Week in 1938, but the Federation was in charge of it.)

Yet despite its growing success, the Federation was hard-pressed to stay solvent those first few years. It was saved by another sort of Ding Darling wildlife stamp. NWF legend has it that in late 1937, Darling got a letter from a Kansas supporter (whose name has been lost), asking: "Why don't you paint some wildlife pictures and have them printed on paper with glue on the back and sell them to lovers of wildlife all over the country?" Darling must have liked the idea, because he painted the first set of sixteen prints himself, reproducing them in sheets of one hundred stamps that sold for a dollar. Darling presented the first run of National Wildlife Restoration Week stamps to FDR in a White House ceremony on March 20, 1938. The first year's effort raised sixteen thousand dollars; by 1949 they were netting NWF a half-million dollars a year.

Like the Duck Stamps, the Wildlife Week stamps quickly became collectors' items. Soon the designs were being painted by such prominent wildlife artists as Roger Tory Peterson and Lynn Bogue Hunt. After the first year, the set always included a bit of amateur art as well, as NWF began sponsoring an annual poster contest. The winning entry was used on Wildlife Week posters, but it was also reproduced as one of the new wildlife stamps. The winner for 1939 was a pretty nineteen-year-old from Memphis named Josephine Marie Bradshaw. Her cartoon of a squirrel on a stairway of stamped envelopes netted her a hundred dollars. The Tennessee Wildlife Federation presented the check.

THE INTERNATIONAL ASSOCIATION WRITES THE FIRST MODEL LAW

As much as the NWF did for sportsmen in the 1930s, however, it was not the only national group working to solve the wildlife crisis.

When the Izaak Walton League met in Chicago in April 1934, one of the topics was the hodgepodge of game and fish laws throughout the United States. The law books of every state were choked by a "vast volume of minor and relatively unimportant, and sometimes absurd, legislation," complained Arthur Foran, president of a new group called More Game Birds Foundation, the group that founded Ducks Unlimited in 1938. Consider, Foran said, the Texas statute prohibiting all deer-calling devices "except deer horns which may be rattled," or the state law (he thought it was Oregon's) that classified bullfrogs as songbirds in order to give them greater protection. Even worse were the local laws passed to satisfy the whims of politicians and selfish sportsmen.

In fact, the only states with thriving wildlife programs were those run not by politicians but by nonpartisan citizen commissions—states like Michigan and Pennsylvania. Shortly after its Chicago meeting, the Izaak Walton League put a formal request to the International Association of Game, Fish and Conservation Commissioners. Design a uniform game and fish law for us, they said, and we'll help get it adopted in every state.

With their 1934 annual meeting just five months away, the members of the International Association lost no time. They appointed an ad hoc committee chaired by former U.S.

Senator Harry B. Hawes, author of the 1926 Hawes Act restricting interstate commercial shipment of black bass. His committee included Ding Darling, still at the Biological Survey; Seth
Gordon, former executive director of the Pennsylvania Game Commission and president of
the American Game Protective Association; Carl Shoemaker, secretary of the Senate Special
Committee on the Conservation of Wildlife Resources; Frank T. Bell, commissioner of the
federal Bureau of Fisheries; More Game Birds' Arthur Foran; and six others. Legal expertise
and correct legal wording would be furnished by attorneys from the Biological Survey (in
Agriculture) and the Bureau of Fisheries (in Commerce). (In 1940, these two agencies would
join as the U.S. Fish and Wildlife Service in the Department of Interior.)

To assure that the document would fairly reflect a consensus point of view, Hawes sent
a lengthy questionnaire to commissioners, leading sportsmen and sportsmen's organizations.
Their replies, he said, "indicated a widespread and active interest." Yet they also reminded
the committee that "different geographical, climatic, political and other conditions ... might
make [a single model law] inappropriate for adoption in all the states."

What Hawes and his committee ultimately presented to the International's convention
in Montreal in September 1934 was a trio of options: a comprehensive "Model State Game
and Fish Law Setup"; an abridged version; and some dozen or so "supplemental suggestions"
for making spot remedies to existing game management systems. In all cases, of course, each
state would be free to adapt the law to its own peculiar needs.

The most significant feature of the law was its recommendation for an autonomous, five-
member game and fish commission, appointed to staggered terms and serving without pay.
The agency itself should operate as much as possible on license fees and other revenues and
avoid mingling its own funds with state appropriations. (After 1937, of course, Pittman-
Robertson would make this feature imperative.) While the commission system "may not be
practical in some of the states," admitted Chairman Hawes, "the sentiment expressed in the
replies to the questionnaire and the practical experience of longtime observers demonstrate
that the overwhelming thought is for the commission form."

The bill went on to list the various prerogatives and duties of the commission, including
the right to fix seasons and bag limits; acquire and designate refuges, hatcheries and hunting lands; propagate, stock and manage species; and enter into cooperative agreements. It
authorized the commission to hire a director to serve "for an indefinite term"; to approve
the director's choice of conservation officers; and to set and manage the agency's budget. It
also prohibited all political activity—other than voting—for employees and officers of the commission. And, under the brief section labeled "Repeals," the model law provided that all acts,
"whether general, local, special, or private" which were inconsistent with the provisions of
the model law be immediately repealed upon passage of the model law.

Clearly, the committee was seeking in a single document to right the most severe wrongs
of typical wildlife administrations.

There was, however, one peculiar feature. Although the bill stipulated that "[n]o person
shall be appointed ... unless he shall be well informed on the subject of wildlife conservation and restoration," the privilege of appointing these men was given to the governor "by
and with the advice and consent of the Senate." Considering how sportsmen presumably

felt about political interference, this clause seems a bit out of character. On the other hand, it may merely reflect the fact that Senator Hawes and several other members of the committee were politicians themselves. At any rate, states were free to strike that provision from their own versions of the model law, and many of them did so (including Tennessee).

The model law was unanimously accepted by the International's voting members. Within days, copies were being distributed to game and fish agencies, sportsmen's groups and outdoor writers across the country. To the sportsmen's groups in particular, the model law was a godsend, drafted by the best wildlife managers in the country, fine-tuned by sympathetic politicians and properly worded by experienced lawyers. Sportsmen had been gnashing their teeth for years about the politicization of their game and fish programs, but the system was so deeply entrenched that it seemed immoveable.

Thus when the IAFGCC's model law hit the streets, the nation's organized sportsmen seized upon it; some turned it into proposed legislation in a matter of weeks. Iowa introduced a commission bill in the very next session of its legislature. Missouri's sportsmen helped pass a model Fish and Game Commission Act in 1936; Kentucky passed a modified version of the bill the same year. Idaho created an independent commission in 1938. In 1944 the citizens of Arkansas created a game and fish commission by constitutional amendment. By the mid-1950s, almost every state in the union was using the commission form of wildlife management as recommended by the International Association's model law.

As for the new Tennessee Federation of Sportsmen, its members had been poised to run with the bill as soon as it landed on their desks.

CHAPTER 2

1935-1945
LAYING THE GROUNDWORK

*I sincerely believe that the Tennessee Federation of Sportsmen can be the most
powerful influence for seeing that our conservation program is carried on
year after year uninterrupted. This can be the greatest single contribution
that this organization can make to the state.*

—Sam Brewster, Tennessee commissioner of Conservation,
to the Tennessee Federation of Sportsmen, April 1937

THE POLITICAL SPOILS SYSTEM

By the 1930s, most sportsmen had come to despise the single-commissioner system of game management, otherwise known as the "state game warden plan," since wardenships were the stock in trade in this form of political horse-trading.

The confrontation had been brewing since 1903, when Tennessee first put Tennessee's wildlife program in the hands of a political appointee. The first state game warden, Colonel Joseph Acklen, was appointed by Governor James B. Frazier for a two-year term. In 1905 a new bill—and a new governor—set the chief warden's term at eight years, and Acklen, by all accounts an outstanding wildlife manager, was reappointed. In 1915, there was yet another reorganization, as Governor Tom Rye created a Department of Game and Fish. The head wildlife administrator was now called the state game and fish warden, and he served the same two-year terms as the governor. (Tennessee's governors didn't start serving four-year terms until 1953.) The head warden was authorized to appoint deputy game wardens for each county, but in practice he did so only with the input and approval of the governor.

At first the deputy wardens' pay was 100 percent of whatever fines they managed to collect; after the 1915 reorganization, they were paid a dollar for each day on the job, plus half of collected fines. If wardens were chosen for their professional training and integrity, this system might not have been so bad, even with the fairly rapid turnover. But as Herman Baggenstoss once said, neither personal merit nor special qualifications had much to do with it. It was no secret that wardenships were gross political currency which a governor might exchange in return for political support or as a reward for political favors. The result was that few appointees knew anything about wildlife management, or cared. Even if they did, their brief tenure gave them little incentive to start new programs, since they would probably be scrapped by the next administration. In 1922 (during the height of prohibition), state game warden Claude P. Williams grumbled, "Good deputy wardens are about as hard to find as they say good liquor is."

The extent of the problem, and the depth of the sportsmen's feeling about it, were summed up in a September 1938 editorial by Tennessee Wildlife Federation President Herman Baggenstoss in *Tennessee Wildlife*, the Federation's monthly magazine.

> *Where To Now?* ... is the question that has confronted every Division dealing with conservation since their early establishment. No administration, regardless of how good, has been able to erase this question—Where To Now?—at the end of their terms. ...
>
> The absence of any stability, and the lack of any continuity, is wildlife's number one enemy in this state.
>
> Capable men are prevented from applying for positions by this uncertainty. It is responsible for the discharge of experienced game men, it has prevented the Department from enacting a training school for its employees, it has permitted the State to violate trusts in the establishment of refuge areas and to violate contracts with individuals, corporations, and the U.S. Government. It has bred distrust for the State of Tennessee.
>
> Recently a conservation officer's position was offered to twelve good men, all employed, in a certain county. All of them, to a man, turned down the position. Why?
>
> Insecurity, possible political interference, and possible reflection on character were among reasons given.
>
> Is it possible that a position with the State of Tennessee as Game Warden is looked upon by the citizens in such a suspicious attitude? If so, who is responsible? No one. What is responsible? The spoils system.

THE MESS AT GAME AND FISH

It was not merely their lack of training and job security that discouraged game wardens from constructive wildlife work. It was also the extraordinary emphasis on law enforcement. Of the $160,000 spent by Game and Fish in 1937-38 (the last year before Pittman-Robertson funds began arriving), nearly half—$70,354.55 to be exact—was spent tracking down and prosecuting violators. That was almost nine times the amount spent on fish hatcheries, five times the investment in education and twice the expenditure for the Buffalo Springs game farm. While it was important to stop lawbreakers and promote public respect for game and fish laws, the sportsmen argued, these ends would ultimately be better achieved by education—both of the wardens and the hunting and fishing public.

There was an added problem in the way game wardens were compensated. The more successful arrests a warden made, the more money he made. The lure of cash was not an idle factor in post-Depression Tennessee, when some workers earned less than $100 a year and farmers as little as $250. Moreover, the hard economic times guaranteed plenty of violators to arrest. Much of the illegal hunting and fishing was done by rural folks who genuinely needed the food or the handful of change their illegal take provided. And even though a fellow could hunt *and* fish for two dollars a year, many—perhaps most—sportsmen never bothered to buy a license at all. Surveys taken as late as 1961 showed that one in five hunters hunted without a license, and one in every *three* fishermen fished without one.

Moreover, said the sportsmen, whatever monies were taken in by the department did not necessarily stay there, though they were supposed to. Revenues from license sales, commercial fishing permits, fines and so on were deposited in the Game and Fish Protection Fund (created in 1915), out of which came all the expenses of the agency, including salaries and per diems. Apparently, however, the state's general fund was also helping itself to a share and using the money for everything from schools to roads to prisons. The sportsmen had tried several times to stop this practice, and in 1927, the seemed to have succeeded. The general appropriations bill that year stipulated that Game and Fish revenues were "specifically appropriated to the use and for the behalf of the Department," nor could "[any] part of the unexpended fund left at the end of each year ... be used for any other purpose, but shall be carried over in said fund and expended during the next year." This law was reiterated in 1935, 1937 and 1939. Therefore, if the sportsmen were right—if Game and Fish revenues *were* being siphoned for unrelated purposes—then the state was violating its own edict.

There was one other thing nagging at the sportsmen: their own apathy. In fact, they often said, the sportsmen of Tennessee already had more game and fish than they deserved, because they made no effort to protect it. That was not quite true, of course; they had tried twice—in 1931 and again in 1933—to create an independent game and fish commission. But neither bill had passed, and it was their own fault, they told each other, because they all said, "Let Bob do it!" Ding Darling himself often compared the nation's sportsmen to the old church goer who thanked God salvation was free: "He had been a member of the church for forty years and it hadn't cost him a cent."

To the founders of the Tennessee Federation of Sportsmen, salvation would cost more than just the dollar for membership or the two dollars for a hunting license. In fact, they seemed to say, true redemption could not be bought at all; it had to be earned by active and unremitting effort. Having failed to organize properly in 1931 and 1933, they were determined not to lose a third round.

THE SPORTSMEN ORGANIZE

On April 14, 1934, ten or twelve "serious-minded" sportsmen met at the King Hotel in Murfreesboro to form the Tennessee Federation of Sportsmen—the first statewide sporting group to take hold in Tennessee since the Tennessee Game and Fish Protective Association. The small group elected Matt Thomas of Knoxville to be president and Joel B. Fort, director of the Federal Reserve Bank in Nashville, as treasurer. Executive secretary Howard Ansley agreed to manage the League's business from an office in the War Memorial Building. Besides these three officers, the executive committee included Knoxville attorney Karl Steinmetz; Herman Baggenstoss of Tracy City, Dr. A. F. Ebert of Chattanooga, W. O. Tirrill of Nashville and Dr. S. John House, the first president of the Davy Crockett chapter of the Izaak Walton League and now a gentleman farmer recently retired from the faculty at Vanderbilt Medical School.

While no records appear to have survived from that first meeting of the Federation, its agenda is clear from newspaper accounts and later documents. In *The Knoxville News-Sentinel* of February 16, 1936, for instance, Karl Steinmetz recalled the meeting in a lengthy article in "Sport Talk," a feature normally written by columnist Bob Wilson. (Wilson had "two badly cut fingers" and so couldn't use his typewriter.)

In his article, Steinmetz emphasized that the driving force behind the Federation was members' disgust and frustration with the political spoils system at Game and Fish. "Everybody [knew] how fish and game were getting scarcer and scarcer, many species of both becoming extinct, and the administration of the fish and game laws and the funds derived from the sportsmens' [sic] licenses being dissipated in politics. Nothing constructive done. No real effort for restocking, conservation, protection or law enforcement. Wardens and deputy wardens appointed solely for their political effect and influence."

In order to get politics out of fish and game, the sportsmen realized, they would have to put fish and game into politics. These were two different things, Steinmetz said, as different as pouring coffee into a bag of sugar from pouring "the proper amount of sugar" into the cup of coffee.

At any rate, the sportsmen understood the need for intense organization, especially if they were to have a commission bill ready to present to the 1935 Legislature. Their plan was "to have local sportsmen's organizations in every county of the state banded together in one statewide federation to present a united front to the Legislature and have sufficient power and influence to carry out its objectives and move fish and game affairs out from under the curse of politics."

There was also, Steinmetz continued, that matter of official mooching. "The taxpayers never paid a cent into the game and fish fund. No money was ever appropriated by the Legislature for wildlife conservation, or the operation of the fish and game department from the general fund. On the contrary the voluntary contributions of the sportsmen through hunting and fishing licenses have frequently been encroached upon in the past and over $400,000 of the money thus taken away from them in the past ten years." Since the sportsmen in effect "pay their own way," Steinmetz argued, "it is logically no business of the Legislature how the fish and game department is operated but exclusively the affair of the sportsmen."

Assuming politics could be got out of the picture, what did the sportsmen propose should take its place? Professional wildlife management, said Steinmetz. "[T]he day when natural propagation and replenishment can be expected to supply the needs of sportsmen is gone forever," he declared. "[F]ish and game were now a crop, and must be propagated or manufactured ... or there will surely be no fish and game at all."

THE FEDERATION SETS UP SHOP

Intending as it did to push its commission bill in the very next session of the Legislature, the Federation could not afford to rely strictly on volunteers to do the necessary legwork. They agreed that executive secretary Ansley should work full time, meeting with sportsmen, signing up existing clubs and organizing new ones. According to a 1936 treasurer's report, Ansley received $140 a month, plus whatever expenses he incurred traveling about the state. To guarantee these costs, Federation leaders committed to "sell" a minimum of one hundred life memberships at fifty dollars each, which they did easily. They also offered regular memberships of one dollar; this rate applied whether one joined as an individual or as a member of a local club. Dues paid in excess of this fee were turned over to the sponsoring club to further its own programs, an uncommonly generous arrangement and one that helps account for the rapid growth in Federation affiliates—some fifty clubs by 1937.

The Federation's first office was in the War Memorial Building in downtown Nashville. The 1936 treasurer's report does not mention any rent or lease payments, so it may be that the sportsmen did not pay for this space. In fact, it's possible they used the same basement room that would eventually be occupied by the Department of Conservation when that department was created by Governor Browning's reorganization bill in February 1937. At any rate, the Federation moved out of the War Memorial Building at the same time the Conservation Department moved in. In March 1937, the Federation's monthly magazine, *Tennessee Wildlife,* listed the Federation's new address as the Noel Hotel—"Nashville's Newest and Finest."

The two years in the Noel were the Federation's heyday—vital, exciting and productive. In July 1937 it hosted the first Tennessee Wildlife Conference, with Jay N. "Ding" Darling himself as featured guest. In December 1937 Herman Baggenstoss announced "another milepost" as the club adopted a new constitution, a new membership policy and a new name— the Tennessee Federation of Sportsmen was now the Tennessee Wildlife Federation. "No longer is [the sportsmen's] program selfish," said the editorial in that month's *Tennessee Wildlife.* "No longer are they concerned just with game animals and game fish but with every living thing God created: birds, animals, trees, shrubs, flowers, fish, water and all that goes to make up this wonderful state. With the adoption of the new constitution and new name, the path has been cleared to actively wage the fight necessary to stop pollution, erosion, dust storms, floods, forest fires and other natural and artificial enemies of Nature."

Moreover, the editorial promised, the new membership categories would encourage "[e]very man, woman, and child in this State" to join the Federation, including "Women's Clubs, Boy Scouts, 4-H Clubs, all Civic Clubs and other types of organizations which should be interested in the welfare of the natural resources of Tennessee and the United States." While this projected surge in enrollments never quite materialized, the Federation was definitely on a growth track.

In 1938, it was happy to become the local sponsor of President Roosevelt's National Wildlife Restoration Week, distributing posters, writing press releases recruiting sponsoring businesses and selling wildlife stamps. (Tennessee quickly became the top seller of stamps nationwide.) In January 1939, Herman Baggenstoss announced that the Federation was moving to the fourth floor of the Third National Bank Building "due to the tremendous amount of work confronting the home office ... in the sponsoring of another and larger Wildlife Week and carrying out its enlarged program."

TENNESSEE GETS ITS FIRST GAME AND FISH COMMISSION

From the start, the Federation's main objective was to create the sort of unpaid, nonpartisan wildlife commission that was already so successful in Pennsylvania, Michigan and elsewhere. That the sportsmen intended to present their bill in January 1935, barely eight months after the group was founded, may have seemed a bit precarious, especially considering that similar bills had been rejected by the last two sessions of the Legislature. On the other hand, they now had the support of the International Association and its model administration bill.

The Federation's version (drafted by attorney Steinmetz), followed the prototype closely: like the International's bill, theirs called for the appointment by the governor of five commissioners representing all regions of the state; no more than three could be from the same political party. Their terms would be staggered, and they would get no pay, only expenses. Their bill copied almost word for word the powers to be vested in the commission: the power to fix seasons and bag limits, close or shorten seasons, buy lands for public hunting, train wildlife managers and so on. It even copied exactly the director's compensation: $3,600.

The only surprise, perhaps, was that the Federation chose not to copy the language in the IAFGCC model that called for repealing all laws, private or otherwise, that were inconsistent with the model law. On the contrary, the Federation's bill stressed that it would have no effect on existing regulations. (By 1935, the 1907 repeal of all private acts had long since been overturned.) Given the sportsmen's historical disgust for private acts, one assumes they made a strictly pragmatic decision not to tamper with these sacred cows. If they were to be dislodged, it would have to be *after* the Federation's law was passed and the commission was secure.

It did pass. On February 8, 1935, the Legislature voted to create the Board of Conservation for Game, Fish and Wild Life; the agency itself was now called the Department of Game and Fish Conservation. Hill McAlister, a Democrat just beginning his second term as governor, signed the bill on February 13.

McAlister now appointed the five members of Tennessee's first citizen game and fish commission: L. C. Jacobs of Nashville, Frank W. Latta, Jr., of Dyersburg, Malcolm Hill of Sparta, Dr. W. H. Cheney of Chattanooga and L. W. Hoskins of Knoxville. For their first director, the commissioners chose Damon Headden, Sr., long active in Lake County politics, and a determined advocate of commercial fishing at Reelfoot Lake. (Though no one could know it then, eighteen years later Headden would fight, literally to the death, trying to destroy the second Game and Fish Commission, the one created by the Tennessee Conservation League in 1949.)

Headden, in fact, was not in for an easy tenure now. The first year of the commission's existence was rocky and confrontational, as Headden himself noted in a Federation newsletter. "No doubt the Commission ... made numerous mistakes, and perhaps it will make mistakes in the future," he wrote. "[Y]et steps were taken and will be taken in the future to correct these mistakes and to keep from having a repetition of them." Apparently the commission had locked horns more than once with politicians who were "continually trying to bring pressure upon the Commission and its director, as in the past."

Relations between the commission and the sportsmen, on the other hand, were solid enough that the commissioners voted to give the Federation some of their money. On May 8, 1936, they agreed to give the Federation $2,400 out of the 1936-1937 Game and Fish budget in recognition of "the many good results obtained through the operation of this organization."

SPENDING THE GAME AND FISH BUDGET

At the same May 8 meeting, the commissioners authorized Headden to spend $12,500 on a public education program, including hiring an education specialist for each of the three grand divisions of the state. (One of the new recruits was John Caldwell, a recent Vanderbilt graduate who would later work for the Federation.) According to Headden, the commission felt that one of the state's greatest needs was a "well-planned educational program to familiarize and acquaint the general public [with] the economic and recreational values ... attached to hunting, fishing and other outdoor sports." Although the Division of Education survived only as long as the commission itself—that is, less than two years—it sparked an interest in conservation that extended well beyond schoolrooms. As John Caldwell later noted, in counties where the department conducted an extensive educational program, "game and fish revenues increased from 50 to 200 percent" (presumably sportsmen were now buying licenses), while violations of the law "decreased proportionately."

The great majority of Game and Fish funding, however—$43,700—was designated for enforcement—"the means of accomplishing the ultimate end desired by all true sportsmen," as Headden put it. This sum provided for eighteen district game protectors (six in each grand division) plus one "divisional protector" (the term *warden*, it seemed, was carefully avoided). Fully five thousand dollars of the enforcement budget was earmarked exclusively for Reelfoot Lake.

After all these expenses, there would be some money left to fund constructive projects like lakes and game farms, Headden allowed. But it would not be much. "[T]he great need for the ensuing year is an appropriation large enough to take advantage of" federal matching funds, he said (though it is not clear what funds he was referring to; Pittman-Robertson was still two years away). In the year just ended, Headden reminded the sportsmen, Tennessee had lost out on some of these programs—"worthwhile projects ... that would have been of great benefit to the sporting public"—because the Legislature had taken too big a bite out of the department's revenues. Headden's final appeal to the sportsmen was to convince their legislators to pass laws that would "keep such a thing from happening again."

On an issue already so close to their hearts, the members of the Federation did not need to be asked twice. They were already polling candidates for the upcoming elections to see which ones would agree—"if elected"—to keep their hands off the Game and Fish funds. In the next session—1937—both houses passed yet another bill giving sole use of hunting and fishing revenues to the Game and Fish agency.

It was the third such bill passed in five sessions, but the sportsmen were pleased. After all, they had little else to be pleased about. In the same session, in the middle of February, with "not a hand raised to defend it," their commission form of administration was abolished.

THE END OF THE COMMISSION

To many in the Federation, the repeal of their commission was a severe blow. In the inaugural issue (February 1937) of *Tennessee Wildlife*, Herman Baggenstoss gave vent to his disappointment in a series of rhetorical questions: "Did not the 1935 general assembly set up a Conservation Board for Fish, Game, and Wildlife? Did not the sportsmen fight for six long years for just such a law? Is not this commission form of government the same model plan adopted by the International Game Conference [sic] in 1934 as the best and most sensible plan of game restoration? Has not this plan been successful in numbers of other states? Has not Tennessee risen in rank from thirty-eighth to tenth in conservation program during the past two years?"

Still, many in the Federation had been bracing for such an outcome. Six months earlier, president Matt Thomas had cautioned the sportsmen to stay alert. "Although the commission bill is a reality, still [we] must organize and stay organized as G-men, or at the next session of the Legislature only seven months hence, what we have secured will be discarded, in order that certain selfish interests may get in charge again. Certainly this ugly effort will be made."

Thomas was right, of course. The new governor, Gordon Browning, had made it clear during his candidacy that he favored an umbrella Department of Conservation into which all related (and a few unrelated) divisions would be placed, from Game and Fish to Forestry, Geology and State Parks. (By the end of the year it would also include the Division of State Information and, improbably, Hotel and Restaurant Inspection.) Each division would be headed by a director, who would report directly to a commissioner of Conservation, who in turn would report directly to the governor. There was almost no hope for a policy-making game and fish commission, and some members of the Federation blamed themselves again for not fighting hard enough to save it.

But in fairness to the sportsmen, there may have been little that they could have done. The Game and Fish Commission, everyone agreed, had not been terribly successful. As the Federation's incoming president Dr. John House said, the 1935 commission had "differed in no essential ways from the old-time one-man political setup which it was supposed to have displaced." Director Headden himself had almost certainly been part of the problem. This man who in June 1936 promised that there would be no more "mistakes" had abruptly resigned his position only three months later. His successor was Howell Buntin, a former state fish and game warden and federal wildlife administrator with what Baggenstoss called "a wide and helpful experience in the field."

Moreover, though the first commission was gone, the prospects for a new one did not seem entirely hopeless. Governor Browning's reorganization bill held out the slight possibility that a commission of some sort might one day be appointed. "[T]he Governor may appoint an advisory Committee on Conservation," stipulated the bill, "consisting of six persons interested in conservation work within the state. The members of said committee shall be appointed for overlapping terms of six years, one retiring each year; they shall be non-salaried, but may be paid traveling expenses." Clearly, even if the 1935 commission had been a bust, the *concept* of a commission had not been absolutely rejected.

In fact, for a brief time Federation leaders had held out some hopes that Browning might be persuaded to salvage the independent Game and Fish Commission. They drafted a resolution urging him to do so; some even met with him to make the appeal in person. However, these requests clearly irritated the new governor, who apparently complained about "certain individuals [who took] the abolition of the game and fish commission as a personal affront." Others in the group knew they had to proceed cautiously. If the governor could be persuaded, all the better. But if he could not, the sportsmen did not want to be dismissed as unreasonable and obstinate. Besides, as Baggenstoss noted, most sportsmen were not, after all, fundamentally opposed to a Department of Conservation. "Such a department can do more for the wild life of Tennessee than six departments pulling against each other," he allowed. "However, the department dealing with renewable natural resources must have a *continuity of thought, program* and *action* before it can be successful in a permanent way."

GOVERNOR BROWNING'S DEPARTMENT OF CONSERVATION

In the end, Browning did not convene a commission, advisory or otherwise. He did, however, promise the sportsmen that his commissioner of Conservation would be a competent conservationist, not a career politician. And when on February 27, 1937, he named native Texan Sam Brewster to the post, the Tennessee Federation of Sportsmen declared itself satisfied. "Governor Browning promised a nonpolitical appointment," said a brief article in the March 1937 *Tennessee Wildlife*, presumably written by Baggenstoss or John House, "and we feel that he has kept his word. Mr. Brewster's training is such that he has an intimate knowledge of the many phases of conservation work ... and we feel sure that every member of the federation unites with us in wishing him every success."

In fact, Brewster was a sort of renaissance man with multiple degrees in landscape architecture, a sojourn abroad studying English parks and landscape design, a stint with the Alabama Extension Service and finally a succession of appointments with the federal government, first in the land planning division of TVA, then with TVA's recreation and conservation section and finally a temporary appointment with the National Park Service, where he was conducting a study of national recreational needs when he was tapped by the Browning administration.

If the Federation recognized the wisdom of cooperating with Browning and his men, Browning and his men recognized the wisdom of cooperating with the Federation. One of the first things Brewster did was agree to keep Howell Buntin as director of Game and Fish. Another was to establish a conservation education section with John Caldwell as field manager, Paul Moore as photographer and film maker and Jim Bailey as supervisor. Brewster's choice of Bailey to lead the section was one of the smartest things he did, because Bailey proved to be an irresistible front man for the new department.

But perhaps the most unusual thing Brewster did was agree to recognize the two-month-old *Tennessee Wildlife* as "the official organ of the Conservation Department." Herman

Baggenstoss, who had been editing the sixteen-page publication since its premier issue in February, delightedly made the announcement in the April 1937 issue.

THE PARTNERSHIP WITH TDOC

"We have always wished that Tennessee might have a state magazine such as is now published so successfully by many other states," wrote Baggenstoss. "We may now realize that wish. Beginning with this issue, *Tennessee Wildlife* will carry official news of the work of the department and its divisions." He offered a proper nod of thanks to the new commissioner: "It is a difficult thing to start publication of a magazine, and we have at times wondered if we could make our magazine permanent. We need have no further fears."

Under the cooperative agreement, the Department of Conservation agreed not only to provide copy and photographs and pay for whatever space these used (typically about half of each issue). Remarkably, it also agreed to leave editorial decision-making to the Federation. There can be no doubt that Baggenstoss and the executive committee insisted on this concession, and probably as little doubt that Brewster resisted granting it. The arrangement was really most unusual, but—for a while at least—it worked. Most issues were editorially quite seamless, with upbeat, chatty news about the Federation and its chapters blending smoothly with upbeat, chatty news about state parks, clean restaurants and fish hatcheries. State personnel contributed lengthy, well-researched articles about small game species or the education program; Federation contacts wrote equally substantive pieces about hunting dogs or TVA lakes.

But at other times, particularly during the ongoing debate over commissions, *Tennessee Wildlife* was like two different magazines accidentally stuck together. On the one hand was the pleasant, rather bland propaganda of an official state publication, on the other the pointed criticism of the polemicist.

This occasional schizophrenia was never so overt as in the December 1938 issue. Subtitled "Department of Conservation Edition," the first fourteen pages were little more than a promotional tour of TDOC, with staged photographs and cheerleader headlines: "Taking Conservation Into the Schools," "Men and Wildlife Depend On Forests," "State Parks Protect Wildlife," "Geology Develops New Industries."

Then abruptly, on page 15, is the familiar *Tennessee Wildlife* masthead, with table of contents, subscription information—and an editorial by Herman Baggenstoss blasting the state and its outgoing governor for once again selling out the natural resources of Tennessee:

> Two years ago WE asked Governor Browning to place a "Commission" over the Department of Conservation, with staggered terms for the purpose of establishing its continuity and stabilizing its program. This he did not see his way clear to do, and for that reason his program will go the way of all programs that are built on political sand and dependent upon political expediency for execution. In the same way, through neglect, will go the Natural Resources of Tennessee, the forests up in smoke, the rich topsoil down the river, pollution will continue unabated, and our "wildlife" will remain without a sincere stable friend in the State government.

As one can imagine, such outspokenness did not endear Baggenstoss to some folks. (His wife Mary Elizabeth remembers how, in later years when Herman was editor and publisher of the *Grundy County Herald*, they sometimes came home to find their windows had been shot out.) Nonetheless, such impassioned, plucky eloquence gave the Tennessee Wildlife Federation a visibility and prominence it had never known before.

HERMAN BAGGENSTOSS STEPS TO THE PLATE

When Herman Baggenstoss became editor of the Federation's publications in late 1936, the Federation was facing not one but two important resignations: outgoing president Matt Thomas, and retiring executive secretary Howard Ansley. Though both men would remain active in the Federation, everyone understood that, given the impending shake-up at Game and Fish, finding suitable replacements was more than usually important.

The new president was Dr. Samuel John House, retired Brentwood doctor and the most recent appointee to the Game and Fish Commission. (This was 1936; the commission was not yet abolished.) Conservationists around the state were delighted to learn of House's election to both positions. They would be equally grieved to learn of his death just a year later, following a long illness.

As for the new executive secretary, the top choice was Herman Baggenstoss, a forester from Tracy City. Besides running the Grundy County CCC Camp in the South Cumberlands, the thirty-two-year-old Baggenstoss had just started producing "Turkey Feathers, Boar Bristles

The first issue of Tennessee Wild Life *(February 1937) featured Dr. S. John House, "Our New President," on its cover. By April, the magazine had become the "official organ" of the Tennessee Department of Conservation. Courtesy of Mrs. Herman Baggenstoss.*

and Fish Fins," the Federation's new bulletin. This newsletter with the ungainly title was a two-sided, mimeographed affair, so densely packed with type that it was almost unreadable. Baggenstoss was eager to upgrade the simple publication and saw that he could do so more readily from the executive secretary's chair. He accepted the position in November 1936. (John Caldwell, about to lose his job with the scuttled Game and Fish Commission, agreed to volunteer as associate editor and business manager.)

Barely two months later, the Federation was going to press with its new, illustrated magazine. By December 1937, *Tennessee Wildlife* was frequently running to eighteen, twenty, even twenty-two pages, and though it had regular advertisers, at least 80 percent of its content was editorial. Even with several associate editors, producing it consumed hours of Baggenstoss' time. Yet when Dr. House died the day after Christmas, he willingly took on the presidency of the Federation as well.

In retrospect, it may have been a mistake, allowing one man to do so much. But good or bad, Herman Baggenstoss would be the point man of the Federation for nearly three years. He attended every annual meeting of the National Wildlife Federation, he met constantly with the Game and Fish Division, he coordinated Tennessee Wildlife Week and stamp sales and he appeared regularly on radio programs and as guest speaker before sportsmen's clubs. He also lobbied for forest protection and organized the Tennessee Forestry Committee of the National Fire Prevention Association. Above all, he wrote voluminously on resource protection. Herman's great strength—apart from his extraordinary organizational zeal—was the printed word. This man who ten years later would buy his own newspaper believed strongly in the power of the press.

Before Baggenstoss took over, communications had not been the Federation's strong suit. During the 1934-35 campaign to pass their commission bill, Federation leaders apparently kept in touch by mail or telephone or in person; at any rate, no Federation bulletins or newsletters have survived from those early months, nor did the outdoor columnists mention any such publications in their weekly columns, which they normally did. There was so little conservation news in those days that when a magazine or interesting bit of correspondence reached an outdoor editor's desk, he invariably shared it in some detail with his readers. In late 1935, for instance, R. A. Wilson announced his high hopes for a new outdoor magazine. "We have before us the December and initial issue of the *Southern States Sportsman*, published at Knoxville. It is the successor of the *Tennessee Sportsman*, formerly published in Nashville." He concluded by wishing the new magazine a "long and useful life. The field it has entered is wide and ripe."

However, the *Southern States Sportsman* did not last more than a few issues. For the next year or so, the field remained wide open for a quality outdoor magazine for Tennessee.

THE POWER OF THE OUTDOOR PRESS

At first, it hardly looked as though the Tennessee Federation of Sportsmen would be the one to fill the void. The Federation's first bulletin, dated June 1936, was a simple collation of ten letter-size sheets, folded in half, with hand-lettered covers and simple illustrations. The back cover was an advertisement for Purina Dog Chow; the Ralston Purina Company was acknowledged prominently on the front.

The name of this simple piece was *Organization News of the Tennessee Federation of Sportsmen!* (The exclamation mark was part of the title.) Why it took two years to announce the "organization news" is anybody's guess, but president Matt Thomas' lead article—"Why, the Tennessee Federation of Sportsmen?"—offered a brief summary of all that had taken place since "the days prior to 1935" through the formation of the commission. It concluded with an exhortation in capital letters: "FORWARD MARCH BOYS, THE FIGHT IS ON."

Yet for all its manifest simplicity, the *Organization News* showed signs of a shrewder intelligence. On the heels of Thomas' speech was a questionnaire to be offered all legislative candidates in the coming (1936) election.

♦   *Question One:* Will you ... oppose any effort made to divert or merge the fish and game funds with other revenues of the state?

♦   *Question Two:* Will you pledge yourself ... to continue [the Game and Fish Commission] and to oppose any effort to curtail [its] powers and duties?

♦   *Question Three:* Will you pledge ... to vote for the repeal of local game laws?

The newsletter also included a report from then-Game and Fish Director Damon Headden; a listing of affiliates (forty-six chapters by mid-1936, up from thirty-four the previous year); and a financial report. (The Federation had $426.17 in the bank as of April 30, 1936, and owed half of that.) As *Tennessee Wildlife* would later do, the *Organization News* included news briefs from as many chapters as would send them. The Knox County Chapter, for instance, reported on its quail food project. It even included the formula: 4 percent Sudan grass, 5 percent each of buckwheat and soybeans, 10 percent milo maize, 13 percent Korean lespedeza, 15 percent each of millet and cowpeas and 33 percent sorghum.

As large as the Federation had become, and as barren the field of outdoor journals, there was a ready-made readership for anything the Federation could produce, even something as crude as the *Organization News*. Fortunately, when a willing editor finally did step forward, it was someone with the journalistic skills, conservation fire and marketing acumen of Herman Baggenstoss.

A passionate, articulate and often entertaining writer, Baggenstoss could also be obstinate and bitingly sarcastic. But his oratory was honest, intelligent and dedicated to the ideal that natural resources deserve to be an inviolable part of the public trust. Thanks to his enormous energy and his nose for publicity, he saturated Tennessee's newspapers with conservation headlines for the better part of three years.

As soon as the second issue of *Tennessee Wildlife* was off the press, Baggenstoss sent out a letter to virtually every newspaper in the state—there were several hundred back then—enclosing the March issue and asking the editor's help in publicizing the Federation's activities and mission. His colleagues in the press were grateful for the promise of a steady, meaty correspondence on a topic which was often a newspaper's most popular feature. For three years Baggenstoss kept his contacts supplied with a ceaseless flow of press releases, news stories and photographs; when clips came back he carefully taped them into a scrapbook that today bulges with yellowed newsprint: "Sportsmen Favor Wild Game Bill" (*Kingsport Times*). "Cooper Would Keep Politics Out of Conservation Program" (*Johnson City Chronicle*). "Baggenstoss Denounces State Game Department" (*Memphis Press-Scimitar*). And in early 1939: "Famous Cartoonist Coming to Bristol for Rally in May" (*Bristol Herald*).

DING DARLING COMES TO TENNESSEE

Jay N. "Ding" Darling's appearance at a 1939 sportsmen's rally in Bristol was not the first time the famous Iowan had visited Tennessee. On July 14-16, 1937, Darling had been the featured speaker at the General Wildlife Federation's first Regional Wildlife Conference in Nashville. Other well-known names on the program included Carl Shoemaker, executive secretary of the General Wildlife Federation; Seth Gordon, head of the Pennsylvania Game Commission; Dr. T. Gilbert Pearson, president of the National Association of Audubon Societies; Dr. Carl Russell, chief of the wildlife division of the National Park Service; I. T. Bode of the U.S. Extension Service and at least two dozen others. This august event, hosted jointly with the Tennessee Wildlife Federation, marked the beginning of the Tennessee affiliate's long, strong relationship with national headquarters (and the first of its many annual meetings at the Noel Hotel). The only cost for three days of meetings, receptions and field trips was $2.50 for Thursday's banquet.

The Tennessee Federation of Sportsmen had joined the Washington-based NWF in 1936, when the latter group (then known as the General Wildlife Federation) was formally founded at the first North American Wildlife Conference in Washington. It is likely that Herman Baggenstoss represented Tennessee at that initial meeting; it is certain that he went the following year, and almost every year after that. In February 1937, Baggenstoss and Tennessee Game and Fish director Howell Buntin traveled together to St. Louis, where another fifteen hundred attendees reelected Darling president and endorsed his seven-point program. Among the seven points: establishing complete government jurisdiction over the nation's water resources; and earmarking for conservation purposes the $3.5 million spent annually on hunting and fishing licenses.

At one point Baggenstoss had a chance to address the whole assembly. He told them of the work being done by the Tennessee affiliate and promised its support of the Federation's new program. In their turn, delegates commended the Tennessee group, saying it was the only affiliate that was self-supporting and the only one publishing a monthly magazine.

If he didn't know him before, Baggenstoss got to know Ding Darling now. The two remained friends until Darling's death in 1962. Darling even drew a cartoon for his Swiss friend. (Unfortunately, Mary Elizabeth can no longer find it.) Baggenstoss met most of the other officers of the Federation in St. Louis, including Edward K. Love of Missouri, director of NWF's Region 5. It was probably at this meeting that Baggenstoss was asked to host the first regional conference of the General Wildlife Federation, an honor he was happy to accept.

The conference was no small undertaking. With three hundred people registered at the Noel Hotel, two hundred signed up for field trips to Norris Dam and Pickett State Forest,

The Tennessee Federation of Sportsmen hosts the first Regional Conference of the General Wildlife Federation, July 1937. J. N. "Ding" Darling (second from right) is the featured speaker. Herman Baggenstoss is at the far left. Courtesy of Mrs. Herman Baggenstoss.

and more than thirty speakers on the program, including Governor Browning, the president of the General Wildlife Federation, Tennessee's attorney general and TVA's chief forester, the three-day event took months of planning. John Caldwell, who had been acting as unpaid business manager of *Tennessee Wildlife*, volunteered as the general conference chairman. When it was over, the executive committee of the Tennessee Wildlife Federation hired him full time. His title was managing editor, but he was in fact a good deal more, organizing new chapters, conducting a series of wildlife surveys, writing articles for the magazine and conducting educational programs.

In addition to convincing the Federation that it needed more staff, the conference also had the useful effect of fortifying the relationship between the Federation and the Browning administration. Governor Browning designated the week of July 11-17, 1937, as State Conservation Week and introduced Ding Darling at the Thursday evening banquet. The Department of Conservation, which cohosted the event, also supplied several speakers, including Commissioner Brewster, who delivered the opening address.

In fact, for all their rocky beginnings, the Federation and the Department of Conservation were learning how to work together. In September 1937, Commissioner Brewster began a series of meetings with sportsmen around the state, seeking to "gain a better understanding of [their] problems." The sportsmen were grateful, and nagged without bullying; Commissioner Brewster was receptive, and listened without groveling. Usually they managed to reach some sort of agreement.

For example, one of the first points in the Federation's agenda was that the Game and Fish agency provide a written annual report, something it had never done in thirty-five years.

In September 1938, Baggenstoss thanked Howell Buntin for the financial statement included in the August issue of *Tennessee Wildlife*. "[A]s far as we know, this is the first complete accounting to the public of the Game and Fish revenues and expenditures in the history of the Game and Fish [program]."

But other demands took longer to fulfill—not because the administration was stubborn, but because its two years were up before the program could be gotten underway. This, of course, was the crux of the Federation's complaint. The Federation had started calling for professional training for game wardens (later known as conservation officers) as soon as Sam Brewster took office. In September 1937, Brewster announced that Tennessee would establish a school for wardens "patterned after the one at Ames, Iowa, which has been recognized as the outstanding school of this type in the land." By the following July nothing had happened, and Baggenstoss ended an editorial about game violations with a sarcastic "[t]his reminds us . . . When does our Officer's Training School start?" And again, in September: "Let's get that training school established!"

But 1938 was an election year and the sand was running out on Browning's term. Come January, he was out, a new governor was in—and those well-laid plans for an officer training school had been taken out with Sam Brewster's trash.

GOVERNOR COOPER BANS PRIVATE WILDLIFE ACTS

Several months before the 1938 election, the Federation had put the question of a commission to all three candidates for governor, including the incumbent. What the sportsmen were pushing now, however, was not just a game and fish commission, but a commission with policy-making powers over the entire Department of Conservation. Based on Missouri's conservation commission, their model called for staggered terms without pay, "sufficient" freedom from political hiring and firing and "sufficient" freedom from political influence in all decision-making. It must be stable enough to follow a policy for at least ten years, and it must be allowed to appoint its own "chief executive officer" who in turn must be allowed to hire and fire all personnel. "This vital point," they said, "cannot be compromised."

Predictably, the incumbent Gordon Browning replied that his Conservation Department had been so effective that there was no need to change it. Roy C. Wallace said he favored a separate commission for game and fish—he did not mention how he felt about retaining the Department of Conservation—and he also pledged to train the game wardens. As for Prentice Cooper, he claimed to favor a seven-man commission for the entire Department of Conservation, including Game and Fish, free of political pressures and designed to assure "stable and continuous policy through at least a decade." Cooper won the 1938 election, but the Federation soon had reason to question his campaign promises. Even before the new Conservation Commission was appointed, he went ahead and named its "chief executive": Commissioner of Conservation J. Charles Poe. Richard Turner soon replaced Howell Buntin as head of Game and Fish.

On February 25, 1939, Cooper submitted his administration bill creating the Conservation Commission. But this was not exactly the bill the Federation expected. Instead of a citizen body free from politics, the fifth member of the commission would be the governor himself, with full powers to hire and fire anybody in the department.

Federation members felt rather taken in by all this, but as vice-president Joel Fort noted philosophically, "It was a compromise, and perhaps later we can get the rest." Even Herman Baggenstoss' March editorial was unexpectedly charitable: "In recognition of constructive legislation enacted, Governor Prentice Cooper and the 76th General Assembly deserve the congratulations of all conservationists." Besides creating Tennessee's first Conservation Commission, the new governor had mounted a campaign against local wildlife laws. Fish and game recognize no boundaries, he declared; neither should the laws that protect them.

Cooper promised that, if elected, he would repeal all existing private wildlife acts and refuse to sign any new ones should they make it to his desk. Not since Malcolm Patterson in 1907 had any governor taken so strong a stand against private acts. On March 10, 1939, Cooper signed a bill repealing all local laws. "Even Reelfoot Lake has been brought under the jurisdiction of general state laws," reported *Tennessee Wildlife* triumphantly.

Though Cooper's ban was undone in 1949 with the creation of the Game and Fish Commission, his stand won him the respect of the sportsmen. (When the first Z. Cartter Patten Award was made in 1943, Cooper won it.) Herman Baggenstoss' benign editorial tone continued when the governor finally appointed the first Conservation Commission in May. In his June 1939 editorial, Baggenstoss declared the commission "exceptionally well-balanced." Its good-natured chairman was Dr. George Mayfield, one of the founders of the Tennessee Ornithological Society and professor of German at Vanderbilt. Mayfield was also an officer in the Tennessee Wildlife Federation. Joe Summers of Johnson City was chairman of the Seven-County Conservation Conference in East Tennessee; he, too, served on the Federation's executive committee. Samuel Mossman Nickey, just twenty-eight years old, was already an executive in his father's timber business. He had studied forest conservation in Europe, Mexico and South America and was also a member of the Federation. Only Major Lytle Brown of Franklin, the retired chief of the Army Corps of Engineers in Nashville, did not, it seems, belong to the sportsmen's group.

Satisfactory as the commission was, however, it had taken Cooper almost five months to assemble it, and Baggenstoss had been getting nervous about the delay. The gloves had came off in April 1939, in a brief but scathing editorial titled "$100,000 Loss":

> As a business man, would you fire 90% of your help today from your store, factory or farm and expect to get efficient results tomorrow? If you did, would you replace them with absolutely green hands, waiving all qualifications and examinations? Would you hire or fire them against the advice of your factory superintendent after he had examined their records and passed on their fitness? OF COURSE NOT.
>
> Yet unfortunately that procedure is being followed today in the Division of Game and Fish, in the hiring and firing of its conservation officers. It is unfortunate for the resources of the State, unfortunate for the taxpayer, unfortunate for every citizen and can only lead to the loss of confidence, ruin and bankruptcy in any business and any government.
>
> Job uncertainty, "fear of the axe," and lack of positive leadership for four months has cost the State a $100,000 loss, if not more, in the Division of Game and Fish.

Common sense demands that Governor Cooper appoint the members of the Conservation Commission now so it can establish the policies of the Department of Conservation as required by law, so that Commissioner Poe and his staff can execute those policies promptly, without fear or favor, for conservation and conservation alone.

END OF THE GLORY DAYS

The Cooper administration had been wary of Baggenstoss' tongue for some time. (For that matter, so were some of Baggenstoss' own colleagues.) Apparently this editorial was the last straw. Though his name would appear on the *Tennessee Wildlife* masthead once or twice more, Herman's contentious editorials disappeared, and it seems likely that the April issue was the last one in which he enjoyed full editorial freedom. In June, the Federation's executive committee voted to appoint a board to direct *Tennessee Wildlife*'s editorial policy.

For several months the magazine listed no editor at all. In December 1939, the editor is given as Edward J. Meeman, editor and publisher of the *Memphis Press-Scimitar* and the current president of the Tennessee Wildlife Federation. Baggenstoss continued as executive secretary a few months more, but apparently his heart wasn't in it. In October, he sent Meeman his formal resignation, a letter not by any means vindictive or disappointed, but friendly and ultimately upbeat. After enumerating some of the achievements of the past thirty-five months—seventy-three affiliates, three thousand "bona fide" members, twenty-seven issues of *Tennessee Wildlife* and the "splendid personnel" of the state's first Conservation Commission—he concluded his letter with a tribute to his colleagues. "I feel that I owe a debt of gratitude to my fellow workers and sportsmen of this state. The experience as executive secretary has been invaluable. The association with the conservationists has been a real source of happiness. I am sure you will find the same during your term as president."

A short time later Baggenstoss left Tennessee for Missouri, where he served on the Conservation Commission before joining the Pacific fleet early in World War II as a Seabee. The magazine never formally acknowledged Baggenstoss' leavetaking as editor. However, the December 1939 issue carried this notice: "Beginning with the next issue the *Tennessee Wildlife* will become *The Tennessee Wildlife and Conservationist* and will be published by the Conservation Commissioner in the interest of the Tennessee Wildlife Federation and the Department of Conservation. ... [E]very phase of Federation activity will be covered."

But in fact there would be little such news to cover. In spite of a flurry of activity in late 1939 over a proposed five-year fund-raising program headed by Meeman and his fellow Memphian Lucius E. Burch, Jr., and in spite of the handful of powerful conservationists who continued to serve on the board (among them Z. Cartter Patten, III, Burch and Karl Steinmetz), the Federation was slowly winding down. With Meeman's election, a significant part of the group's leadership had shifted to Memphis, not the easiest point from which to do business in an elongated state. Moreover, the Federation's relationship with the Department of Conservation remained strained. As one observer would write a few years later, "Several of [the Federation's members] have been trying to run the Department of Conservation and the Department doesn't like it." One result of this breakdown was the accelerated takeover of the magazine by the department. By December 1940, the peculiar partnership between

Tennessee Wildlife and *The Tennessee Conservationist* had been dissolved. Thenceforth, the magazine was simply *The Tennessee Conservationist*, and the Federation's presence in it became more and more slight.

MARCHING OFF TO WAR

But the loss of one man, even a Herman Baggenstoss, should not alone have been capable of shutting down what had been, for better than four years, the leading conservation group in the state. In fact, there was another culprit: World War II. By 1940, the war in Europe was already beginning to disrupt the conservation movement; apparently people had other things on their minds. With the attack on Pearl Harbor, the sportsmen's movement found itself unceremoniously shoved aside. For the next four years nonessential travel was restricted and gasoline rationed. Automobile tires wore out and could not be replaced due to the shortage of rubber. Even firearms and ammunition grew scarce as manufacturing was redirected to supply the war effort. Shipping blockades cut off imports of everything from British-made fishing hooks to Chinese tankin cane and hackle feathers for flies and fly rods. As purchases of guns and shells plummeted, so did Tennessee's share of Pittman-Robertson funds, a grim reminder that many of America's hunters were doing their hunting overseas.

Organized conservation activities were pretty much suspended during the war years. The conservation education workshops sponsored by the Tennessee Department of Conservation faded temporarily while their leader, Jim Bailey, served in the Navy. Cabins at many state parks were reserved for military personnel. Other than hosting USO events, park development projects were pretty much frozen by the lack of materials and shortage of workers. The newest state parks, including Cove Lake, Harrison Bay, Watauga, Booker T. Washington, Cumberland Mountain and T. O. Fuller, were all left half-finished until after the war. Negotiations to create a national historic park at Cumberland Gap near Harrogate were temporarily abandoned. Federal hatchery operations were cut back. In 1942 the Civilian Conservation Corps was disbanded so that the CCC boys could serve overseas instead. Like every other state, Tennessee was forced to shut down dozens of CCC camps and conservation projects, including the crew that had been reforesting Copper Hill.

Sportsmen's groups found their programs equally at a standstill as the draft deprived them of their chief growth market—young and middle-aged men. The International Association of Game, Fish and Conservation Commissioners canceled its 1942 meeting, then, as the fighting continued, canceled meetings for 1943, 1944 and 1945. The Tennessee Outdoor Writers Association (TOWA), newly organized in 1942, had time for just one convention in 1943 before going into dormancy in 1944 and 1945. Many of the youngest outdoor writers were drafted, replaced by retired "scribes," as they called themselves, sometimes even by women.

ENTER LOU WILLIAMS

Louis J. ("Lou") Williams was one of those older fellows called in to pinch hit for the local newspaper. Williams, a trout fisherman, amateur woodworker and assistant sales manager at the Penn-Dixie Cement Corp. in Chattanooga, sat in as the outdoor columnist for *The Chattanooga Times* from 1941 to 1946. Williams was an indefatigable worker for any cause he believed in: Boy Scouts, Girls Clubs, Chambers of Commerce, Audubon Societies, Cancer Societies, sportsmen's clubs. Over the years he made a reputed three hundred gavels in different species of wood, eventually donating the entire collection to the new forestry building at the University of the South. (No one seems to know where the gavels are now.) He collected antique fishing tackle and made hand-crafted fly rods, giving them to U.S. presidents and visiting dignitaries as well as his closest friends. It was Williams who helped organize TOWA, Williams who helped develop the Chickamauga Fly and Bait Casting Club and Williams who would spearhead the Tennessee Conservation League as soon as the war was over. Now, Williams got *The Chattanooga Times* and some of his friends in the Chickamauga fishing club to sponsor the Overseas Tackle Fund.

Overseas Tackle started as a joint project to collect used fishing tackle, refurbish it, then ship it to "the boys overseas." By 1944, about a dozen fellows were involved in the project, including E. H. Peckinpaugh, founder of the Chattanooga chapter of the Izaak Walton League and owner of the Peckinpaugh Company, maker of fishing lures shipped all over the world.

The local project soon developed into a national one. The local press wrote features about it; *Field and Stream* did a story. Tackle manufacturers South Bend and Horricks Ibbotson "emptied their warehouses." People sent brand new fishing equipment, new rods, tackle that hadn't even been opened.

Still, when the war finally ended in 1945 and the soldiers started coming home, Williams was elated. He had another fight in mind.

Between 1944 and 1946, the Overseas Tackle Fund shipped four hundred packages of fishing gear to "lonesome homesick boys" in the service. The effort was sponsored by members of the Chickamauga Fly and Bait Casting Club, including E. H. Peckinpaugh (seated, far left) and Lou Williams (standing, right). Courtesy of Joe Halburnt.

Chapter 3

1946-1949

The League And The Model Law

If you will join hands with us, talk with your legislative representatives in advance of the forthcoming elections and get their pledge of support, and otherwise assist the League in this important work, we will win with flying colors. It is not a job for a handful of men. A good portion of the 260,000 license buyers will have to do their part. Can we count on you?

—preface to the draft of the 1949 model law

The Peacetime Conflict Over Game And Fish

If peacetime signaled the end to conflicts overseas, for Tennessee's sportsmen it meant renewing the battle on another front, the fight over control of Tennessee's fish and game. By the end of World War II, Lou Williams would later recall, politics had so wholly taken over the Game and Fish Division that it would be "impossible to fully describe the situation." Were he to attempt it, he said, "those who weren't around then wouldn't believe what was said."

For instance, "influential business and political leaders who called themselves 'sportsmen'" annually slaughtered doves over baited fields. One politician "routinely shipped frozen bob-white quail to the White House, in violation of state game laws." The quail hatchery at Buffalo Springs raised thirty thousand quail, he said, "but a goodly number of them went into the deep-freeze lockers of the 'right' people."

What really irked the sportsmen, though, was that outdoor sport generally, and big game hunting in particular, was still marginal in Tennessee, especially when compared to the progress being made in states like Pennsylvania and Michigan. While these states placed consistently at or near the top of annual wildlife surveys and big game rankings, Tennessee lagged near the bottom, usually around thirty-eighth or thirty-ninth. While allowances had to be made for ground lost during the war, Tennessee's game management programs simply were not making acceptable headway, the sportsmen felt.

The state's quail hatcheries, in place for a decade now, were still losing as much as thirty dollars a bird, yet one official admitted, "We don't know yet whether the program is successful." Game and Fish had had equally underwhelming success with its raccoon restoration program. And as for its turkey propagation efforts, the results by 1943 had been "none too encouraging. Most of these artificially grown birds apparently [were] unable to accustom themselves to the wilds," said a report.

In spite of the fourteen-year moratorium on deer hunting imposed earlier in the century, and in spite of thousands of dollars spent shipping deer in from other states, Tennessee's deer herd remained abysmally small in 1946. No one knew just how many, but in 1937 a game manager had estimated the total herd of white-tails at less than twelve hundred. A decade later, the herd was still too precarious to support more than a briefest of deer seasons. In 1946, the season lasted just four days, and included parts of just six counties, plus the Andrew Johnson game management area in East Tennessee. In 1945, the scheduled Tellico-Citico deer hunt had to be canceled due to lack of prey.

Like the quail hatching efforts, Tennessee's deer restoration program was not noted for its cost-effectiveness. To buy and transport a white-tailed deer from Wisconsin, for instance, cost the state about ninety dollars per animal. Released in wildlife management areas where hunting was prohibited for the next five years, the deer was left to grow and multiply. Yet once the ban was lifted, it could be shot for the price of a two-dollar hunting and fishing license. That was a poor enough return to the state, said the organized sportsmen. But even more absurd, they said, was that a criminal could take the same deer almost as cheaply as the legitimate sportsman. The penalty for poaching, according to Tennessee's game code, was as little as ten dollars, and never more than twenty-five. The sportsmen consistently asked for harsher punishments for scofflaws; they also asked repeatedly for higher license fees to support a stronger wildlife program. In 1945, a combined hunting and fishing license sold for just two dollars, the same price sportsmen had been paying since 1915. (And back then, one was paying for hunting privileges only. Fishing wasn't licensed in Tennessee until 1931.)

NOT SO VERY BAD: THE DIVISION OF GAME AND FISH

However, in fairness to the division—and to the Conservation Commission established in 1939 by Governor Cooper—Tennessee's game and fish program was not altogether a black hole of incompetence in the mid-1940s. By 1946 the division had a staff of wildlife scientists who, though small in number (three game and three fish technicians) were at least professionally trained. Val Solyom, the head game technician, had been appointed in 1937 by Sam Brewster. Solyom had a graduate degree in wildlife management from the University of Michigan and had later worked for the Michigan Department of Conservation. Eugene Kuhne, a fellow Michigan graduate, came on board as chief fish technician in 1938. Though Kuhne was barely out of university, he'd had considerable experience in Michigan's fisheries department as well as the U.S. Bureau of Fisheries in several western states.

Game and Fish also had a reasonably strong enforcement program. Wildlife officers were not required to have much formal schooling, but they all had to attend a training program, and they boasted a strong arrest record. Their conviction rate averaged better than 80 percent, and was steadily improving. But most important of all, perhaps, was the fact that the division could finally boast some stability. In 1946 Howell Buntin was going on his tenth year as director of Game and Fish, a record of staying power. In 1947 he would succeed Paul Mathes as commissioner of the Department of Conservation. And after seven years on the Conservation Commission, Dr. Mayfield, Joe Summers and forestry expert Sam Nickey were still there. (All members should have rotated off after six years, but the war may have held things up.)

So there was a degree of both expertise and continuity in the affairs of Tennessee's wildlife in the 1940s. During the war years, the agency had conducted an extensive survey of fishing and water quality in almost all the state's lakes and streams. Among the most useful findings of this study was its admission that developing and protecting natural habitats was "probably" even more important than artificial propagation, despite the fact that the agency still spent "a great share of [its] energies" on such programs. This was, of course, the same conclusion being reached by everyone else in the game management universe, and Tennessee was already redirecting its resources accordingly. In 1942, the agency paid nearly twenty thousand dollars (using its new Pittman-Robertson money) for the 63,000-acre Catoosa tract on the Cumberland plateau; its plan was to develop the wild area as habitat for deer and wild turkey. And owing to a recent agreement with the U.S. Fish and Wildlife Service, the agency was hoping at last to control the silt and vegetation that were choking Reelfoot Lake. Under that 1941 agreement, the USFWS leased a third of Reelfoot Lake for a National Wildlife Refuge; in return, it agreed to invest a half-million dollars in lake improvements.

Though they had only advisory powers, much of the progress in Game and Fish reflected the integrity of the men on the Conservation Commission. The commissioners had earned the respect of the sportsmen, who appreciated their honesty and their considerable if not perfect familiarity with sportsmen's issues. Nevertheless, the sportsmen said, it wasn't enough. The commission had no real power to influence policy, and with only four citizen members trying to cover six areas of administration, its talents were spread far too thin.

The Department of Conservation now included, besides Game and Fish, the divisions of Forestry, Parks, Geology, State Information and Hotel and Restaurant Inspection. Granted, the Game and Fish share of the budget was about twice that of any other division ($400,000 for fiscal year 1947-48), and the commission appears to have devoted proportionately more of its time to fish and game matters than to any other issue, with the exception, perhaps, of forestry, whose affairs were closely tied to wildlife. Still, the sportsmen argued, Tennessee's wildlife management program deserved its own board of experts, whose powers were not materially shortchanged by the governor, and whose energies were not dissipated by dirty restaurants or tourism brochures. An independent commission had happened before, in 1935. Why, with proper planning and organization, should it not happen again?

This central question had been germinating for years in the minds of some of the state's sportsmen. In late 1945, thanks to a handful of Tennessee's outdoor writers, it finally began to bear fruit.

When the Outdoor Writers Association of America announced that it would hold its 1946 annual meeting in Chattanooga, Joe Halburnt hurried to complete the first issue of his new sporting magazine. The June 1946 issue of Tennessee Valley Sportsman *(later renamed* Dixie Sportsman*) came off the press just in time for the meeting. By way of congratulations, dozens of outdoor writers autographed Halburnt's personal copy. Courtesy of Joe Halburnt.*

TOWA IS BORN, THE TENNESSEE WILDLIFE FEDERATION DIES

In 1945 the Tennessee Outdoor Writers Association had been in existence barely three years. TOWA had formed near Crossville on August 24, 1942, during the dedication of the new Catoosa Game Refuge. The Game and Fish Division, understandably proud of its enormous new hunting grounds, had invited outdoor writers from all over Tennessee to cover the event. Two of the writers who got invitations were Lou Williams and E. T. Bales, both of Chattanooga. To them, the Crossville gathering presented an opportunity for the taking.

Williams, who had recently started writing an outdoor column for *The Chattanooga Times*, and Bales, who wrote for its rival *Chattanooga News-Free Press*, had for some months been hoping to form a Tennessee chapter of the Outdoor Writers Association of America. With most of their prospective members already assembled in Crossville, it would be easy enough to form an affiliate. Bales and Williams dashed off a memo to their fellow writers, then sat down and drafted proposed bylaws for a group to be called the Tennessee Outdoor Writers Association.

The journalists at Crossville elected Lou Williams president and E. T. Bales secretary. Vice president was Frank Vestal of *The Commercial Appeal* in Memphis and treasurer was Paul K. Bryant, better known as the Old Guide on WSM's popular radio show *Wildlife Club of the Air*, broadcast every Saturday afternoon. Other directors included Joe Halburnt of *The*

Knoxville Journal, Paul Fairleigh of the *Memphis Press-Scimitar* and Joe Summers from the Conservation Commission. The group also included Z. (for Zeboim) Cartter Patten, III, scion of one of Chattanooga's first families; and nationally syndicated outdoor writer Nash Buckingham of Memphis. Buckingham's legendary status in Tennessee owed as much to his career as a star fullback at the University of Tennessee at the turn of the century as it did to his fame as an outdoor writer.

Though the founding members of TOWA approved the idea of an independent game and fish commission, their job was shaping public opinion. It was never their plan to lobby the Legislature themselves. Instead, the group hoped to launch a separate group of sportsmen-conservationists, similar to the now-moribund Tennessee Wildlife Federation, perhaps even a reincarnation of it. In fact, TOWA had once editorialized that it was time "some friend" of the Federation and the Conservation Department "propose a settlement of the differences which seem[ed] to exist between them." Tennessee "sorely" needed a strong statewide organization of sportsmen, said the writer, adding, "There is enough left of the old Federation to form a nucleus around which to build the new."

Shortly after this editorial appeared, TOWA itself went into hibernation for the remainder of the war. As for the Tennessee Wildlife Federation, though its pulse was barely detectable, it *was* still breathing. When Herman Baggenstoss returned from duty in the South Pacific, he and a few friends tried to get the Federation's blood pumping again. It is unclear exactly when they first met, but by May 1946, the revived Federation was getting five-dollar memberships "from various places all over the state." Z. Cartter Patten had been elected president, Knoxville attorney Karl Steinmetz was on the constitution committee, and Baggenstoss himself resumed his former place as the Federation's secretary, working out of his home in Tracy City.

As it turned out, the rebirth of the Federation was short-lived. Just how short-lived, we don't know; the records are sketchy. What is clear is that another star was forming at precisely the same time, and the Tennessee Wildlife Federation was soon pulled into its orbit, and swallowed up.

LOU WILLIAMS PROPOSES A LEAGUE OF SPORTSMEN

By the summer of 1945, America's soldiers were at last being released from their long duty overseas. Lou Williams was delighted, and promptly began declaring, via his forum in the *Times*, that it was time to wake up the slumbering Tennessee Outdoor Writers Association. (Williams was, by default, still president of TOWA.) It was also time, he said with his contagious enthusiasm, for all sportsmen to unite into one powerful statewide alliance.

Throughout the fall, Williams sounded out a few of his allies on the prospects for a new conservation group. He must have known that the old Federation was officially back in business, but he had never been affiliated with the Federation, nor had most of the fellows he now talked with. In fact, there seemed to be a vague impression that the efforts of the Federation had "not met with general acceptance"—referring, no doubt, to the turf wars between the Federation and the Department of Conservation.

On the other hand, most everyone seemed to like the idea of a new organization.

Among the first to lock arms with Williams was Nathaniel Taylor Winston, Sr., a Johnson City outdoor writer, founder of the huge Unaka Rod and Gun Club and a shrewd business-man. (By exploiting a regulatory loophole regarding branch banks, Winston had made his Home Federal the largest savings and loan association in the state.) Winston came from a long line of nonconformists. Among his kin were the famous Taylor brothers, Bob and Alf, who had gained national notoriety in 1886 when they ran against each other for governor in what the press dubbed the "War of the Roses." Robert Love Taylor, the Democrat, went on to become one of Tennessee's great conservationist governors and later, a U.S. Senator. (Brother Alfred, the Republican, finally got his own term as governor in the 1920s.)

Nat Winston had grown up on the Taylor family farm in Elizabethton, moving for a time into a remote cabin he built for himself near Roan Mountain. Alone in the rustic cabin for weeks at a time, Winston developed his knack for storytelling, often exaggerating the strong hillbilly dialect of upper East Tennessee. Periodically Winston would ride into Johnson City to mail off one of these stories, selling them to magazines for fifty dollars apiece. It was on one of these trips into town in the 1920s that he caught the eye of his future wife, the gen-teel daughter of a wealthy Maryland family whose properties included the Mayflower Hotel in Washington, D.C. According to the couple's son, Nat Winston, Jr., a physician who now lives in Nashville, his mother told the eccentric mountain man, "If you get a real job I'll marry you." Thus inspired, the senior Winston went door to door through the neighborhoods of Johnson City, collecting money until he had enough to start a bank.

Winston readily agreed to help Lou Williams solicit other sportsmen and TOWA mem-bers to form the nucleus of a new conservation group. By early winter, a dozen or more men had signed on. Even at this point, a few men were still for resurrecting the old Tennessee Wildlife Federation, and it may have been this minority who briefly restarted the Federation. The majority, however, wanted to form something new.

THE BIRTH OF THE TENNESSEE CONSERVATION LEAGUE

"But what about a name?" wrote Williams in his 1971 history of the League.

We wanted to eliminate the use of "sportsman's club," "wildlife society," "hunting and fishing" and the like. Finally, after lengthy and sometimes heated discussions, Ernest Peckinpaugh, known then as "dean of conservation" in the Chattanooga area, came up with "Tennessee Conservation League." In presenting it he emphasized the need for an organization that stood for more than wildlife conservation. He envisioned one which would concern itself with the overall aspects of natural resource conservation. He wanted the new group to advocate programs which would encompass soil, water, forests as well as wildlife. A number of others in the small, determined group felt the same way. When the proposed name was voted upon the approval was unanimous.

The charter of incorporation was filed with Secretary of State Joe Carr on January 30, 1946. It listed fourteen numbered "purposes" (most of which had to do with hunting and fishing, despite the League's catholic name) and was signed by fifteen men, all of them sportsmen, most of them members of TOWA. The founders put up ten dollars each in seed money, not only to pay the charter fee, but to pay for postage and phone calls. Every sportsmen's club in the state had to be notified about the upcoming organizational meeting.

TCL IS DECLARED "A GOING CONCERN"

That meeting was held Tuesday, February 12, 1946, at Chattanooga's Read House. According to the roster included in the minutes of that meeting, a respectable crowd of fifty-three Tennesseans showed up, plus two guest speakers from the game and fish programs of neighboring states. (In his column the following Sunday, Lou Williams aggrandized the turn-out to "almost one hundred sportsmen," though his 1971 history puts the number of local men at fifty-four. This is still one more than the number actually present, presumably because one man, Paul Bonds, was listed twice in the minutes.)

Of the original fifteen incorporators, twelve made it to the Read House. Only John Flippen, Enoch Brown and Frank Vestal could not be there. (In those pre-interstate days, getting from Memphis to Chattanooga was an all-day drive.) The two visiting wildlife officials were Charlie Elliott, director of Georgia's game and fish program, and Tom Ford, an official from Alabama. Both represented states where the commission form of game and fish administration was

Charter members of the Tennessee Conservation League gather at the Read House in Chattanooga, February 12, 1946. Front row, left to right: Lou Williams, Walter Amann, Jr., Paul K. Bryant and Z. Cartter Patten, III. Back row, left to right: Nash Buckingham, Nat Winston, Sr., E. H. Peckinpaugh, Charles J. Murphy, Major B. Harris, Joseph Halburnt, Clifford Curry and Kyle Walker. Not present: John Flippen, Enoch Brown and Frank Vestal. Copyright © The Chattanooga Times. Used with permission.

already in effect—Alabama's since 1939 and Georgia's since 1943.

The remaining attendees were from throughout Tennessee, though the majority were from the eastern half of the state (an imbalance that would prove chronic for many years). They included Herman Baggenstoss, apparently willing to give this competing group a chance against the renascent Wildlife Federation; many outdoor writers; and delegates from twelve or fifteen sportsmen's groups, assigned by their colleagues to see if the new organization were worth supporting.

The meeting began at 2 p.m. Nat Winston was elected president pro tem on a motion by the self-effacing Lou Williams, but from the start it was obvious that Williams was destined to be the group's leader. It was Williams who explained the vision and goals of the new organization and Williams who led the motion to adopt the charter as read. The group did so unanimously, and the Tennessee Conservation League was officially declared "a going concern."

Z. Cartter Patten now moved that Lou Williams be elected president, and after another unanimous vote, Williams took the chair. This charming, fifty-something fellow with the elfin grin, big heart and an admitted drinking problem would serve for the next five years, the longest continuous stretch of any TCL president. Nat Winston became first vice-president, Nash Buckingham second vice-president, Walter Amann secretary and Cartter Patten treasurer. Another thirteen members were named to the first board of directors. (The bylaws stipulated ten members, one from each of the ten Congressional districts then in Tennessee, but this was an organizational meeting, and the delegates voted to waive many of their own rules for the first year.)

THE LEAGUE VOTES TO STOMP ON POLITICAL TOES

Much of this first meeting was spent voting on the nine pages of proposed bylaws. (Several years later these would be amended as "Constitution and Bylaws.") Most of the bylaws were accepted as written. Those that were changed stirred little debate. For instance, the proposed group membership rate—ten dollars for the first fifty members plus twenty cents per additional member—was quickly changed to ten cents per additional member.

One matter, however, drew "much discussion"—the section on goals and objectives.

For the most part, this section was fairly predictable: to conserve the natural resources of Tennessee, to sponsor educational programs, to cooperate with affiliated clubs and so forth. A number of items had to do with legislation, including a pledge to pass favorable game laws and another to oppose "any amendment or act ... that may deprive a law-abiding citizen the right to possess, own, or bear firearms." (These would be removed in 1951 when the League applied for tax exemption.)

Nowhere, however, did the section say anything about removing the fish and game department from political interference and patronage. This was added as an explicit purpose only after much wrangling among members.

In his *Chattanooga Times* column of February 10, two days before the Read House meeting, Lou Williams explained why the patronage issue had been left out of the proposed bylaws. The question was of such "paramount importance," he said, that the organizers thought it should be included only after it had been discussed by the full group, and "only in the event that a majority of those present wanted to include it."

When the matter came up for discussion, Knoxville outdoor writer Joe Halburnt moved that the bylaws should certainly include, as a principal objective, "the removal of [the] State Game and Fish Division of the Conservation Department of [the] State of Tennessee from political control." Cartter Patten seconded the motion, and a protracted discussion followed. Apparently the argument was simply over whether such an objective ranked as a defining purpose, for everyone agreed with the objective itself. In fact, Lou Williams told the group, it was his "burning desire" to get the Conservation Department itself out of politics. He respected Commissioner Paul Mathes and the rest of his department, but he said they were all "hogtied" by political pressures.

BRIEF HOPES FOR AN INDEPENDENT CONSERVATION DEPARTMENT

In 1946 Game and Fish was still a division of the Conservation Department, as it had been since 1937. Though some sportsmen had come to prefer this umbrella structure, including Herman Baggenstoss and Edward Meeman (and even, at one point in the early '40s, Lou Williams himself), others felt that the political problems in Game and Fish had merely metastasized through the whole Department of Conservation. Therefore, they said, instead of taking politics out of Game and Fish alone, why not take politics out of the whole TDOC? Why not create an autonomous Conservation Commission, with policy-making power over *all* branches of conservation—not just wildlife, but forests, state parks, minerals, everything? With no policy-making power, Tennessee's advisory Conservation Commission was really just political window-dressing, doing no harm but not much tangible good either. Though its members were often highly qualified in their respective fields, neither the division heads nor the governor were obligated to follow their advice. And since members served at the pleasure of the governor, the entire commission could be overturned at the next election. (And in fact, it was. When Gordon Browning was elected, he dumped the old crew and created a Conservation Commission of his own, this one with nine members instead of four, plus himself and the commissioner of Conservation as ex officios.)

By the time it came to a vote, Joe Halburnt's motion had been revised to call for the political independence of the entire department, not just its Game and Fish Division. The motion passed unanimously, and "the removal of [the] Conservation Department of the State of Tennessee from political influence" was inserted near the top of the list of objectives.

If Halburnt's motion helped solidify the League's agenda, it also gave the next morning's newspapers something far more meaty to report than merely the founding of a new hunting and fishing club. While others at the Read House were getting ready for Tuesday evening's celebratory dinner (hosted by Chattanoogans, Inc., and *The Chattanooga Times*), Lou Williams was talking to a reporter from the Associated Press. On Wednesday, most of the state's major dailies announced the League's "Campaign to Remove State Conservation Department From Political Control."

Williams' remarks to the Associated Press reporter had been polite and diplomatic—"I have no complaint to make against any of the present department personnel. It's the system I'm complaining about." Nonetheless, news editors saw a good story in the making:

sportsmen take on a powerful cog in Tennessee's political machine.

As always, the press deserved a good share of the credit for making the Read House meeting a success. In the days before and after February 12, outdoor writers across the state applauded the birth of the League, declaring that such a group had been "urgently needed for some time." If there was a local angle—if, for instance, local sportsmen had been elected to the board—the papers included their names. Some also included information about who could join the League, how much a membership cost, even where to send dues.

An editorial in *The Chattanooga Times* was typical: "The Tennessee Conservation League will do this state a great service if it succeeds in having the state as a whole considered from a nonpolitical standpoint in conservation. States which seek to become nationally known recreation centers and which seek to attract true sportsmen must have a nonpolitical policy which conservationists and sportsmen throughout the state would be glad to advance." Media support became especially strong as the sportsmen-journalists—men like Walter Amann, Paul Bryant, Kyle Walker, Edward Meeman and his best *Press-Scimitar* reporter Paul Fairleigh—devoted generous space (and equally generous praise) to the League's activities. It was clear that the League planned to wage its battles no less in the press than on Capitol Hill.

GROWING THE LEAGUE

When it started in February 1946, the League had signed up nine or ten clubs, including the Unaka Rod and Gun Club, the Chickamauga Fly and Bait Casting Club, the Chattanooga Rod and Gun Club, the Chattanooga Trout Association, the Sportsman's Club (of Chattanooga), the Chattanooga Rifle Club, the Kingsport Rod and Gun Club, the Memphis Anglers Club, the Tri-States Game and Fish Association of Memphis and the Knoxville Rod and Reel Club. Within two months, there were fifteen affiliates, representing an aggregate membership of roughly five thousand. Some sportsmen joined individually by paying a dollar (or more), but the bulk of memberships came en masse, at the group rate of ten cents a head. To join the League a club had to have at least ten members, but the average enrollment appears to have been somewhere between one hundred and two hundred members, though some were much larger. The Unaka Rod and Gun Club alone reported 1,250 members.

Still, the League wanted the sort of clout that came not only with big numbers but with statewide geographical coverage. In April 1946 it announced a membership campaign to enroll 25,000 members from all over Tennessee by the end of the year. (This goal would prove wildly unrealistic. By TCL's first annual meeting in February 1947, the number of affiliates had risen to twenty-five, respectable enough considering that Kentucky's federation had attracted only ten affiliates after two years. Still, it represented only around 6,000 sportsmen, far short of the goal of 25,000.)

But Lou Williams and his executive committee had an even more pressing reason for wanting to expand the membership base: they needed worker bees. Though the board met every two or three months or so, the full membership came together only once a year, at the annual meeting. Here, delegates from local clubs (one delegate per fifty members) voted on "pending business." In the meantime, the League expected committees to do most of the League's work. Ten standing committees were specified by the bylaws: legislation, forestry, game, fish, education, credentials, resolutions, program/planning, pure streams and auditing—as well as "special committees as may be necessary." The bylaws further stipulated that each committee have exactly ten members, one from each of the ten divisions. Finding ten members for each committee was not too hard; distributing them by Congressional district was almost impossible. Eventually the League stopped trying. (The ten-member maximum was abandoned also.)

At any rate, by April 1946, only the two most urgent committees were filled.

One of these was the membership committee. Walter Amann, Jr., was named to chair the membership drive. The other was the all-important legislative committee, the one that would design the strategy to reform the game and fish agency. At first, this committee was headed by Colonel James Corn, a Cleveland attorney and Cherokee adopted son who would later be responsible for creating Red Clay State Historical Park. When Karl Steinmetz joined the League shortly after it was founded, Corn willingly gave up his chair.

That Steinmetz decided to join the new organization was a stroke of luck for TCL. Though reputed to be "mean as a rattlesnake," Steinmetz was a talented lawyer who had written the law creating Tennessee's first game and fish commission back in 1935. Though that commission didn't last long, Steinmetz' experience in writing model laws would soon be needed again.

THE QUEST FOR A MODEL LAW

The first annual meeting of the Tennessee Conservation League was held in Johnson City, February 21-22, 1947. More than a hundred delegates attended; all the standing committees were now in place. However, most of the discussions that weekend concerned only one—Karl Steinmetz' legislative committee. The campaign to reform game and fish would dominate the League's activities for the next two years.

The mood on Friday was tense. "The delegates were just plain sick and tired of conditions in Game and Fish," Lou Williams recalled later. Apparently they were spoiling for an immediate showdown, "ready to blow off the lid" during the current legislative session and unwilling to wait until the next one in 1949. Williams, however, urged caution. Two years might seem like a long time, he admitted, but natural resource conservation was a long-range proposition. Besides, the League was barely a year old, "not yet strong enough to live through a serious controversy." Infinite wisdom, of course, but mighty unpopular that Friday night. For a while Williams must have wondered if the showdown were going to take place right there in the Hotel John Sevier. "[M]any delegates ... wanted an immediate change in conditions. I seemed to be almost alone on changing them more slowly."

It was a critical test of Williams' leadership, but he stood firm. By the next morning, the mood had calmed. Most of the dissenters were now willing "to accept the fact that a year or two must pass before there would be any appreciable improvement." Yet the League was already moving forward.

On Saturday morning, during the reading of committee reports, Karl Steinmetz had argued that if the League wanted to have a model game and fish law ready by 1949, it had better start drafting it now. If the members didn't want him or his legislative committee to do it, he said bluntly, that's fine. Just make sure somebody does.

The legislative strategy group now included at least one other attorney besides Steinmetz and Corn: Alan Kelly, a judge from South Pittsburg. The ten other members were Peck Peckinpaugh, Nat Winston, Cartter Patten, Joe Halburnt and Lou DeQuine. Steinmetz promised that their draft would be ready in time for the 1948 convention, but in fact it was ready much sooner. On November 14, 1947, Lou Williams called a special meeting of the executive committee to review the proposed model law.

THE MODEL LAW ENTERS THE PIPELINE

The most noticeable feature of the draft was that it had scrapped the idea of an independent Conservation Commission. The League was now calling only for an independent Game and Fish Commission. This was a deliberate decision, according to Lou Williams. After looking more carefully at the structure and makeup of the Department of Conservation, the board had simply decided it would be "impractical" to try to change the entire TDOC.

Another oddity of the bill was that it would have the effect of reopening the Pandora's box of private wildlife acts. All local wildlife laws had been repealed by Prentice Cooper's administration in 1939, and that ban was still in effect. Because the proposed new law would repeal "all Acts or parts of Acts in conflict with [its] provisions," that meant Governor Cooper's repeal would be overturned along with every other fish and game act to date. Presumably the League's model law could have extended the ban on private acts. However, it chose not to, and this, no doubt, was one reason it passed.

There were several other unique features in Steinmetz' draft. For one thing, it called for nine commissioners instead of five, three per grand division of the state. It gave game wardens the rather fanciful title of "Wild Life Rangers." And it granted an unprecedented degree of oversight to the sportsmen. In fact, it all but gave sportsmen the power to name the commission.

Though the governor would actually appoint the first nine commissioners himself, the bill mandated that he choose them from a list of eighteen names provided by the sportsmen (the number of nominees was later changed to twenty-seven). The method for drawing up this list was carefully spelled out. First, the director of Game and Fish would call a meeting of the sportsmen in each of the three grand divisions of the state. (Notice of the meetings had to be published twice, "in a newspaper of state-wide circulation.") At each of these meetings, the sportsmen would choose six nominees, "well informed on the subject of wild life conservation and restoration." The names would be submitted to the governor, who would pick three names from each list of six. Whenever a commissioner rotated off the board, the Game and Fish director would call another meeting in the division where the vacancy occurred, and follow a similar nominations process.

Though this selection system was used by at least one other state (Lou Williams thought it was Kentucky), it was easily abused, and in 1959 it was abandoned. The governor could then name his own commissioners, but the sportsmen reserved the right to recommend or object to the governor's choices.

Apart from these features, Steinmetz' bill was much like the other wildlife commission bills of the period. It gave the commissioners authority to hire and fire a director, set seasons and bag limits and acquire land. It stipulated that the commission be entirely self-supporting, neither receiving money from, nor paying money into, the general fund. The commission would operate entirely on its own revenues, whether license fees, fines, permits, leases or federal allocations. These monies would go into a Game and Fish Fund, where they would be held "separate and apart" from any other use by the state. The bill gave the commission sole power to fix the budget, to enforce game and fish laws and to buy lands for game farms, fish hatcheries and hunting grounds.

At the 1948 annual meeting, February 27-28 at the Hermitage Hotel in Nashville, the members moved to adopt the draft with only two minor changes. The draft was officially in the pipeline.

Something else of note occurred at the 1948 annual meeting. Lou Williams and Nat Winston each received a Z. Cartter Patten Award for his great accomplishment in organizing the TCL. (Patten had established the state's first conservation award in 1943 under the auspices of TOWA, but in late 1947 it was transferred to the League.) Winston won the award (an inscribed desk clock) for 1946. The award for 1947, some other desk accessory, went to Lou Williams.

"A Concentrated And Skilful Campaign"

Getting the model law ready for the Legislature was only half the job. Now, the League had to get the Legislature ready for the model law. Votes had to be lined up *before* the session, which meant not only a first round of lobbying among the incumbent members of the House and Senate, but a second round of visits to any newcomers likely to be elected in November. The current governor, Jim McCord, would have to be lobbied, along with every contender for his office. Meanwhile, the average sportsman would have to be told about the bill and why it was important. It would be an enormous public relations job; a year was hardly enough time.

League officers began at once to plan "a concentrated and skilful state-wide campaign" in support of the proposed law. The legislative committee drafted a model "sales talk" so that members would concentrate on "similar arguments." They flooded the newspapers with articles and press releases, pushed the law in weekly outdoor columns and wrote letters of support in the editorial pages. They recorded radio spots, set up a speakers' bureau, appeared before civic groups and in general tried to make sure that every sportsman in the state understood what the law was all about.

They were not necessarily preaching to the choir, either. While most sportsmen supported the commission idea, some were bitterly opposed to an independent commission for fear it would become the handmaiden of a few wealthy and self-interested sportsmen. Some clubs fought the League's bill bitterly. In the July-August 1948 issue of *The Tennessee Conservationist*, two members of the Loudoun Sportsmen's Club demanded, "Why should 3 million Tennesseans turn over our wonderful wildlife resources ... to a small organization" of special-interest hunters and fishermen? Don't be fooled, they wrote, by the claim of political independence; the proposed commission will be nothing if not political. But it hardly mattered, they concluded: "Of course, the group's plan has no hope of becoming law." Not surprisingly, the Loudoun club never affiliated with the League.

Clearly, public education was crucial, yet the League still had no newsletter, no magazine, no regular means of communicating with its membership nor its fellow sportsmen statewide. Lou Williams had written a series of detailed articles for *The Chattanooga Times* explaining the model law, but these were no help to sportsmen in other parts of the state. The Tennessee Wildlife Federation's old ally, *The Tennessee Conservationist,* was once again including sportsmen's news, but only sporadically.

Fortunately, the entire text of the model law had been included in the November 1947 issue of the *Dixie Sportsman* (originally the *Tennessee Valley Sportsman*), a struggling monthly published by Knoxville board member Joe Halburnt. The executive committee agreed to order ten thousand reprints of the article, along with explanatory forewords by Williams and Steinmetz. These would be distributed to members through affiliated sportsmen's clubs; they would also be available to legislators.

A few months later, in an effort to boost circulation, Halburnt offered to send the *Dixie Sportsman* to all individual members of the League in return for twenty-five cents of their one-dollar dues. The magazine would serve as the official voice of the League, he said. However, despite selling a fair number of memberships on the strength of this promise, the *Dixie Sportsman* soon folded, and the League found itself sending out felt logo patches as consolation to the disappointed subscribers. (The League's first logo was simple enough, a circle inscribed with the words "Tennessee Conservation League," "Protect Wildlife," and an outline of the state.)

Such an extensive publicity blitz did not come cheaply, yet the League had barely a thousand dollars in its bank account. The *Dixie Sportsman* reprints and assorted other printing costs would consume a fair share of that, and at least some campaign-related travel would have to be reimbursed. At E. H. Peckinpaugh's suggestion, the executive committee voted on November 14 to print two thousand "fund-raising booklets," each containing ten membership "tickets" at a dollar each. The member selling the most tickets would win a boat and motor. If two thousand members sold just a booklet each, perhaps they really could get twenty thousand new members. A short time later they also began selling "Shares in Conservation" (actually a new membership category) for fifty dollars. The board considered raffling a car, but this idea was rejected as too complicated. Instead, they decided that each affiliate might come up with its own fund-raising project and donate some of the proceeds to the parent organization.

THE BOOM YEARS

In fact, affiliate growth was beginning to boom. As the League's stature and momentum grew, clubs that had been watching from the sidelines now hurried to sign up. Others organized expressly so they could affiliate with the League. To take advantage of the emerging club activity, the League in 1948 published a thirty-page handbook called the *How Book for Organizing, Operating and Maintaining Sportsman's and Conservation Clubs in Tennessee* (usually referred to simply as the *How Book*). The booklet included advice on an array of topics, from writing a constitution to sponsoring crow shoots. The League's own bylaws were included as a reference. Five hundred were printed for about two hundred dollars, a significant outlay but one they expected would pay for itself in new affiliates.

In 1948 affiliates were still paying ten dollars a year for the first fifty members and ten cents per additional member. In April 1949 that rate was raised to twenty-five dollars for the first hundred members and twenty-five cents per additional member (later simply twenty-five cents a member). Yet an affiliate's dues were probably never as important to the League as the sheer mass of its ranks. Gross affiliate memberships were at the core of the League's political power: they comprised at least 80 percent of the League's cumulative enrollment and closer to 100 percent of its political force. It was much more impressive for a hunter to be able to tell his senator that he represented twelve thousand others like him, even though only a fraction of that twelve thousand might be actively involved in the League. In fact, the numbers were so attractive that they were often hyperbolized. Paul Fairleigh of the *Memphis Press-Scimitar* routinely credited the League with 25,000 members, though in fact that magical number has probably never been reached, and it assuredly had not been reached in 1949. Total membership then was probably more in the neighborhood of ten thousand.

But ten thousand sportsmen were no small potatoes to a legislator or office-seeker. Even if wildlife protection were not a popular issue, it would be hard if not impossible for a legislator to ignore such a delegation.

THE MODEL LAW GOES INTO THE FINAL STRETCH

In fact, very few did ignore it. During the year-long lobbying effort that ended with the passage of the model law on February 25, 1949, most politicians were at least willing to consider it; some, including Gordon Browning, pledged their immediate support. Browning, the one-time governor whose administration had created the Department of Conservation in 1937, was now running for a second term. Though the former governor had several friends in the League, including C. P. (a.k.a. "Chuck") Swan, it was Lou Williams who paid the requisite office call. (Williams also called on the incumbent, Jim McCord, who received him "graciously" but offered no support.)

Browning, on the other hand, listened attentively while Williams outlined the League's proposed bill. After asking several questions, Williams later recalled, Browning "grasped my hand and said, 'You will be completely satisfied with the plank in my platform concerning this program.'"

On Saturday, May 15, 1948, Browning released a position paper for the Sunday morning papers. The executive committee of the League happened to be meeting in Tellico Plains that evening, and Williams brought with him a copy of the release. It said, in part, "When the Department of Conservation was established by us in 1937, it was thought best to coordinate all phases of that work under one head. We have now reached the stage of development when we need an independent commission to direct our game and fish division so as to insure continuity of policies and also to take the program entirely out of the reach of political influences. The sportsmen who sustain this activity with their money are entitled to a voice in its affairs." A grateful executive committee promptly sent a wire advising the governor of the "hearty gratification of the committee for his commitment and commend-ing him to the favorable consideration of the people for his stand on this important matter."

Browning won the election handily. To the delight of the League, he chose League mem-ber Chuck Swan to be his commissioner of Conservation. A handsome man from Oak Ridge, Swan was also politically astute. It was Swan who warned the League of Browning's possible objections to details in the model law, advisories that led to two called meetings.

On December 12, 1948, some fifty members of the League met in Athens to discuss the first of these sticking points. Apparently Browning would not support the bill unless it in-cluded the governor and commissioner of Conservation as ex officio members. The ques-tion was not settled in Athens, so Williams called a second meeting in Monterey on February 19, 1949, just a week before the bill came to a vote. The governor had added two more con-ditions, both having to do with the nominations process. He wanted at least twenty-seven names to choose from (nine nominees from each grand division). He also wanted the right to reject any list he didn't like, and request another.

Only twenty men, all from East Tennessee, made it to this meeting. Of those, only nine were entitled to vote. A small majority, including Williams, were willing to trust the governor's intentions; the others were fiercely opposed to making what they considered fatal conces-sions, particularly that of giving seats on the commission to the governor and a member of his cabinet. Williams was reluctant to take a vote: the meeting was so hastily called, and the turnout so small and so divided. Technically, however, he had a quorum. And at any rate, there was no time for another meeting. The model law was already in committee. Eight di-rectors voted to accept the bill with all the governor's changes; only one voted against it.

Once again, Williams had shown his fine judgment, and Commissioner Swan must have seen it. For the next several weeks, while the bill moved through committee, Swan worked steadily with League members to keep it afloat. By the time the bill went to the floor, it had almost unanimous support.

The vote came in late February (not March, as Williams reports in his 1971 history). The model law passed 79 to 2 in the House, 26 to 1 in the Senate. On February 25, 1949, it be-came Chapter 50, Public Acts of 1949, creating what was officially designated the Board of Conservation for Game, Fish and Wildlife.

Williams wrote later that while he could not be sure who had cast the three dissenting votes, he was certain that Damon Headden, Sr., a West Tennessee Democrat now in the House, was behind one of them. The same fellow who had been director of the state's first game and fish commission in 1935-37 was now among the most virulent opponents of the new commission. As a representative whose constituency included Reelfoot Lake fishermen, Headden was as determined to preserve commercial crappie fishing as the League was de-termined to end it. For the next four years—in each of the next two General Assemblies—Headden would do his utmost to get the new commission abolished.

"VICTORY"

Folks in the League were well aware that their commission would be challenged. For now, however, they simply savored their victory.

The 1949 annual meeting was held April 22-23 at the Andrew Johnson Hotel in Knoxville, with business sessions across the street in the Knox County Courthouse. It was indeed (as the front page of the program proclaimed) a most delicious victory celebration. In just three years the League had accomplished what others had been trying to do for nearly twenty. Members wore silly paper hats and could hardly congratulate themselves enough.

The board of directors gave Lou Williams an electric clock "in appreciation of the grand job he ha[d] done as president." They read a proclamation in extravagant praise of Karl Steinmetz; they also gave him the fifth annual Z. Cartter Patten Award. Reportedly Steinmetz was so overcome he could not finish his acceptance speech. To special guest Gordon Browning, who flew in on a National Guard plane, they gave a silver-plated life membership card. If Browning's popularity with the League were not already assured, his address Saturday night "left no doubt of the close relationship between the governor and the sportsmen." His remarks—especially his pledge that he would "stand or fall" with the sportsmen in their campaign for wildlife—"endeared [him] in the hearts of all present."

Not even the rank and file went unappreciated. In his opening report, President Williams offered a stirring tribute to the troops, a speech Joe Halburnt called the "Gettysburg address" of conservation. "The new commission hasn't a chance of succeeding unless we stay behind them," said Williams. "The Governor has kept every promise he made to us and we must continue to do our part."

Prominent conservationists from around the country had been invited to Knoxville to help their Tennessee colleagues celebrate an independent wildlife program. Lloyd Swift, chief of the wildlife management division of the U.S. Forest Service, spoke at Friday's lunch; Dr. Ira Gabrielson, president of the Wildlife Management Institute in Washington, D.C., spoke at the closing banquet. Gordon Clapp, chairman of TVA, talked about water quality and fishing. Ed Tayloe, whom Commissioner Swan had recently tapped to head (what was still) the Game and Fish Division, discussed the sportsman's role in enforcement. Wildlife managers from surrounding states talked at length about the challenges and strengths in their own programs. But no one, apparently, talked quite as much as Al Marsh, Tennessee's hot-blooded chief of game management. Marsh's talk on fox and quail studies in Tennessee lasted so long, in fact, that he crowded out the last fellow on the program. The next morning, the delegates voted that "no talk should exceed thirty minutes."

BIRTH OF THE STATE GAME AND FISH COMMISSION

The most welcome speaker of all may well have been Lucius E. Burch, Jr. Burch, the thoughtful, wellborn Memphis attorney, had been elected chairman of the new Tennessee Game and Fish Commission just two weeks before. On the first day of the annual meeting, he gave a "confidence inspiring" talk on the commission's plans for the near and long-term future. Within the next week, he told the audience, all game wardens in the state would be placed on probation. Those interested in retaining their jobs would have to take a written examination along with all other applicants for the ninety-five warden jobs and seven supervisors. Those who passed the exam would be interviewed by a three-man, nonpolitical selection committee. (According to *The Tennessee Conservationist*, most incumbent wardens qualified to stay on.) Those who survived these hurdles would be sent to training school and certified for Civil Service appointment. Burch pledged to abolish the agency's "expensive club houses and cruisers," to plant "an abundance" of quail food and to try to stop the sale of game fish from Reelfoot Lake. The commission would rely mainly on technical information in making these and other policy decisions, he said, but would be "glad to get good advice from any source"—including members of the League.

The commission by then was already a month old; in fact, it had already held one meeting. Its second meeting was the very next day, in the Andrew Johnson Hotel, while the League's convention was still in session. Thus began the commission's long tradition of meeting at least once a year in conjunction with the TCL annual convention.

"BLOOD COUSINS": THE LEAGUE AND THE COMMISSION

It was also, in a way, the formal start of what would be a long and intimate (some might say incestuous) relationship between the League and the Game and Fish Commission. Newspaper writers were already referring to the two groups as "blood cousins." All nine of the original commissioners were members of the League. Besides chairman Burch, they included Joe Curry of Dyersburg, Dr. Hal Baker of Jackson, John Webb of McMinnville, Hal Meadors of Lebanon, Edwin Crutcher of Nashville, M. L. Brickey of Fountain City, James Asbury of Kingsport and LeRoy Rymer of Cleveland. (If a commissioner happened to be on the TCL board when he was elected, however, League policy required that he resign.)

Some sportsmen grumbled louder than ever that the wildlife of the state was now under the thumb of League elitists, but others merely pointed out that League sportsmen were the ones most familiar with the issues. Certainly the nominations process couldn't have been more democratic. As required by the model law, the twenty-seven nominees had been duly chosen by sportsmen at three public meetings across the state.

The town-hall system of nominating commissioners did not survive, however. No one had ever determined who was eligible to vote, and sportsmen and commissioners alike complained that "persons unqualified" were voting. One commissioner, a business owner, was rumored to have given his workers the afternoon off so they could travel to the polls.

In 1953 legislators tried to correct the system but only succeeded in making it more arcane. The nine commissioners now came from each of nine newly-drawn election districts, so that when a vacancy occurred, nominations were held in each *county* in the affected district, with each county choosing one nominee. These names would be placed on a ballot, and on an announced day, all the sportsmen of the district would drive to a central polling place and vote for their top five nominees. The governor made his appointment from the top five vote-getters. But the system was still flawed, and in 1959 the Legislature abolished the business altogether, with TCL's blessings. Since then, the privilege of choosing commissioners has fallen entirely to the governor, though he is still required to mix them up geographically.

Given its role as birth-mother to the wildlife commission, it was probably inevitable that some skeptics would question the relationship. In a very real sense the commission *was* the League's baby, and like any new parent, the League was keenly interested in its care and

When the first Game and Fish Commission was named in April 1949, all nine commissioners belonged to TCL. Seated, left to right: Commissioner of Conservation Charles P. Swan (ex officio); Ed Tayloe, who served briefly as director of the agency; commission chairman Lucius E. Burch, Jr.; and James Asbury, secretary. Standing: H. H. Meadors, John Webb, Dr. Hal A. Baker, LeRoy Rymer, Joe Curry and M. L. Brickey. Edwin Crutcher, vice president, is absent. Courtesy of TWRA.

feeding. Long before the model law was even passed, board members had decided that the fledgling commission would need help getting its program started. This was not hubris; it was the truth. As typical sportsmen themselves, the League's elders knew the sort of men who would be nominated to serve on the commission. They would all be dedicated conservationists, but few if any would have technical knowledge or wildlife management training. In fact, Lucius Burch would later admit bluntly that "none of us [on the first Commission] knew what we were doing .... Everything we did was wrong." While that was surely an exaggeration, the commissioners did need help, and they knew it.

Even before the model law was passed, the League had begun to prepare its "Suggestions for a Long Range Game and Fish Program for Tennessee." They drew on their own knowledge, but they relied primarily on advice from the state's current wildlife program, the recently established Tennessee Stream Pollution Control Board, the U.S. Forest Service, the Outdoor Writers Association, the U.S. Fish and Wildlife Service, TVA and the game and fish programs of Georgia, Kentucky, Missouri and Pennsylvania. Pennsylvania's Ross Leffler School of Conservation, for instance, was recommended as a model for training Tennessee's conservation officers.

The fifty-page report was finished on March 15, 1949. Williams sent copies to Governor Browning, Commissioner Swan, Game and Fish Director Tayloe, League officers and directors, member clubs and each of the daily newspapers. As soon as the new Game and Fish commissioners had been chosen, they got copies, too. Others could buy them for fifty cents.

THE LONG-RANGE GAME AND FISH PROGRAM

If the model law was a warm-up, the League's long-range report was the main event. The writers thought of everything: administration, personnel, programs, organization, game and fish management, law enforcement, public relations. No detail, it appeared, was too small for their attention, nor too big. They recommended a retirement plan, proposed salary ranges, wrote job descriptions. They recommended that every wildlife officer be essentially fired, then rehired only after passing a rigorous examination by a nonpolitical review board. There should be a game officer in every county, a hike in the hunting and fishing license, stiffer fines for violators and a season limit on most species of game. They recommended a youth program and they strongly urged a monthly magazine. Moreover, since "gunning and fishing" morals had "unquestionably deteriorated across the Nation," they also recommended that the clergy of Tennessee scrutinize the ideals of *The Tennessee Conservationist!*

What was perhaps most remarkable about this document (apart from the business about a morality review board) was the scope and strength of its suggestions. With few exceptions, the policies it recommended underlie the state's game and fish program today.

The commissioners, for instance, were reminded of the limitations of their power. "In the interests of good administration, the Commissioners should not, as a group, or individually, issue instructions or orders to any subordinate. Members of the Commission should . . . refrain from permitting employees [to discuss] with them their individual problems or assignments but should establish a system whereby appeals and information reach the Commission through regular channels."

The section on game management also set the tone for the future. It included a lengthy passage by Dr. Clarence Cottam, assistant director of the U.S. Fish and Wildlife Service, warning that most stocking programs were a waste of money. "The urgent need is for the development of favorable habitat—not for stocking." The section on game and fish laws urged Tennessee to coordinate its laws as closely as possible with those of neighboring states. It also recommended that Tennessee form compacts with neighboring states to address pollution on a watershed-wide basis.

At least one recommendation, however, was off base: that the state relax its laws protecting birds of prey. "All except three species of hawks and owls are protected by Tennessee laws," the report noted, "[but] these laws have never been observed and adhered to, and they will never be." If raptors were not wholly to blame for the shortage of small game, the authors said, they had certainly contributed to it. "No one wants to see hawks and owls, any species of them, exterminated in Tennessee," they concluded, but "[i]f a successful balance of wildlife is to be maintained, it seems only reasonable to believe that all predators should be held in check." Fortunately Game and Fish did not agree. Lou Clapper, the commission's public information man, called the League's suggestions "unsound." One of the agency's posters showed a hawk catching a rodent, with the caption *Let the Hawks Do This!*

For its part, the League stressed that its program was merely a guide, not a mandate. "It is not thought that every suggestion will be adopted," said the foreword. Far from resenting the League's program as interference, the new commission adopted the program unanimously at its first meeting.

THE COMMISSION HIRES A DIRECTOR

The commission now enlisted the League's help in another matter. The wildlife agency needed a new director. Ed C. Tayloe, who had been hired as director in January (before the model law was passed), now handed in his resignation, only six months after he began. The official word was that he had contracted something called "undulant fever" during the war and was too sick to continue. However, he was soon healthy enough to go to work as director of State Parks, so one suspects either he or the commissioners preferred to let the commission select its own director. The commission appointed three outside men—Lou Williams, Frank Vestal and Walter Amann—to serve on a search committee along with commissioners Brickey, Rymer and Crutcher.

Williams recalled later that he was besieged with phone calls from politicians and powerbrokers, asking him to appoint this friend or that associate to the directorship. Williams took great pleasure in reminding each caller that the model law was meant to get politics *out* of game and fish. Some folks suggested that Williams himself take the job, but Williams had sworn from the start that he would never accept any position, paid or unpaid, with the wildlife agency, and he never did.

By mid-July the committee had narrowed its field to nine candidates, including League members John Dyche of LaFollette and Grover Rann of Cleveland, and two out-of-state applicants, Georgia Game and Fish Director Charlie Elliott and John Findlay, the youthful

In contrast to the League's long-range plan, which proposed treating hawks as predators, the Game and Fish Commission appreciated the value of raptors. This Game and Fish poster came out in the early 1950s. Courtesy of TWRA.

director of North Carolina's Department of Game and Inland Fisheries. The search committee interviewed all nine applicants in one day-long session at the Read House. Though several of the men were his personal friends, Williams felt that only the two out-of-staters, Elliott
and Findlay, had the professional training the job called for. He moved that the committee
offer the job to Findlay.

A few months later, on October 4, 1949, Findlay made his preliminary report to the commission. Then, Chairman Burch read a letter to Lou Williams, asking him, as president of the
League, to appoint a "Board of Visitors" to evaluate the Game and Fish agency and report on
its long range program.

As Williams would later observe, "[t]his was a most unusual step for a public body to take."
It was also a potentially delicate one. Would Findlay feel as though the commission were
placing him on trial? Whatever its implications, the request "proved beyond a shadow of a
doubt that the Commission was determined to get off on the right foot." It was also, as Williams couldn't help acknowledging, an extraordinary vote of confidence in the League.

CHAPTER 4

1950-1959
SPREADING THE CONSERVATION ETHIC

*It must ever be borne in mind that fish and game, like all
other crops, are products of the soil and water, and that their
abundance and availability are consequently dependent
upon suitable environment and good management. . . . Wise land use
and the conservation of land and water resources are prerequisite
to wildlife and fishery management and conservation.*

—Board of Visitors Survey,
January 1950

THE BOARD OF VISITORS MAKES ITS RECOMMENDATIONS

To some, inviting a visitors committee to look at the long-range program at Game and Fish meant simply another opportunity to repay political favors. Lou Williams found himself once again fending off requests to give a seat to this friend or that associate. But the intent of chairman Burch's letter was clear: the commission wanted "experts" with "technical" and "professional" experience.

Williams had finalized his list by the October 1949 board meeting. On January 22, 1950, the board of visitors arrived in Nashville. Dr. Ira Gabrielson, president of the Wildlife Management Institute, was its chairman. His team included Dr. Clarence Cottam, assistant director of the U.S. Fish and Wildlife Service; Dr. Reuben Eschmeyer, TVA fisheries biologist (and soon to become executive vice-president of the Sport Fishing Institute); W. R. Paddock, supervisor of the Cherokee National Forest; I. T. Bode, director of the Missouri Conservation Commission; Charles Dunn, superintendent of Chickamauga-Chattanooga National Military Park; and P. J. Hoffmaster, director of Michigan's Conservation Commission.

They stayed for five days, spending most of their time interviewing personnel, reviewing records and assessing existing programs. Their findings, detailed in a report a few weeks later, were largely favorable, with caveats.

Among the many findings which impressed the review team was the department's new hiring system based on merit, as well as its competitive pay scale. Most professional positions, such as game technicians, got at least five thousand dollars a year (not bad for state wages almost half a century ago), and even conservation officers, whose chief qualifications were that they had finished high school and weighed at least 160 pounds, earned $2,160. The review team commended the great emphasis the commission proposed to put on education and agreed that wildlife conservation should be taught in the schools, not necessarily on a mandatory basis.

Though the team found the agency on the whole to be well managed and well organized, it was not uniformly impressed. For instance, it questioned the wisdom of allotting half the total fisheries budget to "hatcheries" and urged the fisheries people to avoid "promiscuous fish stocking." It found the deer population "much too small to meet existing needs" and urged the state to develop private-public refuge partnerships with landowners, much as the state had done in the 1920s. On the other hand, they conceded, there was not much point in improving deer habitat if the state did not also do something about poachers and predatory dogs.

But these were all details. The board found at least three systemic weaknesses in Tennessee's game and fish program: a cumbersome and obsolete game and fish code; industrial and organic water pollution; and forest fires.

As it happened, the League was already lobbying for a bigger fire-fighting budget; it was about to embark on a massive antipollution campaign; and it was even then tackling the antiquated fish and game laws of Tennessee.

"VIRILE AND VIGILANT"—THE REVISED GAME AND FISH CODE

Karl Steinmetz may have been one of those fellows who did a thing too well for his own good. Steinmetz was a lawyer in Knoxville, a charter member of the old Izaak Walton League who early on had joined his legal training with his passion for trout fishing. Having written a successful model game and fish administration law, he was now put to work overhauling the game and fish code itself.

The state had been accumulating regulations, piecemeal and willy-nilly, since before the first of the century. The result was a system that was inconsistent, irrational and often discriminatory. (As for private acts, repealed by Prentice Cooper in 1939, they were legal once again, and sure to confuse things even more.) As Ira Gabrielson and his committee had noted, some laws severely penalized "minor or possibly accidental infractions (particularly for a first offender), while the penalties for a hardened and repeating violator [were] altogether too mild." Lou Williams for one had always found it preposterous that a hunter could poach a ninety-dollar deer and get off with a fine as little as ten dollars.

The state needed a code that was both "virile and vigilant," said the visitors, yet it must not be unduly oppressive. "Complicated and unnecessary laws have a tendency to (1) discourage hunting and fishing, (2) engender a feeling of contempt both for the laws and for the enforcement officers, and (3) make more difficult the final conviction when violators are brought before the court." Indeed, some judges seemed to be more scornful of the laws than they were of the fellows who broke them. Though it was illegal, judges frequently imposed a fine with one stroke of the pen, then suspended it with the next.

The revisions took Steinmetz many months and, as he told his friends, cost him thousands of dollars in lost professional fees. When he was done, the draft bill consisted of five chapters, a total of seventy-four sections, spread over twenty-six pages of text. Some of the sections simply reiterated long-standing and central doctrines, such as the precept that all wildlife in Tennessee belonged to the state; others merely set stiffer fines. For instance, the maximum penalty for taking big game illegally was now increased to a minimum of $50 and a maximum of $250—*plus* a prison stay of thirty days to six months.

There were, however, at least three major changes in the proposed code.

First, and most controversial, was the proposed ban on all commercial trade in game and game fish, not excepting Reelfoot Lake crappie.

A board of visiting wildlife experts assembles in Nashville in early 1950 to review Tennessee's new Game and Fish program. Seated, left to right: W. R. Paddock, I. T. Bode, Dr. Ira Gabrielson, Dr. Clarence Cottam and P. J. Hoffmaster. Standing: John Findlay, (director of the commission), Lou Williams and Commissioner of Conservation C. P. Swan. Charles Dunn and R. W. Eschmeyer were absent. Courtesy of TWRA.

Second was a hike in the current hunting and fishing license, from two dollars to three.

And third was the so-called "Big Game Act," a tough new law that required the arresting officer in a big-game case to confiscate any guns, vehicles and other gear used in the violation. For instance, a man who poached a deer with a new rifle and hauled it out of the woods in a new car stood to lose both rifle *and* car—*and* pay the fine—*and* go to jail. If the trial ended in a conviction (and 90 percent of them did), the contraband was sold at auction, with the proceeds going into the Game and Fish Fund. What was especially tough was that, even if the alleged wrongdoer were *acquitted*, he would still not get his property back unless he made a successful appeal to the director of Game and Fish or, failing that, with the Circuit Court in Nashville. It was a harsh penalty, and indeed, the first poacher convicted under the new law challenged it all the way to the state Supreme Court (and lost at every level). The bounty in the case was several guns, a doe and a 1950 Cadillac.

Yet controversial as it was, the Big Game Act survived the legislative gauntlet. Not so the two other contested items. The one-dollar hike in the combined license was struck down, partly because another conflict was brewing overseas (Korea) and lawmakers were unwilling to raise any fees during that tense period. But the sportsmen themselves were not solidly behind an increase, despite the fact that they had been paying the same measly two dollars since 1915. The increase to a three-dollar combination license would not come until 1955.

As for the section banning commercial game fishing, Reelfoot-area lawmakers made such a row about this clause that the entire wildlife code seemed in jeopardy. Conservation Commissioner C. P. Swan had summoned Steinmetz and LeRoy Rymer to Nashville to warn them that Senator Dallas Hall was lining up votes to kill the bill. In an angry meeting with the sportsmen, Senator Hall vowed that if he could not amend the bill to his liking, he'd destroy it.

It was a tough call for the League. Banning once and for all the sale of Tennessee's wildlife was one of its most deeply felt objectives. Moreover, it was not just Reelfoot game fish at stake. Fishermen from Kentucky, Arkansas, Mississippi and elsewhere were catching crappie in their home lakes and "laundering" them through Tennessee wholesalers. On the other hand, Tennessee's own fish biologists could find no hard evidence that commercial fishing was hurting the Reelfoot fishery.

The board finally decided that "half a loaf [was] better than none," as outdoor writer Walter Amann, Jr., put it. When the game and fish code finally reached the Senate floor (having barely survived intact in the House), Senator Hall added an amendment allowing Reelfoot fishermen to continue selling Reelfoot crappie, but only in Obion and Lake Counties. The League agreed not to object, and the Wildlife Protection Act became law on June 1, 1951.

So while the final bill may have been less than what Steinmetz and his colleagues wanted, it was much more than what they previously had. Besides, they pledged to remove the objectionable Reelfoot amendment the next time around.

THE END OF COMMERCIAL CRAPPIE FISHING—FOR A WHILE

The push to outlaw commercial crappie fishing didn't succeed in 1953, either. What the League got instead was a law requiring commercial fishermen to tag all crappie caught and sold in the lake counties. Though several bootleg wholesalers were still willing to handle illegal fish, the tagging law would certainly cut down on some of the crappie trade. Meanwhile, Game and Fish began a study, using its share of the new Dingell-Johnson Federal Aid to Sport Fish Restoration funds, to assess the impacts of commercial fishing in Reelfoot.

That study was completed in 1955. According to its findings, some forms of commercial fishing, including striped jack (yellow bass), did no apparent harm to the fishery. Crappie fishing, on the other hand, did seem to warrant some restrictions. Though there was little baseline data to compare to, the current study suggested that crappie in Reelfoot had gotten smaller and less robust over the past several years. In 1955, Tennessee banned commercial trade in crappie and every other species of game fish in Tennessee except striped jack.

The sportsmen, it seemed, had finally prevailed in their decades-long quest to halt all hunting and game fishing for profit. But the issue was not over yet. Despite the ban, Reelfoot crappie continued to decline. By 1964 the average fish weighed just 4.1 ounces, less than half the 1955 average of 9.4 ounces. Growth rates of one- and two-year-old crappie had dropped also. Biologists were unsure of the cause, but they speculated that too many fish were now competing for too little food. In 1964, the Game and Fish Commission decided to let commercial fishermen start taking crappie during the winter months; it also ruled in favor of letting them use nets. The League was hotly opposed to the use of nets, but it really couldn't quarrel with the effort to restore crappie. The winter harvest continued for several years, with fishermen taking large hauls in those four or five months. Yet the crappie were not getting any bigger. Whatever the problem was, the commercial harvesters no longer seemed to blame. There was something else amiss in the lake, and commercial crappie fishing continued while the biologists tried to figure out what it was.

THE UNIQUE NATURE OF REELFOOT LAKE

Part of the problem was the lake itself. Reelfoot, that great cypress swamp formed almost magically in 1811-1812 by the New Madrid earthquakes, had been trying to fill itself in ever since. West Tennessee has the most erodible soil in the state, and the Reelfoot watershed is full of feeder creeks, carrying silt, topsoil and pesticides into the lake as relentlessly as slow-moving conveyor belts. Loggers had hurried the process by clearing the land for miles around; local farmers did their part by plowing, tilling and fertilizing much of the watershed; land developers built dams and drainage ditches. The lake was so shallow, so silt-laden and stump-filled by the turn of the century that in 1902 the state Supreme Court ruled it unnavigable, allowing private interests to lay claim to the lake and restrict fishing and hunting rights. This ruling caused such lawlessness—including the brief terrorist campaign in 1908 of the Reelfoot Night Riders—that the high court reversed itself in 1913, and the lake returned to the public domain.

Between its spectacular fishing and hunting, its raptors and waterfowl, its Night Riders and its politics and its other-worldly beauty, Reelfoot Lake was one of the most legend-rich places in Tennessee. Its southern shore became the earliest state park when the Reelfoot Lake Park and Fish and Game Preserve was established in 1909, complete with a clubhouse for sportsmen. When Reelfoot Lake State Park opened officially in 1956 it quickly became the third-most popular park in the system. Meanwhile, a 1941 agreement between the state and the U.S. Fish and Wildlife Service resulted in the state's second National Wildlife Refuge. (The first was Lake Isom, five miles south of Reelfoot, established in 1937.)

But none of these recreational improvements solved the problem of siltation and muck. If anything, they made them worse, because recreational use demanded stable lake levels to support everything from boat docks to campgrounds. And stable lake levels appeared to be one of the things choking the fishery. In the old days before dams and drainage projects, the lake periodically rose and fell with the cycle of seasons, of summer droughts and winter floods. The constant movement of new water into and out of the lake, the periodic exposure of large stretches of lake bottom during dry spells, kept the lake healthy, aerated and productive. Since people began regulating lake levels around the turn of the century, however, the lake bottom had gradually stopped breathing. A spillway built in 1930 regulated water levels even more. By the 1950s, the dead and decaying muck on the lake floor contained little or no dissolved oxygen, inhibiting not only the spawning of fish but the sort of healthy plant life and animal organisms that the fish fed on.

This realization would not come for some years, however, and when it did come, it would be many more years in solving. For now, the commercial fisherman was allowed to suffer along with the sport fisherman.

Time Out For Domestic Duties

The League had now created a commission, given it a long-range program and rewritten all its rules. The Game and Fish Commission may have been the League's baby, but it was certainly time to let it walk on its own. The League had other matters to attend to.

For one thing, there was the delicate matter of attrition.

The League had grown like crazy at first. When it formed in 1946, there were seven or eight clubs. By the first convention, there were twenty-five. A year later there were thirty-three. In 1949, there were seventy-seven. By 1950, there were ninety-five. And by the end of 1951, there were 115 clubs on the rolls at TCL—the greatest number in its history, if available records can be trusted.

However, not all were in good standing. At the 1952 convention, membership committee chairman Dr. A. T. Bayless reported that nineteen of the listed clubs had not paid dues since 1950. Another nineteen had not paid since 1949. Five clubs had been dropped altogether. So, strictly speaking, the League could claim only seventy-two dues-paying clubs by 1952, though it sometimes found it convenient to claim the higher numbers.

So valuable were affiliates, in fact, that Lou Williams drove thousands of miles back and forth across the state during his presidency, urging nonmembers to join and rallying member clubs to keep the faith (and recruit their neighbors). He kept an index card file of prospective clubs, mainly in West and Middle Tennessee, the League's base still being in the East. With his gentle manner and guileless grin, Williams must have been an irresistible salesman.

After two or three years, however, even Williams grew tired of doing most of the marketing. In October 1949, the board adopted a regional leadership structure to distribute the responsibility more evenly. Instead of a first and second vice president, there would now be three regional vice-presidents, one to oversee each of the three grand divisions. The board also voted to increase the number of board members to thirty from ten, three per Congressional district.

Soon Williams was handing out his index cards, telling board members to recruit nearby prospects themselves. Each member also got a copy of the 1948 edition of the *How Book* for organizing sportsmen's clubs; the League published an updated version in 1954. Among other things, the *How Book* urged clubs to host lots of activities. The board now agreed that there should also be regional outings every year. In 1951, the "special" membership committee became a standing committee.

If the directors were upbeat about clubs, they tried to be equally optimistic about money. But in fact the League was suffering on both scores. In 1950, the finance committee had suggested a budget of $12,500. The actual figure turned out to be closer to three thousand dollars. A year later, the story was the same: aggressive projections, modest attainments . Thus began another regrettable tradition: TCL's chronic lack of money.

For all their business acumen, the directors did not seem to have much of a knack for fund-raising. True, they always made a few hundred dollars on the annual meeting; and every so often a private business would make a special donation. They raised their main source of income, affiliate dues, from ten cents to twenty-five cents in 1949. But individual dues remained at just a dollar for many years, and the League's first merchandising effort, felt logo patches selling for a dollar each, generated as little as three or four dollars in a typical year. Most of them were given away as gifts.

Since it was first formed by a series of earthquakes, Reelfoot Lake's natural charms have caused no end of conflict and controversy. Courtesy of TWRA.

The single greatest expense, oddly enough, was salaries and withholdings. The League has always considered itself an all-volunteer group until 1972, and in terms of professional staff, that was true. But by 1950 it was paying twenty-five to forty dollars a month to each of the two "girls" in Secretary E. Lee Cross's Morristown office. When John Bailey took over as secretary in 1953, the monthly stipend went to him. By the time the League hired a director in 1972, Bailey was getting $150 a month.

After wages, the greatest of the League's expenses were printing and mailing costs: brochures, stationery, renewal notices, sporadic newsletters and proceedings of annual meetings. The published proceedings stopped when John Bailey took over, but the newsletters became more regular. Every now and then, the League struck a deal with this or that slick new outdoor magazine, offering to pay the publisher a share of member dues in return for a few pages of space in the magazine. But like Joe Halburnt's *Dixie Sportsman*, these invariably folded before the second or third issue got to the membership. *The Tennessee Conservationist* continued to publicize League activities for free, but not reliably.

A considerable expense was the monthly phone bill; the League also reimbursed travel expenses, though most members paid such costs out of their own pockets. There were numerous incidental expenses, such as the annual affiliation fee to the National Wildlife Federation. And periodically the League helped host special events. In 1950, for instance, it donated one hundred dollars for "entertainment" when the International Association of Game, Fish and Conservation Commissioners held its annual convention in Memphis.

The only other regular outlays at TCL were its special gifts and awards. From Governor Browning's silver-plated membership card in 1949 to a color television set for retiring secretary Lee Cross in 1952, the League honored its colleagues generously and often. The first award made on an annual basis (besides Cartter Patten's) was the Old Guide Award, begun in 1954 to honor outstanding affiliates. Named for the late Paul K. Bryant, the outdoor writer who played the Old Guide on WSM's *Wildlife Club of the Air*, it was renamed the Britton-Crossett Award in 1957, later simply the Britton Club Award, for its new sponsors, Bob Britton and Junius Crossett. The giant West Tennessee Sportsmen's Association and the Greene County Hunting and Fishing Club took the award in six of the first seven years.

TCL also liked to recognize top performers in the Game and Fish agency. In 1956, for instance, it gave a special citation to wildlife officer James Hammond for breaking up the giant "duckleg" operation in West Tennessee. In this incident, described by the U.S. Fish and Wildlife Service as the largest of its kind in the Southeast, twenty-six people were convicted of selling migratory waterfowl around Reelfoot Lake. In 1961, the League began recognizing Game and Fish staff on a regular basis, through the John Dyche Professional Award.

Since the sponsors put up at least some of the money to buy the engraved award plaques, it isn't clear how much of the League's budget was spent on these items. However, the most extravagant gifts were probably not bought with regular club funds at all. When Lou Williams stepped down from the presidency in 1951, for instance, his colleagues gave him a new *car*, an Oldsmobile Rocket 98. That extraordinary tribute was almost certainly the result of a quiet fund-raising collection among the members, because the budget that year was still only around three thousand dollars.

Z. Cartter Patten, founder of the state's first conservation award, finally wins an award of his own. In 1970, the League named him Conservationist of the Year. Photo by Charles Jackson. Courtesy of TWRA.

In fact, the budget was amazingly stagnant. By 1960 it had barely topped four thousand dollars. Yet all the while, the League continued to talk seriously about hiring an executive director. In 1951 it even announced the start of a quarter-million-dollar endowment campaign to allow the League to hire "a man" and open an office. Contributions, they promised, would soon be tax-deductible. That part, at least, was feasible.

Lou Williams had applied for a federal income tax exemption in 1949. The League was a charitable institution, he explained to the Internal Revenue Service, established and operating for educational purposes. The IRS, with its tough restrictions on political lobbying, didn't see it that way. Its first ruling, dated January 20, 1950, concluded that the League was not strictly educational inasmuch as "a substantial part" of its time was spent "attempting to influence legislation." The exemption was denied. (In 1976 the IRS changed its rules to allow limited lobbying by tax-exempt nonprofits.)

This was a blow, but not a lasting one. At its 1951 annual meeting, the League simply changed its bylaws to remove any mention of overt legislative activity. Thus, the "legislative" committee now became the "policy" committee; the stream pollution group now promoted "public interest," not "laws." Any item even obliquely suggestive of lobbying was bleached clean of such references. A few items were erased altogether—such as the League's earlier pledge to oppose gun control.

These changes did the trick. The League got its federal income tax exemption on August 29, 1951, and has retained it ever since. The $250,000 trust fund, on the other hand, was a dud. After ten years it contained barely six thousand dollars.

MR. MUSE TACKLES WATER POLLUTION

Fortunately there were plenty of men in the League who were willing to work for free. Some were already legendary in conservation politics, such as Herman Baggenstoss. But other names were virtually unknown before they rose to prominence in TCL.

Mayland H. Muse was an unassuming, even shy fellow from Johnson City who in 1950 undertook a most public campaign to clean up Tennessee's waters. Like the rest of the nation, many of Tennessee's surface and ground waters had been growing increasingly polluted, especially in the wake of the Industrial Revolution. The problem was not simply aesthetic. According to Garland Wiggins, deputy director of Tennessee Division of Water Pollution Control, periodic episodes of yellow fever, cholera, dysentery and typhoid fever were related to poor sanitation and a contaminated water supply. In 1879, an outbreak of yellow fever centered in Memphis killed twenty thousand people in the Mississippi River Valley alone.

In 1877, the General Assembly created a State Board of Health to deal with the issue. This became the Department of Public Health in 1923 as part of Austin Peay's massive reorganization bill. However, the new department focused very little on water quality or water supplies. Its Division of Sanitary Engineering, with its emphasis on sewage treatment plants, was the closest thing Tennessee had to a water pollution agency until 1945.

Other legislative action was few and far between. In 1907, the House tried to outlaw stream pollution from sawdust and other matter; the bill failed in the Senate. A few years later Tennessee's progressive head game warden, Joseph Acklen, tried to get the bill reintroduced, recommending it particularly "[t]o those who have studied the causes and ravages of typhoid fever." The detritus of lumber mills must have been excessive. In 1927, Peay renewed the complaint that sawmills, together with "textile and acid plants" were killing the state's fish.

Manufacturing industries were not much better. The Pigeon River, a mountain stream in East Tennessee, had been badly polluted since 1908, when a paper mill went on line in Canton, North Carolina. In 1929, Governor Henry Horton signed a bill charging that the "lamentable condition" of the Pigeon was "impairing the health and imperilling the lives" of Tennesseans who lived or fished along its shores. The bill authorized ten thousand dollars for a study of the pollution and its causes; it also authorized the governor to negotiate with "adjacent states." (Neither North Carolina nor the mill were directly implicated.) Failing these measures, said the bill, the attorney general was instructed to bring "any necessary lawsuits."

Sewage and industrial wastes fouled hundreds of river miles, especially near urban centers. As early as 1915 the Corps of Engineers had studied pollution in the Cumberland River. A 1937 article by John Caldwell in *Tennessee Wildlife* decried the "decaying, putrefying, stinking sewage" that made the Cumberland a virtual cesspool for twenty miles below Nashville. In the summer of 1944 these septic conditions triggered a massive fish kill that stretched all the way to Clarksville. According to TVA sanitary engineer S. Leary Jones, the carnage of bloated, stinking fish was so thick that a small boat could barely get through.

Yet before the 1940s, almost nothing had been done to control the polluters or clean up the pollution. The state game and fish code supposedly penalized pollution that harmed a fishery, but it was difficult to enforce because the agency had no criteria for what constituted harm. In 1936 the TVA started a series of formal water quality assessments in the Tennessee River Valley. According to these findings, the vast majority of human waste in the Valley flowed untreated into the river and its tributaries—an amount equal to the raw sewage of a half-million people. Of 250 major industrial plants, said the report, only 47 had any sort of treatment, and most of these were inadequate.

TENNESSEE'S STREAM POLLUTION STUDY BOARD

TVA's findings jolted the state into action.

In 1943, the Department of Health, joined by the Department of Conservation, sponsored the state's first serious attempt at pollution control legislation. Though this bill failed, the General Assembly authorized a study board to find out which streams were polluted, how badly, and from which sources. As governor, Prentice Cooper had an ex-officio seat on this Stream Pollution Study Board; so did the Commissioners of Health, Conservation and Agriculture. In addition, Cooper appointed Lytle Brown, retired Corps engineer and a member of the Conservation Commission; Walter Chandler, mayor of Memphis; and industrialists Rutledge Smith of Nashville and W. M. Fulton of Knoxville.

Frankly, the combined expertise of all seven of these men was probably not as valuable as that of their two technical advisors: Roy Morton, associate professor of sanitary engineering at Vanderbilt; and S. Leary Jones, the sanitary engineer on loan from TVA's pollution program. The forty-seven-page report that came out of the study on January 20, 1945, was mainly Jones' work. According to the report, of 114 sewer systems in the state, only 32 provided any kind of treatment. The other eighty-two sent raw sewage straight through the system and into the public waterways. Many more communities had no waste collection system at all, and thousands of households still relied on "backhouses," some of them perched deliberately on the bank of the nearest stream. Altogether, one million people were dumping 100 million gallons of sewage into the state's surface waters every day, 83 percent of which received no treatment whatsoever. Moreover, the treatment given to the remaining 17 percent was so primitive that it corrected less than half the pollution load.

Industrial waste was flowing into the waterways at an estimated 200-400 million gallons a day, said the report, with a pollution load roughly 150 percent that of domestic sewage. Although "many industries" had some type of treatment, they corrected less than 1 percent of the pollution.

Yet even with these data sitting in front of them, it was clear that the researchers had no real idea what they were dealing with. By their reckoning, only 710 miles—less than 5 percent of Tennessee's 15,000 miles of streams—were "seriously affected by pollution," to use the words of technician R. P. Farrell. Another 6 percent were found to be "damaged for many desirable uses." In other words, 300 million to 500 million gallons of untreated effluent every *day*, and only 11 percent of all surface waters in the state were judged in any degree polluted. Compare this to recent water quality reports for Tennessee, which classify roughly a fourth of all streams as partially polluted and some 10 percent as seriously polluted. Obviously, Tennessee's streams are much cleaner today than they were fifty years ago. The difference, said state Water Pollution Control Director Paul Davis, is that water quality engineers now use far more sensitive standards, and far more sophisticated technology, to determine what is polluted and what is not. Fifty years ago, said Davis, "people had no way of knowing just how bad things were."

THE FIRST REAL WATER POLLUTION LAW IN THE NATION

Nevertheless, the Study Board's report was sufficiently alarming to most lawmakers that they immediately passed Chapter 128, Public Acts of 1945—the first viable water pollution control law in Tennessee, and the first, for that matter, in the nation. Soon states began passing their own laws, but it would be three years before Congress enacted the first federal statute, the Water Pollution Control Act of 1948. This law simply authorized the federal government to regulate water pollution. It specified no goals, objectives, limits nor even the simplest guidelines.

Tennessee's law set no standards, either. It merely created a Stream Pollution Control Board within the Department of Health and gave it the power to make and enforce regulations. Leary Jones was hired on as the principal engineer; R. P. Farrell was named technical secretary. Like the Study Board, the Stream Pollution Control Board was a seven-man assembly of three commissioners and four citizens.

The Legislature had neglected to appropriate any money, however, so for two years, all the board could do was develop criteria and begin warning industries and cities to start getting their sewage treatment acts together. Jones and Farrell did manage to wrangle two laboratory trucks from war surplus.

But even when the first appropriations came through in 1947, cleaner water didn't necessarily follow. The polluters were balking. Although a number of industries and municipalities had developed treatment plans, most complained that they couldn't afford to put them into action, at least not right away. Others insisted that since it was the government who ordered the cleanup, the government should pay for it. More than a few continued to question the need for treatment in the first place, and insisted on more studies. In 1949 the Tennessee Municipal League intervened, introducing a bill designed to buy its members more time. The bill passed, and the Stream Pollution Control Board was temporarily suspended while a second study board went to work.

This seven-man board—called the Stream Pollution Study Commission presumably to distinguish it from the Stream Pollution Study Board and the Stream Pollution Control Board—focused mainly on the fiscal side of things, especially financing, fiscal responsibility, available grants and so on. But the commission was also charged with conducting more studies, designing a five-year abatement plan to begin July 1, 1951, and drafting a law that would create an official water pollution control agency.

The completed report was due on Governor Browning's desk by July 1, 1950.

FIGHTING THIS EVIL OF POLLUTION

This was how things stood on May 20, 1950, when Mayland Muse addressed the "discussional meeting" of TCL's pollution committee at the Ocoee Inn near Benton, on Ocoee Lake.

Muse began, with characteristic humility, by apologizing for being there. "He said that some of those present might think that Lou Williams had made a mistake in appointing him Chairman of the Pollution Committee due to the fact that he was a piping contractor and might logically be thought to represent industry's interests rather than those of the sportsmen," the minutes said. But, he hastened to add, "he felt it an honor to have been appointed."

Then he promptly turned the floor over to Lou Williams.

For the next several hours, Muse stood politely aside while one speaker after another offered his views on "this evil of pollution."

No one was as vehement on the topic as Karl Steinmetz. Steinmetz loved trout fishing more than anything except perhaps growing hybridized irises. In his opinion, the man was "a durn fool who gets into virgin territory where it is fit for anything," then loads the waters with human waste "until they are so repulsive he can no longer stand them, then he spends millions of dollars to purify them."

Why in the world do we need more studies? he demanded. If the water's polluted, he said, "you can see it; and if you can't see it, you can smell it."

Lou Williams, always the voice of calm and compromise, intervened. The League must "refrain from attacking" the issue with force, he said, approaching it instead with "education and leadership." Look at Chattanooga Creek, he pointed out, one of the filthiest streams in the nation. For years the town of Chattanooga refused to do anything about it. But then "a public meeting was called; ... the newspapers cooperated by running pictures certainly not a credit to any community, and ... public sentiment became such that the citizens voted $5 million for a sewage treatment plant." This even though Chattanooga was "already pretty heavy in debt." Similar good-faith efforts were happening with industry, he said. Tennessee Copper Company had already spent $300,000 on research and $500,000 on equipment to clean up its chemical waste at Copperhill. With proper education and encouragement, said Williams, other towns and industries could be persuaded to do likewise. "The League's function," he insisted, was to "create interest on the part of the citizens so that they would demand that something be done and would be willing to pay for it."

Nor, he said, would the League score points by approaching the program from a purely recreational standpoint. "No big industry would spend money to make waters pure just so fishermen could catch fish." They must approach the issue broadly, "from a standpoint of public health and other legitimate uses." On the other hand, he was quick to add, "the League did not have to offer any apologies for protecting the recreational uses of our waters."

When the meeting was over, Muse stood up only long enough to thank everyone for coming. But in his unobtrusive way, he had been preparing his own speeches.

"BE A GOOD RIVER NEIGHBOR"

As promised, the study commission delivered its report to Governor Browning on June 30, 1950. For dozens of cities, towns and industries across Tennessee, the grace period was over. A few—mainly the smallest towns and the biggest industries—had already started building treatment plants. But for modest businesses operating on small profit margins, and large cities needing multimillion dollar treatment plants, the prospect of a government mandate caused them to dig in their heels.

The main problem was that they weren't getting much help with financing. Congress was still waffling on a bill that would allow industries to amortize their construction costs. And while loans were available to cities as part of the federal Water Pollution Control Act, the most they could qualify for was $250,000 or one-third the cost of construction, whichever was less. For most big cities, that was the merest drop in the bucket for a project that could easily cost more than ten million dollars. The only way to raise that kind of money was through bonds, presumably to be repaid through sewer user fees. But to most city officials and voters alike, "user fee" sounded suspiciously like "tax," and in city after city, from Nashville to Memphis to Knoxville, voters rejected bond proposals by overwhelming majorities. In Kingsport, for instance, a bond issue lost by as much as 97 percent—twice. Even in Chattanooga, where five million dollars in bonds had already been approved, officials were now standing around idly while the state Supreme Court decided whether sewer fees were even legal. And all the while the Tennessee Municipal League was subtly spreading the gospel that while stream pollution control was probably a good thing, new taxes probably were not.

Mayland Muse decided it would be his mission to convince taxpayers otherwise. Armed with the slogan "Be a Good River Neighbor," he embarked on what would ultimately be a ten-year odyssey of meetings, out-of-state conferences, research projects, public hearings, briefings, speeches and presentations. There were others on the pollution committee, of course, but it was Muse who did the heavy lifting, though he always referred to himself in the third person. "A member of your committee gave a talk to this industry," he would say, or "a member of your committee paid a visit to that councilman." He was as self-effacing as a ghost, but wherever he went, it seemed, sewer plants followed.

In September 1951, for instance, Muse met with officials in Morristown; the following spring a treatment plant was underway. In October 1951 he gave his pitch to a meeting of all the Chambers of Commerce in the state; the following March, Nashville passed an eleven-million-dollar bond issue by a margin of 6 to 1. Knoxville, Bristol, Erwin, Clarksville, Dickson, Franklin, Springfield were all following suit. By the end of 1952 Memphis was the only major urban center in the state without a major treatment plant in the works. (Memphis' position, apparently, was that when you have as big a toilet bowl as the Mississippi River, you don't need to treat your sewage.)

Muse's work wasn't always so gratifying, however. When TVA impounded Boone Reservoir in the early '50s, for instance, fisheries experts doubted whether fish could even survive in its waters, given the appalling quality of the streams supplying it—the Watauga, which flowed out of Elizabethton and Johnson City, and the South Fork Holston out of Bluff City and Bristol. Bristol had a secondary treatment plant by then, but it didn't work well; it also had an unimproved paper mill. Bluff City dumped raw sewage, and both Elizabethton and Johnson City were bustling manufacturing centers whose waste streams were a lethal sludge of human and industrial garbage. Yet in 1952, even as Boone Reservoir was being flooded, Johnson City voters rejected a $3.2 million bond issue for a municipal sewage plant. Muse hated to admit it, but Johnson City was his hometown.

Several years later, while writing his doctoral thesis on community conservation projects, TCL secretary John Bailey would recall how Muse "[a]lmost single-handed . . . started appearing before the many civic clubs in Johnson City asking for a new vote." Muse succeeded in getting another referendum scheduled. Meanwhile, he pulled out a secret weapon: comic books. Apparently the U.S. Department of Health, Education and Welfare had teamed up with Mark Trail comics to produce a colored booklet called *The Fight to Save America's Waters.* Muse ordered four thousand copies, distributing them among Johnson City's school-

Thirty-four years after winning it the first time, Mayland Muse receives a second Z. Cartter Patten Award in 1987 for cleaning up Tennessee's waters. President Mitchell Parks makes the presentation. TCL file photo.

rooms. The kids must have taken the books home to their parents, for when the time the bond issue came up a second time, it passed easily. Over the next few years, 25,000 school kids in Kingsport and Bluff City would get comic books of their own—and Kingsport and Bluff City would get sewage treatment plants.

A PROGRESS REPORT

In 1945, only thirty-two municipal sewage systems in Tennessee provided any kind of treatment before releasing the waste into the nearest waterway. By 1958, this number had grown to 144, another 49 were in the planning stages, and only 23 were operating with neither treatment works nor plans for building them. Memphis alone was still holding out. The largest city in the state would not complete its first major wastewater treatment facility until 1975. But throughout the state, the rivers were running much clearer.

Of the 238 industries known to be discharging wastes, 199 were either treating their wastes, planning to treat their wastes, or, in a growing number of cases, recovering their wastes. Mayland Muse liked to point to the Embreeville Iron Company, which had reclaimed $37 million worth of zinc dust simply by running its wastewater through a series of settling basins en route to discharge in the Nolichucky River.

In 1953 Muse won the Z. Cartter Patten Award for his pollution campaign. (He won it again in 1986 for the same reason, making him one of three double winners: TOWA journalists Evan Means and Henry Reynolds.) The same weekend, Muse was elected president of the

League. He soon had to cut his presidency short, because in 1954 Governor Frank Clement appointed Muse to his new Conservation Commission. But the tribute that may have pleased Muse more than any other was a letter from S. Leary Jones in 1958. By this time, the Stream Pollution Control Board was a freestanding agency, and Jones was its director. However, said Jones, for years the agency had nowhere near enough staff, nor enough funding, to complete its mission. Between them, he said, the League and Mayland Muse helped keep Tennessee's pollution program alive.

THE BIRTH OF KEEP TENNESSEE GREEN

Next to water, forests were the other great resource issue of the mid-century. Almost half of Tennessee's 26.9 million acres was forested—somewhere between thirteen million and fourteen million acres, depending on whose account you read, and when it was written. (The difference was that as much as a million acres of forest were considered "marginal," so badly scarred by logging, disease and forest fires that they weren't even counted as forest.) At any rate, of that thirteen (or fourteen) million acres, about a million acres belonged to the federal government, either as the Cherokee National Forest or the Great Smoky Mountains National Park. (In 1974, Washington would claim several thousand more acres when it authorized the Big South Fork National River and Recreation Area.) Another 200,000 or so acres were state-owned, either as state parks or state forests, though this number fluctuated also, because of the rapid rate at which the state was buying parks. The remainder, roughly 90 percent of the total, was in private hands: logging companies, paper mills, farms and assorted other interests.

Forests were not only big, they were big business, contributing an estimated $200 million to the state's economy. Their value to water quality, to recreation, to the sportsman—these were incalculable. Obviously such a resource was worth protecting.

In 1874, Joseph B. Killebrew, secretary of what was then called the Tennessee Bureau of Agriculture, wrote, "More is involved in [the question of forest protection] than mere money. ... Happiness, contentment, progress, refinement, and the civilization of humanity depend, in a measure, upon the production of our forests." But Tennessee's first forester wasn't hired until 1914, a Bureau of Forestry wasn't created until 1921, and the first forest fire controls weren't in place until 1922. By 1950, when the Tennessee Conservation League first began talking about a "Keep Tennessee Green" program, barely a third of the state's ninety-five counties had forest fire protection.

In 1941, Tennessee had introduced a cooperative forest fire management program whereby counties had the option of "buying" coverage. In return for a share of the costs, counties were entitled to fire lookout towers, the services of "motorized fire fighting units" (which simply meant crews of trained men who arrived on trucks) and assorted other fire-fighting tools. Granted, the county share was very modest—usually no more than two thousand dollars a year. And the rate was lowest for the most forested counties. Nonetheless, as of July 1, 1950, only thirty-five counties had voted to join the system, leaving more than five and a half million acres vulnerable. If a fire broke out in an unprotected county, the state would presumably send crews to fight it—but the whole point of fire protection was early detection and intervention.

Moreover, critics charged, the state didn't provide enough protection in the limited acreage it did patrol. Tennessee had one of the worst records in the country both for numbers of acres burned every year and numbers of dollars spent on fire control. By July 1, 1950, there were only sixty-seven fireproof lookout towers in the whole state, all of them built in the 1930s by the Civilian Conservation Corps. Fire fighting was still done entirely on foot and by hand; the new "mechanized fire fighting units" (heavy-duty tractor plows) did not arrive until 1952, and even then there were only two of them.

What timber did survive from one year to the next was not of the highest quality. Though Tennessee ranked third in the nation in sheer volume of hardwood lumber production, in general her timber stands were considered inferior, with too much space taken up by culls and junk species. "To sum it all up," said the Division of Forestry's 1952 biennial report, "the average acre of forest land in Tennessee is growing about 100 board feet of wood per year whereas the growth could be three times that much."

In 1946 Governor Jim McCord had been so disturbed by such statistics that he commissioned the Society of American Foresters to do a complete evaluation of the state's forestry picture. The report, submitted to the governor in 1947, concluded that the "[f]orests of Tennessee [were] sadly depleted." The state forestry organization needed strengthening, the budget needed to be greatly enlarged, and Tennessee altogether needed a comprehensive state forest policy, "executed by competent, professionally trained personnel."

None of this was news to the League, which had been pressing for a stronger forestry program since the organization was founded. At the 1948 annual meeting, Cartter Patten presented the Society's recommendations to the League as an eleven-point resolution. It passed unanimously.

Patten had a vested interest in forests. In 1943 he had purchased the so-called Horseshoe Properties near Chattanooga, twenty thousand "overgrazed, overburned and overcut" acres on Waldens Ridge. But Patten wasn't the only member of TCL who was interested in forests. Herman Baggenstoss operated one of the state's first registered tree farms, and it was Baggenstoss who soon took the lead in TCL's campaign for better forest protection.

Baggenstoss had been fighting passionately for Tennessee's forests since at least the early 1930s, when he founded Grundy Camp P-62, the only CCC forest camp on the Cumberland Plateau. Baggenstoss persuaded his foremen to join with local citizens in buying 211 acres of mountainside and deeding it to the state as Grundy Forest—now part of the South Cumberland State Recreation Area (which Baggenstoss also helped create some forty years later). In 1945 he helped organize the Tennessee Timber Growers Association, and in 1949 he started the annual Tennessee Forest Festival, a three-day event complete with skidder parades and the annual crowning of "Queen Sylva" (not to be confused with the Catfish Queen).

It was Baggenstoss who lobbied to get a U.S. Forest Service research lab established at Sewanee in the late '50s (and who fought ardently—but vainly—to save it from Ronald Reagan's budgetary axe in the early 1980s). And it was always Baggenstoss who, whether as a CCC supervisor or as a private tree farmer or as chairman of the Conservation Commission, pushed lawmakers unremittingly to invest more money in forest fire control.

So naturally Baggenstoss was pleased when the League joined a movement called "Keep Green." Keep Green was a national network of forest protection programs in twenty-seven states, concerned with all aspects of timber management but mainly with forest fire control.

Yet the introductory event of Keep Tennessee Green had nothing to do with forest fires. It was deforestation of another sort: the moonscape known as the Copper Basin.

THE GREENING OF COPPER HILL

On Saturday, May 27, 1950, several hundred people, including Governor Gordon Browning, drove to the golf course just outside Copperhill, in Polk County in the extreme southeastern corner of the state. There, framed by fairways and putting greens, Lou Williams welcomed the visitors to an unlikely event: the reclamation of a once-dead landscape.

A century earlier, the basin—called Ducktown Basin then—had been as green as any other settlement in those mountains. But in 1843, or so legend has it, a farmer named Lemmon discovered some yellowish rocks in his potato patch. At first he thought he'd found gold, and was disappointed when he realized his error. But it turned out to be something of considerable value anyway—copper. By 1850 the first of many copper mines was hauling ore out of the basin.

At first, miners carted the ore to Georgia for processing, but by the time the Civil War began, operators were smelting the ore on site, "heap-roasting" the rocks in small, open kilns scattered throughout what was now called the Copper Basin. Acres of trees were cut down to fuel the kilns; what little vegetation remained was soon choked by sulfur dioxide escaping from the kilns. Aquatic life disappeared from North Potato and other local creeks, suffocated not so much by the poisonous atmosphere as by the great loads of sediment that swept into the streams every time it rained. By the turn of the century, the Copper Basin was as barren as a parking lot.

For obvious economic reasons, the state of Tennessee turned a blind eye to the pollution. The neighboring state of Georgia, however, had no such vested interest, and in 1907, it got an injunction from the U.S. Supreme Court halting open smelting in the Basin. By now, all the little mines had been consolidated into one giant complex, the Tennessee Copper Company. As it turned out, however, Tennessee Copper would not be shut down for long by the injunction. The company had recently developed a closed smelting process that allowed it to recover the sulfur fumes as sulfuric acid, a highly marketable product thanks to the development of new "superphosphate" fertilizers. In 1908, having promised to report any stray emissions daily to the state of Georgia, Tennessee Copper resumed operations in the Basin using this new process.

The damage to the landscape remained, however, a persistent if mute accusation of corporate arrogance and official irresponsibility. By the late 1930s, Copperhill schoolchildren were marching into the gullies, planting pine seedlings in an attempt to bring the basin back to life. Finally the copper company itself (with the help of TVA, the U.S. Forest Service and the state of Tennessee) decided to see if something so dead as the Copper Basin could possibly be made to live again. In 1941, a CCC camp moved into the basin. On a five hundred-acre test plot, CCC teams fertilized and mulched soil, planted pine striplings, seeded for weeping lovegrass and sericea lespedeza. When the CCC folded in 1942, the copper company took over, planting another three million pine and black locust seedlings across fifteen hundred acres—about a fifth of the most severely eroded land. By 1950, the restoration project had made enough progress that the community could actually support a golf course. Guests at the League's "forestry meeting" were invited to see the results for themselves on a drive-through tour.

The League had decided to hold this meeting in the Copper Basin partly to demonstrate the merits of scientific reforestation methods. But it also wanted to make a point about a new program it was about to launch.

"Prevent Forest Fires—Grow More Trees"

When Conservation Commissioner C. P. Swan took his turn in the Copperhill program, it was mainly to endorse Keep Tennessee Green, the League's new forestry initiative. Actually, the League wasn't sure just what to call KTG at that point. Other states, such as Arkansas, had formed whole organizations around the Keep Green banner. But the League already had a forestry committee, and Tennessee already had a Timber Growers Association. All the League knew for sure was that it liked Keep Green's no-nonsense slogan: "prevent forest fires, grow more trees."

Herman Baggenstoss contemplates the view overlooking Savage Gulf. Baggenstoss was passionately fond of the region, helping preserve Savage Gulf as a state natural area, establishing Grundy State Forest and lending his name to the nature center at South Cumberland State Recreation Area. Photo by Charles Nicholas. Copyright © The Commercial Appeal, Memphis, TN. Used with permission.

In the end, however, the League decided that Keep Tennessee Green should be a free-standing organization. (In 1971, it was renamed the Tennessee Forestry Association.) On a snowy Thursday morning in February, on the first day of the League's 1951 annual meeting, Governor Browning played host to four hundred KTG "delegates" in the War Memorial Auditorium in Nashville. Lou Williams was introduced as their new president.

For Williams, it must have been an emotional time. Not only was he presiding over a new organization; he was stepping down from a beloved old one. C. J. Murphy of Nashville was the new president of TCL. Williams gave an eloquent if lengthy speech at Friday evening's awards banquet, and drove home the next day in his new Oldsmobile.

As president of Keep Tennessee Green, Williams' first job was to push for more money for fire protection. The entire forestry budget for the coming year—from all sources, including federal aid—was $825,000. Less than $700,000 of that was allocated for fire fighting, including $80,000 from the thirty-five counties enrolled in the fire-protection program. State forester Carl I. Peterson estimated that it would take $1.5 million a year to protect the whole state, plus $1,400,000 in onetime capital purchases.

Lou Williams was advised to ask the Legislature for at least a million a year for the next biennium (1953-1955). Herman Baggenstoss, now the chairman of the Conservation Commission, seconded the appeal.

But before the matter could be voted on, the fires started.

"CREEPING DEATH": THE FIRES OF 1952

The first few months of 1952 had not been uncommonly dry. By April, however, folks began to suspect that the spring rains were not coming. By June, some fire crews were already at work. By July, Tennessee was sweltering in one of the worst droughts on record, and fires were breaking out almost hourly. A false lull came in August, but by September, every fire fighter in the state was summoned to active duty.

Then, in October, disaster struck. A dramatic article *The Tennessee Conservationist* called it "Creeping Death":

> Fire struck the heavily-wooded and remote sections of the North Cumberlands—a rugged and almost primitive section, extremely inaccessible to mechanized fire fighting equipment.
> Fires blazed up then in the South Cumberlands—in the heavily wooded sections of east Tennessee—in spots of middle Tennessee and in west Tennessee. ...
> When the big fires began to rage, the Forestry Division's mechanized equipment—trucks, tractors and fire plows—and all its trained forces were tied up all over the state.
> ... The men had been working for weeks, twenty-four hours a day, and were at the point of exhaustion.

The fire danger reached Grundy County the first week of November, according to another chronicler, Charles Page. Herman Baggenstoss worked around the clock for four days straight, organizing volunteers and dispatching relief units. Though he was now almost fifty years old, he fought some of the fires himself. More volunteers were summoned: foresters, state police, TVA maintenance workers. But the flames were relentless. By Sunday morning, November 9, three separate fires came within a half-hour of Tracy City's shops and homes.

"Hundreds of desperate volunteers joined the weary state crews in last-ditch efforts," wrote Page. "Heavy equipment continued plowing fire breaks. As the flames reached within a half mile of the town at one point, a few drops of rain fell, then more drops." Soon the drops became a steady downpour, and the danger was past. All that remained was cleaning up. And recrimination.

THE FIERY RHETORIC OF HERMAN BAGGENSTOSS

The fires of 1952 destroyed more than a million acres of forest and cost the state "upwards of $30 million," according to Lou Williams. In Hamilton County, where the Horseshoe Properties blazed along with the rest of Waldens Ridge, Cartter Patten estimated the disaster "set [his] program back by three to five years." Fortunately, no lives were lost, but the acrid taste of the disaster, like the smoke that had hung over the state for weeks, lingered.

Frank Clement had been elected governor on November 4, 1952. The Conservation Commission planned to meet on December 2 to do a postmortem of the fire. On November 25, Herman Baggenstoss wrote to the governor-elect, urging him to attend the meeting. Surely Clement "would welcome the opportunity to be briefed on the State Conservation Commission and its functions," said Baggenstoss. Besides, he added slyly, the commission wanted to advise Clement of a growing fomentation among the citizenry. Coalitions were even then forming "with the idea" of producing "a real constructive [forest fire] program."

It is not known whether Clement went to the December meeting; but as he certainly knew the main reason for Baggenstoss' invitation, he may well have stayed away. The bee in Baggenstoss' bonnet was not simply a matter of forestry funding. For more than a year now, Baggenstoss had been lobbying anew for an independent Conservation Commission, with policy-making power over everything from forestry budgets to parks personnel. It galled him that the Conservation Commission had no authority, no continuity. No matter how technically sound or economically prudent its advice might be, the administration was under no obligation to follow it.

As it happened, the new governor did not follow the commission's advice on forestry funding. Clement recommended, and the lawmakers approved, a fairly modest increase in the state's appropriation, to $650,000. Lou Williams termed the increase "insignificant," but in general the League chose to steer around this controversy.

Baggenstoss, on the other hand, was furious—so angry, in fact, that he resigned from the Conservation Commission in protest. In a letter made public at the League's annual meeting in Jackson on April 2, 1953, he told Clement, "I have failed in my efforts to convince you, as Governor of this great Forest State, of the dire and urgent need for sufficient appropriations for the purpose of controlling Forest Fires. ... I bow out in protest of the values you have set on our greatest renewable resource as evidenced by the complete lack of faith shown in the recommendations advocated by the State Advisory Commission [on Forests]."

With his resignation announced on front pages throughout the state, Baggenstoss carried his point with his usual bravura. But the truth was, he was probably out of a job already. The Legislature, at the governor's request, was about to abolish the current Conservation Commission.

In its place they created yet another. The new commission appointed by Frank Clement had six members instead of eleven, but it was still strictly advisory. As Baggenstoss perceived, probably correctly, the new commission was a convenient way to get rid of personnel who had become troublesome.

When Clement proclaimed the second week of November 1953 "Keep Tennessee Forests Green Week," Baggenstoss may well have bristled. But the ironic fact was, the outlook for Tennessee's forests had never been better. In 1953 there would still be lots of fires—roughly 4,300 compared to 1953's record 6,000—but they were never out of control, and they involved less than a tenth of the previous year's acreage—91,000 acres compared to the million acres burned in 1952. The size of the average fire was also smaller, 21 acres compared to an average 174 acres the year before. And only thirteen fires burned more than five hundred acres. In 1952, there had been 166 fires that large. Fortunately, 1953 was no fluke. Over the next six years, the size of the average fire dropped to less than ten acres. The total area burned averaged less than thirty thousand acres.

Why were things so much better? For one thing, it rained more. A new public awareness program also helped. But the state really was better prepared. By 1959, seventy-two counties were enrolled in the forest fire protection program. The Division of Forestry now had a round-the-clock radio communications system, its own airplane, 20 monitoring stations, more than 150 fire towers and 44 mechanized fire plow units. And though the majority of fires were caused by simple carelessness, the division had also acquired a fire-law enforcement specialist who investigated cases of suspected arson.

As if to underscore the state's progress over the last ten years, in 1962 Tennessee won an award for excellence in forest fire control. Called the Beichler Award (a statuette of Smoky Bear), it honored the Southeastern state whose fire record in the past year showed the most improvement over the five previous years. Texas had won the first Beichler award in 1961. In 1963, Tennessee won the Beichler Award for the second time. Then it won it again, in 1964. Whether or not Herman Baggenstoss had anything to do with it, Tennessee's fire danger was clearly past.

FENDING OFF POLITICAL ASSAILANTS

To be honest, the loss of the old Conservation Commission was not especially distressing to the League. After all, the commission had been restructured before, and it would no doubt be restructured again. (In fact, Clement himself would do so. In 1963, after sitting out a term to Buford Ellington, Clement returned to the governor's office and promptly eliminated the Conservation Commission a second time. The 1963 commission would hold *fifteen* members.)

At any rate, Clement in 1953 lost no time choosing a new set of commissioners. One of them was Mayland Muse, the League's current president. (According to TCL's bylaws, Muse had to surrender the presidency, which he did.) As for the insult to their colleague Herman

Baggenstoss, that was unfortunate, but in March 1953 the League was too busy worrying about the Game and Fish Commission to think about much else.

The Game and Fish Commission was under the worst attack of its brief history.

It had been challenged at least once already, in the 1951 General Assembly, in an assault led by the League's nemesis, Damon Headden, Sr. But Governor Browning had won reelection, so the model law had been secure for two more years. But now there was a new governor in power, and Frank Clement, it soon became clear, did not wish to be overly chummy with the Conservation League. He publicly questioned the wisdom of a law that had made Game and Fish "virtually a government unto itself"; he even doubted that the League represented the majority of Tennessee sportsmen. On the contrary, he said, most sportsmen resented the fact that "city sportsmen now consider the game of this State as their private property." *City sportsman*, of course, was a term of high contempt.

So frosty was this new administration to the League that for the first time in four years its leaders had serious fears for their model law—and so did their allies in the outdoor press, including Walter Amann, Jr., who followed the debate closely in *The Knoxville Journal*. "This administration wants the commission to fall, with game and fish put back into the conservation department," Amann wrote in early March. "Any political realist alive knows full well that a Browning-appointed commission has about as much chance for survival at the hands of an opposition administration as a snowball in you-know-where."

Things certainly looked that way. Early in the 1953 session, Greeneville Representative James Hardin introduced a bill to abolish the Game and Fish Commission and return its functions to the Department of Conservation. His chief cosponsor was Representative Damon Headden, *Jr.*, chair of the House Game, Fish and Forestry Committee. According to these two, Tennessee's game and fish agency was more politicized now than ever. Hardin even rumored that Commissioners Lucius Burch and Dr. B. H. Plunk (both prominent leaders in the League) had used their positions to get Game and Fish lakes built near their homes. The charges were unfounded, of course. Humboldt Lake had been built even before Plunk joined the commission, and Fisherville Lake had been sited with a compass to be near a population center. That it was also near the home of a powerful attorney was entirely accidental. Nonetheless, the rumors fed latent prejudices, and soon the Legislature seemed to be burning with an anti-commission fever.

Damon Headden, Sr., who hated the model law so much that he considered running for governor himself in order to overturn it, was delighted by this agreeable shift in the political wind. He scorned the League as a club of "city hunters and game hogs" who did not have the support of "the real hunters and fishermen of Tennessee." When his son the committee chairman contrived an excuse to deny the sportsmen a hearing before the Game, Fish and Forestry Committee, the elder Headden positively gloated. "We have enough votes to kill the commission ... any day we want to bring it up."

"THE MOST DELICIOUS MESS OF CROW I'VE EVER HAD TO EAT"

Headden wasn't the only one predicting the commission's funeral. Walter Amann himself was ready to sign the death warrant. On March 10, he reported glumly to his readers, a delegation including Dr. Plunk, M. L. Brickey, Lee Cross, Cecil Branstetter, Will Roper and *Tennessean* writer Bob Steber had met with Hardin, Headden and the rest of the anti-commission bloc in hopes of reaching a compromise. Instead, said Amann, the sportsmen were "pounced on" by the legislators. In the face of such hostility, he said, "[n]o compromise was possible"; the demise of the commission was "a foregone conclusion."

But Amann hadn't figured on the rallying power of the men in the League. Members flooded their legislators with calls, letters and visits. In just four years, they reminded the lawmakers, Tennessee's wildlife program had become a model for the nation (this was true); its wildlife program had rocketed from thirty-seventh place to third (this was also true). Some of the League lobbyists added mild warnings. "If Clement signs any legislation throwing wildlife to the political spoils system," said Dr. Plunk, "he'll find out who's representing whom the next time he presents himself for election."

By March 19, 1953, the day the House was to consider Hardin's bill, it was clear that the League "had the oppositionists licked," Walter Amann reported incredulously. "[T]he governor also threw up his hands in surrender."

Together the two groups worked out an extremely mild compromise bill. The sportsmen agreed to change the way they voted for commissioners (described at length in the last chapter). And they agreed—reluctantly—to allow the commissioner of Conservation veto power over all hirings and firings in Game and Fish. (Presumably this power was never abused. But the mere potential for abuse was so aggravating to the League that in 1956 members began actively lobbying against it. In 1959 the so-called "veto power" clause was repealed.)

In a way, the 1953 vote to retain the commission was an even more important victory than the law creating it in the first place. Commissions came and went on Capitol Hill as routinely as the nameplates outside legislative offices. The notion that a commission might actually be permanent was such a novel idea that some legislators never did get used to it. Damon Headden, Sr., didn't have a chance to. He died of a massive blood clot just days after the compromise bill passed.

The League knew that this challenge would by no means be the last. Still, members were proud and relieved. As for Walter Amann, he declared to his readers on March 22 that he was about to eat some crow—and it was going to be "the tastiest, most delicious mess of crow" he'd ever had to eat.

THE GLORY DAYS OF CONSERVATION EDUCATION

For most members, of course, life at the League was not always fighting forest fires or negotiating with governors or rushing to eleventh-hour meetings with legislative chairmen. In fact, most League activity was fairly prosaic.

Much of it, of course, was meetings: meetings of the small game committee, meetings of the credentials committee, even meetings of the annual meeting committee. Moreover, though most of the issues that concerned the League in the early days had to do with hunting and fishing, very little official League activity *was* hunting and fishing. True, the League promoted regional field days (often fishing or trap shooting followed by a cookout), but these were always run by the host clubs. The League didn't sponsor organized hunts; it didn't book

Jim Bailey, the man who taught thousands of teachers and students at Fall Creek Falls State Park, stands at the entrance to a new trail there. Courtesy of The Tennessee Conservationist / *Tennessee Department of Environment and Conservation.*

big-game tours or deep-sea fishing expeditions; it rarely even arranged for a few hours' fishing during annual meetings. These were certainly the sorts of things members did, either as affiliates or as individuals. But as social as its members were, the League itself was not—and really never has been—primarily a social club.

It was, as it told the IRS, primarily an educational organization—if education can be taken very broadly to mean educating the voting public and policy-makers about the need for this or that policy. Most of its public education, therefore, took the form of communications: either written—as in newsletters, brochures, reports, reviews, letters and press releases—or verbal—speeches, seminars, conferences, legislative testimony, task forces and so on. But from the start, the League also meant "education" to extend to traditional conservation education for kids and teachers. In fact, the education committee was eventually renamed the youth and education committee.

Fortunately for them, the 1950s happened to be the glory days for conservation education in Tennessee. And much of that owed to the efforts of one man, James L. Bailey, Jr., the education specialist at the Department of Conservation.

Jim Bailey had been working for the Department almost since it was created by the Browning administration in 1937. In fact, Bailey was practically the first person hired by Conservation Commissioner Sam Brewster. As Bailey recalled it many years later, the central office in those days was a single large room in the basement of the War Memorial Building. The conservation program was still in the planning stages, and Bailey's job wasn't really education at all. He had been hired for his expertise in soil erosion and other rural resource issues, having most recently worked for Roosevelt's Emergency Recovery Program in the Department of Agriculture.

However, Jim Bailey also had a certificate from the State Teacher's College at Murfreesboro, and it didn't take Sam Brewster long to realize that his new employee, with his double major in wise land use and education, would make a fine apostle for the teachings of the new department. In October 1937, Brewster set up a new Conservation Education section within the Department, headed by Jim Bailey and funded by thirteen thousand dollars from the budgets of the various TDOC divisions. Bailey had two staffers: photographer Paul Moore and assistant John Caldwell, late of the Tennessee Wildlife Federation.

The education section was an instant and overwhelming success. Bailey and Caldwell were swamped with requests to speak before school groups, garden clubs, rotary clubs. Sometimes they scheduled six engagements in a single day, but even so, they had to turn down hundreds of requests every year. In the spring of 1938 they began hitting the road towing a nineteen-foot "conservation trailer," a traveling exhibit complete with public address system, portable generator and 16mm movie projector. (The education section was already doing a brisk business loaning conservation films, many of which were produced by Paul Moore in the department's own darkroom.) Within months the TDOC trailer had logged tens of thousands of miles traveling to schools and libraries and county fairs, where the local citizenry were happy to wander among the stuffed birds, animal skins, geological specimens and exhibits of hunting and fishing tackle.

GETTING THE TEACHERS INVOLVED

Jim Bailey figured out soon enough that if he was going to teach conservation to all the kids in the state, he had to have help. In 1938 he began signing up the first of three hundred public schools to take part in "conservation teaching units." Teachers in these units agreed to integrate conservation training in their regular coursework for at least a year. The Department of Conservation would supply materials, and staff would stop by for periodic visits. The point, however, was always to use local resources and apply them to actual issues. One of the most famous of these demonstration schools (also called community schools or conservation schools) was the Campaign School in Warren County, whose barren school yard had been gouged and gullied by decades of unchecked erosion. Using check dams, ground cover, state-supplied seedlings and Jim Bailey's teachings, the school grounds by the mid-'40s were lush, level and productive. No less productive, however, were the relationships these conservation teaching units fostered between Bailey and his minions. Teachers, school kids and parents alike adored this short, sweet-tempered fellow who never talked down to them and who took such a passionate interest in their efforts.

At the same time he was developing demonstration schools, Bailey and his assistant John Caldwell began working with the students at George Peabody College for Teachers in Nashville to develop new conservation materials (they called them "bulletins") for distribution to classrooms in Tennessee. Since 1921 Tennessee law had mandated a certain amount of conservation instruction in the public schools, though by the 1930s, the requirement applied only to fifth graders. (In 1963 the mandate was abolished altogether.) Eventually Bailey and Caldwell would write numerous teaching guides themselves, including the popular textbook, *Our Land and Our Living*, but this book didn't come out until 1940 or so. In the meantime, Bailey tried to get all the teachers' colleges in the state to offer conservation courses as part of their regular program, or at least as special summer workshops.

East Tennessee Teachers College in Johnson City offered its first summer program in 1938: ninety-six teachers signed up. The college president said he had never seen so much interest in conservation. Apparently it was true everywhere. The University of Tennessee, Tusculum College, Austin Peay Normal, Bethel College, Murfreesboro—all the teachers' colleges were designing conservation courses not only for their own students but for nonstudents as well. Summer workshops were enormously popular with both groups, as they were reasonably priced and conveniently short: usually three to seven days, though in 1939 the Department of Conservation hosted a six-week course at Norris.) Intended mainly for teachers and school principals, summer workshops also evolved for garden clubbers and housewives, Scout troops and 4-H'ers, even for hunters and fishermen. The annual Forestry Training Camp for Future Farmers of America began in 1950; by 1974 it was still going strong, only by then

The Department of Conservation began sponsoring the annual Forestry Training Camps for Future Farmers of America in 1950. Courtesy of The Tennessee Conservationist / Tennessee Department of Environment and Conservation.

it was called the Environmental Study Camp and it had enrolled the first girl in its history.

That only one girl should sign up for the Forestry Camp in twenty-four years was a bit ironic, considering that women were the heart of the state's conservation education program. Literally thousands of women took the workshops, requested the booklets, rented the movies. In 1941, the Education Service sponsored its first annual Women's Conservation Conference. But the demand seemed only to grow. Jim Bailey's annual Fall Creek Falls workshops with the Tennessee Federation of Garden Clubs, for instance, went on undiminished until he retired in 1976. (The job then fell to his heir apparent, Mack Prichard, who had joined the Department of Conservation in 1954 as a park naturalist. Prichard soon developed as ardent and diverse a following as Bailey himself.)

As late as the 1950s, teaching conservation was acknowledged to be a vital part of Tennessee's "total education program." Although conservation training was never required for formal teacher certification, as long as the state continued to encourage it, the conservation workshops continued to thrive.

For some reason, though, the workshops at East Tennessee Teachers College thrived more than most. Perhaps it was because there were so many of them, sometimes three or four different seminars in a year. Perhaps it was the setting: most of them were held not on campus but at Buffalo Mountain Methodist Camp, five miles outside Johnson City. Or perhaps it was the faculty. East Tennessee workshops drew some of the biggest names in conservation teaching nationally. And there were at least one or two outstanding professors right there on campus—such as John Bailey.

TCL JUMPS ON THE CONSERVATION EDUCATION BANDWAGON

In 1952 John H. Bailey (no relation to Jim, though they were both short and stocky) was a biology professor and chairman of the science and conservation education department at East Tennessee Teachers College in Johnson City (soon to be known as East Tennessee State College). That was the year the League jumped on the workshop bandwagon, hosting the first Buffalo Mountain Science and Conservation Workshop Camp for Teachers, in October. It's not clear whether the League knew John Bailey before the Buffalo Mountain Camp—Bailey was never really much of a sportsman—but they certainly knew him afterwards. The following year, John Bailey was not only in charge of the League's conservation camp from start to finish. He also became the League's new secretary, a job he held, with only a short hiatus while he went to graduate school, for almost twenty years.

The League's Science and Conservation Camps were really a joint venture with the Department of Conservation and, to a lesser extent, the Game and Fish Commission. Teachers especially liked them because their travel and meals were paid through grants: the League got three hundred dollars from the Game and Fish Commission and nine hundred dollars from the National Wildlife Federation. (The NWF gave the 1952 Buffalo Mountain camp second place in its annual conservation-education contest.) Each camp lasted three days, with sessions covering the usual array of topics: water, forests, wildlife and so on. They were taught by the two Baileys, Jim and John, and a mixture of East Tennessee faculty, Game and Fish personnel, staff from assorted federal agencies and the various divisions of the Department of Conservation.

Although the League's role in hosting them appears to have petered out by the end of the decade, the Buffalo Mountain Teacher Camps continued well into the 1960s. And when John Bailey retired from East Tennessee State in 1973, he was still involved in conservation programs at Buffalo Mountain—only now they were conservation camps for kids.

The League was lucky to have someone like Bailey in charge of so prominent and well-received an educational program. Bailey honestly *enjoyed* teaching; he did it for a living. His fellow League members were happy to give him their encouragement; they were happy to give him a budget; in 1954 they even gave him their highest honor, the Z. Cartter Patten Award, despite the fact that Bailey had been with the League for barely a year. Though the award certainly showed how much the men in the League valued conservation education, it probably also showed how grateful they were that somebody was actually *doing* it. Frankly, for many members of the League, conservation education was more attractive in principle than in the execution. Judging by actual League activity (as opposed to mission statements and formal professions of interest), most members would rather serve on the small game committee or the fishing committee or the policy committee. By the mid-1960s, there doesn't appear to have been any formal education program at all, other than the League's ongoing sponsorship of National Wildlife Week, chaired by John Bailey and Game and Fish Director Fred Stanberry.

Nonetheless, the League sincerely believed in what it preached, and always encouraged education programs hosted by local affiliates: fishing rodeos, skeet shoots, nature hikes and the like. Besides, there were always a handful of members who, like John Bailey, liked to work with kids. Education committee member John Jared, for instance, helped organize youth clubs, taught at a conservation camp on Signal Mountain, displayed mounted birds and animals in classrooms and led dozens of kids in taking the "Conservation Pledge": "I give my pledge as an American to save and faithfully to defend from waste the natural resources of my country—its soil and mineral, its forests, waters and wildlife."

A DECADE OF PROGRESS

In retrospect, those first few years of the 1950s were a sort of milestone for the League, with 1953 in particular opening onto a long, smooth straightaway of relative stability and progress. Not only were the conservation camps off and running. The model law had emerged almost intact from the legislative attacks of 1953; the game and fish code was reforming not only the violators but the judges who prosecuted them. Sewage plants were going up, forest fires were going down and Keep Tennessee Green was going strong. (By the mid-1960s, KTG had its own magazine and a full-time executive director, long before the League.)

So it was icing on the cake, really, when the National Wildlife Federation named the League its "Most Outstanding Affiliate" for 1953. Mayland Muse and John Bailey accepted the honor from Federation President Claude Kelley at the Federation's eighteenth annual meeting in Chicago in March 1954. The citation noted the League's "broad and balanced program" as well as its ability to involve "the cooperation of people of all ages and all interests." Considering that there were forty-eight state affiliates in the Federation—with forty-six of them on hand in Chicago—the League regarded its award as a once-in-a-lifetime honor. But it wasn't a onetime thing. TCL won the same award the very next year.

They had accomplished a great deal since 1946, the League knew. But the bottom line was—had fishing and hunting improved? The answer was an unequivocal "yes." In 1951, the state held its first managed turkey hunt ever, in the Ocoee and Shelby Wildlife Management Areas. By the 1959 season, hunters had killed fifty-seven turkeys statewide: "not many," the agency conceded, but "a start." In 1954, the total deer herd was estimated at fifteen to twenty thousand, and hunters bagged a total of 1,737 animals, a threefold increase in just two years and the best season in the agency's history. "Even some biologists were surprised," said Lou Clapper, the popular Game and Fish staffer who would later become the head lobbyist at the National Wildlife Federation. "Many people expressed wonder at even the existence of that many deer in the State." By 1959, all or parts of forty-one counties had been stocked, and the yearly kill exceeded two thousand.

These increases were directly tied to increases in the numbers of hunting and fishing areas open to the public. In 1949 there had been just two state-owned wildlife management areas open to hunting, yielding "a grand total of 136 animals." By 1959, there were twenty-one WMAs, and hunters carried home 42,764 carcasses. "This was not slaughter," the agency hastened to add, "only removal of the normal annual harvest." Cooperative arrangements with farmers and other private landowners yielded two million quail in 1959, two million squirrels and one-and-a-half million rabbits.

Three new state lakes opened during the decade, and a new fish hatchery. The fish management budget had doubled, allowing the section to add four new fisheries biologists. Woods Reservoir at the Arnold Engineering Development Center opened to fishing on Memorial Day weekend, 1953. The agreement creating the AEDC Wildlife Management Area was formalized a year later.

Tennessee's share of federal funds had also grown throughout the period, because the sale of hunting and fishing licenses had grown. In 1958-59, agents sold 416,000 combined hunting and fishing licenses, roughly double the number sold in 1946, and a 30-percent increase since the beginning of the decade. These increases confirmed the findings of a 1955 survey, the first of the well-known Crossley, S–D surveys of fishing and hunting in America. According to the report, 40.9 percent of Tennessee households had at least one angler or hunter, a total of 561,000 fishermen and 356,000 hunters, licensed or otherwise. The dollar value to the state's economy was more than sixty million dollars. And in 1957, Tennessee's two-dollar license finally became history, when the General Assembly voted to increase the fee to three dollars.

In fact, only one misfortune arrived to throw a brief cloud over this period of relative sunniness. On November 17, 1959, Karl Edison Steinmetz died in his Knoxville home at the age of seventy-three. The man who had been responsible for so many of the League's achievements was now leaving them for others to enjoy.

CHAPTER 5

1960-1971
"THESE ARE RAPIDLY CHANGING AND CRITICAL TIMES"

*Many citizens, for the first time in their lives,
have come to realize that conservation of the state's
natural resources might well be a matter of survival.*

—Lou Doney, John Dyche and Lou Williams,
notes for the special evaluation, fall 1970

THE DECEPTIVE QUIET OF THE EARLY '60S

The death of Karl Steinmetz had been a shock. But the Conservation League was full of aging men, and they took the loss of their colleague in stride, and with their usual gestures of thoughtfulness. They collected money for a memorial, and on March 18, 1961, after the annual convention in Cleveland, they all drove out to Tellico Plains. Here, in a moving ceremony beside the North River, they dedicated a large bronze plaque to Steinmetz—"lawyer, naturalist and top-flight trout fisherman."

On the whole, however, nothing especially new or exciting happened to the League in the early 1960s. Affiliate membership remained constant—hovering between 100 and 110 clubs. Though at least one document claimed 146 clubs in 1964 and an aggregate enrollment of twenty thousand, this was at least partly an exaggeration. Only a hundred clubs were listed on the 1964 annual meeting program. The estimate of twenty thousand members, on the other hand, may have been closer to the truth. Though the typical club membership appears to have been fifty to seventy-five members (judging from annual dues assessments), some clubs had many more. Lucius Burch's West Tennessee Sportsmen's Association, for instance, though shrunk considerably from the five thousand members it claimed in the 1940s, was still the largest sportsman's group in the state, with as many as two thousand members in the '60s. Nat Winston's Unaka Rod and Gun Club had dwindled also, but at five hundred to a thousand members, it was still one of the largest in the League.

Fuzzy as its numbers may have been, one thing was clear about the League's membership, and that is that it was nearly as homogeneous as ever: sportsmen and sportsmen's clubs, give or take a few women and the occasional (and always short-lived) garden club. The concerns of the League remained pretty constant also. Apart from one or two new issues such as pesticides and abandoned strip mines, and the old worries about water pollution and forest fires, the items on the League's agenda turned on pretty much the same hunting and fishing issues that it had always cared most about, only now there were committees for just about every subgenre of outdoor sport: a coon committee, a bowhunting committee, a foxhunting committee, a waterfowl committee.

Nor had the institutional scope of the League changed much. The board was enormous—more than sixty members now, including the executive committee—but the League's budget remained stalled somewhere between four and five thousand dollars. Individual dues had finally been raised—the basic membership was now three dollars—but affiliate dues were still a mere twenty-five cents a member. The League's main office was still in "The Baileywick"—the basement of John Bailey's home in Johnson City. Its official publication was still a sheet or two of plain white paper, densely typed on both sides, folded, stapled and mailed to club officers and leaders on a more or less monthly basis.

THE CENTRAL ROLE OF AFFILIATES

However, while the turn of the decade may not have been a particularly dynamic time for the League in general, for many of its affiliates it was a time of growth. In 1961, affiliates

Knoxville-based Tennessee Valley Sportsmen's Club heads out for a work day on Douglas Reservoir, clearing brush for fish habitat in Rankin Bottoms. That's Bob Burns, standing cener, with the chain saw. Courtesy of the Tennessee Valley Sportsmen's Club.

hosted the League's first regional meetings, a good idea that would be revived from time to time. Local clubs were also getting increasingly involved in regional issues. The Wolf River Sportsman Association, for instance, started its own snagging operations in the Wolf River in an effort to avoid channelizing; the West Tennessee Sportsman's Association initiated a hunter ethics program that, among other things, reimbursed farmers up to a hundred dollars for any damage done by its members. (The "I Ask to Hunt" idea was later adopted by the League for all its members.) In East Tennessee, the thousand-member Unaka Rod and Gun Club sponsored a sizable junior chapter as well as one of the state's few women's rifle teams.

Suddenly there was real competition for the annual Britton Club Award. In 1961, the Unaka club finally broke the virtual monopoly on the award held for so long by the West Tennessee Sportsmen's Association and the Greene County Hunting and Fishing Club. From that point until the award was discontinued in 1971, no affiliate won the Britton Award twice, and neither West Tennessee nor Greene County won it at all.

The first two years of the '60s were also notable for bringing to the League two of its most valuable affiliates and some of its most loyal members. The Knoxville-based Tennessee Valley Sportsmen's Club joined the League the same year it was chartered, 1961. The TVSC got quickly and deeply involved in League affairs, and several of its leaders, such as Bob Burns and Jim Wilbanks, soon became leaders in the larger organization. In fact, by the end of the

The 1960 Tellico bear and boar party hunt yields some of each for members of the Highland Sportsman Club: Herschel Green, Nick Demos, Jake Hinds, Bill Hicks, A. J. Smith and Don Smith. Courtesy of the Highland Sportsman Club.

decade they would help save its life. For that favor, the League gave the Tennessee Valley Sportsmen its 1970 (and final) Britton Club Award.

The Highland Sportsman Club of Chattanooga also joined the League as soon as it incorporated in 1960, according to founding member Loyd Ezell. Highland was at once typical and atypical of the League's member clubs. Few if any clubs required new members to buy a stock debenture in order to join, but Highland did. Highland also had a maximum number of memberships (100 then, 150 now), with a permanent waiting list and a policy, understood if unwritten, that women were not allowed. (Like most clubs, HSC offered a "Ladies Auxiliary.")

A handful of League affiliates have always owned their own clubhouses and sporting grounds, and Highland was one of the lucky ones, buying the old Boy Scout camp on North Chickamauga Creek in 1968. The massive stone fireplace in the great hall bears the construction date—1925—as well as the well-known name of the original benefactor: John A. Patten, kin to Z. Cartter Patten. Today the rustic hall looks like something out of a medieval romance, its wood-panelled walls hung with the heraldry of animal skins and mounted heads, forty-three trophies in all.

The Highland Sportsman Club started out, as so many clubs did, with a bunch of fellows who liked to hunt and fish together: Gurney Owens, Larry Lowe, Bob McConnell, A. J. Smith, the Ezell brothers (Loyd, Leonard and Joe), the father-son team of Bob and Richard Simms and numerous others. Most of them worked for DuPont, and when Tellico began sponsoring its annual bear and boar party dog hunts in the early 1950s, they would sign up as a group. There were six hunts available, two days each, with a minimum per party of sixty and a maximum of one hundred. Every year they'd submit a list of sixty names to the Game and Fish Commission, then they'd gather in the public square in Tellico Plains for the late-summer drawing that determined which parties would hunt, and where, and when. For the first few years the group from DuPont hired a local outfitter, but around 1959 they decided to haul their gear themselves, and that's when the Highland Sportsman Club was born.

According to Loyd Ezell, the question in those days was not whether the Highland team would hunt, but which area it would be hunting in, and on which days. Now, he said, the competition is so keen that no one is guaranteed a slot at all. Of course, Tellico in the 1950s didn't have nearly as much big game as it does now, and a lot of fellows lost their shirt tails (the penalty for missing a shot). Still, said Ezell, most times they managed to come home with at least one bear, and sometimes as many as eight or nine wild hogs.

THE STRANGE CASE OF CLUDIE FARLEY

Big game continued to be the leading success story at Game and Fish. All big-game species—bear, hogs, wild turkey, white-tailed deer—were showing steady if not explosive improvement. By 1964 the total deer kill was approaching five thousand, more than double what it had been four years earlier, and the Game and Fish Commission opened the first two-deer season in its history. Meanwhile, the state in 1963 held the first year-round trout fishing season ever. The commission was also putting more and better conservation officers in the field. After 1960, all game and fish wardens were required to have graduated from an

Wildlife officers such as Tellico's Jack Rodgers (shown here in the early 1960s with Charles Darling, left, and a 164-pound buck) were expected to be a mixture of policeman, game manager and public relations expert. Courtesy of the Highland Sportsman Club.

accredited four-year college or university (though they could substitute "experience in certain allied work" for up to two years of college). In many respects, Tennessee's sportsmen had never had it so good.

Still, there were grumblings. By 1960, the state was selling roughly 420,000 combination hunting and fishing licenses, an increase of more than 30 percent since 1950. Since the number of animals available for killing could barely keep up with the number of hunters applying for licenses, some sportsmen continued to complain that game was "disappearing" in Tennessee. Given the steady climb in almost all species, there was obviously no truth to their complaints. On the other hand, something was disappearing at Game and Fish: money. The reserves in the Game and Fish Fund were being depleted faster than they could be replenished. By 1963 the commissioners were again hinting for another increase in the combined license, this time to five dollars.

They did so gingerly, however. Every time the commission asked for a fee increase, it seemed the Legislature used the request as an excuse to nitpick the agency's operations. And there had been some fairly recent controversies. In particular, there had been several rather nasty disputes over the Big Game Act, that section of the game and fish code that allowed for the confiscation of hunting gear in big game cases. So far, the Big Game Act had always been upheld in the courts. But then there was the strange case of Cludie Farley.

Farley, "one of [Cookeville's] very finest citizens," in the words of his state senator, had been charged in 1961 with illegally taking a ten-point buck at Catoosa. As the law provided, both his gun and the animal had been confiscated, and Farley was taken before the General Sessions Court judge in Crossville. After a "hotly contested trial," the judge dismissed the case. Farley, of course, wanted his property back, but according to the law written by Karl Steinmetz back in 1951, his only recourse was to request a hearing with the Game and Fish director in Nashville. If that didn't work, he could appeal in the Davidson County Circuit Court. Apparently Farley decided a $150 gun wasn't worth the lawyers' fees, the travel and the witnesses' expenses. So he did not appeal. He did, however, ask for the return of his trophy deer.

According to Farley's senator, Cookeville lawyer Jared Maddux, Farley got his deer back—but only after it was no good to anyone. The carcass had "putrefied," said Maddux, and "all of [its] hair [had fallen] off." Whatever there may have been of usable meat had been removed. Someone had even cut off the trophy rack, then, "apparently due to remorse of conscience," tried to glue the antlers back on the head.

The case created such a major "hue and cry" in the local press, said Maddux, that at the request of "hundreds of citizens" he introduced a bill in 1963 to amend the Big Game Act. Under this amendment, a defendant found not guilty of a big game violation would get his confiscated property back as soon as he left the court.

The League protested. As Herman Baggenstoss pointed out in a letter to Maddux, the Big Game Act was the most effective weapon the state had against poaching, and it was not used lightly. Game and Fish officers had a conviction rate of 90 percent, and as far as Baggenstoss was concerned, that ten percent was probably just lucky. "I see scores of violations in every deer hunt that cannot be pinned down," he told Maddux, "and the culprits are not brought to justice." If it were not for the threat of confiscation, he said, there would be many more. "Remove this power and you will find pot shooting, shooting out of season, doe killing and buckshotting on an ever-increasing scale."

Maddux appeared to sympathize, promising Baggenstoss he would tone down his bill. Under the proposed amendment, he said, the acquitted defendant would still lose his property, would still have to go before Game and Fish to get it back and would still have the right to an appeal. The only difference, said Maddux, was that he could file the appeal in the court nearest his home, rather than in Davidson County.

However, the amendment passed by the 1963 Legislature did no such thing. In fact, it seemed to thumb its nose at the commission. According to the new law, the defendant *would* get his things back as soon as he was acquitted. And if the director of Game and Fish didn't like, he could appeal the ruling—in the circuit court where the alleged violation took place.

The publicity surrounding the Cludie Farley case left the commission with a seriously blackened eye. For some sportsmen, it added fuel to their growing contention that the commission wasn't doing its job.

COMPETING FOR HABITAT

Part of the problem was that there really was a shortage of certain species. Though it wasn't strictly the commission's fault, small game, upland game birds, waterfowl and even some fish were all under pressure in the early '60s. The chief culprit in virtually every case was lost or degraded habitat. There had been a persistent and troubling rise in the number of reported fish kills: twenty-three in 1959-60, twenty-four the following year, twenty-seven the year after that, thirty-two the year after that. In 1964-65 alone, an estimated 2.2 million fish died in contaminated streams across the state. Sometimes the source could be traced to a factory or municipal sewage plant, but sometimes the reason for the kill remained a mystery. In 1962, the U.S. Department of Health, Education and Welfare gave the Tennessee Game and Fish Commission a three-year, $150,000 grant to train conservation officers to recognize, sample and respond to polluted waters.

At the same time, another water crisis had been brewing ... in Canada. Waterfowl nesting grounds in the provinces were in "critical condition," according to the Game and Fish Commission's 1961-62 annual report, and the effects were being felt throughout West Tennessee. Duck populations took a dive, and in the fall of 1961 the commission reduced shooting hours until populations revived. While part of the loss could be blamed on a recent drought, waterfowl biologists like Tennessee's Calvin Barstow blamed much of the decline on drainage and filling projects all along the birds' migration route. As a member of the Mississippi Flyway Council, Tennessee was doing what it could by restricting seasons, planting waterfowl feeding areas and buying new wetlands. Tigrett, Cheatham and Moss Island, for example, were all acquired around 1959-60. The commission was also trying to persuade private and public landowners—including the U.S. Army Corps of Engineers—to design their drainage and flood-control projects so as not to damage waterfowl feeding grounds. But it had no jurisdiction in most cases, and in 1961, it could only watch nervously, and hope for the best, as the Corps began channelizing the Obion and Forked Deer River basin—a project that would have disastrous results by the end of the decade.

As for small game and farmland game—the rabbits, the squirrels, the grouse, the quail—these were merely the humblest victims of an unprecedented rush to clear, pave, plant, drain, dam and otherwise develop the state of Tennessee. Had it not been for the sportsmen, very few people, it seems, would have noticed their disappearance at all.

"Industry! Industry! Industry!"

Tennessee, in fact, seemed to have gone a little development-crazy in the 1960s. Even the Department of Conservation had been briefly renamed, during Governor Buford Ellington's first term, the Department of Conservation and Commerce. Suddenly the industrialist was regarded as the highest form of patriot. A July 1961 article in *The Tennessee Conservationist* called on every right-minded citizen to "take responsibility" for attracting new jobs, new factories, new investors. "Industry! Industry! Industry!" had become the "great cry" of every Tennessean.

For the League, many of whose members were industrialists themselves, there was nothing inherently wrong with this trend. The unfortunate by-products of development—the pollution, the pesticides, the clear-cuts, the erosion, even the occasional loss of wildlife—were probably as necessary in their way as the *products* of development—the goods, the roads, the electricity, the food, the convenience, the jobs. Everybody benefitted, they said, so everybody should be willing to pay a reasonable share of the costs—even costs to the environment.

What the League objected to, as Lou Williams said at the 1966 annual meeting, was when one interest ruined it for all the others. Take, for example, the indiscriminate use of pesticides. "[W]e would not want to oppose all use of such chemicals," said Williams. "But we should insist that those who use the chemicals know more about them and what their use will do to other land and water values. To use insecticides to accomplish one objective and in the process destroy other values is, to put it mildly, a thoughtless act."

Chemical pesticides were one of the new generation of menaces drawing increasing attention in the 1960s. In 1963, the theme of National Wildlife Week was "Handle With Care: Chemical Pesticides Are Poison." But the Conservation League had been concerned about the environmental effects of pesticides even earlier than 1963—even before biologist Rachel Carson published *Silent Spring* , the 1962 cautionary for which she was named NWF's Conservationist of the Year. In 1961, the League's small game committee had filed a complaint with the Game and Fish Commission that herbicide spraying along utility lines was killing the small game that congregated in the clearings. The commission said it could not prohibit utility-line spraying. But it agreed to monitor it more closely and evaluate any biological damages.

It seemed like a reasonable trade-off, and the League was always willing to accept a reasonable compromise. The trouble was, sometimes the compromises were not so reasonable. Sometimes there seemed to be no compromising at all.

TWO FIGHTS IN THE TELLICO

Two prominent cases involved the Tellico—a dam and a road. The dam was TVA's proposed hydroelectric project on the Little Tennessee River near Lenoir City. The road was a proposed fifty-mile scenic route from Tellico Plains to Robbinsville, North Carolina, through the heart of the Tellico Wildlife Management Area. Both projects were hotly contested by sportsmen, environmentalists and some local citizens. Both were started in spite of the protests. Both were stymied midway through construction. And both were eventually completed, tens of millions of dollars over original budget projections.

TVA had first proposed the Tellico Dam at the mouth of the Little T in 1942. But it wasn't until 1962 that Congress finally gave the go-ahead, and five years more before construction actually began. TVA's position was that the region needed the industry, urbanization and jobs that dams were supposed to attract. The position of the sportsmen, the environmentalists, the Game and Fish Commission, the Department of Conservation, the local farmers and even some businesses was that the Little T was worth more to the region in its free-flowing state.

Few issues provoked the outdoor writers to such heights of rhetorical fury as the prospect of losing the Little T, one of the state's best-loved trout streams. In a series of articles in *Tennessee Out-Of-Doors*, Carl Bolton rejected all the purported benefits, stating flatly that the dam was being built "to keep a huge government agency busy, period."

According to Joe Halburnt, then with the *Maryville Daily Times*, TVA "lied to the people" from beginning to end about the Tellico Dam. "They told 'em if they didn't want [the dam] they wouldn't build it. .... I went down there and visited every farmer on that river and didn't find but one who wanted it." Halburnt reported his findings in the *Times*, he said, and the result was that he lost his job.

Verland H. ("Doc") Jernigan agreed that the only people who wanted the dam built were the ones building it. In his September 10, 1965, column in the *Manchester Times*, Jernigan countered each of TVA's objectives for the dam, beginning with the claim that local residents wanted one. "Actually the people living in the area have fought hard to keep their farms intact and unflooded," he wrote. Neither was there a demand for new industrial sites. "[E]ven if industry wanted locations, there are many excellent sites available now." Recreation and tourism were the area's biggest businesses, he pointed out, yet the lake would flood "many historic shrines" and wipe out some excellent canoeing. But the real crux of the League's argument was that the dam would destroy "probably the best trout float-fishing stream in the entire Eastern part of the United States." The Tennessee Department of Conservation echoed the outdoor community in condemning the proposal.

Despite such protests, construction got underway on the dam in 1967. The new environmental protections of the 1970s managed to halt construction more than once over the next fifteen years, as the next chapter will point out. But the Tellico Dam was finally completed, and the river impounded, by 1980.

THE ROAD THROUGH THE MOUNTAINS

The Tellico-Robbinsville Road had a similar history, though it dragged on even longer.

First proposed by the Tellico Plains Kiwanis Club in 1958, the road from Tellico Plains to Robbinsville was to be a fifty-mile scenic route through the rugged mountains of the Cherokee and Nantahala National Forests, bringing tourist dollars and new business to an almost inaccessible and economically barren area—barren, that is, except for the popular hiking trails in the Joyce Kilmer Memorial Forest and the matchless hunting and trout fishing on both sides of the state line.

In September 1962, League president M. L. Brickey appointed an ad hoc committee to mount a formal protest. But it was too late. In October Congress approved a $6.6 million request for the road from the Tennessee and North Carolina delegations.

The original plan included widening the existing road that snaked along the North River, the trout stream Karl Steinmetz had favored over all others. The sportsmen howled, especially Lou Doney (who owned a cabin in the Cherokee) and Doc Jernigan. The runoff from road building would destroy the trout fishing, they said, and the traffic and tourism would destroy the hunting. After brief consideration, the Federal Highway Commission decided to offer an alternative.

The alternative plan placed the road high above the river, along the ridge that divides the North River and Citico Creek watersheds, crossing Laurel Branch, passing through a stand of virgin timber and roughly bisecting the whole wildlife management area. This route was not acceptable to the sportsmen, either, who could not understand why a road had to be built through the Tellico hunting grounds at all. Could it not skirt around the area and get to Robbinsville that way?

Apparently not. Construction began on both ends of the road in 1965. Frustrated and disgusted with what he perceived as the "apathy" of his fellow sportsmen, Doc Jernigan gave up the fight for lost. But a few years later the battle was joined by unexpected allies: the hikers and pro-wilderness groups spawned by the nascent environmental movement. They did not care much about fishing and hunting, but they did worry that the road would disrupt the virgin forests of Joyce Kilmer.

For the next fifteen years work was stopped in North Carolina while the various parties in the dispute tried to reach an agreement. The Tennessee section, however, kept inching determinedly eastward—until, that is, it was stymied by the mountains themselves. In the mid-1980s, not far from the North Carolina line, the road encountered rock formations containing anakeesta shale, a high-sulphur stone which, when mixed with rainwater, produces a runoff roughly as acidic as the drainage from a strip mine. Fish kills in nearby trout streams again brought construction to a halt, but not permanently. Road engineers figured out a way to cover the exposed rock (at a cost of four million dollars) and in 1996 the two halves of the fifty-mile roadway finally shook hands.

On October 12, 1996, just in time for the fall foliage season, the Cherohala Skyway was declared officially open. In the end, the scenic drive across the mountains cost $100 million, *fifteen* times the original estimate. But to call it a total defeat would not be quite fair. Doc Jernigan and his supporters had managed to stop the original route along the river bed, in itself an extraordinary victory. For that the League gave Jernigan its Z. Cartter Patten Award for 1968.

SHARE AND SHARE ALIKE: LAND GRABS AT AEDC

About the time the road appeared to be a lost cause, Jernigan, now president of the League, was getting drawn into another: the whittling away of wildlife habitat at the Arnold Engineering Development Center in Coffee County, near Tullahoma.

The 42,000-acre wildlife management area at AEDC was formally established in 1954 via a cooperative agreement between the U.S. Air Force and the Tennessee Game and Fish Commission. The Elk River had been impounded a year earlier to create Woods Reservoir. In 1960 AEDC received its first shipment of five dozen deer and fifteen hundred quail; the first deer hunt took place five years later. By the end of the decade AEDC's deer herd had quadrupled, and a few turkeys were being bagged, too. With the small-game plantings provided by local farmers, the excellent crappie and walleye fishing provided by the reservoir and the duck hunting provided by natural winter flooding, AEDC was considered one of the most attractive all-around sporting grounds in Middle Tennessee. In 1966 the area even won an Air Force award for its conservation program.

The trouble was, everyone wanted a piece of it. Lumber interests wanted some of its forests, and local government agencies wanted chunks of "surplus" government land for everything from high schools to industrial parks. By the early 1970s, nearly a third of the original wildlife area had been converted into buildings, parking lots and pine forests.

The men in the League still believed in share-and-share-alike. But some interests seemed determined to take more than their fair share of available public lands. It was, if not exactly a revelation, at least a disturbing development. Since the founding of the Tellico in 1936, Tennessee's sportsmen had been acquiring hunting and fishing grounds at an almost exponential rate. For decades, the most common land-use question was, how can this or that piece of land be improved for hunting and fishing? Now, the major question seemed to be, *should* this land be used for hunting and fishing? Or should it be used for something else?

Tennessee had been quietly shifting from a rural, agrarian society to an urban and industrial one for some years now. As Tommy Hines of the Game and Fish Commission noted in 1970, "It [did] not take much insight to see that land use in Tennessee ha[d] changed in the last fifteen years and [would] continue to change." Yet many sportsmen still regarded the supply of undeveloped lands as a vast if not inexhaustible resource. Clearly, that was no longer the case.

THE NATIONAL PUSH FOR RECREATION AND PUBLIC LANDS

The League's concern about land use had been growing for several years. As early as 1961, it had supported the County Conservation Board bill authorizing counties to buy and develop their own parks, county forests and nature preserves. In 1958, members had endorsed an act formally declaring all state parks as wildlife preserves, even though this meant they

Verland H. "Doc" Jernigan bags three mallards at Woods Reservoir, part of the AEDC empire he was so determined to protect. Courtesy of V. H. Jernigan.

could no longer hunt in state parks except for those administered as state forests.

The League's new urgency to protect public lands reached a peak in 1964, when it compiled a list of conservation priorities for the coming year. Of twelve items in the list, seven had to do with protecting outdoor recreation, wilderness and public lands. One item "reaffirm[ed] the conviction that significant portions of suitable Federal lands should be preserved and maintained as inviolate wilderness." Another commended TVA for its new recreation-demonstration project called "Land Between the Lakes."

The list also endorsed the principle of multiple-use management, especially when public outdoor recreation was included as one of the managed uses. It called upon private landowners to "provide public outdoor recreational facilities where suitable." It supported the Interior Department's plan to preserve selected rivers "in their natural, or wild, free-flowing conditions without impoundments or diversions." It applauded the Army Corps of Engineers' new policy of acquiring a three hundred-foot buffer zone around all of its reservoirs and making these strips of shoreline available for picnic areas and other public use. And it endorsed the creation of a federal Land and Water Conservation Fund "to finance State and Federal programs for public outdoor recreation."

The Land and Water Conservation Fund Act became law on September 3, 1964. Like nearly all of the public-lands initiatives to come out of Washington during this period, the LWCF was a result of President Dwight D. Eisenhower's Outdoor Recreation Resources Review Commission, established in 1958. Among the recommendations of this commission was a federal Bureau of Outdoor Recreation, established in the Department of Interior in 1963, followed by the Wilderness Act of 1964 creating a National Wilderness Preservation System. In 1964 also, Congress created a Public Land Law Review Commission to evaluate policies and laws affecting federal lands, and in 1965, the Federal Water Project Recreation Act required that dams, lakes and similar projects give "full consideration" to recreation and wildlife values during planning and implementation. The National Wild and Scenic Rivers Act passed in 1968, along with an act to create a system of National Scenic Trails.

These may have been federal laws, but their impact was felt instantly in Tennessee. Although just two National Scenic Trails were initially designated by the National Trails System Act, one of them, the Appalachian Trail from Maine to Georgia, ran along the easternmost edge of Tennessee, taking in its way such classic natural areas as Roan Mountain and the Smokies. The National Wild and Scenic Rivers Act listed two Tennessee streams for possible designation: the Buffalo River and the Big South Fork of the Cumberland. The Buffalo was not ultimately included, but the Big South Fork was, when Congress authorized the Big South Fork National River and Recreation Area in 1974. In 1976, after hard lobbying by the Tennessee Scenic Rivers Association, the League and others, four different streams in the Obed watershed were also designated Wild and Scenic.

Both national trails and national rivers were subsidized in part by the Land and Water Conservation Fund, a remarkably versatile piece of legislation similar in concept to the Pittman-Robertson and Dingell-Johnson acts. Tennessee's first designated state natural areas, including Savage Gulf near Tracy City, Ozone Falls in Cumberland County and Big Cypress Tree in Weakley County, were made possible in part by the fund, along with dozens of na-

"Free public access" to recreation was apparently so novel an idea that the Game and Fish Commission advertised it at a TCL convention in the mid-1960s. Photo by David Murrian. Courtesy of TWRA.

ture centers, hiking trails, greenways and playgrounds. Over the years, the LWCF has financed more than 650 projects statewide, at a cost of more than $25 million.

Money in the LWCF comes from so-called "sin taxes," proceeds from various forms of resource exploitation, mainly oil and gas drilling on the continental shelf but also the sale of surplus federal lands and taxes on motorboat fuel. However, only half of a project can be financed by federal aid. The other half must come from the recipient, whether in state or municipal bonds or private donations. When Radnor Lake became available for purchase, for example, the citizen-led Radnor Lake Preservation Association raised a half-million dollars.

The Land and Water Conservation Fund Act also required each state to prepare its own State Comprehensive Outdoor Recreation Plan, or SCORP. Tennessee's first SCORP (there have been several updates and revisions over the years) was prepared by the Department of Conservation with input from the Game and Fish Commission. Since the LWCF would pay up to half the costs of approved projects, Tennessee was happy to find fault with its own facilities. The Department of Conservation, for instance, complained in its 1965 biennial report that Tennessee had only twenty-one state parks, and they were so heavily used that they "[would] not last another twenty-five years." Trees were dying in picnic and camping areas "because too many feet [had] walked dirt off their roots and packed soil like concrete." The writer urged the state acquire thirty new parks as soon as possible, "before the prime areas

. . . are preempted for other uses." For its part, the Game and Fish Commission discovered that it needed to promote more nonconsumptive recreation, like wildlife viewing and nature study. (In 1969, the commission hired a Game and Fish Planner to oversee the wildlife phase of SCORP.) In 1965, Governor Clement supported a $5.5 million bond issue to raise the necessary matching funds, and before long, LWCF money began trickling—at times even pouring—into Tennessee.

NEW GROUPS ON THE BLOCK: TSRA

Washington's burgeoning interest in outdoor recreation was paralleled by a flood of similar activity in the states. In 1968, even before Congress passed the National Wild and Scenic Rivers Act, Tennessee passed its own scenic rivers bill, the first such statute in the country. In fact, members of the Tennessee Scenic Rivers Association had been invited to Washington to speak on behalf of the national law.

TSRA was part of a striking phenomenon that began in the mid-1960s and peaked in the early 1970s: the sudden rise of outdoor activist groups (soon to be known collectively as environmentalists, or what Stewart Udall called the "Third Wave" of conservationists). Like many of these other groups (indeed, like the sportsmen's clubs themselves), TSRA was formed in response to a perceived threat to a resource, in this case, free-flowing streams.

As founding member Bill Griswold tells it, TSRA had its beginnings during a late-summer fishing trip on the Collins River in 1966. The Collins was a pretty, pastoral stream, but like most streams, it occasionally flooded, and local farmers were demanding that it be dredged and straightened—in other words, channelized. Bob Miller, one of the men in the boat, was gloomily discussing the prospect with his companion. As a geologist for the Department of Conservation, Miller understood that channelizing was not likely to eliminate flooding in the Collins. But it was *very* likely to turn the stream into a muddy, lifeless ditch.

Back in Nashville, Miller persuaded a dozen like-minded friends to rally around the Collins. At a meeting in September, they tried to choose a name. Save the Collins? Collins River Preservation Association? Too limiting, said some. Why not something more generic? And so the Tennessee Scenic Rivers Association was born.

At first, TSRA focused strictly on legislation, and the Collins was eventually saved from the dredge. But soon its members began paddling the streams, and teaching others to paddle. They would load up whatever they had that would float, from V-bottom fishing boats to a prototype for an indestructible whitewater canoe. (The Blue Hole OCA, designed by Griswold and Bob Lantz and produced, at first, in a shop on Blue Hole Road in Nashville, was for many years the most popular canoe on Tennessee's rivers.) The paddlers started with the easy rivers—the Buffalo, the Harpeth, the Duck—then gradually progressed to faster water—the Obed, the Hiwassee, the Nolichucky. All the time, they were making note not only of the best ways to run the streams but also the quality of the water, erosion problems, unusual scenic features. Some streams, they decided, were worth special protection.

In 1968, Bob Miller and two other TSRA members, Oak Ridge National Laboratory scientists Liane and Bill Russell, successfully drafted legislation creating a State Scenic Rivers system. The Tennessee Scenic Rivers Act of 1968 designated all or parts of eight streams: the

Collins, the Hiwassee, the Harpeth, the Buffalo, the French Broad, Roaring River, Blackburn Fork and Spring Creek. (Tuckahoe Creek was added by an amendment.) Within a year or two, the trio were hard at work on a new bill. This bill, however, was designed to protect wilderness. For that effort, they turned to a second group.

MORE NEW GROUPS ON THE BLOCK: TCWP AND TTA

Lee and Bill Russell had founded Tennessee Citizens for Wilderness Planning in 1966, the same year TSRA organized. The two groups had much in common: TSRA's goal was to preserve free-flowing rivers; TCWP's stated mission was to preserve "optimum areas of wild lands and waters" from "increasing man-made infringements." However, the Russells' real passion was wilderness. They had been appalled when the 1964 federal Wilderness Act included no wilderness in Tennessee. But they and their friends were also worried about the fate of such privately-owned natural areas as Frozen Head, May Prairie and Dunbar Cave.

The legislation drafted by the Russells and Bob Miller proposed a system to classify and protect not only rugged wild lands but any natural area of outstanding scenic or scientific value, from cedar glades to waterfalls. Their first attempt to pass a natural areas bill failed (probably because it tried to combine scenic preservation with historic preservation). But the following year, thanks in large measure to the guidance of Knoxville Representative Victor Ashe, the Legislature passed the State Natural Areas Preservation Act on May 15, 1971.

As it happened, the General Assembly had only weeks earlier passed another piece of outdoor legislation, lobbied by yet another outdoor group. The Tennessee Trails System Act passed in April 1971, the culmination of three years' work by the Tennessee Trails Association. TTA had been founded in 1968 to push for a state trails system, with the Cumberland Trail its pilot project.

TTA was an unusually broad-based group. According to outdoor writer Evan Means, the idea started with Lou Doney, then president of the League, but its earliest supporters included state naturalist (and sometime archeologist) Mack Prichard; Stan Murray, chair of the Appalachian Trail Conference; Carl Leathers, a leader in the Sierra Club; and Ted Dungjen, an executive with Bowater Southern, the paper company. Bowater created the nation's first Pocket Wilderness Area in 1970 (Angel Falls); it also had developed its own trails network. (In 1971, Bowater's Laurel-Snow Trail was named one of twenty-seven National Recreation Trails when Congress expanded the National Trails System.)

Though hiking and canoeing may have been the activities that brought them together, virtually all of these new activist groups had a political agenda. And though they may have been inexperienced lobbyists at first, they at least had the advantages of new blood and idealism. Tennesseans for Wilderness Planning, for instance, was barely a year old when, in 1967, it took on one of the most intractable industries in the state: strip mining.

BETTER THAN NOTHING: TENNESSEE'S FIRST STRIP MINE BILL

Strip mining—blasting away successive layers of earth and rock to reveal the coal (or other minerals) beneath—may have been more cost-effective than pit mining, but it tended to be far more destructive to the environment. Its massive earth-moving machines uprooted forests and sheered off tons of topsoil; its man-made mountains of spoil and overburden created safety hazards; its toxic effluents of acid, metals and chemicals polluted nearby streams and ground waters. Yet by 1970, nearly forty thousand acres of lands atop the Cumberland Mountain coal belt had been affected by active or orphaned mines.

An active mine was hellish enough, a Dantesque landscape of noise, dirt and heavy machinery. But an abandoned mine was even more depressing, a desolate and deeply gullied wasteland, barren of all but the poorest vegetation, often still oozing with rust-colored runoff. Yet dozens of poor rural families lived in the shadows of these abandoned "highwalls," the vertical drops created as the mining operation sunk its mechanical teeth ever deeper into the earth.

Mining had been among the state's most important industries since early statehood. (In fact, the first natural resource manager in Tennessee was not a game manager nor even a forester, but a state geologist. Dr. Gerard Troost, professor of mineralogy, geology and chemistry at the University of Nashville, was hired in 1831 to "develop" the state's mineral resource.) Coal was first mined in the late 1800s. In those early days, virtually all coal extraction was done in underground pits and shafts. After World War I, however, strip mining began to grow increasingly popular. By 1967, fully half the coal mined in Tennessee was surface mined.

Yet the state had never yet regulated surface mines. It had tried to do so as early as 1942, but miners were a sort of outlaw culture, and most legislators considered strip mining the political equivalent of a hand grenade. The League itself had been uncommonly quiet on the matter. However, if there was one man willing to handle a live grenade, it was Herman Baggenstoss. Baggenstoss, whose home was in the middle of coal country, had been calling for surface mine regulation for years. In 1957, he wrote an editorial on the subject in his weekly newspaper, the *Grundy County Herald*. The piece was called—with Baggenstoss' usual flair for drama—"The Land Cries Out in Anguish."

> Stripping has come to the little community of Sanders Crossing. … Never again will the Village look the same … never again will the people be the same because of it. … Never again will the school children run up and down the green hill behind the school, for that tree-covered hill is no more.
>
> The strip mining has passed by, with day and night chugging of its giant "Page," the roar of its "Euclid" and the blastings that shook the foundation of Sanders Crossing School and sent the school children and teachers scurrying home. …
>
> The stripping has moved across the highway, railroad tracks and the old Altamont Road, shoving everything out of its path to take a swipe at Blue Ribbon Hill,… Hobbs Hill and on until a big ditch will encircle most of the town of Tracy City, creating a land condition that not a single student of the Sanders Crossing School will see corrected … bleak, bare hills towering high above the Oaks … a man-made curse to mankind.

In 1959, Baggenstoss undertook to write his own strip mine legislation. The powerful mining lobby defeated that bill, however, and several subsequent attempts. But that was about to change.

Early in the 1967 session, Oak Ridge-area legislators introduced two new reclamation bills, one in each house. The reception to the bills was predictably cool, and one newspaper predicted "rough sledding." Yet the winds of environmental awareness were already shifting. On February 9, 1967, TCWP hosted a public forum on the issue at an Oak Ridge church. More than two hundred people showed up. Lee Russell had invited Herman Baggenstoss to speak; Evan Means, outdoor columnist for *The Oak Ridger*, showed slides. When it was over, the crowd formed a committee to push the bills through the Legislature. On April 4, 1967, Tennessee finally got its first strip mine law, and the Department of Conservation got a new division: Strip Mining and Land Reclamation.

It was not a strong law, nor was it a strong division, and there would be numerous attempts to toughen both. (In 1985, the federal Office of Surface Mining got tired of waiting, and took the program away from Tennessee.) But change comes slowly in the hollers, and some folks thought this change would never come at all.

The Green Soldiers

It soon became clear that TCWP's ability to mobilize the troops was part of a trend. Similar citizen-led efforts were happening all over the country. Almost overnight, it seemed, environmental lobbying had became an established branch of legal, political and public discourse. The Environmental Defense Fund was founded in 1967, the Environmental Law Institute in 1969, the Natural Resources Defense Council in 1970, the League of Conservation Voters the same year. Meanwhile, a veritable army of citizen soldiers was coming forward to enlist. By the mid-1970s, there was a Sierra Club, a Wilderness Society or an Audubon Society—and sometimes all three—in the major population centers in Tennessee. Student groups formed on college campuses; mothers organized to protest nuclear power.

While some of these new organizations were actively opposed to hunting, such as Greenpeace, most groups simply *didn't* hunt, and had little to do with groups that did. At any rate, none of the new environmental groups joined the Conservation League. In some ways it was an ironic segregation: the League had supported, even been instrumental in passing the strip mine act, the scenic rivers act and the scenic trails act. Yet apparently it was still perceived as primarily a men's hunting and fishing club.

Interestingly, many of the country's new activists did join the National Wildlife Federation, helping the League's parent group make the transition from huge sporting fraternity to the largest broad-based environmental coalition in the nation. NWF enrolled 240 new affiliates and 40,000 new individual members in 1969 alone, many of them "young people, academia, college administrators and politicians," according to NWF president Dr. Donald Zinn. Thousands of these initiates were women. (In 1970, the Federation hired a director of women's activities.) A good many of the new members were families with kids. In July 1970, the first NWF Conservation Summit in the Colorado Rockies attracted 842 families. Land Between the Lakes hosted NWF's first "Camp Energy" for kids in the same year. NWF was also becoming multiethnic and multinational: in 1972, NWF officials attended the first United Nations Conference on the Human Environment in Stockholm, where it distributed its first World Environmental Quality Index. (NWF began issuing a national EQ Index in 1969.)

Yet NWF didn't have to work very hard to recruit these new members. Nothing galvanized the new generation of activists like the growing list of national eco-disasters: the Torrey Canyon oil spill in California in 1967, the fires on the Cuyahoga River in 1969, the toxic waste leaks at Love Canal in 1971, the mutated bodies of eaglets poisoned by DDT. Some of the datelines were Tennessee, such as Hollywood dump in Memphis, an ironic name for one of the country's worst hazardous waste sites. Then there were the fish kills, a virtual epidemic by the late 1960s. One of the worst in Tennessee happened in Boone Reservoir in May 1969, when "empty" barrels used for flotation rusted out, leaking residues of a highly toxic mercury compound and killing more than two million fish. A few months later, a similar leak in the Watauga arm of the same reservoir killed another half-million fish. By 1970 the state was posting Pickwick Lake, the Hiwassee River and the North Fork of the Holston against widespread mercury contamination.

The federal government responded to the growing crisis with the most concentrated and far-reaching surge of environmental legislation in any period before or since. Between 1965 and 1972 Congress passed more than a dozen ground-breaking environmental laws, including three progressively stronger water quality acts: the Water Quality Control Act of 1965, the Clean Water Restoration Act of 1966 and the Clean Water Act of 1972, whose historic amendments included Section 404, the first real wetlands protection law in the nation. Congress passed the Solid Waste Disposal Act in 1965 and an endangered species act in 1966, followed by two much stronger versions in 1969 and 1973. The second Clean Air Act passed in 1970 (the first was in 1963), along with the nation's first law (the Resource Conservation and Recovery Act) for managing hazardous and solid waste. 1972 alone saw the Environmental Pesticide Control Act, the Coastal Zone Management Act, the Marine Protection, Research

Mack Prichard, state naturalist with the Department of Conservation (now TDEC) speaks to the Tennessee Valley Sportsmen's Club in 1985. Prichard probably helped establish more environmental groups than anyone in the state, from the Sierra Club to the Cumberland-Harpeth Audubon Society to Tennessee Trails. Yet he always had great respect for the sportsmen. Courtesy of the Tennessee Valley Sportsmen's Club.

and Sanctuaries Act and the Marine Mammal Protection Act.

On New Year's Day 1970, President Nixon signed into law the single most important bill of all, the National Environmental Policy Act of 1969. NEPA—the law that created an Environmental Protection Agency, established a citizen review panel and required an environmental impact statement for any federal project likely to harm the environment—was arguably the most significant environmental protection statute of the entire century.

Tennessee meanwhile was responding with its own laws. Its first air quality law was passed in 1967, its first solid waste disposal act in 1969, a stronger water quality act in 1971 and a more effective strip mining bill in 1972. And in 1970, a mild-mannered dentist from West Tennessee made history by campaigning for governor on a strong environmental platform—and winning, the first Republican in that office since Alfred Taylor in 1921.

Before 1970, Winfield Dunn had never held elected office. In fact, he had never really even paid that much attention to the environment. But that didn't stop Edward Thackston from giving him a call. Ed Thackston was a young professor in what was then known as the department of environmental and water resources engineering at Vanderbilt. He was keenly interested in everything from water quality to air pollution to strip mining. In fact, he was one of the main organizers of Earth Day on the Vanderbilt campus.

"I offered to write him a position on every issue," Thackston said, if Dunn would agree to support the platform from the governor's office. Dunn was elected, of course, and promptly hired Thackston to be his environmental policy assistant. He also made good on his promise. Over the next four years, Dunn's administration would pass a new Water Quality Control Act, the Scenic Trails Act, the Natural Areas Act, a stronger Surface Mining Act and the state's first Nongame and Endangered Species Act. He also, not incidentally, threw the power of his office behind the struggling Game and Fish Commission.

ANOTHER BIRTHING: THE TENNESSEE ENVIRONMENTAL COUNCIL

Exciting as some of these changes were, the Tennessee Conservation League had not exactly been seized with revolutionary zeal. On the contrary, as millions of Americans rushed toward the first Earth Day celebrations in April 1970, the League, just coming out of its 1970 annual meeting, had all it could do not to get trampled.

The fact was, the League was not quite sure where it was going. Things had been changing at almost lightning speed, and the League had neither the resources, nor the expertise, nor for that matter the energy or the will to keep up. The environmental issues of the '70s were simply too numerous and too complex for a group of novices to handle by themselves—even if they had wanted to.

That was why, shortly before Christmas 1969, a small group of board members, including Lucius Burch, Jr., Lester Dudney and Nashville attorney Cecil Branstetter, proposed that the League form a new umbrella organization to take some of the pressure off the League. They envisioned a sort of environmental think tank and information clearing house for emerging issues, from pesticides to air pollution to solid waste to solar energy. Like the League, it would be a membership organization, but unlike the League, it would have a full-time office, and it would be as broad-based as possible. Among its earliest affiliates were the League of Women Voters, the Tennessee chapter of the American Lung Association, the Tennessee Federation of Garden Clubs and even the Nashville Junior League. (At its height the coalition would list more than seventy member groups.)

The Tennessee Environmental Council (TEC) was chartered in December 1970. Dr. Ruth Neff, a research biologist at Vanderbilt University, was hired as its executive director the following year. In the meantime, Cecil Branstetter, the Council's first president, had agreed to let the fledgling organization work out of his Third Avenue law office until it could afford space of its own. Getting TEC started proved to be no easy task. In fact, Branstetter later described it as "one of the most frustrating" experiences of his life. But slowly the coalition came together. The founders hosted panel discussions around the state, signing up more affiliates and a growing number of individuals. In 1971, TEC got its first government grant, a five thousand-dollar contract to revise the strip mine laws. By the end of the decade, the Tennessee Environmental Council was as solidly established, and as highly respected, as the League itself.

Giving birth to the Council was one of the smartest things the League had ever done, and one of the best things to befall the environmental movement in Tennessee. But now there was another birthday pending, and everyone hoped it would be as happy.

PLANNING FOR A BIRTHDAY—OR A FUNERAL

In 1971 the Tennessee Conservation League would turn twenty-five years old. The silver anniversary would be celebrated at the annual convention in Jackson in March, and hundreds of members would be there, including many who had been on hand for the inaugural meeting in 1946.

Lou Williams, of course, would be a centerpiece. Williams, now retired from his second career as a banker, had been spending the last three or four years "reading through a mass of pages of yellowed musty papers [and] ancient law books" while researching a book-length history of the League and Tennessee's conservation movement. He hoped to have copies ready in time for the annual meeting. (Unfortunately, publication came two months late.)

Meanwhile, *The Tennessee Conservationist* devoted its entire March 1971 issue to the League and its achievements. Evan Means, Dr. Dudney and Anson Galyon of the Game and

Bob Simms' familiar deer-in-the-hand logo was designed for the League's 1960 annual meeting in Chattanooga, but members liked it so well they adopted it as the official TCL seal.

Leaders in a time of transition: these men were TCL's officers for 1971-1972, the period of reorganization: president Charlie Rhea, vice presidents Bob Burns, Greer Ricketson and Travis McNatt, and secretary John Bailey. Photo by Charles Jackson. Courtesy of TWRA.

Fish Commission were all contributing articles. The cover of the magazine was a watercolor adaptation of the League's new logo: an outstretched palm, holding a deer and a tree.

The Conservationist attributed this interesting piece of artwork to staff artist Evelyn Underwood (who in 1974 would soon design the logo for the new Tennessee Wildlife Resources Agency). However, the design was actually the work of Robert H. Simms, a TCL member and bow hunter from Chattanooga. Simms had created the deer-in-the-hand design for a billboard during the 1969 convention in Chattanooga. The original design included an outline of the state of Tennessee as backdrop. Simms' art had been an instant hit. The directors liked it so well they immediately adopted it as the new logo they had been searching for since the 1950s. Lou Williams had it embossed on the cover of his book.

The pleasure of planning a birthday party was tempered, however, by the uneasy sense that the organizers might as easily be planning a funeral. The League had been diminishing, little by little, over the past several years. Though the same hundred or so clubs were still listed on the rolls, nearly a fifth of these no longer existed, and nearly half hadn't paid their dues in more than a year. Though the League had taken in nine thousand dollars in 1969 (more than ever in its history), revenues barely covered expenses. Poor John Bailey, who "work[ed] harder for the League than he [did] earning his living," according to one colleague, had to fight the board for every typewriter and filing cabinet he could squeeze out of them.

The League finally decided to raise affiliate dues in 1970, from twenty-five cents to fifty cents per member. It had also been trying various fund-raising schemes. In 1969, for instance, it endorsed a life insurance program in return for a share of sales; this returned more than a thousand dollars. For a few years TCL even raffled off a new car at the annual convention.

In 1969 the car raffle was the most lucrative item in the budget, clearing more than three thousand dollars. The League was also earning several hundred dollars a year from its executive director endowment fund (which now stood at about twenty thousand dollars).

And in 1965, along with every other affiliate in the country, it signed onto NWF's conservation achievement awards program. For years (until 1993, in fact) the Sears, Roebuck Foundation funded the awards. Though the amount from Sears varied from year to year, the average annual donation to TCL seems to have been around fifteen hundred dollars. Some of that was used to buy the elaborate wildlife statuettes provided through the NWF: the fish for Water Conservationist of the Year, the bear for Conservation Legislator, and so one—ten in all. (TCL's top award, the bald eagle, was dubbed the Governor's Award at first, because each state affiliate had to get the endorsement of its governor before it could take part. By the mid-1970s, however, it was called simply Conservationist of the Year.)

Another chronic discontent at the League was that it still had no formal publication to call its own, other than the crude, mimeographed sheet John Bailey had been producing for almost twenty years.

Finally, there were problems at Game and Fish. Despite a fee increase to five dollars in 1965, the commission was now looking for another increase, this time to ten dollars. It didn't happen, not for many years. Instead, the Legislature began once again to abuse the commission as an incompetent dictatorship. And now the critics had a perfect lightning rod for their attacks. The agency had recently moved into new quarters on the plantation-like grounds of the Ellington Agricultural Center. The total cost—$1.3 million—had been financed, interest-free, by the state's general fund, but was being repaid with sportsmen's money at the rate of $32,800 a year for forty years. (In fact, the debt was paid off twenty-seven years early, with a lump-sum payment of nearly a million dollars in 1983.) But to determined skeptics, that was a minor detail. To them, the new building was proof that an unaccountable agency was out of control.

The League itself was not entirely happy with the way things were being run at Game and Fish. Apparently some commissioners were getting a bit tyrannical. But TCL still took an almost paternal interest in the well-being of the commission, many of whose current members—Greer Ricketson, Ray Strong, Larry Lowe, Smith Howard, Jim Beasley and Bill Blackburn among them—all belonged to the League. When the commission was attacked, the League tended to take it personally.

"HOW DID THINGS GET SO BAD?"

Most members shared the uncomfortable sense that the League was in trouble, but Bob Burns and Jim Wilbanks actually did something about it. Burns was the first president of the Tennessee Valley Sportsman's Club; Wilbanks was its current president. The Knoxville-based TVSC had been a member of the League since 1961, and few clubs took so earnest an interest in its affairs. In the summer of 1970, Wilbanks and Burns had a long talk with League president Penn Foreman (later the assistant commissioner of Conservation under Buck Allison). They agreed that something had to be done.

On August 19, 1970, they called a special eastern regional meeting of the League at

Norris Dam State Park. The purpose was to discuss the League's future—if, indeed, it had one. According to Bob Burns, 125 people showed up for this meeting, including most of the League's officers, dozens of members from East Tennessee, representatives of the outdoor press and several commissioners and other top brass from the Game and Fish Commission.

"These are rapidly changing and critical times in the field of conservation, the environment, and wildlife restoration," Wilbanks began. "Many of us have been interested in these things for many years. But now, because conditions have reached the crisis stage, so to speak, the general public, and some of the informed politicians have awakened to the problems.

"How did things get so bad? Was it that we did not set our sights high enough? Have we been too academic in our approach? Has there been too much light and not enough heat? . . . Have we not recognized too little effort as achievement? It is any wonder that these are critical times? . . . Now, is the time to get involved. Now, is also the time of opportunity. But, let us remember, talk alone won't get the job done. It's going to take action and then follow-up action."

Wilbanks had four recommendations:

First, he said, the League could no longer afford to be "all things to all people." The leadership would have to agree on specific working objectives. (Among the new objectives was returning the Game and Fish Commission to its former glory.)

Second, Wilbanks continued, it was more important than ever to hire a full-time executive secretary. Though this would certainly mean a major fund-raising effort, Wilbanks said, "the need is now" for an informed, aggressive professional. It was also time to move the League's center of business from John Bailey's basement to a real office in a central location, presumably Nashville.

Third, Wilbanks continued, standing committees must be made stronger and more accountable. They should function year-round, not just in the few weeks before and after annual conventions.

Finally, he said, the League needed better communications. A monthly newsletter, perhaps supported by advertising, should be one of the chief duties of a full-time staff. Such a publication would not only allow an "effective, timely and factual" flow of information, said Wilbanks. It would build interest and attract new members. And perhaps most important, it would help hold onto the old ones, the thousands of outdoor lovers who had been the backbone of the League since 1946.

If the League had been teetering on the edge of dissolution, the Norris Dam meeting snatched it back to safety. Everyone approved Wilbanks' sentiments; the thing now was to put them into action. That fall, Lou Williams, Lou Doney and John Dyche met in Chattanooga for a planning session that lasted nearly six hours. The notes from that "gabfest," presented to the board at its January 1971 meeting, would form the next step in the revitalization of the League.

"Any organization, whether it be religious, patriotic, cultural or what have you ought to be restudied once in 25 years," began their report. "Such a proposed study is timely for two reasons, viz.—It commemorates the 25th anniversary and indicates that the officers are aware of the need for such a study and how it might be helpful to the League." The other reason was that conservation seemed to be "on the lips of everyone nowadays." That being the case, they said, "the stage [was] set for some sort of a financing campaign."

The writers urged that a committee of "not more than a dozen members" be appointed at once so that by June they could report on such questions as whether the League should offer corporate memberships and how it could finance a full-time staff. Come to think of it, they said, such an important study "ought not be rushed. May be better to give it a full year."

THE WELCOME RETURN OF MR. BURCH

The special evaluation committee, named at the January board meeting, ultimately included twenty-nine members and "advisors," including some of the most venerable names in TCL's history—Lou Williams, Z. Cartter Patten, John Bailey, Judge Lee Asbury, even Lucius Burch, Jr. For years, Burch had been one of the League's staunchest supporters, president in the mid-'50s, winner of the Z. Cartter Patten Award for 1950, leader of one of its biggest affiliates (the West Tennessee Sportsmen's Association) and first chairman of the Game and Fish Commission. But in recent years Burch's involvement had dwindled because, as he later explained, the League had grown too narrow, too parochial, representing "only the hunters and fishermen in the state." Meanwhile, Burch's own remarkable vision had been growing even broader.

Lucius Burch was now one of the most prominent civil rights activists in the nation. This Southern white man—this man of wealth, rank and privilege, son of the Dean of the Vanderbilt Medical School and himself a 1936 graduate of the exclusive (and segregated) Vanderbilt Law School—had been the first white member of the Memphis chapter of the National Association for the Advancement of Colored People. Dr. Martin Luther King, Jr., had been one of his clients. In fact, on the day Dr. King was assassinated, Burch had been in federal court on behalf of the great civil rights leader. Like others in the League, Burch was a hunter and fly fisherman. But he was also an avid hiker, a deep-sea diver, an aviator and a naturalist. The larger his world got, the smaller the world of the League must have seemed to him.

Now, however, with the promise of a more inclusive, more progressive agenda, Burch once again put his extraordinary abilities behind the League, agreeing not only to serve on the evaluation team but to act as its chairman. Other members included retiring Game and Fish chairman Greer Ricketson, Penn Foreman, Charlie Rhea, Travis McNatt, Jack Ramsey, John Dyche, Daniel Boone, Will Roper, M. L. Brickey, Lester Dudney, Elmer Walker, Ray Strong, A. T. Bayless, Cecil Branstetter, Tom Worden, Emmet Guy, Al Ballinger and NWF representative Bill Reavely. Lou Doney had been named to the committee also, but when he died unexpectedly, in April 1971, his wife Virginia stepped in. Eventually she was joined by a second woman, Shirley Caldwell Patterson of Nashville. Patterson was as interesting and unconventional as her friend Lucius Burch. A member of another prominent Nashville family, Patterson was an accomplished outdoorswoman, an amateur archeologist and a leader in the Sierra Club, the Tennessee Environmental Council and the local Democratic party.

The full committee met for the first time on March 12, 1971, during the League's twenty-fifth annual convention in Memphis. Chairman Burch named two subcommittees, one in charge of "office, director and finance," the other in charge of "objectives and membership."

The latter was chaired by Gainesboro physician Lester R. Dudney, a former chairman of the Game and Fish Commission. His preliminary report was one of the most interesting, because on of the most penetrating, documents to come out of the evaluation process.

Too Narrow, Too White, Too Male

After reviewing the activities, priorities and membership patterns of the League over the previous twenty-five years, Dudney's subcommittee concluded that the organization had simply become too white, too male and altogether too narrow for its own good. A "true" conservation league, their report said, is concerned with all environmental matters, not just "the harvesting of wildlife crops." In their opinion, the League had grown "too limited in concept, concern and action." Relations with affiliates had grown irregular and hollow, communications were poor to nonexistent, the education program was sporadic and superficial, and the League's public image had become tired and irrelevant. It was even failing in its basic pledge to protect natural resources. Though more and more cases of resource abuse required aggressive action, even legal remedies, the League lacked the resources and expertise to pursue them.

Because of these failings, the report charged, the League was no longer growing. Its focus on hunting and fishing had the effect not only of alienating existing members—witness Lucius Burch—but of shutting out thousands of potential newcomers. The League's membership—overwhelmingly "Caucasian, of the older male sex and coming from sportsman clubs"—served as a *de facto* ban on blacks, women, even many of their fellow conservationists. "Effective and valuable people from other organizations, societies, colleges and universities are not encouraged and are not utilized," the report said.

Nor was the League's apparent bigotry entirely accidental. True, the League had never *actively* excluded African Americans, but only because no blacks had ever tried to join. The 1971 subcommittee reported some evidence, albeit "very limited," of racism in the League. While their report did not elaborate, there can be no doubt that at least some members were opposed to an integrated League. Unfortunate as this was, it was perhaps only to be expected of the segregationist age in which most members had grown up.

Black And White: The Issue Of Race

Like pretty much everything else in the state before the late '60s, outdoor recreation had been segregated by race. When T. O. Fuller State Park near Memphis was dedicated in June 1942, *The Tennessee Conservationist* noted proudly that it was, "so far as we know," the first state park in the country dedicated "to the use of Negroes." Technically, it was not the first. TVA had leased the land for both T. O. Fuller and Booker T. Washington, its other "Negro park," to the state in 1938, but Booker T. Washington was acquired a few months earlier. This small plot of land on Chickamauga Lake was just across Harrison Bay from Tennessee's first state park, a former TVA demonstration area called, appropriately, Harrison Bay. The state acquired the properties almost simultaneously, but Harrison Bay was four times larger, more extensively developed, and of course, reserved for whites only.

By 1943 the state had plans for additional parks to serve the "colored" populations of

The Nashville Sportsman's Club was founded even earlier than the League, in 1945. And like the League, its leadership was dominated by successful, professional men. Yet it would be nearly thirty years before they were welcomed into TCL. Here, from left, Dale Crowder, Dr. H. H. Walker, Tom Stalin, C. J. Kincaid and Dr. E. L. Sasser head for one of the few stocked hunting grounds open to black Americans in the 1950s. Courtesy of the Nashville Sportsman's Club.

Nashville, Jackson and northeast Tennessee. But as Bevley Coleman observed in his 1963 dissertation on the history of Tennessee's state parks, "nothing came of the proposal," presumably because whites wouldn't allow it. Both the Division of State Parks and the State Planning Commission (formed in 1933) decided not to push the issue, explaining that "there would probably be objection to establishing a Negro park near any center of white population" in Tennessee—or, for that matter, "on any site within the state." The question of sharing facilities, of course, was not even raised: state law forbade it.

The state obviously felt some obligation to provide reasonable facilities, however. Between them, Booker T. Washington and T. O. Fuller eventually had two swimming pools, several bathhouses, a marina, a golf course, a group camp, tenting grounds, play fields, concession stands and lots of picnic tables. By the 1950s, the Department of Conservation's Education Service was sending black camp counselors to work with black campers. But the parks were tiny—a total of 1,350 acres out of the quarter-million acres in the entire state park system by the mid-'60s. And even when Governor Buford Ellington "ended" the parks' segregation policy in 1962 (restaurants and swimming pools excepted), the state made no formal or public announcement of the fact.

The Game and Fish Commission does not appear to have had a formal racial policy for its wildlife management areas, but black men probably did not feel entirely welcome. (A 1970 survey by the Game and Fish Commission found that 95 percent of license holders in Tennessee were white.) However, according to a history of the all-black Nashville Sportsman's Club, "fifty years ago Blacks had a difficult time locating farm land that was stocked with game where they could hunt or fish." A 1954 survey found that while most black farmers said they didn't mind hunters using their land without permission, almost all white farmers said they did mind. "Racial intolerance," observed the survey, "undoubtedly played a role in their answer." The Nashville Sportsman's Club bought land in Hendersonville in order to have a place to hunt, said past president H. C. Hardy, but the property was flooded when Old Hickory Lake was impounded in the 1950s.

At any rate, racial separation was both the written and the unwritten law of the land for many years, and judging by available records, the League appears to have accepted it without comment—with one noteworthy exception. In 1950, Lou Williams had approached the board with a plan to "sponsor and encourage Negro Sportsmen's Clubs." It is impossible to say how many black clubs existed at that time, but the Nashville Sportsman's Club had been around even before the League itself, first proposed in 1943 and incorporated in 1945. Like the League's, its leaders were white-collar professionals—physicians, college professors, clergy and the like. However, there was "some objection" to Williams' motion, and it was permanently tabled. It would not be until 1973 that the NSC would be invited to join the League. It has been one of the most dedicated affiliates ever since.

WOMEN: THE OTHER 7 PERCENT

The absence of women, while not as acute nor as deliberate as that of African Americans, was likewise noticeable in TCL. One or two garden clubs had joined (and as quickly dropped out) over the decades; in recent years there had also been a handful of "conservation clubs," such as the East Tennessee Wildlife Improvement Club, whose membership was partly female. Still, most of the women who participated in the League did so via their husbands or their fathers, through the "ladies' auxiliary." They may have cooked the wild game, but few actually hunted it: in 1970, only 7 percent of Tennessee license holders were women.

A notable exception was Vivian Burch, who with her husband Bob operated the fishing dock on Fort Loudoun Lake at Concord. (Bob Burch later became a public information officer with the Tennessee Game and Fish Commission.) Vivian Burch had taken part in the very first Tellico wild boar hunt in 1936; she was also an outstanding fly fisherman—even better than some of the men, according to Joe Halburnt. When Bob Burch was drafted into World War II, said Halburnt in a recent interview, "he asked me to make sure Vivian got to Tellico for the opening day of trout season.

"We left before daylight," Halburnt said. "I had Vivian and two men. Right off, I could see the problems on [the men's] faces in the rearview mirror. When we stopped they got me off to one side and reamed me out: 'Who's gonna wet-nurse that woman?' They were fussing and moaning. I told them, 'Don't worry about her.'"

At the campground, the group broke up, Vivian heading upstream by herself, the three men downstream. At lunchtime, the fellows returned to camp as planned. "There was no Vivian," said Halburnt, "and no trout either. Nobody had caught anything. The guys were still fussing. 'She's probably up there with a broken leg, but I'm not going after her.' I told them, 'Don't *worry* about her.'"

Sure enough, Burch showed up, healthy and happy, a few minutes later. "Catch anything?" the men asked sullenly. "The limit," said Vivian Burch. "Their jaws dropped," said Joe Halburnt.

Of course, even if the League had gone out of its way to recruit women, it's doubtful it would have found many takers. The men's-club atmosphere was simply too overwhelming. Even Shirley Patterson, a woman who could live happily for weeks in a tent in a Middle Eastern desert, later recalled feeling isolated and uncomfortable at the League's 1971 annual meeting in Jackson.

Of course, all of these conditions—the subtle sexism, the implicit racism, the clubbiness— were by no means uncommon for the era, and the League (and Lucius Burch and Dr. Dudney in particular) deserve credit for confronting them as frankly as they did. In his eloquent final report for the special evaluation committee, chairman Burch acknowledged that the report was "not a final solution" to these problems, but rather "a modest proposal of how to make a reasonable start."

THE SPECIAL EVALUATION COMMITTEE FILES ITS REPORT

In its way, the report of the special evaluation committee was as central to the history of Tennessee's modern environmental movement as, say, *Silent Spring* was to the history of the movement nationwide. Signed by Burch over the names of the twenty-eight other participants, the fifteen-page document reflected both the legal correctness of the lawyer and the almost religious fervor of the nature lover.

> [A] general awareness has suddenly come upon almost all persons interested in conservation that a segmented approach to the ecological problems of today and tomorrow is bound to fail. The day is forever gone when there was sufficient natural habitat to support an acceptable wildlife level in the state. There is an increasing awareness that the fish in the streams are creatures of the forest—of the watershed—and that every living thing, including man, is dependent upon clean air, pure water and that esthetic resources which feed the mind and soul should receive attention at least equal to that given those resources which can be consumed or used in a tangible way.

While the League continued to be "beyond argument" the strongest conservation group in the state, the report said, "it is now nowhere nearly sufficient to deal with the general problems" currently facing it. "[W]hat is needed is to have within the framework of one organization every aspect of the conservation movement, which will include the individuals and organizations interested in scenic rivers, gardening, forestry, botany, watershed conservation, green belts, hiking, camping, boating, and every aspect of outdoors activity which causes participants to be particularly concerned with ecological problems."

This new umbrella, the report suggested, might be called the Environmental Committee, consisting of three subcommittees: "products of the land" (such as game, forests and rivers); "special interest action groups" (such as Sierra Club, Tennessee Trails and Ducks Unlimited); and "problem areas" (stream pollution, land-use zoning, erosion and so on). The new environmental committee would rank "among the most important and prestigious groups of the League, and second only to the Directors in the promulgation of League policy."

Though neither the names nor the three-part structure stuck, the evaluation knew that TCL needed a broadened agenda if it were to survive. However, they also knew that it would make some members uneasy, others downright rebellious. The evaluation committee hastened to defuse the anticipated objections. "[I]n no way" did the reorganization imply "a diminished interest in the League's traditional concern with wildlife," the report insisted. On the contrary, by attracting the support and participation of "those citizens who ... have not been attracted to the League because of its heretofore more limited objectives," the directors would be able to do an even better job of promoting hunting and fishing.

And, not incidentally, they could also hire an executive director.

THE SEARCH FOR AN EXECUTIVE DIRECTOR

For many on the board, the most tangible proof of the League's renovation would be a permanent office with a professional staff.

The notion of a professional administrator was by no means a new one. That the League would eventually hire a director had been considered such a certainty that provisions for hiring one had been written into the original bylaws. As early as March 1948, the board had been discussing the matter as if it were imminent. Lou Williams had broached the subject first, saying that, in his opinion, "the business of the League was of sufficient importance to justify the employment of a $5,000-a-year man." Though Williams knew as well as anyone that the League's finances could not support such a step at present, he hoped it was something the board would consider in the near future. Karl Steinmetz moved that the executive committee start thinking of a suitable candidate at once, "preferably a G. I." Nothing came of the motion, however, though the subject would be revisited with great energy and regularity for the next twenty years. In 1951, the League had even embarked on its $250,000 fund-raising drive.

Twenty years later, that drive had raised barely fifteen thousand dollars, mostly through life memberships. Yet hiring a director had ceased to be a matter of wish-list fantasy; it was a necessity. As NWF representative Bill Reavely told the evaluation committee, eighteen of the Federation's forty-odd affiliates already had full-time directors; another thirteen were in the process of hiring one. So great was the demand for trained administrators, in fact, that the NWF had prepared a "blueprint" for affiliates to use in hiring a suitable candidate. Since most affiliates operated on a shoestring, national headquarters also offered free financial advice. Reavely recommended that the League look into federal grants, private endowments and corporate sponsorships; he also mentioned Sherman Kelly, a professional fund-raiser who had made a comfortable career managing solicitation drives and donor lists for sportsmen's groups.

The budgetary leap would be a significant one, according to the finance subcommittee's estimates. For the last few years, the League's income had hovered between eight thousand and ten thousand dollars, though in 1970 it suddenly shot up to fifteen thousand. (For some reason, the Sears grant that year was $4,500.) But that was still only enough to cover the director's proposed salary, let alone his payroll taxes. Add to that at least four thousand dollars for a secretary, six thousand dollars in travel expenses, seven thousand dollars in rent and utilities and as much as five thousand dollars for furniture, office equipment and contingencies, and the total first-year costs could be as high as $38,000.

THE GENEROUS LEGACY OF EDWARD MEEMAN

Fortunately, Lucius Burch had an idea how the League might meet this goal. Five years earlier, when Memphis newspaper editor and publisher Edward J. Meeman died in November 1966, he had willed that a large share of his considerable estate be used in the cause of conservation. Burch had known Ed Meeman since at least the late 1930s, when both men served on the board of the old Tennessee Wildlife Federation. (Ironically, they had kicked off a major fund-raising campaign for that group also.)

As chairman of the funding subcommittee, Burch now approached the directors of the Meeman Foundation to ask their support. The Foundation agreed to give the League $100,000 dollars—providing it could raise an equal endowment within five years. The trust agreement, signed in April 1972, provided that in the meantime, the grant money would be held in trust or invested. (It was invested in securities, though not very profitably. After five years the corpus had shrunk to about $83,000.)

If, after five years, the League had failed to raise the matching funds, the original $100,000 (or what was left of it) would be turned over to The Nature Conservancy's national headquarters. (The Conservancy did not establish a Tennessee office until 1978.) If, on the other hand, the League managed to raise the match, then Meeman's $100,000 would be added to the League's $100,000, and together they would be held in perpetuity as the Edward J. Meeman Conservation Trust Fund. The income alone would be used for the "general corporate purposes" of the League.

There was one final hitch. In order to collect on the grant, the League also had to demonstrate that it had satisfied the various recommendations of the special evaluation committee, from diversifying its membership base to starting a publication. If it failed on any point—even if it succeeded in raising the $100,000—the League would still forfeit the Meeman grant to The Nature Conservancy.

TCL leaders were ecstatic. Even with these strings attached, the grant seemed a virtual guarantee that their reorganization plan would succeed. It was time to move from evaluation to implementation.

Chapter Six

1972-1979

The Rise Of The Professional Conservationist

*I hear that the new office is doing well. We are beginning to move,
I believe. I have confidence in the future of the League. Believe we have
something to sell, but we need to get it on the market,
and my opinion is that your office is the key.*

—Bob Burns, in a letter to
Tony Campbell, August 2, 1972

TCL HIRES A DIRECTOR

With the evaluation committee's report finished and the Meeman grant finalized, Lucius Burch now turned his attention back to his Memphis law practice, leaving Bob Burns in charge of the follow-up committee, and his nephew, Nashville attorney Lucius Burch, III, in charge of fund-raising. The reorganization team was now bigger than ever: forty men deployed over four subcommittees. Clenton Smith headed the largest group, sixteen members, who would study the final report and figure out how its recommendations could be put in motion. Cecil Branstetter was in charge of the foursome who would review and amend the bylaws. The fourth subcommittee, the six-man team headed by M. L. Brickey, would mount the search for the League's new executive director.

Brickey's committee faced an interesting task. The proposed job requirements filled nearly two pages of text, yet the successful candidate would receive no more than fifteen thousand dollars a year. This man was expected to be adept in public relations, political science, office administration and budget management; to have a college degree or proven track record in biology or other conservation science; and to show a "keen appreciation" of the outdoors and the natural resources of Tennessee. He must be articulate, mobile and no more than forty years old (the age requirement was soon dropped). He would be responsible for setting up an office, raising funds, producing a newsletter, working with the press, monitoring the legislature, dealing with government agencies, speaking to outside groups, attending seminars, conducting membership campaigns, formulating programs, nurturing affiliates and performing "any other duties" the directors saw fit to assign him.

By mid-January 1972, resumes had begun trickling in. By March, Brickey's subcommittee had heard from about two dozen applicants, interviewed more than half of these and narrowed the list to three finalists. On March 27, following a special called meeting at Henry Horton State Park, the board offered the job to Anthony J. Campbell, thirty-two, of Ft. Bayard, New Mexico. Campbell recalls that his starting salary was twelve thousand dollars.

Tony Campbell was a native Pennsylvanian with four years in the Air Force and a B.S. in wildlife management from New Mexico State University. He had been working for the New Mexico Department of Game and Fish since 1966 as a research biologist, information officer and law enforcement investigator. He was young, intelligent, hard working and instinctively political, equally at ease among legislators and good old boys, but always aware of the differences between them.

Though he wasn't to start work until June, Campbell flew to Tennessee the weekend of April 6 to be officially introduced to the League during its 1972 annual meeting in Gatlinburg. "Everyone who met you was impressed," Bob Burns wrote Campbell soon afterwards, including the young *Knoxville News Sentinel* writer Sam Venable and even Bob Steber of *The Tennessean*—"and he is not easily impressed."

Campbell's arrival was eagerly awaited by all the leaders of the League, but few were as eager as Bob Burns. From the start, the TVA engineer kept in constant touch with his protégé via letters, notes and phone calls, offering (always "for what it [was] worth") a steady stream of observations, encouragements and mild precautions about whom to watch and what to expect.

Tony Campbell, a wildlife biologist in New Mexico's Department of Game and Fish, was thirty-two years old when he became executive director of the Tennessee Conservation League. He fit in well from the first. The cowboy boots probably helped. TCL file photo.

Campbell didn't have long to bask in the glow of celebrity, however. The League had leased a small office in the Mid-State Medical Center at 2010 Church Street for $217 a month, and he barely had time to unpack before he was out shopping for lamps, furniture and do-it-yourself shelving. (He would be packing it all up again within twenty-four months: the League moved to 1205 Eighth Avenue, South, in June 1974. In 1977 it moved again, to 1720 West End Avenue.) He put a down-payment on an electric typewriter, hired a secretary (Tricia Truman) and began the prolonged and often rocky process of consolidating the scattered operations of the League in one location. The League's finances had to be transferred from Covington (home of treasurer Julian Whitley) to a local bank; its nonprofit mailing permit had to be moved from Johnson City (home of secretary John Bailey) to the main post office in Nashville. The latter task prompted a frantic search for the League's 1951 letter from the IRS granting a tax exemption. Meanwhile, since no one had told him otherwise, Campbell was blithely ignoring the IRS requirement to deposit payroll taxes every month.

In short, as he confessed ruefully to one member who had written to ask why she had not yet received her membership card, "Although I didn't anticipate too many problems arising from this move I am finding that it is not a small job."

Campbell also seems to have encountered some slight awkwardness in weaning John Bailey from the job he had held for nearly twenty years. Bailey had hoped—even expected—to be tapped for the new executive director's job, and given his long devotion to the League, this was a natural if not altogether realistic ambition. No one doubted Bailey's dedication, nor his abilities. Chairman of the science department at East Tennessee State University, he held a doctorate in conservation education from Cornell; his thesis there had focused on community conservation projects in the South. However, he was nearing retirement age, and the search committee was clearly hoping for a younger, more aggressive and perhaps more politically savvy fellow to be their new chief executive.

Nonetheless, their decision to look elsewhere must have caused them some unease. In June 1972, and partly in response to Bailey's own appeals, the board voted to pay him a regular "honorarium" of a hundred dollars a month for the next year while the League made the transition from Johnson City to Nashville. But there was another touchy matter. For years, Bailey had served as the League's main delegate to the National Wildlife Federation, attending its annual conventions, voting on behalf of its Tennessee members and painstakingly filling out its various report forms. These tasks would now fall to Tony Campbell as executive director. Whether Bailey complained about the change is not known, but in June, the board agreed to pay his way to the next NWF convention as Campbell's alternate.

Bailey himself would later insist that moving the League's offices to Nashville was "great." Certainly he did not miss the demands of what had become a full-time job at part-time pay. (By 1972 he was getting $150 a month, plus expenses.) Still, it could not have been easy for him when, one July afternoon, Tony Campbell showed up in Johnson City with a rented trailer, ready to load up the old Addressograph and other equipment and haul it all to Nashville. Unfortunately, since Bailey planned to keep the office going a while longer, Campbell did not also load up the endless volumes of League records—meeting notes, minutes, correspondence, brochures, news clippings, resolutions and so on—that had been accumulating since

1946. Apparently the files never did get turned over to the League; at any rate, no one can account for them now. And since John Bailey died in 1983, they are probably gone for good.

But in 1972, Tony Campbell wasn't worrying about the League's past. He was too busy worrying about the immediate future. In particular, he was debating what to do about Game and Fish.

GATHERING STORM CLOUDS OVER GAME AND FISH

From the start, the relationship between the Game and Fish Commission and the Tennessee Conservation League had been unusually close (some would say just plain unusual). Although it had been years since the sportsmen actually elected commissioners, many TCL leaders had served on, or were still serving on, the commission, including Lucius Burch, Jr., M. L. Brickey, Edwin Crutcher, LeRoy Rymer, Jim Asbury, Joe Curry, Milburn Jolly, Will Roper, Travis McNatt, William Harwell, Hugh McDade, Lester Dudney, Charlie Rhea, Hubert Fry, Smith Howard, Jim Beasley, Ray Strong, Karl Smith, Greer Ricketson, Dr. Bill Blackburn, Larry Lowe and many others. There was always someone from the League at commission meetings (Tony Campbell believes he missed no more than five or six meetings in more than twenty years.) The commission, in its turn, always scheduled one of its regular meetings during the League's annual convention. Without actually getting into the other's pocket, the two organizations had, in fact, formed an intensely close partnership.

Thus the League had been understandably concerned when the agency began having serious problems in the late 1960s. For one thing, sportsmen were noting a marked decline in small game, waterbirds and some other wildlife populations. Some of the declines, of course, were temporary, such as the sudden drop in squirrels in 1969 following a hard winter. But others—including the fish kills and the waterfowl losses—could be traced to such chronic and growing menaces as habitat loss and stream pollution. Therefore, they could and probably should be addressed by the wildlife agency.

As Wilbanks had noted at Norris Dam, the commission really was in some danger of "going broke," because the Legislature still refused to grant a fee increase. Game and Fish was the only agency in state government that received absolutely no funding from the state's general fund. Instead, Game and Fish operations were supported entirely by the sportsmen themselves, either through hunting and fishing licenses, boat rentals and so forth; or through federal excise taxes on hunting and fishing equipment, the so-called Pittman-Robertson and Dingell-Johnson funds. (Boating revenues were administered by the commission but were otherwise considered separately.)

The single largest source of revenue at Game and Fish was the combined hunting and fishing license: nearly a half-million sold in 1973-74 for $2.35 million. However, the current five-dollar fee, set in 1966, was the lowest in the nation, and the surplus left over from previous years was quickly running out. Yet rather than grant the agency's repeated requests for an increase, hostile lawmakers were threatening to abolish the commission altogether.

Complaints against the commission were varied. State Senator William D. Baird, a Democrat from Lebanon, was one of the agency's most vehement critics. The Game and Fish Commission was not only "extravagant and wasteful," Baird contended; it did "absolutely nothing for the small game hunter." Baird was an old quail hunter who desperately wanted the agency to resume its long-abandoned program of stocking bobwhite quail, despite the fact that every state in the union had long since abandoned quail stocking as a waste of time and money. "I know you can have a successful quail release program," insisted Baird, but those "crazy biologists" at the wildlife agency "just don't believe me."

Whether or not they were reasonable, such debates made good public theater and so were often played out in the newspapers, embarrassing the agency and generally making the commissioners look like they deserved at least some of the scorn that was being heaped upon them. In fact, in 1973 Baird sponsored a bill that would have given sportsmen the power to elect their own commissioners, as they had done (with great awkwardness) in the '50s.

Some of the worst media attacks came from Amon C. Evans, publisher of *The Nashville Tennessean* (now *The Tennessean*). In March 1971, Evans had authorized a series of articles and editorials that were highly critical of the commission, especially the law enforcement branch, which was "loosely operated, lacked supervision and generally abused its privilege." The series charged that wildlife officers went hunting together, "staked out" the best blind locations and made comparatively few arrests given the number of hours they spent in the field. One officer reportedly took sick leave on the opening day of duck season because a local judge had asked the fellow to take him hunting.

Officers not only spent on-duty time drumming up support for a fee increase, said the newspaper; the funds the agency did collect were wildly misappropriated. For instance, said one editorial, while only $29,000 had been spent on pollution control, $339,000 had been spent on an extravagant public relations program.

In another piece, reporter Jerry Thompson observed that agency director Fred Stanberry had been asked to resign after he told a legislative review committee that the commission had been "more responsive to the affluent," a common and long-standing complaint. (According to Greer Ricketson, who was chairman of the commission at the time, Stanberry had been fired following a series of indiscretions.)

Some insiders said Amon Evans was mad at the commission because he lost his favorite duck blind on the Tennessee River near Camden. The river was under TVA jurisdiction, but Evans decided to tighten the screws on Game and Fish anyway, assigning a team of reporters to scrutinize the agency's records. "When I heard he was going to do this," said Ricketson, "I told him we would be cooperative. In return, [we wanted] no innuendos. If you print something," Ricketson told him, "print it as fact."

No such luck, said Ricketson. Unable to find hard evidence of wrongdoing, he said, the reporters resorted to half-truths and insinuation. For instance, there had been a question about private use of agency-owned equipment, such as its fleet of aluminum fishing boats. Purchased for public use on agency lakes, these boats were occasionally borrowed by agency staff to use in their free time, said Ricketson. He even remembered clarifying this point to one of the reporters. "But they wrote things like, 'Some people seem to think . . .' or 'There seems to be some question that . . .,'" Ricketson recalled. "They didn't say it right out, just a lot of innuendos. That went on for a week or more."

MISPERCEPTION, MISMANAGEMENT AND MISJUDGMENT

In fairness to the newspaper, these were not isolated complaints. There was an increasing public perception that the wildlife agency had grown inept, inbred, unresponsive, unaccountable and expensive. In an effort to rein in what they saw as an out-of-control behemoth, the legislators in 1970 elevated the commissioner of Conservation, already an ex officio member of the commission, to full voting status.

That did not satisfy, however. In 1971, following a harsh review of the commission's operations, lawmakers in both houses introduced bills that would have dissolved the commission altogether, placing it back under the thumb of the Department of Conservation. Both bills failed, but they were back two years later, sponsored by, among others, the quail hunter Bill Baird. (Interestingly, one of the 1971 cosponsors, Granville Hinton, was now commissioner of Conservation under Winfield Dunn, sparking rumors that a "Judas" with full voting powers was sitting on the commission.)

Feathers had also flown early in 1971, when someone in the agency proposed cancelling the home-county fishing perk—that is, the practice of allowing residents to fish with natural bait in their home counties without a license. That brief firestorm died down when the commission backed off from the proposal.

And some noses were still out of joint that the agency was now working out of its new, $1.3 million headquarters at Ellington Agricultural Center. Never mind that the agency was paying for every brick. And never mind that the three-story building looked about as architecturally interesting as a warehouse. The sight of it was wormwood to people like Senator Baird, who said it looked like "a little Pentagon," adding sourly, "they haven't spent a dime on the small game hunter since 1951." A *Tennessean* editorial on May 27, 1971, found the building equally distasteful, a symbol of the commission's extravagance and a reminder that it was "too closely attuned to the wishes of the few wealthy sportsmen, while ignoring the needs of the little man who pays the bills."

Actually, until now it didn't seem that the "little men" had been paying all that much attention to the Game and Fish controversy. Their loudest outcry had come when the commission had threatened the home-fishing privilege. But in May 1971, the commission's new director, David Goodrich, lit another fuse, one that set off angry waterfowlers throughout the state.

Goodrich, former chief of the law enforcement division, had been assistant director of the commission since 1963, when Fred Stanberry replaced Col. Forrest Durand as director. When Stanberry resigned under pressure in early 1971, the commission tapped Goodrich as his successor. Goodrich took office on May 13; days later he eliminated the entire technical section of the waterfowl management unit, including its popular chief biologist Calvin Barstow and both of his assistants. He explained his move by saying that he wanted to apply the $75,000 savings to "other purposes such as research and planning"—and, he ought to have added, law enforcement. At least some of the money went to the law enforcement section, though it was already under heavy fire for claiming a bigger share of the agency's $4.5 million budget than any other single division, larger than game management, larger than fish management.

The following week the commission began holding a series of public meetings to hear the duck hunters' complaints. The commissioners knew the hunters were mad, but they weren't expecting quite such vehemence. At the first public meeting in Clarksville, a group calling itself the "Committee for Better Game and Fish" charged that the commission was no longer fit to govern the resource. Spokesman Don Ansley, a champion duck caller, TCL member and a leader in Ducks Unlimited, read a prepared statement demanding that the commission hand its authority back to the governor. "Middle Tennessee sportsmen ... are requesting that the Governor set up, with appropriate action of Legislature, a new cabinet-level department of Game and Fish. The single head of this department would be a cabinet-level appointment made by the Governor [and] subject to the approval of the senate. ... Present game and fish commissioners would assume the role of an advisory board."

In other words: undo the 1949 model law. Ansley's speech was followed by dead silence. Commissioners and onlookers were stunned. But Senator Baird must have been rubbing his hands in glee.

By early 1973, Game and Fish seemed hopelessly mired in controversy. A legislative sub-committee, convened to study the agency in the wake of the Goodrich firings, had found almost nothing positive to say about it. For the third time in as many years, the commission had come before the Legislature in quest of a fee increase, and again been sent away empty-handed. *The Tennessean* was again on the attack, charging that "[w]hile rabbit hunters, pole fishermen and conservationists yearned for more programs to benefit them," the commission was catering to "the exotic needs of wealthy hunters" with such extravagances as $200,000 in imported European hogs.

Even Al Marsh, the former commission employee who had talked at such length at the League's 1949 annual meeting, now emptied his thesaurus at the Game and Fish Commission. (The erstwhile chief of game management had been "separated from service" in 1951.) In a 1973 letter to the *Nashville Banner*, Marsh railed at the "intrigue," "dissension," "turmoil," "instability," "inefficiency," "bungled priorities," "discrimination," "gross mismanagement," "inappropriateness" and "incompetence" of the current wildlife agency. The League itself came in for a share of the vitriol. According to Marsh, the League's "self-serving sportsmen" dominated the commission, yet they neither "equitably or adequately" represented "the general public's rights in the wildlife heritage."

A BLUE-RIBBON PANEL EVALUATES THE COMMISSION

The League had been watching these storm clouds gather with growing dismay. Not simply because many of its most respected members continued to serve on the commission, including its chairman, Larry Lowe of Chattanooga, but because it had a good collective memory. "This move would set us back untold years," said Earl Glover, a two-term past president of the League from Old Hickory. "There is no denying that the Commission has had its problems. But show me a branch of state government that hasn't. ... The Commission concept is basically sound."

Tony Campbell meanwhile was doing some investigations of his own. More than three-fifths of the states had independent, governor-appointed game and fish commissions like

Tennessee's. But in recent years, many of them had experienced the same problems as their colleagues in Tennessee. Most had managed to remained autonomous, but a few had been returned to an umbrella agency where, invariably, they lost a measure of control over their operations. At least some states, including Colorado, Arkansas, Ohio and Massachusetts, had settled their problems in great part by submitting to an impartial, outside review, not by political theorists or institutional economists, but by seasoned wildlife management professionals with no political stake in the outcome. In most cases the review team had been put together, and in many cases had been chaired, by Thomas L. Kimball, executive vice president of the National Wildlife Federation.

At a meeting of the commission in early 1973, Tony Campbell described the benefits of a "blue-ribbon evaluation." The commissioners seemed to like the idea. The director, however, did not. Goodrich's stock had never fully recovered since the waterfowl firings, and according to Tony Campbell, he talked the commissioners out of it.

Campbell was not worried. The decision to convene a review was not the director's to make at all, but the governor's. The next time he met with the commissioners, he again proposed a blue-ribbon review, and again they approved of it. But this time Campbell made it impossible for them to back down. He told the commissioners that he planned to feed the story to his contacts in the outdoor press, including Bob Witt of the *Banner*, Bob Steber of *The Tennessean*, Charles Searcy of *The Chattanooga Times* and Henry Reynolds of *The Commercial Appeal*. "I'm going to get these outdoor writers to hear what you're going to do and they'll report it." Which, of course, they did.

On Friday, March 30, 1973, Bob Witt reported that the director of the Conservation League had offered a "constructive suggestion" to the Game and Fish Commission. Said Campbell (who was really a master rhetorician), "I see nothing wrong in requesting a committee of nationally-known professional wildlifers to come in here and evaluate our Game and Fish program. ... "This would be strictly a professional, no-axe-to-grind evaluation and the findings could be presented to the ... Commission and the governor as well."

Suddenly, the future of Game and Fish did not seem quite so bleak. On the following Thursday, April 5, 1973, commission chairman Larry Lowe ended his tenure by formally requesting Governor Winfield Dunn to initiate the evaluation process.

Fortunately, Winfield Dunn's administration had been as friendly to the sportsmen's interests as it had been to those of the environmentalists. In fact, both the governor and his environmental policy advisor, Ed Thackston (still on leave from Vanderbilt) both liked to hunt, and Tony Campbell worked well with them both. (In fact, Thackston would join the TCL board as soon as he returned to Vanderbilt in 1974.) Now, Campbell enlisted Thackston's support in making sure the governor understood and supported the evaluation process.

On May 18, 1973, Dunn wrote to Kimball at the NWF. "I hope that you will ... assist us by selecting a committee of approximately five qualified professionals" to undertake this evaluation, he began. The panel should be "completely independent and nonpolitical, and, if possible, contain one or more members from the southeastern area of the United States, so that the committee will have the benefit of some background concerning the unique problems of this area." The commission would foot the bill, of course, estimated at ten thousand dollars.

Kimball, who knew Tony Campbell personally, had of course been told to expect Dunn's letter. He soon had his team lined up: Charles Kelley, director of Alabama's Division of Game and Fish; John S. Gottschalk, executive vice president of the International Association of Game, Fish and Conservation Commissioners; Richard H. Stroud, executive vice president of the Sport Fishing Institute in Washington, D.C.; and Dr. Douglas L. Gilbert, assistant dean of the college of forestry and natural resources at Colorado State University. Kimball, himself a former game and fish director for both Arizona and Colorado, would serve as chairman. Most asked to be paid their expenses only.

On July 30, 1973, the evaluation team convened in Nashville. For the next week they met with Game and Fish staff, commissioners, legislators and people in the governor's office. They scrutinized procedures and reviewed policies. And for three hours on August 1, they invited members of the public to come forward and air their concerns. Those who could not attend were invited to send in written comments by August 15.

Though one hunter called it a "gripe session," the mood throughout this comment-gathering period was remarkably civil, if critical. "Thank you for your time and consideration of our questions," wrote the members of one club, adding, "[w]e hope we are mistaken about the ineptness of our Game and Fish Commission ... but we know we're not."

Of course, most participants were predictably biased in favor of their own sport and predictably cavalier about the needs of others. "My gripe concerns fishing," said one man. "[L]et the hunters do their own griping." "Up the license fee for fishermen," said another fellow. "[T]he hunter has no interest in hatcheries."

Yet most speakers seemed to agree on several basic points: morale at the agency was low; it was out of touch with its public; it was dominated by the law enforcement section; its wildlife management priorities were poor; its information and education program was ineffective; and its commissioners, some of whom "tried to sort of throw their weight around," as Greer Ricketson put it, needed to understand the limits of their duties. Few believed, however, that these were unpardonable sins. When Nashville's Senator Douglas Henry polled his sporting constituents, he found that most of them wanted to give the agency another chance.

The evaluation team, meanwhile, continued to meet periodically through the fall. By December it had completed its report, a bulky document listing sixty-nine separate items. Some of these items were rejected, such as the suggestion to abolish the eight-year-old boating division, and the suggestion to trim the commission to six voting members from the current ten. But most of the recommendations were adopted, including the demand for a clearer distinction between the commissioners who made policy, and the director and staff who executed it. As it turned out, these two functions were to be separated altogether.

THE RESHAPING OF GAME AND FISH: TWRA AND TWRC

When the reorganization took effect on April 1, 1974, the old Tennessee Game and Fish Commission was no more. It had been recast (via legislative act) in two parts: the band of commissioners was now the Tennessee Wildlife Resources *Commission*; the director and his staff were now the Tennessee Wildlife Resources *Agency*. At long last, the agency had a name that lent itself to easy abbreviation: TWRA. Even the logo had been changed: it now depicted not a deer and a fish, but a fish and a raccoon (a nod, of course, to the new emphasis on both small and nongame wildlife). The design was the work of Evelyn Underwood, the same artist who had inadvertently been credited with the League's new logo three years earlier.

But these were not the most dramatic changes. Probably the most significant difference at Game and Fish—that is, *TWRA*—was the agency's decentralized structure. Before, the commission had overseen its program in all ninety-five counties from its single headquarters in Nashville. Now, in addition to the Ellington Agricultural Center headquarters, the agency had four regional offices in Jackson (Region 1), Murfreesboro (Region II), Crossville (Region III) and Morristown (Region IV). The regional system had already proven itself in a number of other states, including Colorado. Not only was it said to give staff more experience in more areas of administration and operation; it also put Game and Fish personnel in the field, where most people felt they belonged.

Job requirements had also been upgraded, including a mandate that all game wardens (the new "wildlife conservation officers") have college degrees, preferably in conservation or wildlife management. Those already on staff would be offered advanced training. The commission expanded its game management section and created a separate program for small game, nongame and endangered species. The I & E section (Information and Education) finally got its own magazine in 1975, ending nearly four decades of sharing space with *The Tennessee Conservationist*. It was called *Tennessee Wildlife*, the same name Herman Baggenstoss used when he began publishing a magazine for the Tennessee Federation of Sportsmen in 1937.

A final mark of progress came in May 1975, when the General Assembly at last relented and passed the first license increase in ten years. The combined hunting and fishing license fee was now $7.50, not the $10 requested by the commission, but better than nothing. Lawmakers also created a five-dollar nongame "certificate," as well as the first comprehensive "sportsman" license, a thirty-dollar pass good for everything but trout fishing.

The reorganization had not been painless, of course, nor without some loss of life.

Director David Goodrich was the earliest to go. Barely two weeks after the review process got underway, Goodrich quit. In his resignation letter of August 16, 1973, Goodrich told commission chairman Edgar Evins, "It is obvious from my recent discussions with members of the ... Commission that I no longer have their one-hundred per cent support." Of course, as Sam Venable noted in *The Knoxville News-Sentinel*, "[His resignation] was merely a technical thing. Had he not quit he would have been fired." Besides his questionable judgment in firing the waterfowl staff, the former chief of law enforcement had been severely criticized for seeking a pay increase for wildlife officers but no one else.

After Goodrich left, there followed the briefest of interim terms by the well-liked but terminally ill assistant director, Harold Warvel. (Warvel died the following February, having received the League's Conservationist of the Year Award in 1973.) In 1981, when former commissioner Larry Lowe donated two huge purple martin houses to TWRA, the agency held a simple installation ceremony in memory of Warvel.

In September 1973 the commission appointed Harvey Bray, state planning chief for Colorado's Division of Wildlife, to be the new director. Though Bray impressed early observers with his boldness and drive, he eventually fell out of favor with the commissioners, and in the fall of 1977, they asked assistant director Gary T. Myers to step in as acting director. In February 1978 they offered Myers the post for good. After a decade of rapid turnovers, the executive director's chair had finally found some stability. Almost twenty years later, Myers would still be on the job.

Myers, a native Texan, had studied wildlife management at Colorado State, earning a bachelor's and master's degree before going to work for the Colorado game and fish agency. In May 1974 he followed Harvey Bray to Tennessee. Like Bray, he had been recruited in part because of his experience in a regional wildlife administration system. One of his first jobs was to sell the merits of Tennessee's new four-region system to the sportsmen, who, he recalls, "weren't all that enthused" about it.

"I remember the first TCL meeting I ever went to," Myers said in an interview in 1996. "I went into it kind of watching my back. TCL asked hard questions. ... I had a smile on my face but I didn't really trust a lot of people at TCL. I knew we had to get along with them. [But] you're not real comfortable walking into a lion's den, being held accountable for everything under the sun."

Myers continued to be wary of the sportsmen for some time—until he encountered their

Gary Myers congratulates Region IV's Tony Proffitt, named TWRA's Wildlife Officer of the Year for 1988. Many observers credit Myers with restoring morale at the beleaguered Game and Fish agency. Courtesy of TWRA..

unexpected support. "About the third year I was here, [TWRA] decided that these private acts were for the birds," especially the so-called "coon dog laws" which allowed certain counties to extend the dog-training seasons beyond the limits recommended by agency biologists. According to the scientists, raccoons were seriously weakened by dog chases, especially nursing females. But over the years, dozens of counties had persuaded the General Assembly to pass local laws that favored the hunters, not the coons.

Eventually the General Assembly decided to hold hearings across the state to determine the effectiveness of TWRA in these and other matters. Myers represented the agency at those hearings.

The first hearing was tough enough, said Myers, but the second one, in the town of Woodbury, was worse. "The coon hunters turned out *en masse* and pretty well crucified us. … I felt like the Lone Ranger."

A few days later Myers described the massacre to Tony Campbell. The League, of course, had been fighting private wildlife acts from the first; in 1985 it would sue the state in an effort to ban local exemptions.

"Tony got TCL to attend the rest of the meetings," said Myers, "and that's when it dawned on me that these guys are our friends—they're not our enemies. They have questions about programs, concerns about things. But when you get right down to it they really care about the well-being of the agency and the well-being of the programs."

Gary Myers trusted TCL after that. "I know that, if we misbehave, we'll likely be called to task—and we should. If our programs flounder, we'll likely be called to task—and we should. But if anyone wants to demolish us, TCL will be there."

TRYING TO PRIME THE CASH PUMP

Bob Burns likes to tell how, shortly after accepting the executive director's job, Tony Campbell spent the night in Knoxville with Burns and his wife. "Tony said to me, 'One thing I want to know—how are you guys going to pay me?' And I said, 'You have to find it!'"

Burns was only half in jest. Raising money was listed in his job description as one of Campbell's primary tasks; it would soon become one of his most chronic headaches. The board had approved a 1972-73 budget of $43,000, yet by mid-1972, more than half of its affiliates—54 of the 100 clubs still on the rolls—were seriously delinquent. In the confusion of setting up a new office, checks sometimes went undeposited for weeks while they made their way from one forwarding address to the next. Bills went unpaid, and in September, barely three months after opening shop, the League was forced to borrow five thousand dollars from its savings account to cover rent and salaries. In fact, there would be many months when Campbell drew no salary at all. By late 1976, the League owed Campbell (now earning fourteen thousand dollars a year) more than twenty thousand dollars in back pay. (Campbell came to consider this a sort of direct-deposit savings account, as he and his new wife Ronnie were building a house. The deficit, most of it, anyway, would eventually be repaid.)

But tight belts are a way of life with most nonprofits; at any rate, that was how it would always be with the League. Dues went up almost yearly in an effort to keep up with expenses: affiliates were paying $1.50 per member by 1979, and individual dues had doubled to ten dollars. For most of the decade, all of the bookwork was done by the office manager—who also handled most of the typing, the filing, the membership relations, the special events and so on. One hardly wonders that Tony Campbell went through three assistants in the first four years.

By 1976, however, the League had a keeper. Sue Garner, whose husband Kenneth worked for the U.S. Fish and Wildlife Service, took the secretary's job in part because she was a sort of good old girl herself, a woman who liked to hunt and fish and boil crawdads. Garner soon became as much a fixture of the League as Campbell himself, and just as indispensable. Somehow she always managed to get the bills paid, even when the checking account seemed to have run dry.

Part of the problem, of course, was that neither Campbell nor the majority of the board had any experience (and really, no burning interest) in fund raising. Besides Lucius Burch himself, Joe Criswell may have been the most notable exception. When he left on his well-publicized "Bicentenary Conservation Walkathon" in mid-March 1976, the forty-eight-year-old Criswell carried little more than a sack of apples and a stack of conservation literature. (A friend accompanied him on horseback.) When he arrived at Fort Nashboro three weeks and 185 miles later, arriving during the League's 1976 convention, he presented president Al Ballinger with $3,225 in donations and pledges.

It was great public relations. However, getting a few well-wishers to pledge a nickel a mile

Three weeks after he began, Joe Criswell (in the white shirt) completes his 1976 Bicentenary Conservation Walkathon from Dyersburg to Nashville. President Al Ballinger (far left) accepts $3,225 in pledges, most of it raised by Doris Burkhead (far right), who used her CB radio to solicit donations. Gene Fisher accompanied Criswell on horseback while Molly Ward (in costume) walked intermittent stretches. Beside her is Tony Campbell. Photo by Bob Steber. Copyright © The Tennessean. Used with permission.

was one thing. Getting corporations and wealthy individuals to pledge thousands of dollars for the endowment was another. Yet it was thought to be feasible. A Dallas fund-raising consultant told the board in 1973 that the conservation-minded citizens of Tennessee could easily support a $100,000 fund drive; heck, they could support $500,000. The board was delighted to hear it. In October, they announced the start of a half-million dollar fund-raising campaign.

Of course, with neither an aggressive solicitation plan nor a professional fund-raising team, this figure was nothing short of absurd. Trolling successfully for big money takes salesmanship, experience and ceaseless legwork. Tony Campbell would much rather deal with issues, and his board of directors, though they had all vowed their active support, failed to produce more than a handful of significant pledges. As Lucius Burch, Jr., noted, in some annoyance, a year or two into the drive, "We've got a lot of good Chiefs in the Tennessee Conservation League but we seem to be pretty short of Indians."

The result was that the Meeman grant which Burch had worked so hard to secure was in serious jeopardy from the start. To be sure, the first rounds of direct-mail appeals had been encouraging, netting an average pledge of twenty-five dollars from more than a thousand doctors, dentists and other targeted audiences within the first few years. But as Burch saw it, the League had spent $20,000 to raise $25,000—not all of which had been collected. By February 1974, Burch was calling the matching fund campaign "the biggest fiasco that I have seen in a long lifetime of observing efforts to raise money."

THE DIFFICULTY OF DIVERSIFYING

Moreover, despite the high ambitions of the 1971 special evaluation report, TCL still was not linking up with the hundreds of potential supporters in such groups as the Sierra Club

Sue Garner joined the League in 1976 as office manager, bookkeeper and pretty much everything else. Garner loved hunting and fishing, she loved LSU football and she especially loved the members of TCL—and they her. TCL file photo.

and the Audubon Societies. The League "ha[d] been working very closely with these groups" on certain issues, Tony Campbell hastened to assure Burch in June 1973, and, he was pleased to note, it had recently affiliated with the all-black Nashville Sportsman's Club. The League had even briefly considered merging with the Tennessee Environmental Council, the broadest of the broad-based environmental groups. But that suggestion had gone nowhere, nor does former TEC director Ruth Neff recall any formal efforts by the League to recruit TEC members. In short, Campbell told Burch, "we seem to have run up against a brick wall" in creating the diversified base of support required by the Meeman grant.

But the clock was still ticking toward that $100,000 deadline. On the first weekend in December 1974, the League made another effort to plot a wider course when it hosted the third annual "Intergroup Conference" at Henry Horton State Park. Intergroup had started in 1972, when Tennessee Citizens for Wilderness Planning hosted a large gathering of environmental leaders for a weekend of seminars and discussions on wilderness issues. So enthusiastic was the response that Ruth Neff and the TEC agreed to organize a second Intergroup the following year. But coordinating speakers, housing, meals, meeting space and entertainment for many dozens of people was no small task. When the 1973 meeting was over, the major groups, TCL among them, agreed to try rotating the job on an annual basis. Thus it was that the League came to be in charge of Intergroup '74, focusing on the theme of water resources. The rotation idea did not stick, however. By 1976, the responsibility for hosting Intergroup had lodged permanently with TEC.

In its early years especially, Intergroup was a dynamic, exciting weekend event, and the League, naturally, had hoped to find some common ground, perhaps even pick up a few new members. But that did not happen. The sort of folks who enjoyed Intergroup were not, frankly, the sort of folks who enjoyed hunting and fishing and dressing up in camouflage. Eventually the League hardly went to Intergroup at all.

THE LEAGUE MAKES THE MEEMAN DEADLINE

Clearly, the League was still hampered by its reputation as a hunting and fishing club for men, and to many mainstream environmentalists, anything to do with guns or blood sports was repugnant. Never mind that the League's emphasis was supposed to be changing; the perception was still there, and it was hard to shake. Some members, apparently, did not care to try. According to Ruth Neff, "some TCL members were not very welcoming" to this new generation of activists; there was even, she said, some "active hostility." (At a land-use planning symposium in 1975, one TCL member actually called Dr. Neff a communist.) This failure to connect was unfortunate for both sides, of course, but perhaps more so for TCL: without new blood, the League might forfeit the Meeman grant.

In fact, it came dangerously close to doing so. Though the League's budget had risen to more than $60,000 by the end of 1976, only a few months before the Meeman deadline, only $27,000 had been deposited in the endowment account, barely a fourth of the $100,000 needed to secure the grant (and a laughable fraction of the half-million-dollar fantasy figure set in 1973). In fact, the only reason the League was able to announce, in May of 1977, that it had finally reached the Meeman goal was that the entire unmet balance—slightly more than

$77,000—had been quietly paid by a single individual.

Though the League had no desire to publicize either the gift or its terms, the donor was J. Clark Akers, III, a wealthy Nashville contractor and one of four duck hunters who sued the U.S. Army Corps of Engineers in 1970 to stop its channelization project in the Obion and Forked Deer River Basin. There were certain strings attached to the gift, however. Over the next four years, the League had to donate one-half the amount of Akers' gift—roughly $38,000—back to the National Ecological Foundation.

The board, of course, could hardly afford to quibble. The interest alone on the Meeman endowment—fifteen thousand to twenty thousand dollars a year—should be more than enough to pay the commitment to the NEF.

So even though the Meeman challenge did not, strictly speaking, attract the broad financial support it was designed to do, it did leave the League with a sizable endowment. Moreover, there can be little doubt that this five-year carrot helped spur the League to comply (partly if not perfectly) with the goals outlined in the 1971 evaluation report.

THE DEBUT OF *TENNESSEE OUT-OF-DOORS*

In at least partial fulfillment of its pledge to improve communications, the League could now hold up not one but two regular publications. *Tennessee Tracks* was a briefing paper mailed to the membership on a more or less monthly basis, sometimes less often, but sometimes weekly during legislative sessions. Much more substantial was *Tennessee Out-Of-Doors*, which debuted in August 1973 following a brief, failed partnership with something called *Tennessee Sportsman News,* another in the long series of short-lived outdoor magazines.

Tennessee Out-Of-Doors was a sixteen-page, tabloid-style newsletter, mailed free each month to every TCL member, including members of affiliate clubs. The format of the paper, and roughly half of its editorial content, including Lou Clapper's "Washington Watch," were provided for a fee by the National Wildlife Federation. The other half was devoted to League news, items from affiliates and a more or less monthly message from Tony Campbell (who was listed on the masthead as editor). Since the paper was a costly undertaking (eight hundred to a thousand dollars per issue), it also contained advertising. By the end of the decade, the League was letting its affiliates sell the lucrative centerfold ads in return for a share of the revenues.

Apparently the newspapers were expensive for the National Wildlife Federation as well. In early 1982, the Federation advised its affiliates that it would no longer be offering the newspaper service. *T-O-D* ceased publication during the summer months while the board debated whether it could continue producing the newsletter without NWF's help.

They decided they had no choice. For many members, *T-O-D* was the best conservation news they got. In September 1982, *Tennessee Out-Of-Doors* reappeared, a few pages shorter and without the usual wildlife sketches on the cover (no great loss), but otherwise not much changed. True, it no longer had the benefit of Lou Clapper's excellent political commentary, and it now came out only every other month. But all things considered, *T-O-D* continued to be a commendable effort, particularly given that the League never had a bona fide editor nor even a full-time communications professional.

BROADENING HORIZONS

The League had also, after some resistance, reworked the old committee structure. In 1973, the "committee to restructure the composition of committees" reshaped the board into two categories: five "action" committees (wildlife; fisheries; environmental quality; outdoor recreation; sportsmen); and ten "administrative" committees (credentials; awards; resolutions; legislative affairs; constitution and bylaws; nominating; program, planning and agenda; audit, budget and dues; national affairs; environmental information, education, publications and public relations). By the time chairman Charles Rhea died in summer 1976, the new structure was functioning reasonably well, though many committee heads continued to respond "no report" when called on for an update of their activities.

Even the League's efforts to diversify had not been entirely fruitless. In 1972, for instance, it had managed to recruit its first female board member. Nashvillian Carol Knauth was not a hunter but a birder who wrote natural history and birding columns for the *Nashville Banner, The Tennessee Conservationist* and sometimes *T-O-D* itself. Though she served for one term only, her presence was an important milestone. As Knauth herself said in her resignation letter, "A woman on the board (or women) and one or more non-hunters were essential to the new concept of the TCL, and I was willing to serve as both, symbolically, to break the ice, which has been done."

The board was also trying to build a more active relationship with Tennessee businesses. In 1974 it created nine at-large seats, partly in hopes of attracting "the brains and ability" of the private sector. Soon thereafter, Hugh McDade, a public relations executive with ALCOA and a former Game and Fish chairman, became the League's first official representative from industry. In that same year, the League even took a stand for the physically disabled. Tom Rollins, a popular outdoor writer from Clinton, was confined to a wheelchair. Though an avid fisherman and occasional hunter, Rollins sometimes fell out of his wheelchair on uneven ground, an awkward and at times embarrassing situation for both him and his companions. In 1974 TCL led a call, successfully, for handicapped-accessible fishing platforms on some of Tennessee's fishing lakes.

A WIDER AGENDA: THE ENVIRONMENTAL BOARDS

As its demographic profile had widened, so had the League's agenda. By degrees, hunting and fishing issues were making way for wider-reaching ones as scenic beauty, energy conservation and endangered species. In 1974, the League helped pass Tennessee's first nongame protections via the Nongame and Endangered or Threatened Wildlife Species Conservation Act. By the end of the decade it was speaking out against billboards and litter and calling for container deposit legislation, otherwise known as the bottle bill. Though TCL never took more than a polite interest in things like wind power or solar energy (leadership on these issues fell to the Environmental Council and the Tennessee Solar Energy Association), it at least gave them fairly regular coverage in *Tennessee Out-Of-Doors*. (When the gas crunch of 1974 forced TCL to cancel the winter board meeting, the debate suddenly became more than academic.)

Beginning around 1971, the League had also accepted a formal role on both of the state's environmental regulatory boards. These were not mere sinecures. Both the Air Pollution Control Board and the Water Quality Control Board were rule-making bodies; they also served as the jury in case of an appeal. Though both boards were dominated by private and municipal interests, both had designated one seat specifically for "a representative of conservation interests." As the best-known conservation group in the state, it often fell to TCL to name the water board designee. In the case of the air pollution board, TCL *had* to choose the nominee under the terms of the air quality control law.

Often (though not always) the League chose from its own ranks. The early records are sketchy, but according to Ron Culberson, chief administrative officer for the division, TCL's first nominee to the Air Pollution Control Board was Erlewood Barden, a TCL member and businessman from Memphis (and later a member of the Conservation Commission and the State Parks Foundation). Barden was succeeded by another TCL member, Nashville attorney Edward G. Holt. Vanderbilt engineering professor (and non-TCL member) Dr. Karl Schnelle served two terms, followed by retired TVA engineer (and League stalwart) Bob Burns in 1986. (Ten years later, Burns was still there, hoping to finish a third term.)

TCL's first appointment to the Water Quality Control Board was Dr. Lester Dudney, a past TCL president and former Game and Fish chairman. Dudney served two terms, but in later years the League would nominate members from the Environmental Council, the League of Women Voters and the Scenic Rivers Association. TSRA's Ann Tidwell, for instance, who served in the mid-'80s, was considered one of the most competent members in the board's history. Obviously, what mattered to the League was not whether the appointee belonged to the League, but whether he or she knew anything about clean water—or even cared.

Unfortunately, neither could be said about Dr. Clifton Timanus. In 1978, ignoring the nominees offered by TCL and the Tennessee Environmental Council, Governor Ray Blanton appointed Dr. Timanus to the "conservation interests" seat on the Water Quality Control Board.

The problem was, nobody in the conservation community had ever heard of Clifton Timanus. The only credential he could claim was membership in the Wally Byron Caravan Club International. The Humboldt dentist did not even know what he had been appointed to. "What is this Water Quality Board anyway?" he asked reporters. "I still don't know what it involves."

The League and the Environmental Council threatened a lawsuit. But before they could act, Timanus quit the board "voluntarily." According to *The Jackson Sun,* Timanus said that he resigned because staying on was not worth "all the fuss and fight." But in fact, Timanus had already been sued by the state's attorney general. Timanus had allegedly tried to bribe two water quality officials into hurrying through some strip mining permits. Timanus called the charges "trumped up," and pointed out that they had been dropped. That was true, acknowledged *The Sun*—but only because the attorney general had agreed to drop them if Timanus agreed to leave quietly.

LAND-USE PLANNING: FIRST RIPPLES IN THE WAVE OF THE FUTURE

As Tony Campbell noted in one of his letters to Lucius Burch, the League in the mid-1970s made its first formal entry into one of the newest of the new environmental issues: land-use planning. Until now, land had been the most neglected of the country's nonrenewable natural resources. As Ruth Neff noted in a series of articles (1973-1976) in *The Tennessee Conservationist*, "While our population is growing, our supply of land remains constant. ... We no longer have any frontier; we have no land where a landowner may 'do as he pleases' with his land without affecting his neighbors—individually and collectively."

Neff went on to list some of the typical sources of conflict: prime farm lands lost to shopping centers and subdivisions. Wetlands drained and channelized for farms. Established neighborhoods disrupted by highways. Parks lost to condominiums. Industries forced to locate miles from the work force. Ecosystems sacrificed for strip malls. "Examples are legion," she concluded; "the need for integrated land-use planning and management is clear." Yet by 1974 a bill to establish a statewide land-use policy and process had already been rejected three times by the General Assembly.

In February 1975, supported by a grant from the Tennessee Committee for the Humanities, TEC and TCL cosponsored a land-use planning symposium at Henry Horton State Park. The day-long event drew 250 people, including developers, academics, city and county planners, conservationists, zoning officials and representatives of the agriculture and forest products industries. Though this was the same meeting where Ruth Neff was accused of being a communist, Tony Campbell would later describe the symposium as the start of "an outstanding, continuing dialogue."

By the end of the year TCL had formed something called the Resource Agency Coordinating Committee, an effort to keep the discussion going, at least among federal and state agencies. (Other than TCL itself, no citizen groups were included.) Among its member agencies were TVA, EPA, the U.S. Fish and Wildlife Service, the Soil Conservation Service, the Corps of Engineers, TWRA (that is, the old Game and Fish Commission), the Department of Conservation and the various environmental quality divisions of the Tennessee Department of Public Health. Only the local heads of these agencies were invited, said Campbell; no substitutions allowed.

"There were always battles down in the lower levels," Campbell explained; "turf fights. We figured if you could ever get the heads together you could prevent these problems." Their afternoon meetings were informal, and usually featured a Mexican meal prepared by Campbell himself. But despite its "laid-back" tone, he said, the committee stayed active for four or five years. Colonel Henry Hatch of the Corps of Engineers "actually drew up a constitution."

One of the issues that came out of the Henry Horton meeting was the need for tax relief for those who chose, for public-spirited reasons, *not* to develop all of their land. Land values were skyrocketing, especially around urban areas. But because property was assessed according to its *potential* value, not its current use, a farm in Brentwood might pay the same taxes as if it were being used for an office park.

Bill Terry was with the State Planning Office at the time; Terry was also a leader in the Tennessee Chapter of the Sierra Club. With the help of Ed Thackston, who was now on TCL's board, Terry drafted a conservation easement bill for agricultural and forest lands. It provoked, as they knew it would, much discussion. State Representative Mike Murphy wanted the bill to include tax breaks for urban open space. K. C. Dodson of the Tennessee Farm Bureau Federation wanted the bill to remove penalties should a farmer later want to sell previously covenanted lands. By the time it passed, said Terry, the bill didn't look much like the one he had written. But at least it was on the books. The Agricultural, Forest and Open Space Land Act passed in 1976.

The Greenbelt Law, as it was called, was widely abused, and even the Resource Agency Coordinating Committee eventually petered out. Nonetheless, these early nods to land-use planning were significant, if only because they got people talking about what was sure to be a persistent problem, with implications not only for the environment but for the economy, the legal system, even patterns of social and cultural behavior.

Yet as stubborn as these and other issues may have been (the League never did get a bottle bill passed, for instance), what mattered was that they were being tackled at all. Having broadened TCL's horizons, having diversified its goals as well as its membership, the board could now consider its debt to Ed Meeman discharged.

THE BATTLE TO BAN LEAD SHOT

Of course, some hunting and fishing issues were every bit as contentious as land-use planning or any of those other "broad-based" issues. A case in point was the long and bitter fight to ban lead shot in the 1970s. The Game and Fish Commission supported the ban relatively early in the debate; but the general membership of the League stubbornly refused to concede for nearly a decade. The League always liked to say that its decisions were based on evidence, not emotion. However, its rejection of nontoxic steel shot was clearly based on neither: it was based almost entirely on economics.

For almost a century the evidence had been mounting that lead pellets from hunters' shotguns, when swallowed by feeding waterfowl, eventually poisoned the birds. The alarm had been sounded as early as 1894, when George Bird Grinnell warned in the February 1894 issue of *Forest and Stream* that lead-poisoned ducks were "dumpy, stupid and stagger in their walk," and suffered from convulsions, vomiting and respiratory problems.

In the years that followed, numerous studies backed up Grinnell's observations. In 1919, a biologist with the Bureau of Biological Survey determined that as few as two or three swallowed pellets could be fatal; gizzards taken from poisoned birds often contained as many as forty. By the 1970s, the U.S. Fish and Wildlife Service reported that as many as two million or more waterfowl were dying from lead poisoning each year—one for every bird killed intentionally by duck hunters.

In 1965 the Mississippi Flyway Council, of which Tennessee was a part, urged that the waterfowl-hunting industry find an alternative to lead shot. In 1970 the International Association of Game, Fish and Conservation Commissioners recommended the use of nontoxic steel (actually soft iron) by all waterfowlers. In 1972, the National Wildlife Federation put a similar request to the Interior Department, and in 1976, having completed a final environmental impact statement, the U.S. Fish and Wildlife Service announced that it was imposing a gradual, nationwide ban on lead shot, commencing with the Atlantic Flyway where mortality was greatest. (By 1977 the ban included parts of Tennessee.)

Ronnie Pritchard, Bill Hackett, Jack Beasley and Steve McCord get their opening-day limit at Camden Wildlife Management Area in the late '70s. According to Pritchard, his party had "excellent results" using steel shot. Courtesy of Ronnie Pritchard.

The resulting clamor was immediate. Most duck hunters refused to believe that lead poisoning was anything but a bureaucratic tempest in a teapot. Because the victims tended to die quietly and by degrees, few hunters were aware that they had even seen poisoned waterfowl, much less contributed to their deaths. Besides, complained the hunters, steel shot cost twice as much as lead. (This was true.) They also said it would ruin their guns, but this was not true. It may have been true at first, but ballistics engineers had eventually corrected the problem. They said the shorter trajectory and slighter impact of steel would result in greater numbers of maimed and crippled birds, but this was not true, either. Extensive tests conducted by Remington and other firearms manufacturers proved that a hunter could soon adapt his aim to the different ballistic properties of steel. Finally, the hunters whined, steel shot might even cripple *them*, since it often exploded inside gun barrels. This charge was true only in the rarest and most preventable of instances.

In 1976 the National Rifle Association sued the U.S. Fish and Wildlife Service, charging that a steel-shot mandate would lead to more firearms injuries. That suit was promptly rejected, but Congress kept the issue burning by declaring in 1978 that it was up to the states whether or not to ban lead shot. (This ruling, an amendment to the Interior Department's appropriations bill, forbade the use of federal funds to impose or enforce a ban on lead shot without the state's consent.)

The Stevens Amendment, as the ruling was called, created a major headache for state wildlife agencies. As TWRA biologist and information officer Ged Petit wrote in *Tennessee Wildlife* in 1978, the agency was "far from happy" over the issue. Nevertheless, said Petit, when TWRA researchers opened the gizzards of eight hundred ducks in a 1977-1978 study, they found a "significant" percentage of ducks had ingested lead. Petit was an avid hunter himself, but the resource had to come first: TWRA would side with its fellow state agencies in supporting the ban. (When Ged Petit died in a single-car accident in 1992 at fifty-three, the League created the Ged Petit TWRA Education Award in his honor.)

Back in 1978, however, even Ged Petit's tactful diplomacy failed to impress most of the state's sportsmen—not even those in the Tennessee Conservation League. Though Tony Campbell supported the ban and offered numerous studies to support it, he could not force the membership to go along. For years, their official position was one of "let's wait and see."

Outdoor writer Sam Venable covered the League's 1977 annual convention in Jackson. Someone had filed a resolution rejecting the ban, but before it came to a vote, Campbell made one last appeal. Delegates listened politely enough, then voted to reject the ban anyway.

"It was probably one of the few times I saw Tony really frustrated," recalled Venable. "You really missed this one," he told the delegates. "You let petty interests get the better of you."

It was not until the early 1980s, when a handful of bald eagles died after eating lead-poisoned prey, that the League finally relented. A resolution passed at the 1985 annual convention in Nashville represented a complete reversal of all the League's earlier objections.

"ILLITERATE BOOZING SLOBS": THE ANTI-HUNTING DEBATE

There may have been another reason besides "petty interests" that the nation's sportsmen were so slow to accept steel shot. They may have resented the ban as another attempt to restrict—in however roundabout a way—their freedom to bear arms. It was an issue they were particularly sensitive about in the mid-'70s. The national debate over gun control and its corollary, the anti-hunting movement, had been smoldering since at least the late 1960s. Cleveland Amory's Fund for Animals had tried, for instance, to ban bowhunting in California in 1974; the Humane Society had earlier sued the Interior Department to ban archery and muzzleloader hunts on certain federal wildlife refuges. Both these efforts had outraged sportsmen across the country.

But nothing galvanized them like *The Guns of Autumn*.

The Guns of Autumn was a ninety-minute TV special that aired on CBS on September 5, 1975. Even to an impartial observer it seemed deliberately inflammatory, showing waterfowlers opening fire thirty minutes before legal shooting time, deer hunters dragging a struggling animal out of the woods and big-game hunters picking off bears at the city dump.

The response from the hunting public was instant, deafening—and furious. "*The Guns of Autumn* ... should receive an award for the most biased TV reporting of the year, possibly of the decade," wrote C. Boyd Pfeiffer in the *Washington Post*. The show was "an insult, a deliberate affront to the vast majority of hunters who know and love their sport, their game and the outdoors."

"This is the most distorted picture of the American hunter I have ever seen," said Thomas Washington, head of the Michigan United Conservation Clubs. The MUCC had agreed to help CBS make the documentary, Washington said, "only after assurance by the documentary producer, Mr. Irv Drasnin, that the show would be used to promote hunting as a wholesome recreational pursuit and in the best tradition of its American heritage." Instead, Washington fumed, "Mr. Drasnin and CBS have attempted to brand some twenty million American hunters as illiterate boozing slobs." Filmed sequences were "grossly exaggerated" or "falsely portrayed," he said; his own words were taken out of context or used to provide voiceovers for sequences he had no part in producing. (The MUCC eventually filed a $300 million libel suit against CBS, but it was not successful.)

In Tennessee, outdoor writers flayed the program with equal vehemence in their columns. "In a half century, I have never seen anything during actual hunting to equal the atrocious and brutal scene of spurious hunters repeatedly shooting a white deer with a handgun, eventually making pictures of it gasping," sputtered Doc Jernigan in the *Manchester Times*. Robert S. "Doc" Hines, a Cleveland dentist and another past president of the League, fired off an angry protest letter to one of the show's advertisers, then sent a copy to Tony Campbell, adding in a postscript, "I don't know what your thoughts are, but we are mad as an old wet hen."

The League, in fact, was flooded by calls and letters. Members clearly expected a strong response from their executive director. Campbell was as disgusted as anyone by what he referred to as "a 'documentary' (ha-ha)." Only months earlier, he had worked with TWRA and a Nashville production company to design a sixty-second public-service announcement promoting hunting as a morally-acceptable sport. (The spot featured country singer Loretta Lynn and her husband Mooney, chatting in their kitchen. According to the storyboard, Mooney was to make the point that for most hunters, enjoying nature was more important than shooting some defenseless critter: "i.e. he went hunting the other day and bagged no game, but saw a bald eagle soaring which made the outing worthwhile and memorable.")

However, as head of an organization whose members in fact were *not* all hunters, who even, in a few cases, favored strong gun controls, Campbell could not afford the pleasure of name-calling. Whatever his response, he knew that it would be judged not only by his own constituency but by members of the press, the Legislature and the non-hunting environmental groups the League was still hoping to attract. But Campbell was a shrewd rhetorical strategist, his style a well-balanced blend of firmness and tact, of concession and demand, always tailored to the needs and prejudices of his audience.

"I am sure that no informed hunter will deny that hunters such as [those] portrayed [*in The Guns of Autumn*] exist," he began in a protest letter to CBS. "[B]ut we feel that the vast majority of America's twenty million hunters do not even resemble those seen on the show." In a letter to the Federal Communications Commission, he noted that "[i]n a time when the credibility of the electronic media (especially television) is suffering, we feel it behooves the [FCC] to require CBS to produce a factual documentary on hunting and wildlife conservation in America." And to a Dunlap physician who wrote that he had spent many hours "looking for bullets in corpses," and who wanted to know the League's position on gun control before he sent in his renewal check, Campbell replied soothingly, "Like you, I have laid [sic] awake many nights trying to analyze the problem and in my own mind find some way to come to grips with it."

Whether or not the doctor renewed his membership is not known, but Campbell was right when he said that the League had a "somewhat middle-of-the-road attitude" on firearms control. It was true, of course, that "all of our members are very concerned with the increase in all types of crime in recent years." But it was also true (though Campbell did not mention it) that "protect[ing] the right to bear arms" was one of the League's founding purposes, included in the original bylaws and later deleted only so TCL could qualify for an IRS tax exemption. He also did not mention that the Tennessee State Rifle Association, an NRA affiliate, was not only one of the largest member groups of the League; its newsletter was being carried each month in the pages of *Tennessee Out-Of-Doors*. (This arrangement did not last long, however.)

Not that the League had any quarrel with the National Rifle Association in those days, said Campbell. In fact, at one time both the League and the National Wildlife Federation worked closely with the NRA to teach gun safety and hunter education to youngsters. No longer. Now, said Campbell, "They're paranoid. . . . You have to understand that the NRA has changed over the years." Not long ago, he said, "I was telling [an NRA representative] about those old hunter safety programs we used to do with the kids. 'Oh,' he said, 'we'd really oppose that now.'"

Passionate as folks were about the anti-hunting and gun control debate, however, it really did not rank as a major issue for the League. For most of the '70s it remained a background issue, blazing up from time to time but usually dying down just as quickly. If *The Guns of Autumn* was a brush fire, however, the West Tennessee Tributaries Flood Control Project was a conflagration—a vast, hot, unthinkably complex issue that burned on for years, sometimes quietly, sometimes violently, consuming vast quantities of time, money and energy, and often igniting the many other issues that lay in its path.

OBION-FORKED DEER: THE BIG BATTLE OVER THE BIG DITCH

One of the most interesting lessons in man-made geography can be had by comparing a modern map of Tennessee to a map from the turn of the century. On an old map, in the northwest quadrant of the state dominated by the Obion and Forked Deer Rivers, the observer will see a bloom of tributaries spreading eastward from the Mississippi River like a network of tiny veins across a retina. It is hard to tell where one stream leaves off and another starts. In fact, though the Obion is technically one river system and the Forked Deer to its south is another, they are part of the same vast watershed, a series of primary and secondary forks that finally come together at Moss Island before flowing the last few miles into the Mississippi.

Now, look at a modern map of the same area. Instead of oxbows and meanders, the watershed looks like a pile of pick-up sticks, all angles and straightedges. This odd regularity doesn't look natural, and it isn't. It's the result of decades of flood control via channelization—the physical straightening of naturally meandering rivers.

Congress authorized the West Tennessee Tributaries Flood Control Project (WTTP) in 1948, though the work didn't begin until 1961. The plan called for the U.S. Army Corps of Engineers to channelize 241 of the roughly 350 miles of streams in the Obion and Forked Deer River Basin in an effort to minimize flood damage to surrounding farmlands. In those days, channelization was one of the Corps' preferred means of floodplain management, with projects from the Platte River in Nebraska to the Kissimmee in Florida. (The Kissimmee River

Canal, dug in the mid-'60s, proved such an ecological disaster by the 1970s that the Florida Legislature made the Corps undo it.)

In West Tennessee, a region where streams are known to overflow their banks for half the days in a year, channelization dated almost to the turn of the century. One old-timer remembered watching in 1918 as a wooden dredgeboat a hundred feet long and sixty-nine feet wide ploughed furrows in the Forked Deer near Dyersburg. During the 1920s and 1930s, private interests did "extensive dredging" in nearly all the major rivers in the region, including the Loosahatchie and the Wolf as well as the Obion and Forked Deer. (Today, only the main stem of the Hatchie has never been channelized).

What they were trying to do, of course, was keep the rivers from flooding so often, for such long periods and at such inconvenient times, that is, during the spring planting season. The nearly three million acres that comprise the Obion-Forked Deer watershed contain some of the most productive agricultural lands in the state, as well as extensive bottomland hardwoods and nearly a fifth of the state's total cropland. Because the basin is so flat, however, it doesn't take much of a downpour before the surrounding floodplain is under water, drowning crops, killing timber stands and ruining homes and outbuildings. Moreover, because so much of the area has been cleared for planting, and because its soils are already so highly erodible (mostly a mixture of sand and loess), the basin also has the highest rate of erosion in the state, an estimated 25 million tons of topsoil washed away each year.

As the rivers flow slowly on toward the Mississippi, they deposit this silt load along their outer edges, where the waters move slowest. Eventually these deposits constrict the waterway, creating small levees and sandbars and slowing the stream even further. Sometimes trees and other debris get hung up on the sandbars, creating a sort of natural dam. A meandering stream, one that hasn't been tampered with, will usually just flow around these obstructions, creating a new oxbow here, a small island there. However, if the waters happen to be particularly high, as they often are in winter and early spring, the river floods. It is all part of a marvelously efficient natural system, and nobody would complain if nobody lived in the river. (Technically, a river is defined not by its center line but by the area it reliably floods in various cycles, such as the ten-year or hundred-year floodplain.)

The logical solution, one might think, would be to prohibit people from buying, building or planting in these flood zones. In fact, the 1961 Tennessee General Assembly even considered a Comprehensive Flood Land Use Planning Act to "prevent unwise encroachment and building development" within critical areas of floodplain.

Unfortunately, no amount of human intervention has ever fully succeeded in correcting what is the fundamental folly of living or planting in a floodplain. Frequent flooding is a natural part of the hydrologic cycle in West Tennessee. Floodplains serve as the stabilizers that allow flood waters to recede by degrees, minimizing erosion, reducing siltation and safeguarding aquatic life. At the same time, each flood serves to recharge the surrounding wetlands—those soggy, ecologically teeming transitional zones that act as natural sponges for the watershed, soaking up floodwaters, filtering out silt and other impurities, maintaining groundwater levels and providing vital habitat for a rich variety of plants, fish, waterfowl, birds, insects and assorted useful microorganisms.

Yet as recently as twenty or thirty years ago, wetlands were still reviled as "swamps" in this country. Landowners were allowed, even encouraged, to drain, clear, fill and farm every last acre of them. During droughts, they rushed to plant the exposed bottoms. Then, when the rains returned, they howled in dismay as their new crops disappeared from view. Some farmers climbed into their bulldozers and drove out into the streams and opened the channels themselves. Others built levees or constructed crude dams. Still others took their complaints to their legislators. And the legislators, unwilling to tell their constituents they shouldn't be living in a floodplain in the first place, took their complaints to the agency in charge of channels: the U.S. Army Corps of Engineers. Thus it was that in 1948, Congress gave the Corps the go-ahead to dredge the Obion and Forked Deer Rivers.

Before the West Tennessee Tributaries Project could get underway, however, the nation had begun its slow drift toward environmentalism. In 1958, a new Fish and Wildlife Coordination Act stipulated that "wildlife conservation shall receive equal consideration and be coordinated with other features of [federal] water-resource development programs." It also stated that if a single-purpose federal project destroyed wildlife habitat, the agency building the project "shall" mitigate the damage to the habitat. Since the WTTP was a single-purpose project (its purpose being to improve agriculture), the 1958 Coordination Act almost certainly would apply.

After all, farming wasn't the only thing folks did in West Tennessee. According to the Tennessee Game and Fish Commission, waterfowl hunting was worth an estimated $2.25 million a year to the local economy by 1958. In fact, the commission had recently made it a priority to add to its meager waterfowl hunting grounds in the area, identifying at least seven wetlands for acquisition. In 1958, it had finally scraped together enough money to buy the first two tracts: 1,500 acres on the Forked Deer near Tigrett and 3,500 acres on Moss Island, a stone's throw from the Mississippi on the Obion. Gooch WMA, also on the Obion, was acquired a few years later.

In 1958, and with a sizable real estate investment now at stake, the Game and Fish Commission began conducting its own studies of the proposed drainage project. Charles Hendrix, wetlands project leader for the commission, summed up his findings in a July 1959 article in *The Tennessee Conservationist.* "If the drainage project is done as a single purpose project without regard for wildlife[,] then our waterfowl hunting would be greatly damaged if not completely ruined," he wrote. But "[i]f this is carried out as a multipurpose project with wildlife given the consideration deserved, then waterfowl hunting might not be hurt too badly, if at all." A spokesman for the Corps seemed to agree, pointing out that his agency had "very effectively" incorporated the multiple-use concept in recent projects on the Cumberland River. Nonetheless, he added significantly, Corps projects "must ultimately provide the greatest good for the greatest number of people."

In 1961, the first subcontractors went to work. Over the next decade, they would channelize (or re-channelize) seventy-seven miles of the basin, mostly along the Obion. But in April 1970, the dredging suddenly stopped—and would not resume again for fifteen years. The way had been blocked by four Nashville duck hunters.

Joking around at Reelfoot Lake, J. Clark Akers makes a hat out of a lily pad. But he wasn't joking in 1970, when he and three fellow duck hunters went after the Corps of Engineers, charging that channelization in the Obion-Forked Deer River Basin was destroying prime wetlands and bottomland hardwoods. A federal court agreed. Courtesy of Clark Akers.

The Mice That Roared

As part owners of two hunting clubs on the Obion, the four men—J. Clark Akers, III, William W. Dillon, III, Dr. John Tudor and Dr. Sam Harwell—together laid claim to about 1,350 acres in the basin. It was a land of wild timber and pin oak, submerged throughout much of the fall and winter migration season—"a duck hunter's paradise," as one man put it. Unfortunately, the section of river that flowed through their property had been channelized before, and it was one of the first scheduled for dredging now. Several years earlier, a massive log jam at the Gooch railroad bridge had caused a severe flood, "swamping out" thousands of acres of good timber all the way into Weakley County. To the Corps, there was only one way to prevent such a thing from happening again: open up the old channel.

In 1963, Clark Akers recalls, the Corps contacted the twelve landowners, asking them to donate an easement so the project could proceed. Akers refused; so did three others. So the Corps simply condemned the land. Soon, what few trees had not been claimed by the flood were now felled by machines; the river became a broad, muddy ditch. The project lowered the river thirty feet; all the feeder creeks eroded down to the level of the main stream. Neighboring farmers "cleared every remaining tree and bush up to the banks and converted as many acres of timber as they could burn into bean fields."

Almost overnight, the duck hunter's paradise had become a duck hunter's nightmare.

For the next six years, said Akers, no more work was done in his area. But in 1969, he learned that the Corps had let a new contract that would extend the ditch into Weakley County—and into some of the best remaining duck habitat in the basin. Akers knew nothing about any Fish and Wildlife Coordination Act, but he decided to pay a visit to the Corps engineers anyway. Given the disaster in 1963, he said, shouldn't you guys at least *study* the effects of what you've done so far, before you do any more?

What Akers was suggesting, though of course he didn't realize it, was an environmental impact statement. The EIS did not come into official existence until New Year's Day 1970, when President Richard Nixon signed into law something called the National Environmental Policy Act. Section 102(C) of NEPA required that any "major federal actions … significantly affecting the quality of the human environment" must first prepare a detailed statement of impact, including a list of alternatives. Moreover, since NEPA could apply to projects started before 1970, the new law could—and eventually would—be applied to West Tennessee Tribs.

But NEPA was still a year away. As for the Fish and Wildlife Coordination Act, in the almost twelve years of its existence, it had never once been used to challenge a federal water project. Consequently, the Corps' spokesman saw no reason to accommodate his visitor. He listened politely, then replied, "If Congress gives us money, we're going to dig ditches."

THE LONG, SLOW ROAD OF LITIGATION

On April 23, 1970, Akers and his three fellow duck hunters sued the Secretary of the Army in U.S. District Court in Nashville. For legal reasons, *Akers v. Resor* also named the head of the Department of Interior, Tennessee Governor Buford Ellington, Tennessee Highway Commissioner Charles Speight and even Greer Ricketson as chairman of the Game and Fish Commission, though in fact all of these agencies sympathized with the plaintiffs and at least one of them, the Game and Fish Commission, was considering entering the lawsuit on their behalf. The channelization project had already destroyed some of the wetlands at Gooch Wildlife Management Area, and Tigrett would be next. The commission was demanding 44,000 acres of prime wetlands from the Corps as mitigation for the ones it was destroying. (Calvin Barstow, the Game and Fish biologist who wrote the mitigation plan, was named Wildlife Conservationist of the Year for 1970 by TCL.)

The 1970 lawsuit was by every measure a remarkable action. Suits brought by private individuals against giant government bureaucracies are fairly common nowadays, but not so in 1970. The idea that four duck hunters could overturn an entire economy was preposterous, unthinkable, un-American. In West Tennessee, whole towns sided with the Corps; Eighth District Congressman Ed Jones declared the drainage project "essential to the health and well-being" of every citizen. An editorial in *The Dyersburg Mirror* railed against wealthy sportsmen who "[sat] comfortably in their plush offices" in Nashville while Dyer County farmers braced for the next season of floods. Ironically, the floods were worse now than ever, but that was beside the point. "[I]t may have been a big mistake to have started the dredging years ago," conceded Henry Pierce, an outspoken landowner from Dyersburg, "but now that they have [started], they just can't leave us here to drown in a half-finished job."

Akers may have been brave, but he wasn't foolhardy. He and his partners knew that most judges would take a dim view of four people claiming to represent the conservation interests of the entire state. That was why they hired Charles H. Warfield, "one of the best courtroom lawyers in the state," according to Tony Campbell, and partly why they organized under the impressive-sounding name of the "National Ecological Foundation." It was also why they sought the support of the Conservation League.

THE CORPS, THE COURT AND THE PLAINTIFFS

In January 1971, the Tennessee Conservation League petitioned to enter the lawsuit as coplaintiff, along with its much bigger brother, the National Wildlife Federation. (The Sierra Club and the International Association of Game, Fish and Wildlife Commissioners intervened as friends of the court.) NWF and the League retained Charles Newman, a Memphis attorney who was already gaining some experience with NEPA.

Newman was the plaintiffs' attorney in what had become the highly visible Overton Park case. In 1969, two environmental groups had sued the U.S. Department of Transportation over the planned routing of Interstate 40 through Overton Park in Memphis. They based their case on a section of the Transportation Act of 1966 that said federal roads must avoid parks, wildlife areas and so on, unless no "feasible and prudent alternative" could be found. In 1970, Federal District Court Judge Bailey Brown dismissed the case, but it was appealed all the way to the U.S. Supreme Court. On March 2, 1971, the nine justices unanimously overturned the lower court's ruling. In the meantime, of course, NEPA had become law, so now, in addition to looking for alternative routes under the Transportation Act, the USDOT also had to prepare an environmental impact statement. In the end, the plaintiffs won. The stretch of Interstate 40 through Overton Park was abandoned. Today, the highway simply ends several blocks east of the park—diverts onto city streets—then picks up again several blocks to the west.

At any rate, the League was fortunate to have a good Memphis lawyer: at the Corps' request, *Akers v. Resor* had been moved from Nashville to Memphis. Thanks to the inevitable delays, continuances, hearings, injunctions and general quibblings, however, it would not actually go to trial until April 1972. In the meantime, the Corps was enjoined from doing further work in the basin while it prepared a mitigation plan. Its first proposal, offered for public review in early 1971, offered to give the state 14,400 acres of wetlands, including 9,000 acres next to the Gooch and Tigrett WMAs, in compensation for the wetlands it had destroyed. Speaking for the Game and Fish Commission, chairman Greer Ricketson doubted that 14,400 acres was a fair trade for the 220,000 acres likely to be affected by West Tennessee Tribs; 44,000 acres (the figure recommended by Cal Barstow) was more like it.

At about this time (early 1972), the U.S. attorney in the case, Thomas Turley, reminded the court that, under the Flood Control Act of 1936, the Corps of Engineers must have a local sponsoring agency to maintain the channels once they were cleared. Buford Ellington had volunteered the state of Tennessee to be the sponsoring agency back around 1960 when the WTTP first began. The Highway Department was put in charge of the maintenance work, even though "they didn't have so much as a canoe," as Clark Akers put it. In 1970, however, the General Assembly failed to make its usual appropriation for the channel work; no one seems to know exactly why. At any rate, in 1972, the state created an all-new sponsoring agency, the Obion-Forked Deer Basin Authority, to work with the Corps and generally "develop" the water and land resources in the basin.

When at last the case went to trial, the judge was Bailey Brown—the same judge who had ruled against the plaintiffs in the first stages of the Overton Park case. It could be a bad omen. But on the other hand, as one journalist noted, Overton Park had become a "hot potato" for Bailey Brown. He could be in no hurry to get burned again.

Testimony in the WTTP case lasted little more than a week, most of it not very flattering to the Corps. Expert witnesses testified how up to 95 percent of fish and wildlife habitat was at risk from the channelization; how farmers were already getting government subsidies *not* to farm in the floodplain; how the projected benefit-to-cost ratio of 1.1 to 1 was wildly exaggerated; even how the basin would in all likelihood continue to flood even *after* the project was finished. In fact, after pointed questioning, the head of the Dyer County Levee and Drainage District finally acknowledged that channelization upstream of Obion County would almost certainly make things worse for the folks in his county.

In May, Judge Brown delivered his ruling. The EIS was inadequate, he said. Until the Corps' engineers could come up with a better one, they would have to sit tight on their West Tennessee Tributaries Project.

For the next several years the ball went back and forth between the Corps, the courts and the plaintiffs. First, the Corps appealed Judge Brown's injunction. The plaintiffs agreed to let the Corps proceed on a single stretch of the Obion—the so-called Mengelwood item— but only because Mengelwood was flooding worse than ever, thanks to channelization upstream, where the Corps had scoured a ditch three hundred feet wide and thirty feet deep. In 1973, the plaintiffs and their attorneys met with the Corps, the Game and Fish Commission, the EPA and envoys from the offices of U.S. Senator Howard Baker and Congressman Ed Jones. At length they reached what Tony Campbell deemed "a fair settlement." Chief among its provisions was a compromise mitigation plan: 32,000 acres of prime basin wetlands as compensation for the damage already done. In return for the mitigation lands *and* an acceptable EIS, Akers implied, he and his fellow plaintiffs would drop the lawsuit.

Things seemed to be nearing a resolution; the newspaper even hailed it as such. But in 1976 the plaintiffs realized that the mitigation lands being purchased by the Corps were not in the designated areas. Back to court they went. Meanwhile, the Corps presented its revised EIS, two thousand pages of data, studies and comments. Judge Brown held another hearing to consider its merits, and TCL board members Ed Thackston and Chester McConnell offered expert testimony. When it was over, Judge Brown ruled for a *second* time that the EIS was inadequate, the only time in the history of NEPA that an EIS had been rejected twice. The judge renewed his injunction against further digging, and again ordered the Corps to produce an acceptable EIS. The plaintiffs were winning, it seemed, yet the whole affair was enormously fractious, complex and exhausting.

THE BASIN AUTHORITY IS "MORTALLY WOUNDED"

Meanwhile, another storm was brewing. Though the Corps' hands were pretty much tied during the injunction period, the Obion-Forked Deer Basin Authority could, and eventually did, go to work "maintaining" the existing channels. The problem was, contends Clark Akers, the authority wasn't maintaining old channels so much as it was digging new ones—at an average cost to taxpayers of $27,000 per mile. As Akers exasperatedly put it, "The basin authority had become a surrogate Corps of Engineers."

But that was not all. The authority was also operating without a Section 404 permit. Section 404 of the 1972 Clean Water Act was the first real protection of wetlands at the federal level. In essence, Section 404 requires a permit to deposit dredged or fill material "into the navigable waters" of the United States. While the 1972 provision did not specifically mention wetlands, a U.S. District Court judge in March 1975 ruled that Section 404 did indeed apply to "adjacent wetlands," as well as tributaries and feeder streams. The Corps of Engineers was the permitting authority. (The Corps had been in charge of dredge-and-fill permits since they were first required by the River and Harbor Act of 1899, but back then they had nothing to do with protecting clean water, just commercial navigation.)

In September 1977, TCL board member Chester McConnell, a passionate, even obsessive opponent of channelization, told the board that the OFDBA's activity was making things worse in the basin. Far from simply "maintaining" channels, it was enlarging them with its heavy-handed clearing methods, using draglines where a winch and chain saw would do, destroying streamside vegetation, adding to already disastrous levels of erosion and generally making a mess of the environment at an unconscionable cost to taxpayers. The program was not only destroying much of the remaining wetlands in the basin, he said; it was also threatening to undermine bridges. (In 1983 the U.S. Geological Survey would implicate channelization in the collapses of at least seven bridges, resulting in six deaths, since the WTTP began.)

Game and Fish biologist Cal Barstow (front, left) was named Wildlife Conservationist of the Year in 1971 for his work on the Obion-Forked Deer mitigation plan. Other winners in 1971 were (front row) John Bartlett, forests; Lib Roller, education; Carl Bolton, communications; and Dr. Lester Dudney, Conservationist of the Year. Back row: Bill Alley, youth; David J. Wilson, water; Glen Elkins, soil; and Dennis Gibson for the Children's Museum of Nashville, Conservation Organization of the Year. Lieutenant Governor John Wilder was Conservation Legislator. Courtesy of TWRA.

Single-minded he certainly was, but McConnell knew what he was talking about. The former Game and Fish biologist was now regional representative of the Wildlife Management Institute, an organization as old and respected as the National Wildlife Federation itself. He had probably spent more hours observing the rivers, reading reports and preparing testimony than anyone else in the case, with the possible exceptions of Clark Akers, Tony Campbell and E.B. Dyer of the Soil Conservation Service. (Dyer, a TCL board member from Brentwood, was named Land and Soil Conservationist of the Year in 1979 for convincing the SCS to mend its own channelizing ways.) McConnell now proposed to the board that it pass a resolution declaring the League "opposed to the channel work currently being carried out by the basin authority and [asking it] to pursue alternative methods."

The OFDBA was in for trouble. On September 27, 1978, the National Ecological Foundation sued the Corps again. By allowing the basin authority to operate without the necessary permits, said the lawsuit, the Corps was violating NEPA and just about everything else, including the River and Harbor Act, the Water Pollution Control Act, the Fish and Wildlife Coordination Act and the Administrative Procedures Act. This time, the basin authority itself was named as a codefendant. Actually, it named the Governor of Tennessee operating through the OFDBA, but that did not make things any easier for Richard Swaim.

Swaim, West Tennessee vice-president of the League as well as its president in 1977-78, also happened to be the executive director of the Obion-Forked Deer Basin Authority. He had worked closely with the League from the moment he was hired by the authority in September 1973, telling the board that he wanted TCL to be the "chief source of the environmental input" to the Obion-Forked Deer project.

Thus it was not an easy matter when, on October 1, 1978, the TCL board met to decide whether to join the National Ecological Foundation in its new lawsuit against the basin authority. The discussion lasted several grueling hours, hairsplitting in its detail and often painfully heated. Much of the input came from Chester McConnell, Ed Thackston and Jim Whoric, who had earlier been appointed by president Loyd Ezell to investigate the authority's practices. The trio had spent several days in the basin, traveling the streams in a small boat. Their report to the board was not very hopeful. Swaim argued earnestly against the legal action, but when the vote was counted, it was almost two-to-one in favor of joining the suit, with one abstention.

Richard Swaim was apparently so distressed by the board's action, according to TCL administrator Sue Garner, that he avoided the League from that moment. Yet as difficult as the confrontation was, Tony Campbell remembers that meeting as his "proudest moment" in twenty years as head of the League. "It took all day to come to that decision and Richard was right there. ... I thought it really said a lot about the ability of our board to look at an issue carefully, honestly, and make a decision about it."

It also said something about the League's instinct for backing the right horse. The basin authority was soon afterwards audited by the state, a process which left the agency "mortally wounded," as Campbell put it. Auditors faulted the OFDBA for everything from excessive costs and inept use of federal funds, to shortsighted planning and misleading assessments.

Almost eight years had passed since the battle over the Big Ditch was first joined, but the problems of flooding and habitat loss in the basin had not gone away. Perhaps it was time to try a new tack. In 1980, the League asked Governor Lamar Alexander to call together the various agencies involved in the issue, including the state Departments of Conservation and Agriculture, the basin authority, TWRA, the Corps of Engineers and the Fish and Wildlife Service. Out of that meeting evolved the (first) Governor's West Tennessee Tributaries Task Force. Though the issue was still far from settled, and in fact would remain so for years to come, at least now the Corps seemed ready to deal.

THE LITTLE FISH IN THE LITTLE T

The West Tennessee Tribs project was not the only federal water project blocked by the new environmental laws of the '70s. The Tellico Dam had been deadlocked since 1972, when the Environmental Defense Fund and other groups sued TVA, charging that the agency was in violation of NEPA, the National Environmental Policy Act of 1969. The League joined that suit, with support from the legal staff of the National Wildlife Federation. But even as TVA was preparing an environmental impact statement under NEPA, it appeared the dam might be blocked by an even newer law, the Endangered Species Act of 1973.

In the summer of 1973, University of Tennessee ichthyologist David Etnier, snorkeling with a colleague in the Little Tennessee River, had spotted a small fish he could not identify. It was, he decided, a new species of darter, and it appeared to live on tiny snails at the bottom of the Little T—and nowhere else in the country. (That was later found not to be the case.)

In 1976 the snail darter was added to the Interior Department's list of federally endangered species. Several groups now used the darter as the basis of a new lawsuit to scrap the dam once and for all. This time, however, the National Wildlife Federation declined to join in the litigation. "To be quite frank," Tom Kimball said at the time, "we don't like to enter a suit unless we think we can win." Kimball may have also feared that Congress would use the lawsuit to scrap the ESA altogether, which was not far wrong. At any rate, the League sat out this round of litigation also, though it continued to protest the project editorially.

The suit did win. On June 15, 1978, the U.S. Supreme Court ruled 6 to 3 in favor of the plaintiffs and the Endangered Species Act. Meanwhile, projected benefit-cost ratios were so abysmal—fifty cents on every dollar, roughly—that the Senate refused to fund the project any longer. The League gave its Conservationist of the Year Award for 1978 to Zygmunt Plater, the former UT law professor who had argued the case before the high court.

But as Tony Campbell put it, each time the Tellico issue seemed to have been extinguished, someone found "another match to rekindle the flames." In 1978, urged by Tennessee's Senator Howard Baker and his fellow Republican Congressman, John Duncan of Knoxville, Congress created the Endangered Species Committee, a sort of parole board for projects that had run afoul of the ESA. Dubbed the "God Squad" because of its life-or-death power over threatened species, the committee included six cabinet-level administrators plus one envoy from the affected state. (President Carter appointed William R. Willis, Jr., an attorney and member of the Game and Fish Commission.)

On January 23, 1979, the committee ruled unanimously in favor of the snail darter. The public interest would be best served, it said, if the Little T stayed a river. It should have been a killing blow, but the dam did not die. Instead, as Congress considered the 1979 Energy and Water Development Appropriations Bill, John Duncan "quietly slipped" on an amendment authorizing funds for the final stages of work on the dam. The House passed the bill, the Senate approved the House version in September and President Jimmy Carter, "with regret," signed the bill into law. Within a few months, East Tennesseans had another TVA lake.

TVA'S AIR POLLUTION PROBLEMS

At about the same time it was sitting out the snail darter suit, TCL chose to pass on another major litigation involving the Tennessee Valley Authority. In 1977, a coalition of public-interest groups led by the Tennessee Environmental Council sued TVA over air pollution from its coal-burning power plants.

TVA began building coal-fired power plants in the early 1950s. By the 1960s, Tennessee's air was seriously degraded. The flyash in particular was so bad, said Air Pollution Control director Harold Hodges, that some mornings he'd look outside and think it had snowed.

The lawsuit demanded TVA reduce by half its sulfur dioxide emissions. There were other provisions, too, but this point was considered crucial. However, when TEC director Ruth Neff went before the TCL board to ask their support, the directors declined, apparently for the same reasons they had not joined the Tellico Dam suit the year before—lack of resources and doubts that it would succeed.

Yet in it did succeed, not only winning a promise to reduce emissions by half within the next five years (beginning in 1980), but helping trigger a new spirit of environmental cooperation in the giant federal agency.

THE START OF A LONG TRADITION: THE YOUTH CONSERVATION CAMPS

Fortunately, not everything was a controversy. For instance, the League was the chief Tennessee sponsor of National Hunting and Fishing Day, a scaled-down version of President Roosevelt's National Wildlife Week. It premiered in 1972 with the endorsement of Governor Dunn.

Then there were the youth camps. Youth Conservation Summits were a sort of summer camp *cum* training ground for teenagers considering a career in natural resource management. There were seminars in wildlife management, plant ecology, forests and fisheries, all taught by volunteer instructors on loan from places like TWRA, the Department of Conservation and Westvaco Corporation, the timber company.

The first youth camp was held in June 1977 at Montgomery Bell State Park. (Most later camps met at the Brandon Springs group camp at Land Between the Lakes.) Camp director for years was Dr. Padgett Kelly, a biology professor at Bethel College who would later head the conservation education curriculum for the Tennessee Department of Education. The rate was just fifty dollars for the week, including meals and housing. Over the years this fee went up, of course, but the youth summits were always a terrific bargain. By the time they closed in 1991, campers were still paying just $170 for the week.

CHAPTER 7

1980-1989
A DECADE OF SHAPING POLICY

*Because of its philosophies and approach to conservation issues and programs,
TCL is the recognized leader among state conservation and environmental
organizations. It has been called upon to provide leadership in many instances.*

—National Wildlife Federation, in naming TCL
Outstanding Affiliate of the Year, March 1980

THE DECADE OF THE TASK FORCE

The 1980s began auspiciously for the League. In March, Tony Campbell's photo made the cover of the first issue of *The Leader*, the National Wildlife Federation's new monthly newsletter for local activists; the headline announced "Tennessee Top State Affiliate." The League had been named Outstanding Affiliate for 1979, cited for, among other things, its comeback growth since the early '70s, its success in forming a Resource Agency Coordinating Committee and its leadership in the Tennessee Alliance for Container Deposit Legislation. League president Ed Thackston, NWF board member Greer Ricketson, Tony Campbell and Clark Akers all went to the NWF's 1980 convention in Miami, where Thackston accepted the Federation's "Connie" Award to the strains of "The Tennessee Waltz." But there was a second Connie for the group from Tennessee. Clark Akers won a whooping crane statuette in honor of his decade-long fight to preserve the Obion-Forked Deer watershed.

The League's win—its first since 1954—was gratifying proof of the progress it had made in the decade just ended. Akers' win, on the other hand, was an omen of the decade to come. This man, this David who had successfully challenged a government Goliath, would come to be seen as a metaphor of '80s activism, a symbol of the growing clout and stamina of the citizen conservation lobby.

Clark Akers, Dr. Greer Ricketson, Tony Campbell and Dr. Edward Thackston pose for pictures during the National Wildlife Federation's 1980 annual convention in Miami. Akers received one of the whooping crane statuettes for his success in stopping the West Tennessee Tributaries Project. Thackston accepted the other "Connie" for the League as outstanding NWF affiliate for 1979. Courtesy of the National Wildlife Federation.

Perhaps nothing epitomized this new power more than the rise of the environmental task force. Throughout the country, complex questions of resource protection were being resolved, or at any rate debated, by dialogue groups, advisory panels and steering committees. Their makeup included not only the regulating agencies but anyone else who might reasonably be judged to have expertise or clear interest in the matter: private citizens, conservation groups, farmers, government functionaries, local officials, small businesses, scientists, academics, neighborhood groups, labor unions and so on.

Naturally, individuals with more experience at mediation and managed argument tended to wield more power in these groups than those who had none. But task forces were valuable for that very reason, that they gave newcomers a chance to gain some expertise in the fine art of environmental negotiation. The result, indeed, was a remarkably democratic (if often cumbersome) attempt to come to terms on issues that an earlier age would probably have settled, if not behind closed doors, at least with precious little outside discussion.

Literally dozens of such groups were convened in Tennessee in the 1980s, and the League's reputation for moderation and expertise earned it a seat on virtually all of them. In many cases, TCL was the only conservation group formally invited to take part; in a few cases, it was the League that suggested them. A few examples:

◆   *Hatchie River Protection Task Force.* The League formed this group in 1981 to develop a management plan for the Hatchie, the last main-stem unchannelized river in West Tennessee and one of the first streams designated a State Scenic River.

◆   *Kentucky Lake Natural Resources Management Team.* This interagency team convened in 1982 to promote the conservation, development and wise use of Kentucky Lake's varied resources. Tony Campbell represented the League as the only conservation group on board, at least initially.

◆   *Metro Creeks Task Force.* This panel was established in June 1983 to assure that public works projects in or near Nashville streams did as little environmental damage as possible. Again, Tony Campbell was the only non-agency person on the task force.

◆   *Dale Hollow Reservoir Clear-Cutting Task Force.* Residents around Dale Hollow, a Corps of Engineers lake, protested the extensive clear-cuts in the Corps' forest management plan. The task force, meeting for several months starting in 1984, finally reached an agreement that included smaller clear-cuts and wider buffer zones.

◆   *Spencer Range Task Force.* When the Tennessee National Guard proposed in 1984 to build a heavy-artillery training site not far from Savage Gulf and Fall Creek Falls, the task force convened to weigh the military needs against the impacts of the noise, air traffic and collateral development. The proposal was eventually withdrawn, in part because of cuts in defense spending.

◆   *MRS Task Force.* When the Department of Energy proposed to build a temporary storage facility ("monitored retrievable storage") for nuclear waste in Oak Ridge in 1985, a task force convened to assess the possible impacts, including transportation hazards and exposure to low-level radiation. By the following year the proposal had been abandoned, killed not only by public opposition and litigation brought by the Tennessee attorney

Citizens, state foresters and federal resource managers discuss the issues at a fall 1984 meeting of the Dale Hollow Clear-Cutting Task Force. Courtesy of TWRA.

general, but by the DOE's own weak rationale in building temporary storage without firm plans for a permanent facility.

◆   *Columbia Dam Task Force.* Like the other controversial TVA dam on the Little T, the Columbia Dam on the Duck River was halted in mid-construction in 1983 when environmentalists sued over an endangered species, the birdwing pearly mussel. At the League's suggestion, the task force came together in 1986 to discuss the impacts to wildlife, water quality and recreation. However, it was mainly poor economic planning—a mere forty cents of estimated benefits for every dollar of cost—that finally scrapped the project.

◆   *TWRA License Increase Task Force.* The last time the Legislature had granted a fee increase was 1981, when the combination hunting-fishing license rose to ten dollars. Inflation made it now seem like much less. Convened in 1987 to look at the agency's needs and options, the task force ultimately agreed to a phased-in increase, beginning with a hike to $15.50 in 1990, then stepping up every two years until it reached $21 in 1996.

◆   *Septic Tanks Siting Task Force.* By the mid-1980s Tennessee was the only state in the country still allowing developers and homeowners to blast into bedrock to make room for septic tanks and overflow field lines. Ed Thackston represented the League on this task force, which convened in 1988 and ended in 1989 with a ban on blasting.

◆   *Governor's Interagency Wetlands Task Force.* Though several wetlands-protection statutes were on the books at both the state and federal level, the various agencies with jurisdiction in Tennessee rarely seemed to agree on what the rules meant or how they were to be applied. At the League's request, Governor Ned McWherter convened this board in 1988, charging members with designing a Tennessee Wetlands Conservation Strategy. It completed the strategy in 1994.

Though the citizen lobby really took off in the '80s, the phenomenon had in fact been gaining momentum for the last ten or twelve years. Earth Day 1970 was an important symbol of the unified citizen voice, but it was really NEPA—the National Environmental Policy Act of 1969—that gave citizens a strong legal mechanism for influencing federal decision-making. Section 102 (C) of NEPA not only required an environmental impact statement for every major federal action significantly affecting the human environment, it also required that interested parties, including the general public, be involved in the review process. NEPA further required that the Council on Environmental Quality (created by the same act) consult regularly with this larger constituency as it developed national policies and reviewed programs.

But as the 1980s progressed, conservationists had more than NEPA to thank for their heightened role in environmental decision-making. The anti-regulation, pro-development bias of President Ronald Reagan's administration, especially his choice of James Watt as Secretary of Interior, inflamed conservationists, who accused Reagan of "ideological warfare" with the environment. During the League's 1982 annual convention in Gatlinburg, Patrick Parenteau of the National Wildlife Federation blasted Reagan's efforts to turn back the clock on almost twenty years of environmental progress. "Under the cry of 'regulatory reform,'" Parenteau said, "we see the destruction of the environmental safety net, and under the rhetoric of 'the new federalism' we find the dumping of responsibilities onto the states without giving the states the wherewithal to carry out these responsibilities." Bob Baker of the National Park Service saw in the trend not only a "major decentralization of power," but an alarming fiscal stinginess toward conservation, wildlife protection and recreation projects.

Among the programs wounded by federal budget cuts were wetlands acquisition programs, pilot projects to promote energy conservation, cost-sharing plans for local sewage treatment plants, the once-influential Council on Environmental Quality, the landmark Land and Water Conservation Fund, even the U.S. Forest Service's Silviculture Laboratory at Sewanee, which was shut down altogether.

Yet if (as Parenteau put it) conservationists were being "held hostage" to the White House, in the end they were probably stronger and wiser for it. Reagan's two terms in office probably gave citizen activists more training and experience than they ever could have gained under a more beneficent leader. The Reagan years, for instance, coincided with a dramatic rise in "Friends" groups at hundreds of state and national parks nationwide, including "Friends of the Smokies," "Friends of Frozen Head" and "Friends of Fall Creek Falls." Before, these people were merely the hikers, the campers or the nature walkers. Now, they were the ones leading the hikes, maintaining the campgrounds and building the nature centers.

THE LEAGUE TAKES UP EAGLE HACKING

One of the federally funded programs that took a direct hit from the Reagan White House was the program to bring bald eagles back to Land Between the Lakes, TVA's recreation-demonstration area between Kentucky and Barkley reservoirs.

Once so prolific that farmers used to shoot them as varmints, bald eagles were now precious rare winter visitors to Tennessee, victims alike of DDT poisoning and habitat loss. Nesting birds were even rarer: the last time a bald eagle was hatched in Tennessee was in 1961. DDT had since been banned, but the great birds were not yet returning on their own.

In 1980, following methods developed at Cornell University, the Tennessee Valley Authority had started a five-year propagation program with one hacking station, two imported eaglets and the help of the U.S. Fish and Wildlife Service and TWRA. (TWRA also began its own hacking program for ospreys and eagles at Reelfoot Lake.) The following summer, three more eaglets, each about two months old, arrived from the Patuxent Wildlife Research Center in Laurel, Maryland, and the Columbus, Ohio, zoo. For the first six or seven weeks, the birds lived in a man-made nest atop forty-foot stilts overlooking Lake Barkley, close to the Kentucky line. Their food arrived via cable trolley from a nearby observation tower. Human attendants fed, watered and constantly monitored the birds but stayed out of sight as much as possible.

When the young eagles were sturdy enough to fly, biologists gingerly fitted each one with a radio transmitter and colored leg bands, then returned to their observation post and released the cage door. One by one, the birds emerged from the nest, made a few tentative test flights, then soon flew away. Three to five years later, assuming they weren't killed in the meantime, the adult eagles should come back to within fifty or seventy-five miles of their adopted home to build nests of their own.

The program went as planned for the first two seasons. Then, early in 1982 (designated the Bicentennial Year of the Bald Eagle by Congress), TVA's budget was slashed. Forced to reduce its nongame programs, the agency eliminated most of the eight thousand dollars set aside for its eagle programs.

The Conservation League decided to take over.

At its 1982 annual convention in March, Tony Campbell explained to the board what the eagle project would entail. First, it would entail cash. Even with three thousand dollars from TVA and continued assistance from TWRA, the League could still expect to pay up to five thousand dollars for two student interns, helicopter and airplane transportation, food for the eagles and transmitters to track them once they were released. Supporters were soon being invited to "adopt an eagle" for twenty-five dollars a day, though by 1984 Eagle Rare Bourbon was picking up most of the tab.

However, Campbell continued, money was only part of it. The League would also have to handle the logistics of air travel, ground travel and visiting hours; coordinate press briefings and news releases; mount a public education program; stay in touch with TWRA's nongame coordinator Bob Hatcher and other raptor specialists; and organize a network of volunteers to eagle-sit during the interns' days off. Nevertheless, he concluded, the payoff in public goodwill should be well worth the investment.

He was right. Few undertakings in the League's history drew the effusive press coverage of the eagle program. When the League's first two birds arrived in Nashville from Patuxent on June 29, 1982 (via complimentary airfare on American, official airline of the eagle project), they were greeted by a horde of cameras, microphones, reporters and wildlife personnel. The crowd loaded into cars and trucks and followed the bird cages west toward Dover, where one media type after another cautiously ascended the tower for one final look at the new arrivals. The birds' release seven weeks later drew many of the same reporters back to Land Between the Lakes for more photos, more stories and more public approval.

The 1983 program generated no less excitement, especially when a baby eagle was discovered in a nest in Stewart County, on land owned by Westvaco Corporation, near the Cross Creeks National Wildlife Refuge just outside the LBL boundary. Though the parents could not be traced to any of the Tennessee-hacked eagles, the first successful birth of a bald eagle in twenty-two years caused statewide rejoicing.

The real celebration, however, came in 1984. That spring, three more eaglets hatched from the same Westvaco nest. (Two of the three died, however, after getting entangled in bailing twine used in their nest.) Then a second nest, this one within the boundaries of LBL, was discovered by a turkey hunter along an isolated stretch of Kentucky Lake. By squinting through spotting scopes at the identifying leg bands, biologists could tell that, sure enough, one of the adults had been reared at LBL. It was one of the second batch of birds released in 1981, but whether it was male or female, they couldn't get close enough to say.

Scientists continued to monitor the nest (from a respectful distance, of course). By May 1984, the pair had produced the first official offspring of the LBL hacking program. The League, the volunteers, the interns, TVA, the TWRA, the newspapers—everyone was jubilant. Though 1984 was the formal end of the five-year program at Land Between the Lakes, the

TVA biologist Marcus Cope (left) and Bob Hatcher, coordinator of TWRA's nongame program, welcome a pair of bald eagles to Tennessee. Courtesy of TWRA.

League continued to support the hacking stations there, as well as several new ones being sponsored by TWRA and others at Dale Hollow Lake, Chickamauga Reservoir and a number of other sites. By the end of the decade, the various hacking towers in the state had released 115 eaglets into the wild. Returning adults had built thirty-four successful nests, giving birth to sixty-one baby birds. By 1995, the National Wildlife Federation's annual eagle count identified 338 bald eagles in the state, and the species was downlisted from endangered to threatened in Tennessee. It was one of the most successful and heartwarming chapters in the history of wildlife management in Tennessee.

THE RETURN OF THE RALLIES

One thing the eagle hacking project made clear to the League: worthy issues and controversies notwithstanding, people really went in for the fun stuff. The baby eagle project was probably the most upbeat, exciting and visible thing the League had ever done, attracting dozens of volunteers as well as new members, some new affiliates and lots of feel-good media coverage. Its value to the League could hardly be overstated. As the National Wildlife Federation advised its affiliates in a 1984 leadership guide, "a voluntary organization ultimately isn't business, it's pleasure." And sportsmen, after all, were a pleasure-loving bunch.

At any rate, that was the premise behind the sportsman's rallies.

Next to the eagles, the rallies were probably the most popular activity sponsored by the League in the 1980s. With their raffles and dozens of donated door prizes, their live music, demonstrations, barbecue dinners, displays, booths and duck-calling contests, they attracted glowing press coverage as well as thousands of sportsmen from all over the Southeast.

Yet when they were first proposed in the spring of 1980, the rallies were seen less as a public relations tool than a way to raise money. The League still owed most of the roughly $38,000 it had pledged to the National Ecological Foundation in 1977 as a condition of Clark Akers' matching contribution toward the $100,000 Meeman grant. In 1979, the directors in each of the four League divisions agreed to raise $2,500 per year, per division, until the commitment was paid off. But—no surprise—this was easier said than done. By April 1980, the directors of Region II (Middle Tennessee) had come up with only $400 of their assigned $2,500, not much better than the other three.

Vice president Jim Whoric suggested the rally as a way to generate the balance. Ducks Unlimited used to host them back in the 1960s, one-day affairs that drew thousands of people and raised thousands of dollars. It could happen again.

And it did, in late September 1980. The first TCL Sportsman's Rally happened on a Thursday evening at the National Guard Armory in Nashville, with nearly a thousand people paying two dollars a head to get in. Most paid another few dollars for a plate of barbecue; others bought a twenty-five dollar membership and got a Bill Dillon nature print as a bonus. Still others paid five dollars to honk, whistle or bleat their way to the finish in the annual Tennessee State Duck Calling Championships. (These fees, however, went to the winner to help pay his way to the World Duck Calling Contest in Stuttgart, Arkansas.)

The rally was an unqualified success. By the time it was over, the directors of Region II had their $2,500 and were already planning the next one. The next year's event drew an even bigger crowd, and other regions began copying the idea in Jackson, Knoxville and Chattanooga. The Nashville rally, however, was always the granddaddy. For several years it even had to move to the state fairgrounds to accommodate the swelling crowds, which at their peak exceeded two thousand. As the attendance grew, so did the list of attractions, including, at one point, a dunking booth with Tony Campbell, TWRA's assistant director Ron Fox and Sue Garner's husband Kenneth as the targets. By the middle of the '80s, proceeds for the four-hour event approached ten thousand dollars.

SOMETHING FOR HUNTERS: BOW TOURNAMENTS AND DEER REGISTRIES

For most of the decade TCL also made a few dollars cosponsoring the Tennessee State Bowhunters Tournament. Though bowhunting was never very prominent in the League, several hundred archers—including a large number of women—always came out for the two-day tournament, hosted by a Rutherford County affiliate, the Necedah Bowhunters. Saturday's shooting always ended with music, dancing, beans, cornbread and beer (Budweiser was a cosponsor). With entry fees only ten or fifteen dollars, the tournaments barely paid for the hours spent organizing them. Their chief value to the League was the fun and goodwill.

Some popular events did have certifiable value, however. The 1984 sportsman's rally, for instance, included the first official Tennessee Deer Registry, cosponsored by the TWRA. The deer registry was essentially a weigh-in for "quality" deer. Employees from TWRA recorded the various measurements and proportions of the mounted antlers—things like number of points, symmetry, widest span and so on—as well as when, where and how each deer was

Larry Marcum, then coordinator of TWRA's deer program, scores a set of antlers at the first Tennessee deer registry at the 1984 Sportsman's Rally in Nashville. Jimmy Adams of Gallatin looks on. Photo by Turner Hutchison. Courtesy of the Nashville Banner. *Copyright © 1984* Nashville Banner *Publishing Co.*

taken. These data were converted into a numeric score. If the score met a prescribed minimum, the deer was duly entered into the Tennessee Deer Registry as well as the national registry established in 1950 by the Boone and Crockett Club. (The Boone and Crockett registry, formally known as the Official Scoring System for North American Big Game Trophies, combined two earlier scoring systems, one copyrighted in 1935 by a Dr. James Clark, the other devised by Mr. Grancel Fitz in 1939.)

Tennessee's first registry scored 450 sets of deer antlers. Of these, eighty-five qualified as trophies. "Guys must've had these big trophy heads hanging around their homes for years," said Larry Marcum, TWRA's chief of game management. The number of qualifying entries fell off sharply after that. Yet the registries remained immensely popular for most of the decade, with sometimes two dozen scheduled in a single year. The hunters got bragging rights, and TWRA got a database that helped monitor the quality of the deer herd. That herd, incidentally, had exploded, going from barely 1,000 animals in 1940 to more than 350,000 in 1984.

Alan Polk was the League's point person in much of this activity. Polk, an active board member from East Tennessee, had been hired in July 1984 specifically to work on such sportsmen-oriented programs as the rallies and deer registries. He also worked on the League's publications, but his real purpose was to upgrade the relationship with sportsmen. Hunters and fishermen were still the core of the League's membership. But lately, with Tony Campbell's time so taken up at the Legislature or in task force meetings, the sportsmen were in some danger of feeling neglected.

Fur trappers, for instance, though a relatively small segment of TCL's population, wanted the League's support in responding to what it considered unreasonable regulations, as well as "all the anti-trapping propaganda in newspapers, magazines and on TV" said Ed Kelly, president of East Tennessee Fur Takers. Trout fishermen wanted the League to help TWRA establish trophy trout reaches in some of the most popular trout streams. They had submitted resolutions at several annual meetings in the mid-'80s, calling for trophy trout reaches on the Hiwassee and Caney Fork. According to Alan Polk, there were economic as well as biological benefits to letting some fish grow to trophy size (typically fourteen to sixteen inches long, and eight or ten pounds). Trout fishing had grown so popular in Tennessee, however, that even with four hatcheries running at full tilt, few individuals could survive to trophy size without some restrictions, whether reduced creel limits, shorter seasons, artificial lures or even catch-and-release zones. TWRA generally supported the idea, but some local fishermen saw trophy zones as government sticking its nose where it didn't belong. In fact, as soon as TWRA ventured to establish trophy zones in the late '80s and early '90s, they were promptly challenged, and some of them were overturned.

EDUCATION NOW

A big part of Polk's job was education. He set up leadership workshops for affiliates and organized the League's end of National Hunting and Fishing Day. He worked with affiliates and TWRA in hosting hunting seminars in 1984, fishing seminars in 1986 and a hunter-ethics program called Operation Game Thief—actually, a confidential way for hunters to report violators. And when a mandatory hunter education bill finally went into effect on January 1, 1985, Polk helped recruit volunteer instructors.

The League had been trying to mandate hunter education since 1973, but the Legislature balked at the word "mandatory." In 1974 it refused to pass the League's first hunter education bill, and several subsequent bills. It did, however, agree that hunters must wear blaze orange. In 1973, at the suggestion of retiring Game and Fish chairman Larry Lowe, the League had urged that Tennessee join almost two dozen other states in requiring big game hunters (turkey hunters excepted) to wear fluorescent orange hunting vests. These other states had all reported "sharp declines" in casualties, Campbell told the lawmakers, who passed the League's blaze-orange bill in 1975. But it would be eight more years before it passed a bill mandating that hunters be educated.

It was a proud day for the League when this bill was finally signed; Tony Campbell considered it one of the most important pieces of legislation he had ever worked on. Effective January 1, 1985, anyone born after January 1, 1969, had to complete an approved hunter education course or be liable to lose his hunting license. TWRA administered the program, trained the instructors in week-long workshops and supplied some of the faculty from its own ranks. By the end of 1985, according to TWRA, nine hundred instructors had been certified by the program, many of these supplied by the League and its affiliates.

Polk also took on some of the responsibility for Project CENTS—Conservation Education Now for Tennessee Students. CENTS was already one of the brightest stars in the League's little galaxy of outreach programs. Initiated in 1983 with funding from Lamar Alexander's Safe Growth Team and leadership from Dr. Padgett Kelly (the same fellow behind the youth conservation camps), Project CENTS was really an amalgam of three existing programs: Project WILD (Wildlife in Learning Design); CLASS Project (Conservation Learning Activities in Science and Social Studies); and Project Learning Tree. All three programs had been designed by professional educators to teach conservation while incidentally teaching such mainstream academic skills as math and science.

Such doubling-up was important, for despite an Environmental Education Act passed by Congress in 1970, getting conservation training into public schools wasn't as easy as it had been in the rural '30s and '40s. The modern curriculum was more regimented now, and most teachers resisted new tasks. The success of Project CENTS was that its lesson plans were designed to supplement traditional course work, not replace it. A math class, for instance, might learn about fractions through an exercise involving ten bears and a limited food supply.

The League did not actually host the teacher workshops that were the heart of Project CENTS. But it consolidated the programs; it enlisted funding; it legitimized the CENTS office as a part of the state Department of Education; and it recruited an impressive list of partners and supporters. Starting with TWRA and the Department of Education, the team of cosponsors eventually grew to include TVA, the Division of Forestry and the Tennessee Forestry Association. By the end of CENTS' first decade, fifteen thousand teachers had been through its workshops; hundreds of thousands of children had pretended to be bears.

FILLING THE HOLES IN THE LEDGER

The popularity of the Nashville rallies endured for most of the decade, but eventually both they and the public seemed to have reached saturation. By 1989, sportsman's rallies had been pretty much abandoned in the outlying regions. And in Nashville, the League knew that the '89 show would be its last. Acknowledging that the crowds had gotten much smaller, Tony Campbell told reporters that the League was probably going to try something else in 1990: a three-day "outdoor show" for the entire state.

There was, indeed, a three-day show in 1990, held at the Johnson City Freedom Hall Civic Center. Similar to the rallies, it offered exhibits, demonstrations and prizes. But unlike the rallies, it was a financial bust. Far from the projected proceeds of ten thousand to twelve thousand dollars, the League made a profit of exactly $62.48.

As proceeds from the rallies had dropped, the League started holding "reverse auctions" (actually high-stakes raffles) to make up the difference. The first such event, organized by TVA's Larry M. Richardson and held during the 1988 annual meeting in Gatlinburg, sold 200 tickets at $150 each; the cash pot was $15,300, with a incredible profit to TCL of $9,000. The 100th ticket drawn, for example, netted the winner $3,000; the holder of grand prize ticket No. 200 got $10,000. (Richardson sold seven of the last ten tickets.) The $150 "donation" (none of which was tax-deductible) also bought cocktails, entertainment and a prime rib dinner for two.

In 1989 the League followed the same format at the annual meeting in Clarksville, only on a grander scale. The 1989 meeting sold 250 tickets, paid $19,000 in prizes, and netted a surplus of more than $15,000.

It seemed the League had a winner. But then *The Tennessean* broke a story about illegal gambling operations. The Tennessee Constitution prohibits gambling of all types, and technically that includes even the most benign games of chance, from church bingo games to "benefit drawings" by nonprofit groups. The state of Tennessee had looked the other way for years. But the newspaper found evidence that some racketeers were masquerading as nonprofit organizations in order to slip by the regulators. Forced to uphold the law under such public scrutiny, the state attorney general in 1989 shut the gate on all games of chance. With the rallies dried up and the raffles banned, the League was suddenly looking at a big hole in the ledger.

THE FINE ART OF GOVERNMENT GRANTSMANSHIP

Money was an ongoing worry for the League throughout the decade. Though annual revenues rose steadily, going from just under $100,000 in 1980 to just over $240,000 in 1989, annual expenses rose right alongside, and five years out of ten ended slightly in the red. Despite annual infusions of interest from the Meeman fund (rarely less than fifteen thousand dollars a year), despite the continued grant from Sears for the awards program, despite occasional large gifts and bequests, including nearly forty thousand dollars when Dr. Dudney died in 1982, despite the donation of a valuable piece of real estate and its monthly rental income—despite all that, cash flow at the League always seemed just slightly obstructed.

A raccoon in a tree by New York wildlife artist Charles Fracé was the first Tennessee Conservation Print and Stamp in 1982. Copyright © 1982 Charles Fracé.

One of the most attractive ways to increase revenue was government contracts—non-bid, short-term work assignments from such agencies as TVA, the Corps of Engineers and the State of Tennessee. Government contracts were not only feathers in the cap of any organization respected enough to earn them; for some, such as the Tennessee Environmental Council in its early years, they were an economic mainstay. Though the assignments usually meant more travel, more expenses and certainly more work, the contracting agencies were prepared to pay for such assistance. As far as they were concerned, they were getting professional consulting at a fraction of the going rate.

The League had already landed a few such jobs in the late '70s. The Corps of Engineers, for instance, hired the League to do an environmental inventory of Nashville's Mill Creek as part of a flood plain study. The sixty-page final report, submitted in April 1980 by Ed Thackston, Tony Campbell and several of Thackston's Vanderbilt students, earned $2,500 for the League. Around the same time, TVA asked the League to prepare a resource management plan for Land Between the Lakes. The board agreed that since Tony Campbell did all the work, the $1,877 fee should go toward paying off his back salary.

In 1980, TVA had another job for the League.

Having recently lost the 1977 lawsuit over its violations of the Clean Air Act, TVA was eager to restore its rather battered public image. Relations with the environmental community already seemed to be mending. Sulfur dioxide emissions were down, environmental accountability seemed to be up, and the agency's progressive new director, S. David Freeman, was succeeding in moving the utility's focus away from nuclear power. In 1980 Freeman met with Tony Campbell and Tom Kimball, head of the National Wildlife Federation, to propose a series of community meetings, one in each of the seven TVA districts. We already know how the conservationists feel about TVA's environmental impacts, Freeman explained. Now we want to hear from the folks who traditionally have not been involved in the discussion—the work force, farmers, labor and industry groups and so forth.

Though this was not the League's usual target audience, Campbell and Kimball agreed that the dialogue was important. Besides, TVA would pay for salaries, office space, phones, supplies and even a part-time secretary who could occasionally ease Sue Garner's work load.

The public meetings, which lasted through 1981, succeeded in restoring at least some of the public's trust in the Tennessee Valley Authority. No doubt they also had a part in TVA's decision to consolidate its various environmental functions under one roof, the Office of Natural Resources. As for the League, the contract had been money in the bank. The trouble was, the money wasn't in the bank now. Short-term contracts were, after all, short-term.

Fortunately, the League had other ideas for fund-raising. In 1982, it issued the state's first conservation stamp and matching print, not unlike the wildlife stamps that had proved so profitable for the National Wildlife Federation in the 1930s. The signed, numbered prints by artist Charles Fracé depicted a raccoon, the Tennessee state animal, crouched in a tree. Campbell and Fracé presented the first print to Governor Alexander in a ceremony in the governor's office. Each print included a matching stamp and sold for seventy-five dollars. In coming years, TCL would contract with some of the country's leading wildlife artists, including Ralph McDonald and Johnny Lynch.

In 1986, the League ordered a "limited edition" of commemorative pocket knives, paying thirteen dollars each and selling them for thirty. At one time or another the League sold Christmas cards, cookbooks, purple martin houses and golf shirts. Though the merchandising projects were usually well-received, they were probably worth at least as much for their public relations value as for the relatively small sums of money they produced.

Obviously the League had to find more significant, more permanent sources of income. In particular, it needed to attract more contributing members, that is, individuals who paid at least ten dollars a year (and usually much more). Individual contributions were the single greatest source of income for the League, accounting for as much as half of its annual income. Yet they represented a considerably smaller share of membership overall—usually around three thousand members. (Most individual members also belonged to an affiliate.)

Affiliate clubs, on the other hand, though they represented most of the League's aggregate membership, contributed less than ten percent of the overall budget. In fact, even though the group rate went up twice in the 1980s (to $2 in 1982, then to $2.50 in 1986), total affiliate dues averaged only $5,000 to $8,000 a year.

Which points to a chronic discrepancy. For years, the League had claimed to represent anywhere from fourteen thousand to eighteen thousand members. A 1986 brochure describing the eagle hacking program, for instance, referred to "the League's 18,000 members." The bulk of these, of course, were claimed not as individuals but as members of affiliates. Yet assuming an average dues rate of two dollars a head, the League in the 1980s should have been grossing twenty to thirty thousand dollars a year in affiliate dues, at least four times what it was actually collecting.

According to Tony Campbell, what may look like a shortfall was simply the result of a longstanding if unofficial policy of letting some affiliates pay dues not strictly by the head, but simply as they were able or inclined. This was especially common, he said, among such large affiliates as the Tennessee State Rifle Association (with a reported six to eight thousand members). Apparently the feeling among board members was that, even if it did not translate to hard cash, the collective influence of such numbers was just as valuable as their money. (On the other hand, one wonders how Lou Williams would have felt about letting one group ride free while everyone else paid full fare.)

Campbell's explanation also seems to skirt the question of how the League's affiliate membership could have stayed so robust even as sportsmen's groups all over the state were dwindling. The question has been asked before. But perhaps the answer isn't important. TCL *was* speaking for the sportsmen of Tennessee, whether they were paying for the privilege or not.

THE TOUGH BUSINESS OF FUND-RAISING

Whatever its numbers may have been, the League needed more of them. In 1980, it hired a young fellow named Tim Ryan to conduct a series of direct-mail membership drives; the following year it hired a half-time membership services director, Jim Donahue. With response rates averaging almost 8 percent (3 percent is the industry standard), the fund-raising drives were considered highly successful. However, some of them actually lost money because the costs of printing and postage were so high, to say nothing of staff labor. In 1986, the board contracted with Sherman Kelly and Associates, a firm that had been running membership drives for sportsmen's leagues since at least the early '70s.

Though Sherman Kelly charged $150 a month plus 15 percent of returns, it brought results. By 1989, the number of individual members was the highest in the League's history: 3,687. The bad news was that the number of club members (those reported to the NWF, at any rate) was the lowest in its history: 3,288. The number of affiliated clubs stood at fifty-six.

The League decided it was time to hire a full-time development director. In 1988, it got a three-year grant from Clark Akers to hire a development and communications specialist, and in June, Sandy Ferencz arrived. Ferencz had lots of high hopes, including plans to reactivate TCL's corporate membership council, but she quit within a year. Her replacement was Bobby Stanton. With as much ambition as her predecessor and more staying power, Stanton got the League listed on United Way pledge forms, organized membership contests and helped administer a major grant. But the bottom line was that few of Stanton's ideas raised significant money, such as the fizzled membership contests. And it was Stanton who proposed the ill-fated outdoor show in Johnson City, the one that raised hardly enough for bus fare back to Nashville. Money-raising was a precarious business, and even full-time money-raisers didn't have it down to a science.

TCL AND INDUSTRY: BEDFELLOWS?

The League would have liked more money from private industry. In fact, that was one of the reasons it formed a Corporate Conservation Council in 1982 (the same year a national corporate council was formed by the NWF). Money was never mentioned as an objective, of course. Rather, said the League, the idea was to open lines of communication between industry and conservation leaders.

And to be fair, the League's CCC did do some of that. In 1984, the group cohosted an environmental manufacturing symposium with the Tennessee Manufacturers Association (now the Tennessee Association of Business). And in 1988, Saturn's environmental manager Bill Miller hosted a dozen of his fellow CCC members at Haynes Haven, Saturn's elegant antebellum mansion in Spring Hill. Here, executives from such major-league corporations as Bowater, Tennessee Eastman, Jack Daniel, ALCOA, Olin Corporation and Westvaco spent an afternoon planning a calendar of corporate conservation activities.

CCC members made it a point, almost a matter of policy, to respond frankly to the public's concerns about their respective industries. As soon as Saturn moved to Spring Hill in 1986, it formed a citizen advisory committee to allow local leaders some input in the company's developing environmental policy. At Jack Daniel, environmental manager Doug Clark routinely had environmental types down to Lynchburg to see the distillery's water protection and waste recovery systems (and then, if they were lucky, got them a reservation for lunch at Mrs. Bobo's Boarding House).

Whether or not anything of real significance came out of the CCC, at least there was, as the League always noted, "dialogue." In fact, dialogue may have been the strongest link between TCL and the CCC, because the CCC never did raise all that much money. Though the League always set what seemed like reasonable fund-raising goals for the CCC, it never met them. In 1983, it projected $12,500 from corporate donors; it got $5,000. In 1984, it set a more modest goal of ten thousand dollars; it raised almost none. The CCC then faded out of notice for a few years, rallied briefly in 1988, faded away again, rallied again. In fact, despite the League's admittedly close ties to a number of Tennessee corporations (and despite some critics' belief that TCL is a puppet of big business), corporate funding has never been a major part of the League's budget. Most donations were no more than five hundred or a thousand dollars. In fact, in 1988 the board felt compelled to set a two hundred-dollar minimum for membership in the CCC. A few gifts were larger, of course, but these were almost always earmarked for special projects, such as ALCOA's annual grant of two thousand dollars for the youth conservation camp.

If the League was sometimes accused of being too cozy with corporate sponsors, it was at least partly because the League liked to stay on good terms with them, meeting in their conference rooms, consulting with their engineers, fishing in their private ponds, even drinking their whiskey. Unlike many environmental groups, the League sympathized with the conflicting demands of capitalism and resource protection. It had been that way from the beginning, when Lou Williams urged tolerance and patience for factories trying to clean up their water pollution. Work *with* them, Williams would always say; don't alienate them.

However, though many of its members were executives themselves (Lou Williams once worked for a cement plant and Mayland Muse was a plumbing contractor), TCL had had no formal relationship with industry before the 1970s. In 1971, however, the special evaluation committee had urged the board to "tap the reservoir of brains and ability" of the private sector. By 1975 the board had its first at-large member from industry, ALCOA's Hugh McDade, a former chairman of the Game and Fish Commission. ALCOA was represented on the board for years, along with Bowater, Jack Daniel and Saturn.

Even in the early years of the modern environmental movement, when industry came in for a lot of heavy bashing from the public, the League considered itself "not an enemy of industry but more of a bedfellow with it." Its members, said TCL loyalist George Knox in 1973, understood that they "depend[ed] upon industry for their livelihood" no less than industries "depend[ed] upon the earth's natural resources" for theirs.

Diplomacy, even a sort of cautious advocacy, soon became the League's style. When the state began drafting regulations for deep-well disposal of hazardous wastes in 1983, the League was concerned that the rules might be *too* stringent. "[They] will make it almost impossible to inject waste underground," Tony Campbell told the board. "We need at least one location … in Tennessee [where] hazardous or toxic waste can be disposed of legally."

The League always held that neither its personal nor professional relationships with industry had any bearing on its policies, positions or awards. As much as that is possible, it is probably true. Still, it looked a bit odd when, in 1975, the League named Bowater Southern its Conservation Organization of the Year, putting a huge multinational corporation in with the likes of the Nashville Children's Museum and the Tennessee Federation of Garden Clubs.

Granted, Bowater probably deserved some kind of recognition. This was the company that initiated the Pocket Wilderness System, a public-private effort to preserve bits of ecosystems in the midst of heavily lumbered forests. A tract of Bowater property on the

In 1988, Saturn's Bill Miller (back row, far right) hosts fellow Corporate Conservation Council members at Haynes Haven, Saturn's antebellum mansion in Spring Hill. Tony Campbell and Mitchell Parks are in the back row. TCL file photo.

Cumberland Plateau, Angel Falls, became the first Pocket Wilderness in 1970. A year later, Bowater's Laurel-Snow Trail was named one of twenty-seven National Recreation Trails when Congress expanded the scenic trails act. And the year after that, Bowater started a program of planting wildlife food whenever it planted young pine trees. In November 1974, the corporation got an environmental award from the Bureau of Outdoor Recreation.

The trouble was, though the League in 1975 had an award for just about everything else, including legislators, it did not have a category specifically for industry. The Conservation Organization of the Year award was as close as the awards committee could come, but it clearly wasn't appropriate. When the 1975 ceremonies were over, Tony Campbell contacted the National Wildlife Federation, sponsor of the Conservation Achievement Awards, and asked which statuettes weren't already taken. (When NWF established the awards program in 1965, there were ten designated statuettes, plus another three or four generic beasts that could be assigned as needed.) The awards committee selected the antelope, called it Industrial Conservationist of the Year, and at the next annual meeting (April 1976), presented it to ALCOA.

Over the years, the antelope would go to some of the biggest companies in Tennessee, as well as a few that were not so big: Koppers, Westvaco, Jack Daniel, Tennessee Eastman, Mead Paper, Saturn, Monsanto, Cumberland Mountain Sand Co., even the Knoxville Utilities Board. The awards were highly regarded, even sought after. Tennessee Eastman, for instance, was in the running at least five times before it finally won the award in 1984 for improving its air and water discharges. Yet in at least two of those earlier five years, nobody won the award at all. As awards committee chairman Ed Thackston said, "We won't give an award if we don't see a clear winner." Tennessee Eastman may have been in compliance with government regulations, "but it's not enough just to be in compliance. They have to go beyond compliance."

THE LEAGUE AND THE "THIRD WAVE" CONSERVATIONISTS

Some environmental groups did not think it wise, being so friendly with industry. But then, TCL had never really called itself an environmental group. Somehow it always managed to cling to the old-fashioned term "conservation group."

The distinction was important, said Oak Ridge outdoor writer Evan Means in 1974. Modern environmentalism, he said, was part of what Stewart Udall called the "Third Wave" of conservation, the movement that began around Earth Day and included men like Cleveland Amory and Paul Ehrlich, and groups like Greenpeace and the Environmental Defense Fund. The First Wave, around the turn of the century, was made up of men like Teddy Roosevelt, George Bird Grinnell and Gifford Pinchot. The Second Wave was the hunters and fishermen of the '30s and '40s, men like Ding Darling and Aldo Leopold, Lou Williams and Herman Baggenstoss. The Third Wave became known as the environmentalists.

"They came on strong," wrote Means, "and they didn't apologize for their existence. The old Second Wave conservationists were never very aggressive, but they still got some things done, like the Dingell-Johnson Act and Tennessee's progress in water pollution abatement. The older conservation organizations sought financing from the 'moneyed interests,'" said Means, but not so the environmentalists. "[They] sought their money from their peers, by popular subscription, so they could afford to be more outspoken. They didn't hesitate to beard a bureaucrat in his den."

In many cases, however, these were differences of style rather than substance. For the most part, TCL maintained a polite, if cool, relationship with the new environmental groups, occasionally working together on common causes from scenic rivers to endangered species to the bottle bill. However, though the League obviously shared at least some of the environmentalists' agenda, it always seemed a bit of a loner.

For instance, few League members bought tickets to the annual EAF fund-raiser, a lively benefit for the Environmental Action Fund, a lobbying group founded in 1976 with seed money from actor Robert Redford. And though the League had a seat on the board of the Tennessee Environmental Council, its members almost never attended TEC's annual Intergroup Conference each fall. On the other hand, when the League held *its* annual convention each spring, there were precious few "environmentalists" at those. The fact was, though the two sets of activists had a good deal in common, they were really quite different—structurally, demographically and even, to a degree, philosophically.

The League, for instance, was one of the few groups in the state with a full-time office, a professional staff, substantial programming and a significant budget. Other than TEC, The Nature Conservancy, the Environmental Action Fund and a handful of others, pretty much all the environmental coalitions in the state were run entirely by volunteers, and most were run on a shoestring. The League was also one of the few groups with a strong presence on Capitol Hill, and one of even fewer groups with real friendships there. The League's top leaders *looked* like legislators: mostly men, mostly white, mostly married, mostly middle-aged and mostly conservative. Most of them were white-collar professionals—physicians, lawyers, engineers and businessmen—who had lived in Tennessee for most of their mostly successful careers.

In contrast to TCL, the Third Wave of activists tended to be a good deal younger, as often female as male, often recent transplants from other parts of the country. They were often single, and though most of them were well educated, with solid upper-middle class backgrounds and values, many were just getting started in their careers; many were still in school. Though they had no fear of Capitol Hill, they were received there with indifference, if not outright contempt. Racially, though they were still predominantly white, they were probably more tolerant of diversity. Most were social liberals; the majority were Democrats.

Moreover, while many of the environmentalists could perhaps have learned to overlook the age and gender differences in the League, few, presumably, could ignore the fact (or at any rate the perception) that hunting and fishing were the League's main pursuits. Not necessarily because they objected to hunting and fishing (although a fair number did), but because they personally did not do these things. The environmentalists' favorite recreations were things like hiking, camping, caving, bird watching, canoeing and nature photography—the so-called "nonconsumptive" uses of nature. However, at least some were opposed—strenuously—to hunting and fishing. At one point in the late '80s the Tennessee Environmental Council even signed up a local animal-rights group as an affiliate.

By then, however, TEC and the League were almost completely estranged.

TCL AND TEC: COMMON BONDS, BUT BREAKABLE

The split was unfortunate. After all, TEC had sprung from the loins of the League itself, back in 1969-1970. For years, the two organizations had remained close, or at least as close as TCL ever got to another organization whose members didn't often wear camouflage. TEC and the League shared many of the same positions, many of the same supporters, many of the same government contractors. At one point in the mid-'80s, they even shared the same office space. The Council had developed a reputation as solid as the League's—perhaps, in some respects, even stronger, because it was not so narrowly identified with one special interest. Its first executive director, Dr. Ruth Neff, was a thoughtful, clear-eyed analyst whose

Dr. Ruth Neff left TEC in 1984 to join Lamar Alexander's Safe Growth Team, then stayed on through the McWherter administration. When Neff retired in 1994, the Department of Environment and Conservation named its main conference room after her. Courtesy of TDEC.

understanding of politics was as keen as her understanding of environmental science. Both groups were recognized and respected on Capitol Hill (though Ruth Neff was not by nature the glad-hander that Tony Campbell was) and they were equally in demand on steering committees and advisory boards. And though they did not always stand on the same side of an issue, they both believed firmly in consensus and compromise.

When Neff left the Council in 1984 to join Lamar Alexander's new Safe Growth Team, TEC's mantle passed to Neff's assistant, Mayo Taylor. Though younger and probably more innovative than her predecessor, Taylor had no desire to tinker with the Council's basic program of objective advocacy based on solid technical research. For instance, at a 1985 public hearing on the MRS, a proposed nuclear waste storage facility in Oak Ridge, Taylor delivered a dozen pages of economic, logistic and demographic data to support the Council's decision to oppose the facility. Congressman Bart Gordon later said that it was Taylor's testimony that convinced him to oppose the MRS as well.

Taylor, however, had promised to stay only two years. Her replacement was John Sherman, the twenty-something former director of Vanderbilt's Student Environmental Health Program. Under Sherman's leadership, the Council broke new ground in a number of previously neglected areas, especially recycling and other solid waste issues. Sherman also broadened the Council's membership base, attracting support from Nashville's music and arts communities as well as the growing number of so-called Greens councils, "socially responsible" businesses and community-based waste management groups, notably HALT (Humanity Against Lethal Trash) and BURNT (Bring Urban Recycling to Nashville Today).

In making some of these changes, however, Sherman stepped on a few of the older toes on the TEC board. Not long after he arrived, he convinced the board to abolish the handful of at-large seats reserved for industry, such as DuPont's Roy Johnson and Mitch Magid of Steiner Liff. Though there were many in the Council who welcomed this move, others, including Shirley Patterson, Cecil Branstetter, Tony Campbell and Ruth Neff herself, were disturbed by what they saw as an unnecessary combativeness.

Sherman and some TEC staff also managed to get crossways with state regulatory agencies, suggesting they were too soft on polluters. Jim Tramel, for instance, the director of TEC's toxics program, told reporters that "state government [was] unwilling to implement pollution prevention policies." One result, of course, was that TEC found itself increasingly shut out of policy discussions, both formal and informal. On the other hand, the Council's complaints led to a number of successful lawsuits against noncomplying industries in the early '90s. Nonetheless, when TEC began challenging some of the League's own positions, TCL quietly let its membership expire in 1992. These fences have only recently begun mending, partly because TEC got a new director, Alan Jones, in 1994.

Of course, the Environmental Council wasn't the only organization with a reputation for being unreasonable. Some groups—including some sportsmen's groups—said the same thing about the Conservation League. TCL was bossy and arrogant, they charged, overly intimate with legislators, agencies and industry groups and not intimate enough with citizens groups. Few issues underscored these tensions like the recurring debate over wilderness in the Cherokee National Forest.

THE FIGHT OVER WILDERNESS IN THE CHEROKEE

The argument, which began long before the 1980s, centered on how much acreage in the Cherokee should be open to timber harvests, off-road vehicles, "habitat manipulation" and other mechanical intrusions, and how much should be reserved for more passive, nonconsumptive pursuits such as hiking, back-country camping and whatever hunting and fishing could be managed without benefit of trucks or roads, cabins or motorboats. Proponents of maximum wilderness, especially Tennessee Citizens for Wilderness Planning, the Sierra Club, the Wilderness Society and various hiking clubs, held that the Cherokee could easily afford to set aside 15 percent of its 625,000 acres for deliberate nondevelopment. Opponents of wilderness—especially loggers who benefitted from subsidized timber sales, but also many sportsmen and even some officials of the Forest Service—held that an unmanaged forest is a wasted resource.

Then there was the League, always somewhere in the middle, though with a distinct lean toward "multiple use." The League understood the appeal of a primitive wilderness experience, and said more than once that it supported the concept of wilderness areas. It also acknowledged the potential damage to the environment from logging roads and four-wheelers, as well as the benefits of wilderness to certain species, including black bears, certain rare plants and red-cockaded woodpeckers, an endangered species that nests only in the cavities of old-growth pine forests.

On the other hand, said the League, did the Cherokee really even need designated wilderness? Forest Service records showed that barely twenty percent of the recreational users of the Cherokee were nonsportsmen. (Of course, such statistics could just as well be used to argue *for* wilderness.) At any rate, there were the Smokies, right next door, half-a-million acres of *de facto* if not designated wilderness. (In 1978 Senator Jim Sasser tried to get most of the Smokies declared wilderness—excluding the area around Mt. LeConte Lodge—but the bill did not pass.) Even assuming the pro-wilderness folks *could* make a case for more wilderness, did it have to be in the same places used by hunters and fishermen? And as for the argument that wilderness was its own justification, the League saw that as almost no argument at all. A century of research had shown managed forests to be healthier, more productive and more ecologically diverse than forests left to themselves. In short, though it supported some wilderness set-asides, the League usually voted in favor of multiple use.

A BRIEF HISTORY OF THE CHEROKEE

Congress had inadvertently laid the grounds for the controversy when it passed the Wilderness Act in 1964. The act established the National Wilderness Preservation System, a network of federally owned lands "untrammeled by man" and "affected primarily by the forces of nature." To qualify, an area had to be free of roads, human habitation and "permanent improvements" of any kind; it had to have "outstanding opportunities for solitude or a primitive and unconfined type of recreation"; and it had to be of "sufficient size"—the bill recommended a minimum five thousand acres. Interestingly, wilderness areas were not required to have scenic, scientific, educational or historic value.

The original act designated some 9.5 million acres of wilderness lands, most of them in the 187 million-acre National Forest System, the rest in lands administered by the National Park Service or the Bureau of Land Management. Most of this was in the West, however, and none of it was in the Cherokee, the narrow band of forest that lies in two sections along the easternmost edge of Tennessee, straddling the Great Smoky Mountains National Park. Where the forests of the Cherokee spill into Georgia they become the Chattahoochee National Forest; where they cross into North Carolina, they are known as the Nantahala National Forest in the south and the Pisgah National Forest to the north.

The Wilderness Act was not the first time the nation's forests had been inventoried. In 1891, the Forest Reserve Act had authorized the U.S. Division of Forestry (later the U.S. Forest Service) to buy lands for "forest reserves" nationwide, and in 1900, President William McKinley ordered a study of the Southern Appalachians. (Gifford Pinchot was one of the preparers.) In 1901, President Roosevelt submitted the report to Congress, along with a resolution from Tennessee legislators favoring a national forest reserve in their state.

By June 1920, the U.S. Forest Service had acquired three "purchase units" in East Tennessee—the Unaka, the Pisgah and the Cherokee—and proclaimed all three national forests. In 1936, the three units were combined into one, the Cherokee National Forest. That same year, Tennessee and the Forest Service signed a cooperative management agreement for the Cherokee, creating the Tellico Wildlife Management Area and authorizing others. That fall the Game and Fish Commission held the first managed wild boar hunt in Tellico's—and the nation's—history.

Yet even back then, there was some interest in wilderness. A fellow named Benton MacKaye, for instance, had proposed a "wilderness footpath" from Georgia to Maine as early as 1921. The first efforts to protect the Smokies were underway by the early 1920s, led by men like Ed Meeman, Paul Fink and Paul Adams, who built the first cabin on Mt. LeConte in 1925. In 1935, the Forest Service itself proposed a protected wilderness area in the Cherokee, tentatively named the Citico-Cheoah Primitive Area, near Citico Creek. But nothing ever came of it, and by the time the 1964 Wilderness Act passed, the Forest Service was taking the position that there "[wasn't] any wilderness in the eastern United States" at all.

Some folks believed otherwise. A pro-wilderness group called the Southeastern Coalition for Eastern Wilderness now began lobbying to correct the insult. In 1971, the Forest Service conducted another survey of potential wilderness, the Roadless Area Review and Evaluation.

The first round of RARE proposals, released for comment in 1973, called for three wilderness areas in the southern Cherokee: Cohutta (an extension of the existing Cohutta Wilderness Area in Georgia); Joyce Kilmer-Slickrock (an extension of the Kilmer-Slickrock area in North Carolina); and the Gee Creek Wilderness Area on the Hiwassee River, entirely in Tennessee. The pro-wilderness folks supported all three areas. The League objected only to those sections that fell in the most heavily managed parts of the Tellico and Ocoee Wildlife Management Areas. The Kilmer-Slickrock extension, for instance, would have included seventeen thousand acres of the Citico Creek watershed in the Tellico, including the Double Camp and Big Fodderstack areas. The Cohutta proposal impinged on sixteen thousand acres of the Ocoee WMA, including much of Big Frog Mountain. It would also close one of the main access roads into the area.

The League's members did not much favor the idea of turning intensively managed habitat back into wilderness. In a 1973 statement to the Senate Interior Committee, Tony Campbell urged that the committee remove four thousand acres from both the Cohutta and Kilmer-Slickrock areas; he also urged that public hearings be held to allow "citizen input." The League was certainly not opposed to wilderness, he stressed. But it was not willing to give up previously established hunting grounds. Ed Thackston, still working for Winfield Dunn at the time, made a similar appeal on behalf of the governor. They needn't have worried. When the Eastern Wilderness Areas Act was finalized in 1974, it included only 8,200 acres in Tennessee: a 1,700-acre extension of the Cohutta; a 4,000-acre extension of Joyce Kilmer-Slickrock; and the 2,500-acre Gee Creek Wilderness. Several other areas, including Big Frog Mountain and Citico Creek, were designated for further study.So now the Cherokee was less than two percent wilderness, and the pro-wilderness forces were not pleased.

RARE II: ANOTHER CHANCE FOR WILDERNESS

Jimmy Carter campaigned for President on the promise of more wilderness, and when he got to the White House he kept his promise. (In 1979, Carter was the first President to be named Conservationist of the Year by the National Wildlife Federation.) In 1977, the U.S. Forest Service began a new evaluation of Eastern wilderness called RARE II. This time, though, it used somewhat relaxed guidelines for defining wilderness: "roadless," for instance, could mean so many miles of primitive logging roads per so many miles of forest. When the draft environmental impact statement came out in 1978, it identified 130,000 additional acres of potential wilderness in the Cherokee, including Citico Creek and twenty other areas. The public had until October 1, 1978, to submit comments.

Greeneville director and two-term League president Mark Benko befriends an osprey on the TCL / TWRA / TVA hacking site on the Nolichucky River. Benko helped formulate TCL's response to the debate over wilderness in the Cherokee. Courtesy of TWRA.

In an interesting coincidence, the Tennessee Wildlife Resources Commission had announced in June 1977 that it was designating the entire Cherokee National Forest as the Cherokee Wildlife Management Area. All the old management units were now absorbed into this giant new WMA, including Tellico, Ocoee, Andrew Johnson, Kettlefoot, Laurel Fork and Unicoi. For some years, TWRA and the Forest Service had been hoping to create a single, forest-wide management area featuring uniform seasons and a single permit good for almost all species. Sportsmen now had more freedoms in the Cherokee than ever, but for some, the consolidation was just one more reason to oppose wilderness.

At any rate, as soon as the draft EIS cam out, an opposition force formed, spearheaded by the Carter County Hunting and Fishing Club, a longtime TCL affiliate. Environmentalists meanwhile had formed a lobby of their own, the Cherokee National Forest Wilderness Coalition. Its coordinator was Will Skelton, a Knoxville lawyer and head of the Tennessee Sierra Club's conservation committee.

Public input was to be a central feature of RARE II; in all, more than two hundred hearings would be held throughout the Eastern United States. Given the scope of the process, the Forest Service had stated at the outset that it would not consider form letters or petitions. Accordingly, the pro-wilderness faction submitted 724 "substantive letters," as Skelton put it, along with a written report of each area. The anti-wilderness folks defied the rules, flooding the Forest Service with 12,586 petition signatures and form letters. But to the consternation of the wilderness coalition, when it came time to tally public opinion, the Forest Service decided to accept the mass-produced opposition.

Meanwhile the League was holding numerous meetings of its own, both with its own members in East Tennessee as well as Forest Service officials. Its conclusion, to no one's surprise, was that designating all or even most of the 130,000 acres under study would be a "poor allocation of the forest resource." "[M]ost areas," it said, "would be best managed under the multiple use concept." In September 1978 TCL submitted its own heavily detailed analysis to the Forest Service: designate four areas as wilderness, hold two for further study—and leave the other twelve as they are.

Once again, pro-wilderness groups hotly protested the League's findings—or, as Campbell mildly stated it in the League's 1978 annual report, "the League's stand was very unpopular with many organizations."

But when the Forest Service's final report came out, the League's looked generous by comparison. Submitted to Congress in January 1979, the Forest Service's recommendations for Eastern wilderness included only one small area in Tennessee, the four thousand-acre Bald River Gorge on the Tellico River. Another five areas—Citico Creek, Big Frog and Little Frog Mountains, Flint Mill and Pond Mountain—were recommended for further study. The others were recommended as nonwilderness. Only after Will Skelton complained to Congress about the Forest Service's sleight-of-hand during the comment period did it add two more small areas, Pond Mountain Addition and Unaka Mountain, to the list for further review.

Wiser and more aggressive now, the wilderness coalition submitted a plan of its own, the Citizens Wilderness Proposal, designating 15 percent wilderness in the Cherokee. It began circulating its own petitions, eventually collecting more than twenty thousand names, and it enlisted the support of Knoxville Republican Congressman John Duncan. Nevertheless, when its draft EIS came out, the Forest Service recommended less than half of Big Frog Mountain, and none of Citico Creek. TCL was again more liberal, calling for wilderness designation of the whole Big Frog area and roughly two-thirds of Citico Creek. Both TWRA and the Department of Conservation had recommended both areas be included in their entirety.

In 1983, Congressman Duncan introduced a bill giving wilderness protection to all of Citico Creek, Big Frog Mountain and Bald River Gorge. Tennessee's Senators Howard Baker and Jim Sasser introduced a similar bill in the Senate, and when the Tennessee Wilderness Act was finally enacted on October 30, 1984, it included all three areas, a total of some 25,000 acres.

Wilderness was finally on a roll. In 1985, the Forest Service recommended six more wilderness areas, including four in the neglected northern half of the Cherokee: Pond Mountain, Sampson Mountain, Big Laurel Branch and Unaka Mountain. With the support of Congressmen Duncan and Jim Quillen and Senators Sasser and Al Gore, the 1986 Tennessee Wilderness Act passed. (The following year Sasser tried once more to pass a Smokies wilderness bill, but his colleagues must have thought they'd granted enough wilderness in his part of the country. At any rate, the bill failed.)

Nonetheless, Tennessee now had 11 wilderness areas covering more than 66,000 acres, or slightly more than 10 percent of the Cherokee. To show that there were no hard feelings, the League named Will Skelton Forest Conservationist of the Year for 1986.

NOT THROUGH YET: THE CHEROKEE MANAGEMENT PLAN

But it wasn't long before the League would again be at odds with the Sierra Club, this time over the Cherokee National Forest Management Plan.

Congress passed the National Forest Management Act in 1976, requiring each National Forest to draw up a long-range management plan for all of its various uses and resources, from logging and wildlife management to education and wilderness recreation. Moreover, Congress required that there be extensive public participation in the planning process.

For the next several years, the administrators at the Cherokee worked up a number of possible scenarios for how the Cherokee might be operated over the next half-century. In January 1985, it released for public review a total of six alternatives. Alternative 1, calling for no changes at all to the current plan, served as a baseline; the other five differed mainly according to how much land was slated for logging, how much for wilderness and how much for new roads. The Forest Service's preference was Alternative 6, which called for some added wilderness, continued clear-cutting and new roads that would, however, be closed during wet seasons when logging is most destructive to the environment.

League director Mark Benko worked closely with TWRA and the Forest Service scrutinizing the alternatives and discussing them with local sportsmen. What Benko and other board members finally recommended was a slightly more restrictive version of the Forest Service's preferred alternative. In fact, when the Forest Service released its final plan in February 1986, its recommendation—a new Alternative 7—was "just about identical" to the League's proposal, as Tony Campbell noted with obvious pride.

However, Alternative 7 was not acceptable to a pro-wilderness faction that now included Will Skelton's Sierra Club, the Wilderness Society, Tennessee Citizens for Wilderness Planning, the Tennessee Audubon Council and the Smoky Mountain Hiking Club. The five organizations filed an appeal, challenging (among other things) that the plan allowed excessive logging and citing the Forest Service's own accounts that it was losing more than a million dollars a year on below-cost timber sales in the Cherokee. Though the two sides eventually signed a settlement agreement in August 1988, there would continue to be periodic uprisings over issues like road closings, use of ORVs and timber harvesting.

DRAWING SWORDS OVER REELFOOT DRAWDOWNS

Like the Cherokee wilderness, another resource issue of the '80s dated back many decades. Despite the 1941 lease agreement that gave the U.S. Fish and Wildlife Service control of a third of Reelfoot Lake in return for a half-million dollars worth of improvements, Reelfoot did not appear to be much improved. The muck bottom was muckier than ever. The water was more burdened with pesticides, herbicides and topsoil from area farms. Channelized feeder streams carried in still more silt.

The problem seemed to be made worse by the Fish and Wildlife Service itself. Every spring (when water levels are normally at their highest), the USFWS opened the spillway gates on the southern end of the lake in order to drain water off 2,800 acres of farmland at the northern end—including 1,200 acres within its Reelfoot National Wildlife Refuge. The USFWS then planted this property with waterfowl food for the next winter's crop of migrating ducks and geese. (Meanwhile, farmers on the adjacent 1,600 acres got a bonus planting season, courtesy of the taxpayer.)

TWRA liked ducks and geese, too, of course, but it also had a responsibility to the overall management of the lake. Though Reelfoot was still one of the most productive lakes in the state, it was not as healthy as it once was. Crappie, for instance, still averaged just 4.1 ounces, compared to 9 ounces in the early '50s. One of the problems, TWRA biologists now knew, was eutrophication: the lake was too rich in plant nutrients and vegetation, and dangerously low in dissolved oxygen. In a sense, the lake was choking. And one of the causes, TWRA knew, was that Reelfoot, which normally would have frequent periods of high and low water like all the other shallow waters in these parts, was being kept at the same tourist-friendly level all year round.

No one was quite sure why, but the U.S. Fish and Wildlife Service had been controlling lake levels at Reelfoot for years. In 1984, the Legislature named TWRA the lead administering agency for the lake, and TWRA began looking for ways to correct the lake's problems.

That August, TWRA announced—with the USFWS concurring—that it proposed to lower the lake level about six feet below normal pool, beginning in May 1985, and let it stay down for about five months. By exposing fifty percent of the lake's bottom to sun and air, the agency believed, the extended drawdown would compact the muck enough to oxygenate the lake and revitalize the fishery.

It was a controversial plan at best. Hundreds of lake residents made a living from fishing and other forms of tourism, and the drawdown would leave cabins and boat docks high and dry. TWRA admitted that the exposed muck and algae were sure to smell as bad as they looked, and there were concerns about possible fish kills. Nor would the process end with the first drawdown. TWRA said it would probably have to lower the lake at least partially, every ten years or so.

To no one's surprise, the plan got virtually no local support. The League itself hesitated to stake a position at first. Hundreds of its members fished on the lake, and at least one of them, Al Hamilton, owned a sportsmen's lodge there. In fact, some folks believed it was because of Hamilton that the lake was getting so much attention in the first place. Hamilton had founded the Reelfoot Lake Development Council to organize local residents on behalf of the lake; in 1984, TCL named him Conservationist of the Year. Nevertheless, after hearing the rationale for a drawdown, including the fact that similar actions had worked in Florida, the League in 1985 passed a resolution in full support of the drawdown.

The landowners still weren't buying. Shortly after the drawdown began, they sued TWRA and the U.S. Fish and Wildlife Service in Federal District Court in Memphis, demanding an environmental impact statement under NEPA. Judge Odell Horton agreed, and ordered the drawdown stopped while the USFWS, as the federal agency with control of the spillway under the 1941 lease, prepared the EIS. TWRA appealed the ruling to the U.S. Circuit Court of Appeals for the Sixth Circuit but lost on appeal.

When the EIS was finally completed in July 1989, more than three years overdue, the court found it acceptable. In September, USFWS and TWRA announced they were resuming the drawdown. Again local residents sued the two agencies in Federal District Court, challenging the sufficiency of the EIS. Though the League's directors still believed the drawdown was biologically sound, in September 1990 they voted to join the lawsuit as friends of the court in support of the plaintiffs. "What we're interested in is getting the case before the court," said West Tennessee director Sam Anderson, "and get[ting] the issues concerning state water laws resolved, as well as determining who is truly responsible for overall management of Reelfoot Lake."

This time, however, the court ruled for the defendants. The lawsuit was dismissed.

But still the drawdown did not proceed. It seemed the spillway—one of the oldest in the state, built in 1930—could not handle the proposed drawdown; another would have to built. Then another question arose: word had it TWRA's water level management plan included *raising* lake levels from time to time, in addition to lowering them. This aspect of TWRA's proposal implicated property rights issues of adjacent private landowners in Tennessee, as well as a small group of large, politically powerful farmers in Kentucky. As a result, TWRA's plan to artificially fluctuate Reelfoot water levels got moved to a back burner. As of early 1997, that's where it remained.

A DECADE OF LEADERSHIP TRAINING

The debate over drawdowns was unusual in one respect. The League's leadership in the issue, at least in the final years, came at least as much from regional director Sam Anderson as it did from Tony Campbell. Anderson briefed the board as new developments arose; he researched the complicated history of the 1941 lease; he even wrote a three-part series explaining the issue in *The Weakley County Press*. According to League policy, this was exactly how it should be: one of the jobs of regional director was to provide local leadership in local issues.

Yet it hadn't always worked that way. While the League had an unusually active and gifted board by most standards, it often struggled to keep all the members involved. On several occasions, so few came to meetings that they couldn't make a quorum. For their part, members complained they weren't always notified properly, weren't kept informed, weren't delegated to. At one point a group of directors from the western region (Region 1) even formed a "Cottonmouth Coalition," vowing not to communicate with headquarters until headquarters communicated better with them. Unfortunately, they were only partly joking: the weight of leadership at TCL *was* rather unevenly distributed.

One of the reasons, ironically, was simply that the League had a staff who did much, perhaps too much, of the League's work. Before 1972, those responsibilities were spread among as many as forty or fifty directors and at least as many committee members. When Tony Campbell was hired, the dynamic of labor shifted. Those who chose to slack off found it remarkably easy to do so. Those who wished to stay involved could certainly do so. But the new director proved almost *too* competent, said four-time League president Larry M. Richardson. A self-starter with a strong independent streak, Campbell often preferred to figure a thing out for himself rather than wait on others to help him. It seemed to the board, said Richardson, that it had become almost "a rubber stamp" for the director's policies and projects.

Another problem was simply that the board structure was so ungainly. For many years, it had been partitioned into just three regions (West, Middle and East), each represented by a vice president. In 1974 the board had tried to make things more efficient by subdividing further, into twelve districts. In 1977, it divided further still, grouping the twelve districts into four regions, each with a vice president. In 1981, in an effort to make them more equitable and cohesive, president Ed Thackston and a committee redrew both district and regional boundaries. But none of these measures solved the basic problem of leader involvement.

In 1979, the four regional vice presidents—Jim Whoric, Jim Wilkes, Dallas Prince and Herman Carrick—went to a leadership conference in Asheville, North Carolina, sponsored by the National Wildlife Federation. There, they learned about a region-based system of leadership in which all district and regional directors were expected to do a lot more than any of them had ever done before: make monthly written reports, submit newsletter articles, recruit affiliates, attend public hearings, talk to other clubs and generally serve as the League's point men. In turn, the central office was supposed to be more responsive to their needs.

It worked for a little while. Whoric, Wilkes and several directors were especially faithful to their new duties, writing articles, reporting at every board meeting and holding regional meetings. Others, however, were not so zealous. Frankly, this drove Ed Thackston up the wall. A two-term League president from 1979 to 1981, Thackston had joined the board in 1974 when he left the governor's office to return to Vanderbilt. Dr. Thackston was one of the League's most talented and devoted board members, performing his responsibilities with

Between them, Larry M. Richardson (left) and Edward L. Thackston have served nearly forty years on TCL's board of directors. Both were heavily involved in the League's multiple efforts to restructure. Courtesy of Larry Richardson and Edward Thackston.

an almost military diligence and expecting his colleagues to do likewise. When they did not, the engineer in him looked for ways to correct the problem.

Thus emerged the Yellow Notebooks. Each three-ring notebook contained a list of directors' duties, the constitution and bylaws, a directory, a set of monthly report forms, a copy of past resolutions and a set of the most recent minutes. Subsequent minutes would be distributed with the holes pre-punched so they could go right in the notebook with the others.

In June 1983 the board held a leadership retreat at Tims Ford State Park. Here, members agreed to restructure the operating committees and add a new one: long-range planning. Planning committee members included Tom Talley and the four regional vice presidents: Mitchell Parks, William David Smith, Don Byerly and Tracey Simpson. Its chairman was Ed Thackston. By October, the committee had developed four pages of goals and objectives: strong affiliates, a strong education program, even a conservation education center. They also passed around ten pages of office policies and procedures, the first time the League had ever had such a document. There were policies for everything from how many coffee breaks employees could take to how much they could spend on breakfast on the road. It included a vacation policy, an antidiscrimination policy, policies for hiring and travel, even a policy for how staff dressed for work ("a manner generally accepted to be acceptable").

These changes no doubt did some good, but apparently the sense of something amiss lingered, because by 1987 another major planning process was in the works. This one was dubbed the strategic planning process, and its key word was "stakeholders." The way to run a volunteer organization, said Charles "Buzz" Buffington, recently elected to the executive committee, was to run it like a business. (The Izaak Walton League said the same thing in 1927.) Thus the strategic planning process used words like clients, employees and competitors. Members talked about marketing strategies, economic trend and performance evaluations. Committees were again restructured, new ones were added, bylaws were again revised. And again they pressed the need for a conservation resource center.

THE LONG ROAD TOWARD A RESOURCE CENTER

The idea for a conservation resource center had started with Mitchell Parks. Parks, a leader in the all-black Nashville Sportsman's Club, joined the League as an at-large member of the board in 1980. Though he liked to fish and hunt, Parks did not consider himself an expert in matters of wildlife management. Rather, he preferred that his contributions reflect the sort of things he did in his day job. Parks was director of the Tennessee office of the U.S. Department of Commerce's Economic Development Administration. His goal was to develop the economy of the Conservation League.

Parks had barely been on board three months when, midway through the June 7, 1980, board meeting, he brought up an idea he had been chewing on for some weeks. The conservation community needed an education resource center; the League would benefit from owning its own headquarters. Was there any reason, he asked, why the two facilities could not be combined? The other directors were intrigued by the prospect of what Parks called a "one-stop shopping center" for conservation materials, reports, slideshows and the like. Even better if it could double as the League's permanent offices.

It was a good thing Parks had staying power. He would pursue this rather elusive dream for the next ten years (including two terms as president, and eight months in the hospital in 1987 following a near-fatal car wreck that cost him both legs).

Parks' original vision was a handsome new facility, built with donated funds on what he

Mitchell Parks' dream for a Conservation Resource Center survived ten years of slow fund-raising, a half-dozen failed building sites and a car wreck that cost him both legs. TCL file photo.

hoped would be donated land. Early on, he and Ed Thackston enlisted a leading Nashville architectural and engineering firm, Barge, Waggoner, Sumner and Cannon, to help with planning and design.

Unfortunately, sketching the center on paper was easy compared to finding the projected $300,000 for the building and an appropriate lot to build it on. The 130-acre Croft farm on Nolensville Road, owned in trust by the Cumberland Museum and Science Center, seemed a possibility at first, but there were complications, and the site was eventually used for the new Grassmere Wildlife Park. Then, in late 1981, the League received a donation of 15.2 acres of Mill Creek flood plain on Murfreesboro Road, just south of downtown Nashville. The area was a nesting site for black-crowned night herons, a threatened species in Tennessee, and Mitchell Parks had encouraged the owners, Mandell Cypress and Jerome Guttman, to donate it to the League for a resource center and nature preserve. The board was delighted, and reporters were advised to stand by as construction should be starting almost any day. But it never happened.

Next, Parks and his team of housing sleuths tried to get permission to build next to TWRA's headquarters at Ellington Agricultural Center. TWRA didn't mind, but the state did. They then got an easement from the Corps of Engineers to build near Percy Priest Dam, an attractive site, but that fell through also. So it went, year after year.

Meanwhile, the money came in—at a trickle. If Parks had expected the board would set the tone for the capital campaign, he was right—unfortunately. Several years into the campaign, two-thirds of the directors had put nothing in the building fund, and the response from businesses was just as underwhelming. In 1985 Parks persuaded the board to hire a private fund-raising firm, Don Elliott and Associates.

With professionals in charge, contributions picked up immediately. By the time Parks was elected League president in 1986 (the first African American ever to hold that position), the fund boasted nearly $128,000 in cash, pledges and in-kind contributions. This sudden outpouring soon dried up, however, and by decade's end, the $300,000 building fund contained barely $140,000, very little of which was in ready cash. In the meantime, of course, the cost of new construction continued to skyrocket. Mitchell Parks would have to be patient a while longer.

BOTTLE BILLS, BILLBOARDS, AND THE CAMPAIGN FOR SCENIC BEAUTY

The League's Mill Creek acreage never was developed. But that does not mean it was a drain on the budget. There was a lone billboard on the property, and it was earning the League eight hundred dollars a year in rental income.

Billboards were still an emerging conservation issue in the 1980s. At issue was so-called visual clutter, the destruction of the viewshed. By the time Lady Bird Johnson's Highway Beautification Act passed in 1965, the nation was looking more critically at roadside advertising as well as other forms of visual pollution, including litter and unscreened junkyards. A handful of states banned billboards altogether—Hawaii, Vermont and Maine among them—and a growing number of cities. Brentwood, Germantown and Farragut were among the first Tennessee towns to restrict obtrusive signs. In Sevierville, where hundreds of garish tourist

When Governor Lamar Alexander proposed a Cleaner Highways program in 1986, Tony Campbell was his liaison with the conservation and environmental community. Photo by Dave Murrian. Courtesy of TWRA.

signs line Highway 441 into the Smokies, city administrators had erected a small plaque apologizing for the clutter.

The League itself had complained about billboards from time to time, especially the "selective cutting" of trees along public highways by the billboard companies. A 1980 article in *Tennessee Out-Of-Doors* called it "vandalism for private gain" and declared that government agencies that wink at the practice should be indicted. In 1979 and 1980, TCL supported legislation banning the practice, but neither bill passed.

When Lamar Alexander became governor in 1979, scenic beauty was one of the first issues he faced. The movement to pass a bottle bill was just then gaining momentum, led by the Conservation League and supported by a wide range of citizen groups and even some industries, notably ALCOA. The first round of legislation failed. By 1980, however, supporters thought they had enough votes for passage.

According to Ruth Neff, that was when "Alexander's folks decided to punt." The governor wanted to "develop a viable alternative" to the bottle bill, she said, one with "a little bit broader coverage." The result was Alexander's Safe Growth Plan, a fifty-page program of environmental and public health initiatives unveiled in January 1981. On the matter of throwaway containers, the plan recommended voluntary recycling, as well as continued use of government and prison crews to pick up roadside trash. As for billboards, it recommended stricter limits on size and placement, as well as higher permit fees (the present fees paid only a fraction of what it cost the state to collect them). The plan also urged tighter controls on "indiscriminate" tree cutting and urged the state Department of Transportation (TDOT) to "step up" efforts to acquire the seven thousand nonconforming billboards.

To implement some of these proposals, Alexander created a Safe Growth Action Team as part of the governor's office. TDOT planner Ben Smith was brought on board as director; his policy assistant was Day Lohman from the Tennessee office of The Nature Conservancy. (Ruth Neff would succeed Lohman in 1984.) By the time Ned McWherter dissolved the Safe Growth Team in 1987 (actually, he just gave it a different name, the Environmental Policy Group, and moved it to a different department), it had accomplished some impressive things: a clean water initiative, wetlands protection, natural areas planning. However, there had been little movement on billboards, until the final year of Alexander's tenure.

In January 1986, Alexander called a press conference to announce a new administrative measure called Cleaner Highways. Cleaner Highways called for many of the same measures outlined in his earlier Safe Growth Plan, including stricter billboard controls, screened junkyards and uniform "logo signs" at highway exits. Unlike the Safe Growth Plan, however, these measures were immediately drafted into a bill and put into the legislative hopper.

A citizens' coalition sprang up at once, led by the League and a new group called Tennesseans for Scenic Beauty, an affiliate of the national Coalition for Scenic Beauty. (The groups are now called Scenic Tennessee and Scenic America.) Its members included not only environmental groups but garden clubs, municipal planners, neighborhood organizations, landscape architects and an assortment of tourism-related businesses. As the most experienced negotiator in the group, Tony Campbell soon became the unofficial leader of the lobbying effort.

For three months, volunteers polled voters, distributed fact sheets, met with legislators and even tied yellow ribbons around roadside trees. When Commissioner of Conservation Charles Howell began wearing a yellow tie to work, everyone in the campaign started wearing yellow. The group got free legal advice not only from the national coalition in Washington but also from the Southern Environmental Law Center in Virginia, whose sign-control experts had successfully challenged the First Amendment rights of billboards and other forms of commercial speech.

Cleaner Highways did not pass, however. Though supporters can probably take credit for hastening the use of logo signs, they were no match for the well-financed lobbyists of the billboard industry, especially Lamar Advertising, one of the largest firms in the Southeast. Lamar's sometimes hostile business tactics had been investigated in North Carolina and elsewhere; the Cleaner Highways coalition had often cited those findings as it tried to make its case in Tennessee.

The irony was, it was Lamar Advertising sending the League a check for eight hundred dollars every April.

Not that the League could have done anything about it at that point, even had it wanted to. It was locked into a five-year lease that would not expire until 1988. But the League had no intention of canceling the lease, according to Ed Thackston. "We never opposed billboards on urban, commercial property," he said, "only on rural or residential or agricultural land." Of course, one might argue that urban, commercial areas are precisely where billboard controls are needed most. At any rate, as of 1997 a sign still stood on the Murfreesboro Road property, and the League was still collecting rent on it.

THE LEAGUE TAKES AIM AT PRIVATE ACTS

In fairness to the League, running a nonprofit group was expensive, and few things were as expensive as lawsuits. And in late 1985, just as the billboard controversy was about to boil over, the League had finally gone to court over private wildlife acts.

The board had been considering a lawsuit against private (county-wide as opposed to statewide) wildlife laws since 1980, but now a pair of private acts regarding raccoon hunting had pushed the board into motion. Though the lawsuit specifically targeted only these two so-called "coon laws," the plaintiffs hoped its effect would be to undermine the constitutional basis for all local wildlife acts. Yet such laws were deeply entrenched in the culture and politics of rural Tennessee.

As a matter of fact, the very first wildlife acts passed in Tennessee were not statewide at all, but local. In 1870, the General Assembly passed three such acts. One banned deer hunting with dogs in Benton and Humphreys counties. Another set a closed season on game birds, songbirds and deer in the counties of Fayette, Rutherford and Shelby. And the third banned the use of seines and fishing nets in Davidson, Rutherford, Robertson, Maury, Williamson, Cheatham and six other counties, all in Middle Tennessee.

The second private act came exactly one year later, when six of the twelve Middle Tennessee counties opted out of the 1870 act. Thus was set the tone for wildlife legislation in Tennessee. From then on, laws were routinely made in one session only to be repealed in the next. In fact, when the General Assembly finally did pass its first *statewide* game law in 1875—a ban on songbird hunting, and a ban on most seining and trapping—it concluded with the names of forty counties to be exempted from the act—as well as a blanket exemption for every East Tennessee county not already named.

Getting an exemption passed was apparently not a very difficult matter. First, a band of constituents petitioned for the change with the county commission. The commission approved the request and forwarded it to the county's delegation in Nashville. Senator and Representative So-and-So put the petition in the form of a bill and introduced it in the next session of the General Assembly. Thanks to the quaint but questionable practice of "legislative courtesy," these acts usually passed with little or no debate.

The result was a constantly shifting patchwork of seasons, bag limits, gear requirements and hunting regulations, often unintelligible in their rationale. One law, for instance, prohibited Hamblen County hunters from shooting a raccoon out of a tree with a gun, but did allow knocking it out of the tree with a club. Frustrating as the laws must have been for administrators and game wardens, they occasionally stymied the sportsmen themselves. In the 1950s, for instance, some Davidson County coon hunters found themselves trying to repeal their own earlier law allowing year-round dog training. Apparently, coon dogs had wiped out their private cache of fifty imported raccoons.

And yet, absurd as it was, the practice of county-by-county wildlife management was not only upheld but specifically provided for by the Tennessee Constitution. Section 13, Article XI, of the 1870 Constitution (the one still in effect today) added this new provision: "The General Assembly shall have power to enact laws for the protection and preservation of game and fish, within the state, and such laws may be enacted for and applied and enforced in particular counties or geographical districts, designated by the General Assembly."

The trouble with this provision was that the typical member of the General Assembly had no more idea what constituted sound wildlife policy than the typical wildlife manager understood what constituted sound fiscal policy. That was why lawmakers created an independent Game and Fish Commission in the first place. The 1949 law creating the commission gave the agency exclusive jurisdiction over the wildlife resources of the state. The commission alone, it said, had the authority to decide "whether or not the supply of game and/or fish [was] at any time adequate to allow the taking thereof without the danger of extinction or undue depletion."

For the legislators periodically to abrogate that power was either arrogance—since it assumed they knew more about wildlife management than the people who did it for a living—or self-serving politics—since it subjected the interests of the many to the demands of the few. It may also have been unconstitutional. Another provision of the 1870 Constitution, Section 8 of Article XI, prohibits laws "for the benefit of individuals inconsistent with the general laws of the land." Obviously there was considerable wiggle room for deciding what was a benefit and what was not.

Over the years, periodic attempts were made to undo the ill effects of Section 13. In 1907, the General Assembly under Governor Malcolm Patterson repealed all local wildlife laws except for open seasons on squirrels and doves. "A law that is good enough for one county should be good enough for all the state," huffed state game warden Joseph Acklen. But Patterson's repeal was itself repealed in 1915 by Governor Tom Rye's reorganization bill. In 1939, Governor Prentice Cooper would try again, repealing all local laws and setting a moratorium on new ones. Like Patterson's bill, however, Cooper's bill was overturned by a radical change in the game and fish administration: the so-called model law of 1949.

BARKING LEGISLATORS

By 1980, the Tennessee Code contained more than 120 local wildlife laws, 78 for raccoons alone, and more were being slipped into the hopper all the time. A 1983 bill, for instance, proposed to give the county courts *all* regulation over coon hunting, including seasons, methods and bag limits. Another proposed to set a six-month training season for coon dogs, even stipulating the starting date. As Tony Campbell said in disgust, "the Legislature doesn't need to be in the business of setting season dates for anything." If the laws were a joke, the chambers were a circus. When coon laws came up for discussion, lawmakers often barked, bayed and howled until they had to quit for laughing.

The TCL board first broached the possibility of a lawsuit in 1980. By the 1982 annual meeting, Campbell reported on what would amount to a sort of class action. "This [suit] would take any act ever passed by the Legislature regulating wildlife and analyze each and every one of them," he said. "It would make no difference whether they were private acts or general acts with local application or general acts with statewide application. We would challenge all of them."

But in a series of meetings with the Nashville law firm of Willis and Knight, the League eventually decided to narrow the suit to coon laws only. After all, this would not be an easy case to win, cautioned William R. Willis, Jr., a former chairman of the Wildlife Resources Commission. (Willis had been Tennessee's representative on the Endangered Species Committee in 1978 when it refused to exempt the Tellico Dam from the Endangered Species Act.) The advantage of focusing on a single species was that there was plenty of recent data on raccoons, including a 1983 survey by the TWRA.

According to that survey, coon populations were indeed shrinking, especially in East Tennessee. "There aren't enough coons in East Tennessee to make a good coat," grumbled outdoor writer Don Kirk. In portions of Hawkins, Sullivan, Blount, Loudoun and Union counties, there were no coons at all. A good deal of coon hunting was done illegally, according to Mike Pelton, professor of wildlife management at the University of Tennessee. In the late 1970s, after tagging raccoons in a three-county area of East Tennessee, Pelton and his students found that hunters killed more than half the coons out of season.

Yet coon hunters and hunting clubs such as the East Tennessee Houndsmen's Association seemed unmoved by the data. After a futile effort to reach a compromise uniform season, the Wildlife Resources Commission in 1982 had banned *all* coon hunting and coon-dog training east of Highway 56 (or roughly one-third of the state). The following year, lawmakers showed their displeasure by setting their own seasons for the area east of Highway 56. In 1983, they established a *minimum* six-month open season for training, and a *minimum* six-week season for hunting. Nonetheless, the new laws failed to satisfy some area residents, who insisted on having the same seasons as their friends further west: a year-round training season, with four months for hunting. In 1984 the lawmakers tried to compromise by moving the dividing line a bit further to the right, to Highway 27. The restricted area now occupied only about one-fourth of the state.

Of course, to Campbell and the lawyers, it hardly mattered if the area was the size of a postage stamp; what mattered was that the Legislature was setting seasons at all. It was about this time that they decided to target only the two Highway 27 laws—the one setting a six-month coon dog training season and the other a six-week hunting season.

"The basic strategy," Campbell explained in a letter seeking funds to defray the costs of the lawsuit, "is that *if* the judge rules that these acts are illegal, then using his ruling we can ask the Attorney General to rule the other private acts unconstitutional." Campbell's letter must have been convincing. Even though the lawyers on the case were working almost for free, other expenses were expected to top four thousand dollars. Campbell suggested a sixty-dollar donation from each of the League's affiliates. Many responded with checks for one hundred, two hundred, even five hundred dollars. Eventually the League collected five thousand dollars.

Twenty-six drafts later, the suit was finally filed in Davidson County Chancery Court on November 7, 1985. Besides asking the court to declare both the Highway 27 laws unconstitutional, the lawsuit also asked that the TWRC impose a statewide closed season on hunting and chasing raccoons while it conducted a survey to determine what *would* be appropriate seasons.

The chief defendant named in the suit was W. J. Michael Cody as attorney general for the state of Tennessee. Two other defendants were Larry Nunn as chairman of the Tennessee

Wildlife Resources Commission and Gary Myers as executive director of TWRA. Of course, both Myers and Nunn were squarely behind the League. The agency and the commission were named, as often happens in such cases, only because they administered the laws in question.

Chancellor Irvin Kilcrease heard the case on June 4 and 5, 1986. The League's case had commanded plenty of convincing testimony, much press and a good deal of sympathy. Even the state's counsel, Assistant State Attorney General Mary Walker, acknowledged that the Legislature's method of setting seasons at the request of one or two legislators was not "the best way" to manage wildlife.

Nevertheless, said Walker, "The wisdom of what the Legislature has done is a matter exclusively reserved to the Legislature." Besides, she added pointedly, the Legislature could "eliminate the Wildlife Commission if [it] wanted to."

On August 20, 1986, Chancellor Kilcrease rejected the League's suit. According to an Associated Press report, the Chancellor was not convinced that the raccoon bills "[did] not tend to protect and preserve raccoons."

Disappointed but unbowed, the League appealed to the state Supreme Court. But that appeal too was shot down, unanimously and in much the same language used in the lower court. "One might conclude from [the expert testimony] the Legislature did not choose the very best means to protect and preserve the raccoon population," conceded Special Justice Thomas A. Greer in a decision dated September 21, 1987. "However, without question, it cannot be said these statutes do not 'tend' to preserve and protect the raccoon population." Besides, he noted (with striking if unintentional irony), "We know of no other discipline where it is insisted the Legislature is bound to follow the opinions of the best experts in the given field. This certainly is not true in taxation, finances, public health, schools, or other areas of governmental regulations."

No doubt it is true, Greer concluded, that as society changes, so do its values. We may well have a different regard for raccoons today than our forebears did a hundred years ago. Nevertheless, "[f]or this court to impose its judgment or discretion in this case would be a usurpation of a judgmental act specifically granted to the Legislature."

Clearly TCL's leaders had underestimated the extraordinary deference with which the courts regarded legislative powers. It cost them a lawsuit. But the effort earned them the respect of many who watched from the sidelines.

PROGRESS, BUT JUST BARELY, ON OBION-FORKED DEER

Meanwhile, although it did so at a positively glacial pace, another lawsuit inched closer to a resolution.

The Obion-Forked Deer Task Force convened by Governor Alexander in 1980 had in fact hammered out a settlement of sorts between the plaintiffs and the Corps of Engineers by late 1982—though for various reasons it was not formally accepted by the federal court for another two-and-a-half years.

Under the terms of the consent decree, which was signed in 1985 by Federal District Court Judge Odell Horton, the Corps could (in theory) complete the 150 or so miles of channels remaining in the West Tennessee Tributaries Project. However, before it could begin work on any one item, it must first hand over to the state a corresponding parcel of wetlands, until it reached the required total of 32,000 prime mitigation acres agreed to back in 1973. (The Corps had been buying some wetlands, but so far the state had not taken delivery on a single acre.) The settlement also required that at least 20 percent of funding for the project be spent on mitigation.

The settlement further required that the project use less destructive methods for working in the rivers, similar to the Stream Obstruction Removal Guidelines (SORG) developed by the Wildlife Society and the American Fisheries Society in 1983. For instance, channels were to be worked as much as possible from one side of the waterway only, leaving trees and other vegetation intact on the opposite bank. The Obion-Forked Deer Basin Authority could continue to do stream maintenance, but it must use SORG techniques also, for instance, using chain saws instead of bulldozers to clear blockages and, where possible, allowing ox-bows to return to their natural, meandering path. Moreover, the basin authority must agree to run its work plan by a technical review committee before proceeding on any of it.

But even that was not all. As a final term for dropping their lawsuit, the plaintiffs had stipulated that before any new or maintenance work could be done on a given stretch of river, the basin authority must first acquire protective conservation easements on 30 percent of the remaining bottomland hardwoods in the work area (a basin-wide total of about 45,000 acres) *and* on 80 percent of woodlands affected by lateral drainage. In other words, basin landowners had to sign legally-binding agreements never to clear, farm or build on the affected property. In return, they would qualify for a tax break—and, for what it was worth, the satisfaction of helping preserve the area's natural ecosystem. If even one landowner refused to grant a necessary easement (which was quite likely, given such limited carrots), then neither the Corps nor the basin authority could proceed.

It was less than the plaintiffs had hoped for, but probably as much as they were going to get. As Tony Campbell told the TCL board in 1984, "we can't ask for any more and win."

Chester McConnell, though no longer on the board, alone remained fiercely opposed to the settlement. It was a devastation to wetlands, he said, a waste of resources and a fraud against the American people. Far from signing it, he argued, the League should sue the Corps again. While the others agreed with his objections in principle, they were weary pragmatists now.

"Chester is right," said Tony Campbell. "But folks, we have an environmental lawsuit and that lawsuit cannot address whether it is a waste of money or not. The judge is going to say that Congress makes the decision on whether or not we should waste our money and the courts have nothing to say about how we waste our money. They are going to tell us that Congress makes the decision on whether or not we should save wetlands and whether a duck is worth a damn to anybody." When the issue came to a vote, the board voted unanimously to accept the terms of the agreement. In May 1985 the settlement was accepted by the Federal District Court in Memphis.

At last, fifteen years after it began, the Obion-Forked Deer lawsuit was finally settled. Maybe.

WETLANDS ACQUISITION IN TENNESSEE AND CANADA

What was certainly not settled was the larger issue of wetlands loss in general.

By the early 1980s, as many as half of all wetlands in the United States had been dredged, filled, drained or otherwise destroyed. (In Tennessee, possibly as many as 2.8 million acres of original wetlands had dwindled to barely 800,000.) Waterfowl populations, critically threatened by habitat loss in Canada, were equally at risk from drainage and development projects all along their migration route. There had been important federal measures, of course, such as the "swampbuster" and "sodbuster" provisions of the 1985 Farm Bill, which penalized farmers for planting in wetlands or erodible soil, as well as Sections 401 and 404 of the Clean Water Act. But they all had their limitations.

Clearly, Tennessee needed a firm wetlands policy at the state level. In the mid-1980s, a legislative task force began considering the state's proper role in regulating wetlands, or indeed whether it should regulate them at all. Perhaps, said some, the state should simply *buy* some wetlands, and guarantee their protection that way. But where would Tennessee get that kind of money?

Chuck Cook, head of The Nature Conservancy, told the committee about an option that seemed to be working in Florida. There, a percentage of the real estate transfer tax went into a fund for buying wetlands. That's what the members of Tennessee's task force decided to do. In 1986, they introduced the wetlands acquisition bill, a proposal to increase the real estate transfer tax from twenty-six cents per hundred dollars of value to thirty cents. The additional four cents would be placed in a fund administered by TWRA and the Commissioner of Agriculture and earmarked strictly for wetlands acquisition. (This designation was somewhat illusory, however. In 1991, the Legislature approved the use of four million dollars from the fund to buy the Royal Blue Wildlife Management Area on the Cumberland Plateau.)

The proposal seemed friendly enough: who would object to paying another forty dollars on a hundred thousand-dollar house? Well, the Tennessee Association of Realtors did. In a field already buggered by points and closing costs, an added tax was most unwelcome, and a tax that would take land out of potential development was even less so. Eventually, supporters reached a compromise with the realtors. They would reduce the tax hike by half, from four cents to two, then make up the difference by allotting two cents of the existing transfer tax to the wetlands fund. They also agreed to a ten-year sunset provision, meaning the act would be cancelled in ten years unless new legislation came along to extend it. (In 1991, Legislators not only repealed the sunset clause, they approved another four-cent tax for buying parks and recreation lands.) Finally, to quiet the complaints of local governments, the bill stipulated that the state would pay local property taxes on any wetlands purchased with the fund. Yet even with these concessions, the fund would still generate an estimated three million dollars a year, enough to buy three, perhaps four thousand acres of wetlands.

The bill passed on April 9, 1986. TWRA made its first purchase of wetlands, 1,298 acres of prime bottomland hardwoods in Lauderdale County, almost exactly a year later. Tony Campbell, who had lobbied hard for the bill, called the Wetlands Acquisition Act "the greatest piece of natural resources legislation to come along in years." Gary Myers of the TWRA said the General Assembly deserved "a gold star."

GARY MYERS' "SCREWBALL IDEA" TO SAVE WETLANDS

Myers had reason to be pleased. He was now not only head of the TWRA; he was the current president of the International Association of Fish and Wildlife Agencies (the first Tennessean in that post since Joseph Acklen in 1912). For years, the IAFWA had supported the United States and Canada in their efforts to forge a joint management plan for North America's wetlands, especially the vast prairie pothole region of central Canada. Those efforts were finally about to bear fruit. In May 1986, U.S. Interior Secretary Don Hodel and Canada's Environment Minister Thomas McMillan signed the North American Waterfowl Management Plan.

There was only one problem. It would cost as much as $1.5 billion to implement the plan over the next 15 years, but the NAWMP document had provided no funding. Moreover, the plan stipulated that the United States would pay 75 percent of the costs in Canada, because U.S. hunters kill 75 percent of the ducks. The U.S. Fish and Wildlife Service now asked Gary Myers to serve on a scoping committee, along with Larry Jahn of the Wildlife Management Institute and Hazard Campbell, president of Ducks Unlimited. They held their first meeting in Gary Myers' hotel room in September 1986, during the IAFWA's annual meeting in Providence, Rhode Island.

There in the hotel room, Myers "laid out this screwball idea." If the IAFWA could raise a million dollars in seed money from the states, he said, it could ask for matching funds from Ducks Unlimited. Then those two million could be matched by the National Fish and Wildlife Foundation. And *those* funds, suggested Canada's Jim Peterson, could be matched by the Canadian provinces and the Canadian government.

Myers' colleagues didn't think the idea was so screwy: twelve states eventually came up with a total of one million dollars. (TCL even contributed a little.) Ducks Unlimited kicked in another million; the National Fish and Wildlife Foundation matched the two million, and Canada matched that. Eventually they had almost ten million dollars. Meanwhile, people were busy gathering duck-banding data (to document the need for more money); a video (to show how Quill Lake in Saskatchewan would spend the first four million dollars); enabling legislation (to authorize the joint venture with Canada); and finally, said Myers, someone "to figure out what a joint venture [was]." The first meeting ever of an international joint venture in the United States occurred at the Stouffer Hotel in Nashville, said Myers; that's where they were invented.

In December 1989, Congress formalized the implementation plan as the North American Wetlands Conservation Act. Interior Secretary Manuel Lujan appointed Myers to the nine-member Wetlands Conservation Council. Myers would now be responsible for spending the money he had helped raise. And (as he told the League four months later in accepting their Conservationist of the Year award for 1989) at least $700,000 of the Council's funds would be spent in Tennessee.

CHAPTER 8

1990-1996

MARKING MILESTONES, PLANNING FOR THE FUTURE

As the Tennessee Conservation League moves into its fifty-first year,
we are challenged with more complex issues facing our environment
than ever before. We believe that we can integrate a healthy environment
with a healthy economy. We must make sure that the very things that
make our state so special ... remain for future generations.

—Prospectus for the Lucius E. Burch Center
for Conservation Planning, January 1997

THE LEAGUE ISSUES AN ENVIRONMENTAL REPORT CARD

On April 22, 1990, Tennessee and the rest of the nation celebrated the twentieth anniversary of Earth Day. The League decided to mark the occasion with a major retrospective, a look back that served equally as a look into the future.

Released the first week of April, the *Tennessee Environmental Quality Index 1970–1990* (subtitled *How Are We Doing?*) summarized twenty years of progress in the state's environmental programs. Dubbed the EQ Index, or simply EQI, the report was modeled after a national review issued annually since 1969 by the National Wildlife Federation. The League's report analyzed air quality, water quality, solid waste control, land and soil use, forest management and wildlife protection. The report closed with a brief epilogue summing up all of these findings.

To those fearing (or expecting) a more dire accounting, the summary was surprisingly temperate. Tennessee's environment was "not as well off as [it] ought to be," it concluded, but neither was it "as bad off" as it might be. The authors of the twelve-page report were all environmental professionals: Vanderbilt environmental engineering professor Dr. Edward L. Thackston, Saturn's environmental affairs manager William R. Miller, environmental consultant Larry R. Richardson and state natural areas coordinator Daryl Durham. Their manner was likewise professional, neither understated nor embellished. Old threats had been controlled; new ones were emerging: that was the gist of their report. Their tone was one of statistical precision, technical circumspection and, from time to time, cautious optimism.

Air quality, for instance, had improved greatly since 1970, when the federal Clean Air Act began reining in such major polluters as power plants and automobiles. On the other hand, a growing list of industrial chemicals was not regulated at all. Hydrocarbons continued to erode the ozone layer and sulfur dioxide emissions continued to cause acid rain. Meanwhile, such everyday hazards as tobacco smoke and the formaldehyde in wallboard paneling were drawing attention to the air *inside* homes, schools and office buildings.

As with air quality, said the report, Tennessee's waters had been vastly upgraded over the last two decades as most industrial and municipal dischargers came into compliance with new federal and state pollution laws. On the other hand, Tennessee waters now faced serious threats from more elusive sources, such as urban and agricultural runoff, erosion and acid drainage from strip mines, as well as small concentrations of previously undetected contaminants.

Solid waste got the same mixed reviews. The state had long ago outlawed open dumps, regulated hazardous wastes and tentatively promoted recycling. A task force was already drafting a comprehensive waste management plan that would include not merely landfills but also recycling and public education. (The Solid Waste Management Act was signed into law on May 31, 1991.) But in the meantime, said the Environmental Quality Index, the sanitary landfills of the '70s were already overflowing, and the state still had not figured out how best to deal with the public's vehement NIMBY response ("not in my back yard") to new landfills.

The prognosis for forests and wildlife was likewise guarded. The state's timber harvest was larger than ever, but the quality of the harvest had declined. Aggressive management had helped restore white-tailed deer, bear, wild turkey and Canada geese. But certain other species, small game and wetland game birds in particular, were running out of suitable habitat. As for the hundreds of nongame species that comprised 94 percent of the state's wildlife, the bald eagle was a well-known success story, but other nongame species got precious little active management, if any.

In short, the EQ Index took a determinedly balanced view of things, delivered with roughly the same degree of emotion as an IRS audit. Yet for all its lack of fireworks, it attracted lavish media attention. Headlines announced, "State's Environment Has Improved." *The Greeneville Sun* ran an eight-day series. *The Tennessee Conservationist* reproduced the entire report in its July-August issue.

Given the national clamor over Earth Day 1990, such attention was to be expected. But the League's EQ Index would probably have been newsworthy in any case, because it was followed, just one week later, by the publication of a much more damning environmental review, and much more ominous headlines: *State Ranked Near Bottom On Environment.*

A Second Opinion On Tennessee's Environmental Health

In its report, dubbed the "Green Index," the nonprofit Institute for Southern Studies in Durham, North Carolina, had placed Tennessee fourth-from-worst in the nation in environmental quality and public health. Only South Carolina, Louisiana, Mississippi and Alabama ranked lower. Bob Hall, research director for the institute, blamed the abysmal ratings on the South's "backward resistance" to environmental reforms. "The South not only has become the nation's biggest waste dump," said Hall. "The region also has a disproportionate share of hazardous jobs, contaminated water, homes lacking complete plumbing and industries spewing cancer-causing chemicals." A similar assessment by Washington, D.C.-based Renew America had been even less forgiving. Its 1989 "State of the States" report had placed Tennessee forty-ninth out of fifty.

Both of these national rankings were based largely on government data, in particular the Environmental Protection Agency's first Toxics Release Inventory (TRI), published in 1989. The TRI was a compilation of emissions data for more than three hundred hazardous chemicals from the nation's largest manufacturers. The EPA had been collecting such information for years, of course. In fact, the National Wildlife Foundation in 1979 had used EPA data to rank the relative toxic safety of each state. Until the Toxics Release Inventory came out, however, EPA's emissions data had not been readily available to the public.

In 1986, the public was granted regular if limited access to hazardous waste information when Congress passed the Superfund Amendments and Reauthorization Act (SARA). Section 313 of SARA (the so-called Emergency Planning and Community Right-to-Know Act) required that EPA publish an annual Toxics Release Inventory for every state and every major industry, ranked by weight (volume) and subdivided according to "pathways"—air, landfills, underground injection, surface water, municipal sewage treatment plants or off-site transfers. Emissions into the air always topped the list.

The TRI did not purport to be an entirely accurate measure of the nation's total chemical load. For one thing, the index tracked only a fraction of the thousands of chemicals in use in the United States. For another, it left the reporting to the industries themselves, with no independent audit required. Emissions below a certain minimum threshold were exempt from the TRI, nor did it apply to any plant employing fewer than ten workers. And what was perhaps its greatest weakness of all, the TRI exempted power plants, government facilities and all emissions of sulfur dioxide, carbon monoxide and nitrogen dioxide, since these were covered under federal standards for ambient air quality.

But even with these caveats, the TRI numbers were—to put it mildly—impressive. The first Toxics Release Inventory, published in April 1989 but representing data collected in 1987, showed that the nation's factories released three and a half *billion* pounds of toxics in 1987. Texas ranked first, at 350 million pounds. And number two after Texas, with 293 million pounds, was Tennessee.

The League had been aware of the EPA data when it published the EQ Index. In fact, in August 1989, it had issued a press release on the TRI, along with a recap of the top one hundred Tennessee companies on the list and a statement from Tony Campbell that Tennessee still had "some serious problems." However, Campbell had stressed, just because a facility was listed in the TRI did not necessarily mean the local population and wildlife were in danger. "Since the rankings in the report are based on total weight and not on types of emissions which are likely to be most dangerous, the report can be misleading," Campbell had said at the time. "The biggest numbers are usually for substances which are not very toxic."

(The National Wildlife Foundation had said basically the same thing ten years earlier when it analyzed EPA emissions data for 1979. In what they called a "need-response index," NWF's scientists had ranked each state not simply by total volume of toxic wastes but also by what they judged the adequacy of the state's "response" to that waste. According to their study, Tennessee in 1979 had ranked near the bottom in volume of waste, but twentieth from the top in its ability to handle it. In fact, of the top ten hazardous waste generators in the nation, Tennessee alone had ranked in the top twenty regulatory programs.)

At any rate, the League saw little point in comparing raw poundages to overall environmental quality, nor did it see much sense in comparing the Green Index to its own EQ Index. Nevertheless, some folks did compare them, and the result was that, to skeptics at least, the EQ Index looked a bit like a whitewash, self-serving propaganda from an organization that liked to take credit for cleaning up the environment while catering to the industries that polluted it.

The question of bias resurfaced the following year, when the League released its second Environmental Quality Index, *Checking Our Progress*. Its major theme was that environmental quality would continue to improve, but only if the state anted up the needed funding, including decent wages for regulatory personnel. Nonpoint source water pollution, for instance, had emerged as "the water quality problem of the 1990s," but regulators' hands were tied by a chronic "lack of sufficient resources for regulation, monitoring, inspection and enforcement." Yet even as authors Thackston, Miller and Durham chided Tennessee for its continued stinginess to vital conservation and regulatory programs, they had high hopes for several recent initiatives, including the state's new Comprehensive Solid Waste Management Act, its recent ban on blasting rock for septic tank lines and the reauthorized federal Clean Air Act of 1990. The latter, they said, should result in a "drastic reduction" in air toxics emissions in the next five years.

In the meantime, said the 1991 report, manufacturers were not only reporting their emissions but in some cases reducing them, "even if [the emissions] are legal and do not cause any measurable harm." As for the seventeen most noxious chemicals, these were being targeted by EPA's voluntary "33/50 Program"—33 percent reductions nationwide by 1992, 50 percent by 1995. These were important first steps, said the report, and would no doubt lead to "many more 'real' reductions as manufacturers ... become more aware of just how much their emissions actually are and how much bad public relations can be caused by them."

This statement was clearly intended as a preemptive strike. The latest TRI had just been released by the EPA, and it was sure to send more feathers flying. Though Tennessee's releases had dropped slightly in 1989, to 264 million pounds, the 1991 TRI showed Tennessee still holding onto second place.

No one was surprised, therefore, when both Renew America and the Green Index again placed Tennessee near the bottom of their charts for environmental integrity. But now, the

Tony Campbell joins authors Ed Thackston, Daryl Durham and Larry R. Richardson for a press conference at Legislative Plaza following release of the first Environmental Quality Index, April 1990. Bill Miller couldn't make it. TCL file photo/Sue Garner.

EQ Index came under attack from a more local source. Jim Tramel, coordinator of the toxics program at the Tennessee Environmental Council, warned that the TRI list was "just the tip of the toxic iceberg." He rejected the League's argument that some toxics are less toxic than others. "Who wants to compare damage?" he said. "I think that's offensive to people." Though the League tried to remain diplomatic, it found such challenges increasingly irritating. In fact, it was during one of these recurring clashes over the toxics issue that it finally broke with the Council, canceling the membership it had held since it founded TEC in 1970.

ALL TOXICS ARE NOT CREATED EQUAL

The League decided to go on the offensive. In April 1992, just before the EPA released its fourth TRI, the League issued its own "toxic threat" list for air emissions. This ranking of fifteen Tennessee industries was actually a re-ranking of the top fifteen companies in EPA's toxics release inventory for 1989. However, unlike the TRI, it was adjusted for relative toxicity, based on Occupational Safety and Health Administration limits for each listed chemical. By this formula, a company releasing a million pounds of benzene, a known carcinogen with an OSHA standard of one part per million, would be judged one hundred times more dangerous than a company releasing the same volume of toluene, with an OSHA standard of one *hundred* parts per million. (The League warned that its rough ranking did not take into account other factors, such as local geography or wind direction.)

Thus, although a few companies' rankings stayed the same on both the EPA and TCL lists (DuPont's New Johnsonville plant stayed at third, for instance), others were moved up, or down. Tennessee Eastman's Kingsport facility, for example, which had ranked first on the TRI with 1989 gross air releases of 41 million pounds, dropped to sixth in the TCL analysis, because its emissions consisted mostly of acetone, which has an OSHA standard of 750 parts per million. (After 1993, the TRI stopped listing acetone releases altogether.)

BASF Corporation, on the other hand, second in the TRI ranking, now ranked first with the League, while North American Rayon, fourth on the TRI, now took second place. (Both BASF and NAR release carbon disulfide, a highly toxic chemical with an OSHA standard of four parts per million.)

The League took pains to note, once again, that these threats were strictly theoretical, neither actual nor even imminent. Nonetheless, its list drew indignant protests not only from the companies it named, but also from the thousand-member Tennessee Association of Business, which condemned the new ranking as "unscientific." The criticism stung slightly, of course: the League usually worked well with the TAB and even served on its annual awards committee. But in their hearts, TCL's leaders welcomed the complaints. For too long, the League had been accused of being soft on industry. This tussle, they hoped, would prove otherwise. Any organization that gets attacked from *both* sides of an issue surely could be nobody's patsy.

The League continued to play hardball in its next EQ Index. Though the public was more aware of environmental problems than ever before, said the 1992 report, it was "woefully uninformed about the causes and processes of environmental degradation and the relative severity and risks of various environmental problems." The four authors of the 1992 index (Robert P. Ford, manager of the Tennessee Biodiversity Program, now joined the team of Thackston, Miller and Durham) charged that NIMBY was alive and well in Tennessee. "We all benefit from our high-tech society, but we all want all wastes and hazardous activities taken somewhere else."

Moreover, charged the report, the mass media had not been doing its duty in helping set things straight. "Although there are now many more news media and good reporters interested in reporting on environmental issues," the authors said with studied politeness, "very few reporters have strong enough backgrounds in chemistry, physics and math to understand the technicalities involved." Ironically, the League had tried to fill some of the void in November 1990, when it cohosted an "environmental awareness" seminar for the media at Middle Tennessee State University. Although Senator Al Gore topped the program, most of the panelists were environmental scientists, with few regulators and even fewer practicing journalists. Obviously, the League wanted to impress upon the audience the complexities and ambiguities of technical issues which were too often treated in the press as simple and straightforward.

As if to illustrate its point about an under-informed media, the 1992 EQ Index discussed the "bad publicity" surrounding DuPont's deep-well injection of hazardous wastes at its titanium dioxide plant in New Johnsonville. For almost a quarter of a century, the chemical maker had been disposing its principal waste, a dilute mixture of water, hydrochloric acid and iron chlorides, by pumping it down a mile-long shaft into bedrock, where the acid was neutralized by the limestone and the iron chlorides settled into the earth. The EPA considered deep wells so relatively safe that deep-well releases were often compiled separately from other forms of disposal so as not to skew the latter. The League's EQ Index for 1992 even judged DuPont's system "a net benefit to the environment," since the waste was no longer going into Kentucky Lake, as it had done formerly. Nonetheless, said the report, the public was easily misled "by large numbers and the emotional label 'toxic.'"

Almost as if on cue, *The Tennessean* not long afterward ran a story questioning the safety of DuPont's deep wells. Though reporter Jim East supposedly had access to the League's latest EQ Index, the story contained no reference to it. Instead, it quoted the TEC's controversial Jim Tramel, charging that deep wells were unsafe because the liquid wastes migrate upwards—a claim disputed by most hydrologists and geologists.

The League was losing its patience. By the time its fourth and final EQ Index came out in 1993 (called *Environmental Risk: How Are We Coping With It?*), authors Bill Miller, Ed Thackston, Ruth Neff, Tony Campbell and Larry Richardson were pulling no punches. Environmental threats do exist, they said, but it is a mistake to let our responses be driven "by political expediency, by an overzealous and ... uninformed press, or by a successful scare campaign from a special interest group."

There was too much at stake, they went on, to allow limited energies and resources to be misplaced. "As a society we need to focus on those problems that pose actual risks ... and move away from the mindset which states that any risk at all must be eliminated, or that whatever the concentration of the chemical, however small, it must be reduced. We must move away from the idea that if it can be measured, it is, therefore, of significance. We must challenge the notion that just because someone makes a statement, then it must be true."

THE EQ INDEXES: A POSTSCRIPT

The 1993 report was the last Environmental Quality Index the League produced, at least for the time being. But the dialogue started by the Index did not end there. Tennessee's Department of Environment and Conservation (TDEC) liked the idea so well that in 1994 it began publishing its own annual State of the Environment report (though, as one might expect, it had a distinctly cheerleading tone). At the League's annual meeting in Memphis in March 1993, TDEC Commissioner J. W. Luna announced that, at TCL's urging, his department had just created a new Division of Pollution Prevention and Environmental Awareness, to correct the "continued false perception that Tennessee's environment is polluted to a greater degree than its neighbors." It was to be the centerpiece of something called the Toxics 2000 Initiative, a voluntary emissions-reduction program similar to EPA's 33/50 Program. EPA's program reached its main goal—a 50-percent reduction nationwide of the seventeen worst chemicals—a year early. The state believed it could have comparable success.

NONPOINT SOURCE WATER POLLUTION: BIG NAME FOR A BIG PROBLEM

In January 1987, in its then-latest version of the federal Water Pollution Control Act (popularly called the Clean Water Act, or CWA), Congress had called for each state to do something about the continued threats to water quality. The lawmakers were not referring to factories or city sewers; these polluters had long since been brought under regulatory control. Rather, the states were now being told to clean up something called "nonpoint source pollution" (NPS)—or what one observer defined, accurately if not very gracefully, as "sources you can't really point your finger at."

According to the experts, nonpoint sources were now the nation's number-one cause of water pollution. Though some of them looked innocent enough—a grandmother spraying her roses, a teenager changing the oil in his car—nonpoint sources were far more insidious than the old industrial discharge pipes or municipal sewer systems, precisely because they *were* harder to pinpoint. Some nonpoint pollution happened directly in the waterways, when, for instance, developers dredged a creek, or cattle waded through a stream, or loggers drove heavy equipment across a stream bed. But for the most part, nonpoint pollution happened whenever it rained. One good thunderstorm, and gasoline and motor oil were washed from city streets and parking lots and into storm drains. One good snowmelt, and the detritus of bridge construction floated away with the current. One good downpour, in short, and every unsecured contaminant in the entire watershed was on the move: pesticides, topsoil, detergents, animal waste, even some airborne pollutants.

Surface waters were not alone at risk from nonpoint source pollution. Underground waters were vulnerable as well, especially the vast sand aquifers of West Tennessee that supply drinking water to more than a million people. Faulty septic tanks were the worst culprits, but groundwater could also be contaminated by leaking fuel storage tanks, acid leaching out of strip mines, even household solvents carelessly dumped in the back yard.

As hard as it was to identify, nonpoint source water pollution was even harder to regulate, harder to correct and harder, after all, to hate. Nevertheless, said Congress, the states had to try. According to this directive (Section 319 of the 1987 Clean Water Act), every state had to file a Nonpoint Source Water Pollution Management Plan with EPA by the end of 1989. The plan had to include a four-year calendar of action, a list of existing programs and a plan for using "best management practices," or BMPs, to control nonpoint source pollution. BMPs were the best, if not the only, means a state had to correct a source of pollution that was not, after all, illegal. However, because they were merely advisory, not statutory, BMPs had to rely on the public spirit of the polluters themselves, from weekend gardeners to cattle farmers. Short of changing the pollution laws, all a state could do was develop reasonable BMPs, encourage their use and monitor their results.

Shortly after the 1987 Clean Water Act became law, J. W. Luna, Ned McWherter's commissioner of Health and Environment (as the department was then called), announced the creation of a Nonpoint Source Management Section within the Division of Construction Grants and Loans. He also convened a task force, dubbed the Management Advisory Group (MAG), to develop Tennessee's Nonpoint Source Management Plan. MAG was an enormous body that at one point included seventy members. Tony Campbell represented the League.

MAG spent much of the next two years evaluating the extent of nonpoint source pollution in Tennessee. Of 540,000 acres of lakes and 19,000 miles of streams (of which only half were actually studied), roughly 77,000 acres of lakes and 3,300 miles of rivers were considered harmed by nonpoint sources. Groundwater was at risk primarily from as many as 50,000 malfunctioning septic systems.

In 1991, with vigorous support by TCL, the Environmental Action Fund, TWRA commissioner Tom Hensley and others, lawmakers agreed that a portion of the increase in the real estate transfer tax (under the new State and Local Park and Recreation Partnership Act) could be spent on nonpoint source pollution. It was considered a great coup.

FARMING AND LOGGING: ARE BMPS ENOUGH?

But nonpoint source pollution was too extensive to be fixed by funding alone. The biggest NPS culprit by far was agriculture, accounting for as much as 80 percent of the problem, largely from soil erosion but also from fertilizers, animal wastes, pesticides and drainage projects. Tennessee's nonpoint source management plan contained lots of suggested BMPs for farmers, from integrated pest management to no-till farming. It also recommended farmers seek the free technical advice available from the U.S. Soil Conservation Service and the University of Tennessee Agricultural Extension Service.

As far as the League was concerned, however, farmers who plowed into streams or watered their cattle in the local creek should have to be responsible for their discharges just as they would the discharges from any factory. In Tennessee, however (indeed in most states), routine agricultural pollution was exempt from state regulation. The state could talk to the farmer about it—and often did—but in most cases the farmer was not obligated by law to correct it. Sometimes, of course, the pollutants were so concentrated and excessive as to be considered an actual *point* source—an overflow of manure from a feed lot, for instance, or a leaking chemical storage tank. Such a case might in fact be actionable. That is, the farmer would probably be visited by water pollution control officials, told to clean up the pollutant and possibly fined if he didn't comply. But the small, daily seepage from that same feed lot or holding tank, though perhaps just as offensive over time, would not be subject to water quality permits, controls, inspections or penalties.

A similar situation existed with silviculture. Skidders, flatbed logging trucks and other heavy equipment could tear up a forest appallingly, turning nearby waters into a slough of silt, pesticides, diesel fuel, branches and tree tops. If the land were not promptly seeded and replanted, it could continue to erode long after the loggers moved on. True, silviculture was not nearly as polluting, acre for acre, as farming. And it was also true that the logging industry in general tended to be better at policing itself. In fact, the League had worked closely with the Tennessee Forestry Association developing BMPs for the industry.

Nevertheless, TCL wanted to see both exemptions removed. It had even tried, more than once, to pass legislation mandating forestry BMPs, including fines for those who refused. Mark Benko, Larry Richardson and Ed Thackston had worked hard to pass these bills. They did not pass, however, and most observers felt this was one fight the League had no chance of winning. After all, such exemptions are common in other states.

But the League had a bone between its teeth, and it did not want to let go.

Shortly after the Management Advisory Group submitted its final management plan to EPA in early 1989, Tony Campbell sent a letter to the agency, urging EPA to reject both the agriculture and forestry sections of the plan unless Tennessee first removed both exemptions. EPA would not agree. Instead, EPA Region IV administrator Greer Tidwell, Sr., notified the state that it had approved both exemptions. Tennessee was free to begin implementing its nonpoint source management plan.

Fortunately, the folks in Tennessee's nonpoint source section didn't seem overly sore that the League had just tried to derail the plan it had spent two years and thousands of dollars preparing. On the contrary, in June 1990 the state agreed to pay TCL forty thousand dollars to put together a public education campaign on nonpoint source pollution. Though the League was supposed to put up a share of costs, the match could be anything from storage space to staff time. Meanwhile, even as it developed material promoting voluntary BMPs, the League continued its fight to make them mandatory. As Campbell often said, all the BMPs in the world wouldn't do any good if the folks causing the pollution didn't use them.

"A CARPET WITH PIECES CUT OUT": THE DEBATE OVER CHIP MILLS

That was really the crux of the debate over chip mills: that small loggers who supplied the mills had no incentive to use BMPs, and a big incentive—cash for any thing they could haul out of the woods—to ignore them.

The chip mill controversy had started in May 1989, when a Perry County lumber mill owner announced plans to build a wood chipping operation and barge terminal at Kittrell's Landing on Kentucky Lake. The chips would be shipped down the Tennessee River to another terminal, where they would be sold to paper mills or presswood processors or, in many cases, shipped overseas.

The economics of the proposal seemed attractive enough. Because wood chips may be used in place of whole trees in products like paper and pressboard, a chip mill in Perry County would create a market for the otherwise useless "junk timber" left to rot by more selective harvests. Moreover, said mill owner Tommy Graham, his expanded operation would not only create more jobs and attract new businesses. By encouraging "even-aged management" (otherwise known as clear-cutting), it would actually improve the region's forests.

Most business and community leaders in Perry County hailed Graham's proposal as an economic boon to this thinly-populated, heavily-forested area about a hundred miles southwest of Nashville. As for its potential effect on the resource, the Tennessee Division of Forestry agreed that carefully managed clear-cuts did indeed tend to result in healthier forests and higher-quality hardwoods. Officials also acknowledged that the state's forests could easily support the increased demand. In the past forty years, Tennessee's forested acreage had actually increased by a million acres, thanks to more thoughtful management. In fact, said Dwight Barnett, director of education for the division, the forest cover was so dense that well-managed clear-cuts would simply look "like a carpet with pieces cut out."

But it wasn't up to Forestry to decide. Because the barges would use the Tennessee River, Graham had to get clearance from TVA (which controlled the river banks) and the U.S. Army Corps of Engineers (which controlled navigation).

In February 1990, TVA and the Corps held a packed public hearing at the Perry County high school. While most speakers supported the proposal, a handful argued that the mill would lead to wholesale clear-cutting, severe erosion and excessive river traffic that would turn Kentucky Lake into "a polluted barge canal."

Bill Miller was at the hearing to represent the Tennessee Conservation League; attorney Joe McCaleb was there on behalf of the Middle Tennessee Group of the Sierra Club. For once, the two organizations were in agreement. Neither Miller nor McCaleb rejected the proposal, nor did they endorse it. Instead, they both called for an environmental impact statement under NEPA, the National Environmental Policy Act of 1969.

An EIS was duly ordered. When it was finished, TVA and the Corps announced that the environmental impacts of the proposed mill did not outweigh its benefits, and Tommy Graham could have his permit. (He never did build a chip mill, however. Tony Campbell thinks he never intended to. Instead, he sold the property to Champion International, which now has a chip mill on the site.)

But the chip mill issue had not gone away; in fact, it now got hotter than ever. By March 1991, three more chip mills had been proposed, by three different firms, for three different sites along a twelve-mile stretch of the Tennessee River near Chattanooga. Environmental forces objected more strenuously than ever. They organized into a three-state citizen's group (Tennessee, Georgia and Alabama); they even teamed up with furniture shops and hardwood flooring manufacturers, who feared that high-quality lumber might be fed into the chippers right along with branches and culls.

TVA and the Corps were again obliged to do an EIS. This time, however, the process took much longer, as it had to consider three times the harvest, three times the barge traffic and three times the impact. When the draft EIS came out in summer 1992, Tony Campbell read it carefully, then wrote a letter to Paul Schmierbach, manager of TVA's Environmental Quality Office. Based on the findings of the draft EIS, he said, TVA should deny all three permits. His comments were far more an indictment of Tennessee forestry policy, however, than of the chip mills themselves.

[G]iven the fact that the State of Tennessee, through the Tennessee Division of Forestry and the University of Tennessee Extension Service, has not been willing to invest in programs that would facilitate good forest management practices on private nonindustrial forest land, we feel that under the current conditions there is no assurance that the chip mills would in any way accrue to Tennessee's forest resources or the citizens of the state.

Apparently, both TVA and the Corps agreed. Even though at least one of the applicants, the giant Boise Cascade, promised to buy timber only from loggers using best management practices, all three permits were denied.

The Chips Fall On Champion

But even that was not the end of the chip mill controversy. Wood chips were, after all, the raw material of paper production, and large paper mills, especially those with enormous land holdings, often had chipping operations of their own. And few paper companies owned more timberland in Tennessee than Champion International Corporation—some 245,000 acres by 1994.

Champion already had one chip mill, Tommy Graham's old property on the Tennessee River. The mill it now proposed would be on the eastern edge of the Cumberland Plateau, in an area called New River. However, that mill would not actually be on the New River (which is in fact a branch of the Cumberland). Instead, chips would travel by rail to Champion's big paper mill in Canton, North Carolina, a small town on Interstate 40, about fifty river miles east of Newport, Tennessee, on the Pigeon River.

As Champion did not intend to use the river for transportation, it did not need a permit to clear-cut its 85,000 acres of New River forest land. Instead, the controversy erupted over the fact that it was planning to clear-cut at all. According to some critics, Champion had a cut-and-run mentality when it came to managing its forests, not only in such distant places as Montana and Maine, but right at its own doorstep in Cocke County. Champion, naturally, insisted that it intended to be a good steward of the New River property and a good neighbor to adjoining landowners.

Nevertheless, if some folks remained skeptical, it was understandable. Down around Newport, Champion was an environmental evil of almost Biblical proportions.

The Canton paper mill had been in operation since 1908. Ever since, residents downstream had been complaining about the stench, the foam and the black discharge that fouled the Pigeon, an otherwise scenic whitewater tributary of the French Broad. In 1929, Governor Henry Horton had signed a bill condemning the "lamentable condition" of the Pigeon, charging that it was "impairing the health and imperilling the lives" of citizens in Tennessee. The bill allotted ten thousand dollars for a study by the new Division of Sanitary Engineering; it also authorized "any necessary lawsuits." Nothing, however, seems to have come of these early efforts to clean up the river.

THE LONG STRUGGLE TO CLEAN UP THE PIGEON RIVER

In 1972, over President Nixon's objections, Congress passed the Federal Water Pollution Control Act Amendments of 1972—a.k.a. the Clean Water Act. Besides setting ambitious pollution control goals, the Clean Water Act set tough new standards for industrial waste, including standards for toxic chemicals. But what was even more important to Tennessee officials, the law gave EPA the power to veto any state-issued NPDES (National Pollutant Discharge Elimination System) permit if it failed to protect water quality standards—whether in the host state or in a state downstream.

Forcing North Carolina's hand was no overnight matter, however. Tennessee water quality officials, TWRA and local residents lobbied for years to get EPA to take action. (Their struggle eventually became the basis for an entire book, Richard A. Bartlett's 1995 *Troubled Waters.*) The debate also spawned at least two protest groups, the Pigeon River Action Group and the Dead Pigeon River Council. Yet EPA, it seemed, merely yawned.

Then, in 1980, the Pigeon's pollution readings jumped off the meter.

What had happened had nothing to do with Champion Paper, at least not directly. Rather, it had to do with Carolina Power and Light (CPL) and its hydroelectric storage reservoir some thirty miles downstream from the paper mill. When it was built in the late 1920s, Waterville Reservoir had been equipped with something called a Johnson valve, basically a spigot so huge you could drive a truck through it—assuming you could get a truck down there in the first place. Over the years, the valve (which is located near the base of the dam) had been buried under tons of organic muck and mud.

So when the recently-formed Federal Energy Regulatory Commission (FERC) asked for a demonstration of the Johnson valve in 1979, Carolina Power and Light officials were understandably aghast. Waterville Reservoir is more than a hundred feet deep at that point, its waters impenetrably black. According to David McKinney, chief of environmental services at TWRA, one diver was killed building a temporary coffer dam to contain the valve. But FERC was adamant. The coffer was completed, the gears were turned, the valve cranked opened— and it would not shut. For the next five days, Waterville Lake rushed out through the breach, carrying with it a half-century of muck, mud and paper-mill sediment.

McKinney was working for the Tennessee Division of Water Quality Control at the time. He and another division biologist, David Melgaard, were sent to the Pigeon to investigate. McKinney stresses that the Waterville Lake episode was really just a freak, a spike on a water-quality chart that was "absolutely deplorable" to begin with. Nevertheless, the pollution from that accidental drawdown was one of the determining factors when, in 1983, Tennessee finally sued the state of North Carolina. EPA was taking notice at last.

In 1985, EPA not only rejected Champion's proposed new NPDES permit, it revoked North Carolina's authority to issue one, the first (and only) such action in the history of EPA's Southeast region. The main sticking point was color. Tennessee water quality laws prohibit "objectionable" color, yet North Carolina had not proposed to restrict the color of Champion's effluent at all. Champion officials complained that meeting the proposed color limit could put the mill out of business. So resentful and panicked were mill workers that at one point, EPA officials considered wearing bulletproof vests to a public hearing in Asheville.

In 1988, Champion and EPA worked out a compromise: eighty-five "apparent color units" at the state line (instead of the proposed fifty). All they needed now was a nod from Tennessee. But Governor Ned McWherter, who had made a much-publicized float trip down the river in September 1988 (and who was feeling relentless pressure from the Dead Pigeon River Council), refused to sign the variance. North Carolina and Champion were furious.

Foam streaks the Pigeon River in September 1988 as David McKinney, chief of environmental services at TWRA, gets a water sample. McKinney's 1980 study of the river spurred Tennessee's 1983 lawsuit against North Carolina. Courtesy of Paul Davis.

In 1989, Champion made an announcement that was half-concession, half-defiance. It would spend $200 million modernizing the plant, it said, but it would also cut jobs. That September, EPA granted a five-year permit which retained the fifty-unit color limit but allowed Champion three years to achieve it. In light of the planned modernization, Tennessee officials did not object.

But color wasn't the only thing area residents were worried about. Traces of dioxin had been detected both in the water and in fish tissues. (The river was posted in both states against eating the fish.) Though the science linking dioxin and cancer was still sketchy, residents filed a $5 billion class-action lawsuit against Champion in 1991. The case was finally settled in 1993, following a mistrial, for $6.5 million. Considering the amount of the original lawsuit and Champion's net worth (six billion dollars, according to Richard Bartlett), most observers agreed that Champion had won.

To some people, therefore, it was a breathtaking irony when, at the League's 1994 annual meeting in Gatlinburg, Champion received an environmental award: Forest Conservationist of the Year. Granted, the forestry award had nothing to do with Champion's operations on the Pigeon River. Rather, it cited Champion's use of forestry BMPs, its seventy thousand acres of public-access hunting lands and its use of wildlife-friendly harvesting techniques, such as saving hollow nesting trees and reseeding logging roads with wildlife foods. In fact, said one forestry official, Champion in recent years had become "a model of forest management" in East Tennessee. "The streams are clear where they operate," said Hart Applegate, forest management chief for the Tennessee Division of Forestry. "There's not any degradation of the environment. They really have become a good friend to the forest."

The League was not oblivious to Champion's other problems. In fact, in 1988 it had given its Conservationist of the Year Award to Nelson Ross as cofounder of the Dead Pigeon River Council, citing his fight against "one of the ... most damaging water pollution problems in Tennessee history." But that was water; this was forests. As far as the awards committee was concerned, the two issues were entirely separate.

Nonetheless, the League took a beating for its choice. Television actress Park Overall denounced the award from her home in Hollywood, charging in a letter to *The LaFollette Press* that the Pigeon was still "as black as the Ace of Spades and as deadly as a viper in Timothy grass." In a less poetic complaint to the same newspaper, anti-Champion activist Doug Murray suggested that the award was not as disinterested as one might wish. "Champion gives TCL $15,000 a year to fund one staff position and also helps sponsor TCL's awards banquets," said Murray, a member of Save Our Cumberland Mountains, one of the oldest land-protection groups in Tennessee. "Over the years, winners seem to be picked more on the basis of which polluting corporation needs some good publicity rather than merit."

It wasn't the first time such charges had been lobbed at the League, though of course the TCL awards committee flatly, even angrily, denied them. "Money never influenced the awards committee," said Ed Thackston, who has chaired the awards committee for years, including the one that selected Champion. "We have never given an award to any company with an outstanding permit violation, or of anything else required by law." Perhaps, if the League could be accused of anything, it was a lack of diplomacy.

THE PIGEON RIVER CONTROVERSY: AN UPDATE

Despite the settlement, despite a major plant overhaul, despite a river that really *was* improving, the Champion controversy was far from settled.

When Champion's five-year NPDES permit expired in 1994, it was once again up to North Carolina to issue a new permit. Due to various delays, the new permit was not released until mid-1996. Tennessee officials, waiting expectantly, were disappointed. In their opinion, the new requirements were not sufficiently improved over those in the 1989 permit.

Shortly before Christmas 1996, Tennessee Governor Don Sundquist called a press conference in Newport. Accompanied by a phalanx of officials and advisors (including TCL directors Don Byerly and Ed Thackston, who briefed the governor during the flight from Nashville), Sundquist denounced the continued pollution of the Pigeon River. In January 1997, Tennessee's attorney general filed a petition in North Carolina, asking that the permit be overturned. According to the newspapers, Vice President Al Gore was even sounded out, in hopes, presumably, that he would use the weight of his office to intervene. Meanwhile, Tennessee water quality officials took their case to the Internet. In January 1977 they created a Pigeon River spot on Tennessee's home page.

A REPORT CARD FOR TDOT

Champion International wasn't the only one struggling with image problems in the early '90s. Tennessee's Department of Transportation also had a poor reputation ("probably well deserved," Tony Campbell noted dryly) for making a mess of road- and bridge-building sites. Sometimes adjacent streams became so badly choked with sediment that only the lowest forms of aquatic life survived. In 1992 alone the Division of Water Pollution Control had fined TDOT $5,000 for polluting a creek in Hamilton County, $1,398 for a fish kill in Monroe County, $1,000 for a contractor who dumped concrete into a stream and $150,000—the largest water-pollution fine in the state's history—for erosion caused by Interstate 181 in Unicoi County.

People had been complaining for years about TDOT's sloppiness, but few complained as loudly as the 1,500-member Tennessee Scenic Rivers Association. TSRA knew the rivers of Tennessee as well as any group. It led canoe and kayak trips nearly every weekend, hosted cleanups and organized Adopt-A-Stream volunteers. TSRA president Ann Tidwell had served on the state Water Quality Control Board in the '80s, and in 1991, members helped establish the Tennessee Rivers Assessment Program in the Department of Conservation. Of the dozens of TSRA watchdogs, however, few were as dogged as Ray Norris, a psychology professor at Peabody College of Vanderbilt University. It was Norris, for instance, who in 1986 spearheaded the legal action that opened the door for TDOT to be fined by fellow state agencies.

The case involved the new Lavender Bridge in Morgan County, where Highway 62 crosses White Creek, a tributary of the Obed. The contractor had made only halfhearted efforts to stop dirt and debris from entering the creek. After spending hours canoeing and wading the stream, comparing sediment loads above and below the construction zone and even taking water samples in a snow storm, Norris and his colleagues formally charged TDOT with violating the state's Water Quality Control Act. At first, TDOT held that it was immune from such action, arguing that it was unlawful for one state agency to bring action against another. In the end, however, TDOT conceded that it *was* subject to the terms of Tennessee's water quality laws. Moreover, it agreed that in the future, all TDOT projects likely to disturb streams must first be reviewed by the Division of Water Pollution Control. It was a significant victory "on paper," said Norris, but in practice it didn't have the hoped-for results.

Like TSRA, the League had been wary of road-building projects for years. In 1964, just as the federal interstate highway system was getting into full swing, TCL delegates had passed a resolution warning of the "profound effect[s]" of road building on fish and wildlife, as well as "irreparable damage" to "parks, natural areas and refuges." When a proposed new highway threatened to cut through the Ocoee unit of the Cherokee Wildlife Management Area in 1992, the Conservation League itself prepared to sue.

In the summer of 1992, Tony Campbell urged Governor Ned McWherter to "do something about TDOT." McWherter's reply was to put the League in charge of a full-scale study of the highway department. Examine TDOT's projects, the governor told Tony Campbell, visit the work sites, talk to the supervisors. See where the weak spots are and who's causing them. Then figure out how to keep them from happening again. For this (and a video), TDOT agreed to pay the League seventy thousand dollars a year for two years. At the end of the two years, the agency extended the contract for a third.

CONSERVATION FOR THE NEXT CENTURY: TAKING UP FOR NONGAME

If nonpoint source pollution was one of the subtle disasters of the '90s, so was the loss of habitat for "non-hunted" wildlife. Because the losses were gradual rather than dramatic, few took notice. Nevertheless, as the League had said in its 1990 Environmental Quality Index, the more people understood about even the humblest wildlife species, the more they'd understand about life itself.

In a way, the term "nongame" has always been an unfortunate label, defining a species according to what it is not, like "nonwhite" peoples. Tennessee's nongame menagerie—a vast array of warblers, chipmunks, turtles, butterflies, snakes, eagles, bats and all the rest—are

Travis McNatt, a former Game and Fish chairman and TCL president, was one of 1.7 million Tennesseans— and a sizable number of the League's sportsmen—who enjoyed "nonconsumptive" outdoor pursuits, especially birding. TCL file photo.

not mere biological backdrops for the more prominent game species of turkey, trout and white-tailed deer. On the contrary, nongame species account for 94 percent of the state's 1,272 species of animal life; they also account for nearly a fourth of the state's wildlife-related economy. A survey by the Bureau of the Census and the U.S. Fish and Wildlife Service found that in 1991, Tennesseans spent $295 million on "nonconsumptive wildlife-associated recreation"—primarily bird feeding and bird watching, but also wildlife photography, nature study and so on. In fact, the survey showed that almost twice as many adult Tennesseans— 1.7 million—took part in nonconsumptive activities compared to those who hunted or fished.

Yet for much of this century, virtually 100 percent of wildlife funding in Tennessee had gone to the 6 percent of game species. This was probably only natural, since 100 percent of wildlife funding came from fees and taxes paid by the sportsmen. Nonetheless, the picture had begun to change in 1974, when Tennessee passed a Nongame and Endangered or Threatened Species Conservation Act, created a nongame section in the game and fish agency and pulled Bob Hatcher out of the fish management division to supervise it. The agency created an optional, five-dollar nongame "certificate" to fund the program; it even changed its name from the Game and Fish Commission to the Tennessee *Wildlife* Resources Agency. Its new logo featured a fish and a raccoon, a more inclusive twist on the old deer-and-fish design.

Over the next twenty-two years, Bob Hatcher's nongame program would develop a raptor rehabilitation center, establish wildlife observation areas, build hacking towers, legalize the sport of falconry, help publish the *Tennessee Wildlife Viewing Guide* and certify dozens of volunteer rehabilitators who in turn nursed thousands of injured animals back to health. It developed management plans for red-cockaded woodpeckers, blackcrowned night herons, Ohio River muskellunge, bats, mussels, bobcats, river otters, barn owls, Mississippi kites, osprey, peregrine falcons and, of course, the agency's poster child, the American bald eagle. And it did all on a tiny fraction of the budget allocated to game and sport fish.

However, the agency wasn't selling enough nongame certificates to pay for all this nongame management. Like everything else at TWRA, most of the costs came out of the Game and Fish Fund. Sportsmen were happy to pay their fair share, but as TCL pointed out, with almost two million people enjoying the resource, they shouldn't be expected to foot the entire bill themselves. That was why, from time to time, TWRA asked the Legislature for help from the general fund. These payments ranged from $42,000 in fiscal year 1978-79 (the first general fund appropriation in the agency's history) to $100,000 in 1988-89 and 1989-90. Meanwhile, TCL and the agency continued looking for new sources of revenue.

At its 1977 annual meeting, the League passed a resolution supporting a federal excise tax on outdoor gear, similar to earmarked taxes on fishing and hunting gear. In 1980 Congress agreed to provide nongame funding in its new Fish and Wildlife Coordination Act. But the idea for an excise tax languished, not resurfacing until 1993, when a coalition of eight national organizations, led by the International Association of Fish and Wildlife Agencies, began pushing the Fish and Wildlife Diversity Funding Initiative. The initiative proposed a surcharge of up to five percent on general-use outdoor gear, from backpacks and binoculars to bird feeders and Coleman stoves. By its reckoning, such a tax would generate $350 million annually, to be administered by the same people who handled the Pittman-Robertson and

Wallop-Breaux funds. The money would be divided among the states by a similar formula and matched on a similar basis. Unfortunately, the diversity funding initiative did not gave much Congressional support. By early 1997, backers of the measure were still looking for more corporate sponsors before they introduced it as a bill.

Meanwhile, Tennesseans continued to press legislators and TWRA officials to come up with more immediate sources of nongame funding, and in 1993, they created the Watchable Wildlife Fund, an endowment to which businesses, organizations and individuals would (or so supporters hoped) donate directly. But the fund was not growing very quickly, so at the League's urging, the lawmakers created a special study committee to suggest imaginative ways to build the endowment. Several legislators and agency personnel were on the team, as well as representatives of the Tennessee Ornithological Society, the Environmental Action Fund and Tony Campbell for the League.

Most of their ideas—such as a severance tax on sand and gravel dredging and a surcharge on speeding tickets—were rejected. A third suggestion, however, was more to everyone's liking: a special license plate. In 1994, the Legislature approved the "bluebird" automobile license plate, featuring an Eastern bluebird and the caption "Watchable Wildlife." Motorists would pay an extra twenty-five dollars a year each time they renewed their tags.

Though not as lucrative as some of the other funding options, the bluebird plate was a popular public relations tool. It worked so well, in fact, that it had instant competition. The Tennessee State Parks Foundation's "purple iris" license plate came out at the same time.

ALL SPECIES GREAT AND SMALL: THE TENNESSEE BIODIVERSITY PROJECT

To many minds, some species are more watchable than others. No doubt that was why the TWRA put a bluebird on its license plate, rather than, say, a turkey vulture, and why they chose the male bird, with its pretty russet and blue feathers, over the rather bland female.

Among natural systems biologists, however, the male bluebird is neither more nor less attractive than any other species. For them, the growing interest in nongame is merely part of a larger movement to value all species—and not only animal species, but plants, and not only individual species, but entire communities. Of course, careful observers have understood for at least a century the principles of a healthy ecosystem, what George Perkins Marsh once called "the spontaneous arrangements of the organic [and] the inorganic world." But it was not until the 1970s that Tennessee began taking formal measures to preserve the whole canvas of natural diversity in the state.

The first of these was the Tennessee Natural Areas Program created by the Tennessee Natural Areas Preservation Act of 1971. By 1996, nearly fifty Designated State Natural Areas had been granted formal protection under the act, including Savage Gulf, Fall Creek Falls, May Prairie, even the Lucius Burch, Jr., Forest in Memphis. A still greater number of privately owned natural areas ("registered" as opposed to "designated") were protected under nonbinding cooperative agreements with the landowners.

There was only one hitch. The Department of Conservation (reorganized into the Department of Environment and Conservation in 1991), which identified and administered the natural areas, had little hard data, and virtually no criteria, on which to base its determinations of "natural significance." Fortunately, this was about the time computers were revolutionizing the way information was collected, processed, stored and retrieved. In 1975, using a methodology developed by The Nature Conservancy, TDOC formed a new section to compile and manage the needed databases, species inventories, distribution maps, vegetation plots and so on. The new Tennessee Natural Heritage Program took its place as part of a network of Heritage Programs nationwide.

Meanwhile, other state and federal agencies were creating their own information systems, from TVA's Wildlife and Natural Heritage Program to the Geographic Information Systems of the TWRA to the U.S. Forest Service surveys of land cover and vegetation. By the early 1990s, the collective database on Tennessee's biological landscape was huge. It included TABS (Tennessee Animal Biographies) and TADS (Tennessee Aquatic Database), both managed by the TWRA, as well as TWRA's habitat models, wetlands maps and digitized databases of wildlife management areas. The Department of Environment and Conservation had established several databases of its own, including the rare plant and animal inventories in the Natural Heritage Program, the Tennessee Rivers Assessment Program and something called "vertebrate characterization abstracts."

However, like overlays in an anatomy textbook, each of these databases focused only on one or two elements of the organism: here the skeleton, there the major muscle groups, here the digestive tract. Taken together, they revealed a lot more about how the organism functioned than any single system taken separately. Perhaps it was time to start overlaying the separate data sets onto a map of Tennessee. That way, if there were unprotected areas, or holes in the available data, it should be easy to spot them through a new process known as gap analysis. Eventually, the integrated data could be used to produce one comprehensive plan (or any number of local plans) for protecting Tennessee's biodiversity.

Of course, it would also take public cooperation. In fact, that's really where the Tennessee Biodiversity Project began. Not with satellite images or fancy computer programs, but with the obvious premise that people can't be expected to protect something if they don't know what it is they need to protect.

LAND-USE PLANNING: THE DISCUSSION RESUMES

In 1990, Daryl Durham was one of the newest members of the TCL board, a wildlife manager who had spent considerable time in Africa and Latin America studying land-use patterns and the destruction of Third World ecosystems. She was now coordinator of the state's natural areas program and supervisor of the Natural Heritage Inventory. She worked regularly with the individuals, businesses, farmers, developers, paper companies *et al* who own nine-tenths of the land in Tennessee. Some of these landowners were good stewards of their property, she found. But most were "mak[ing] land-use decisions without ever understanding how they affect[ed] Tennessee's biodiversity."

It occurred to Durham that if these people had good information, they were more likely to make good decisions. Durham shared her ideas with several other natural resource professionals, including Bob Ford, TCL vice president and coordinator of the Hatchie Scenic River. By the end of 1990, they had developed a proposal for the Tennessee Biodiversity

Project, a three-year study of natural systems on the Cumberland Plateau. TCL was to be the host organization. Bob Ford would coordinate the project, with assistance as needed from the Department of Conservation, TWRA, TVA and other agencies. Kay Linder, already active as a TCL volunteer, was hired to lead an extensive public education campaign.

Total cost of the initial three-year project was estimated at a rather extraordinary half-million dollars, though in fact the bulk of funding had already been secured from the Lyndhurst Foundation, the U.S. Fish and Wildlife Service and the National Fish and Wildlife Foundation. Other costs would be borne by the various state and federal agencies furnishing the research teams.

Although information management was a large part of the project, it was probably not the most difficult. The real challenge was changing people's attitudes about private property. It would be no easy thing, for instance, to convince a soybean farmer to make room for migrating ovenbirds in his farm management plans. In Tennessee as everywhere, the early 1990s seemed marked by a growing defensiveness over property rights, a bias reminiscent of the Sagebrush Rebellion of 1980.

This was not the first time the League had gotten involved in the debate over land use. The League had helped write one of the state's first land-use bills, the Agricultural, Forest and Open Space Land Act of 1976. That bill had come out of a land-use planning symposium cosponsored by TCL at Henry Horton State Park in 1975. For several years following that meeting, Tony Campbell had hosted a series of informal land-use discussions among agency heads, collectively known as the Resource Agency Coordinating Committee.

Maybe it was time to try the multi-agency approach again. In 1993, the League hosted thirty people, from the Farm Bureau to the Association of Conservation Districts, for a two-day Natural Resources Dialogue Group at Henry Horton. At times the debate was polarized. But in the end, at least three points of consensus emerged.

First, the participants agreed that Tennessee needed a comprehensive, statewide environmental policy. Second, it needed a user-friendly mechanism (agency, technical board or whatever) to help landowners make reasonable use of their land without hurting the ecosystem. And third, Tennesseans needed to learn to base land-use decisions not on property lines or political boundaries, but on geophysical borders such as watersheds.

Land-use planning based on watersheds was not altogether new. The state's Division of Water Pollution Control had long been accustomed to seeing the state as a system of rivers and hills, crests and valleys—fifty-four watershed units in all. In 1995, the division announced that henceforth it would schedule its management and regulatory activities by watershed rather than, say, by county. By the end of the century, every watershed unit in the state was expected to be functioning under the new system.

CANARIES IN THE GLOBAL COALMINE: THE NEOTROPICAL MIGRANT STUDY

As ambitious as the Biodiversity Project was, it needed a proving ground, a demonstration project on which to test the organizers' theories about ecosystem management.

For their pilot project, Durham and Ford chose an emerging ecological crisis: the gradual disappearance of Neotropical migrant songbirds.

Bob Ford was coordinator of the Hatchie State Scenic River, and Daryl Durham was the state's natural areas coordinator, when they developed the Tennessee Biodiversity Project in 1990. Courtesy of Bob Ford and Daryl Durham.

Neotropical migrants are birds that winter in Central and South America and the Caribbean Basin but that nest and breed in North America's forests. According to Bob Ford, eighty varieties of Neotropical migrant songbirds spend some time in Tennessee each year, a delightful variety that includes tanagers, warblers, swallows, hummingbirds, thrushes, vireos and some waterbirds, including least terns and blue-winged teal. For some years, members of the Tennessee Ornithological Society and their counterparts in other states had noticed a drop in the numbers of these species during their annual bird counts. One cause appeared to be DDT, outlawed in the United States since 1972 but still used in parts of Latin America. But most experts suspected the chief culprit was widespread habitat loss—not only in the northern and southern forests where the birds lived, but along their migratory routes as well.

The League had long been convinced of the global nature of environmental protection, but this was the first time it found itself directly involved in an international project. In 1990, Tony Campbell spent two weeks in Brazil as part of "Partners of the Americas," an economic development program that considered, among other things, the social and environmental implications of clear-cutting the tropical rainforests. A short time later, TCL joined "Partners in Flight—*Aves de las Americas,*" an international conservation project targeting Neotropical migrants. It was through Partners in Flight that the League established its own migrant study, the pilot project dubbed Birds and Biodiversity.

Most of the first three years of the project were spent compiling and analyzing databases, then translating these findings for public consumption. This phase, the public education campaign, was considered vital. Bob Ford and Kay Linder gave dozens of presentations; Ford wrote special reports and a monthly article for *Tennessee Out-Of-Doors*; Project CENTS adapted some of the findings for a special teaching unit called *Birds and Biodiversity: Threads in the Fabric of Life.* In a tentative partnership with the Dominican Republic, Tennessee began looking into the chances of shipping binoculars and fie guides to park rangers there, while promoting coffee grown on migrant-friendly plantations, here.

The Tennessee Biodiversity Project was so successful that most of the sponsors renewed their r even before the first three years were up. In 1993 the project expanded into a partnership that included TWRA, TOS and the neighboring states of Kentucky and Alabama. Ecosystem management was a central theme when the Southeastern Association of Fish and Wildlife Agencies met in Nashville in 1995; wildlife professionals across the country were scrutinizing Tennessee's model for possible use in their own states.

At the League's fiftieth annual meeting in Chattanooga in May 1996, Daryl Durham was named Wildlife Conservationist of the Year. Her concern for even the humblest forms of wildlife had led to the most significant research effort in the League's history.

PEARLS OF GREAT PRICE: THE TENNESSEE RIVER MUSSEL

It is worth noting, however, that the League was lobbying for humble species even before anyone ever thought of the Biodiversity Project. One of these issues involved freshwater mussels, as humble a creature as you could ask for. Yet for all their unassuming looks, mussels are in fact an important link in the Tennessee River ecosystem, especially in Kentucky Lake, where mussel beds might stretch for miles. So acutely sensitive to their habitat are they that one TWRA biologist called them possibly "the best water quality indicator we have in Tennessee." Thus it was no minor worry when, in the 1980s, Tennessee's vast mussel stocks began to decline. Nonpoint source water pollution was suspected, along with habitat destruction, impoundments and overharvesting by commercial mussel harvesters.

Though only twelve of seventy-two species could be legally harvested, and though few people paid any attention to them at all, mussels were an ancient and honored commodity in Tennessee. Indians had used them for utensils, decoration and sometimes food. Shortly before the turn of the century the garment industry began using the pearlescent shell linings for buttons. An estimated one-third of all "pearl" buttons in the country came from the Tennessee River Valley. At its height, the pearl button industry was worth more than six million dollars. The industry faded around World War II with the advent of plastic, but another market for mussel shells was already opening up.

Pearl farmers in Japan and other Asian countries had discovered that pellets ground from North American mussel shells produced particularly high-quality cultured pearls. A bead-shaped nucleus, inserted into the mantle of a pearl oyster, would provoke the mollusk to secrete multiple layers of nacre. After several months, or even several years, the farmer opened the oyster to reveal a perfectly round pearl.

Suddenly the rush was on. So great was the demand for shells, said TWRA's Keith Jones, so vast the supply and so high the return, that mussel licenses soared. The best divers might harvest two thousand pounds, and earn a hundred dollars, in a single day. Those who brokered the shells to Asia, of course, made much more. At first, just three families dominated the shell export business in Tennessee, said Gina Latendresse, president of American Pearl Company of Nashville and Camden. By the 1970s, there were fifteen. One of these was her father. By the late 1960s, John Latendresse was not only Benton County's leading shell exporter. He had figured out how to grow pearls himself, using native mussels as the incubators. By developing a variety of shapes and textures other than the traditional round, Latendresse and his American Pearl Company soon became the only significant contender in the domestic cultured pearl industry.

Yet even with this new competition, the Asian market continued as brisk as ever, said TWRA's Jones. "Ton after ton of Washboard, Maple Leaf, Three Ridge and Ebony shells rattled across the scales" on their way to Japan. "It was beyond the imagination that these tremendous reserves of shells could ever be depleted by men crawling on their hands and knees, groping in the dark waters that covered thousands of acres."

However, like any resource that gets consumed faster than it can be renewed, the reserves *were* shrinking. Roughly the same number of divers were collecting only a fourth as many shells. In the late 1970s, TWRA began a five-year study of the resource. Over the next decade or so, the agency established size limits for the most popular species, introduced new licensing requirements for pearl farmers and, in 1989, increased the price of a commercial license.

Yet even with these precautions, the mussel beds continued to decline. The League, which had been involved in Kentucky Lake management decisions since at least the '70s, now drafted a bill imposing a severance tax on mussels. The bill died its first time out, in 1990. But in 1991, lawmakers passed the equivalent, a fee charged to wholesale buyers and exporters. The extra $100,000 a year allowed TWRA to hire a mussel biologist, a technician and a law enforcement officer to work the mussel beat.

ANOTHER IDENTITY CRISIS

If sheer activity was any indicator, 1990 should have been a time of great momentum and optimism at the League. After all, a new decade had begun, a new millennium was approaching; the League's golden anniversary was just a few years away. But instead of a burning excitement, some people at the League seemed to be feeling just plain burned out. As the 1990 annual report admitted, if there was "any negative aspect" to the League's success, it was that the demand on the League's staff time was "almost overwhelming."

For one thing, the League was again having money trouble. As Tony Campbell glumly pointed out, finances were the worst he had seen them in eight or ten years. A contest to recruit new members had flopped; income from raffles and rallies had dried up; sales of things like cookbooks and knives, though good for public relations, barely covered the cost of producing and marketing them. Despite an annual budget of a quarter of a million dollars, despite the first major dues hike in a decade and a half (individual dues were now fifteen dollars), despite a full-time development director and a supposedly revitalized Corporate Conservation Council—despite all that, the League in some months could barely pay the rent. And that monthly rent, since a recent move to Music Row, was now a thousand dollars.

In fact, if the Biodiversity Project had a drawback, it was that it provided no help with overhead. Though Bob Ford worked out of an office at the League, his duties were supposed to remain separate from those of other staff. Yet naturally the arrangement sometimes meant more work, even if it was just answering Ford's telephone.

The League, in fact, had never been so busy. In a single year—1990—it had produced the Environmental Quality Index, launched the Birds and Biodiversity Project and begun the nonpoint source education campaign. It sponsored an Earth Day poster contest and a ten-year Arbor Day project known as ReLeaf Tennessee. It held its fourteenth annual Youth Con-servation Summit and cohosted the environmental media symposium at MTSU.

Yet despite the seemingly endless energy required to drive all these projects—or maybe because of it—morale at times seemed depressingly low. Despite efforts to coax more team spirit from the leadership, including the "strategic planning process" mapped out in 1987 and 1988, relations between the board and the staff were still somewhat fragile. At the same time, the public seemed to have grown weary of such once-popular programs as the youth camps (canceled after 1991), deer registries (virtually canceled by the affiliates, though TWRA still held them), sportsman's rallies (phased out by 1991), even eagle hacking (handed off to student groups). As enthusiasm for these programs eroded, so did the favorable press cov-erage they had once generated. In fact, the most-publicized TCL story of 1990 (next to the predictable furor over ReLeaf Tennessee, with its endless photo ops of fourth-graders plant-ing tulip poplars) was the Environmental Quality Index.

The EQ Index had generated a great deal of free air time for the League. But just as im-portant, it also seemed to prove a point the League had been trying to make for years: that TCL wasn't just about hunting and fishing. In fact, the Index had barely even mentioned hunt-ing and fishing; its brief discussions about wildlife focused mainly on nongame.

On the other hand, this new image of a more inclusive TCL may have had a downside. Though some observers no doubt welcomed the make-over, others, it appeared, found it puzzling. Did the Tennessee Conservation League care about sportsmen, or didn't it? Was TCL a sporting club, or wasn't it?

The answer, of course, was that the League was both. As president Mark Benko said in the 1990 annual report, "Today, our environmental victories are broader and have an even greater impact on conserving our natural heritage." Yet even as he commended the League's new agenda, he acknowledged that there were those who "would say that addressing these broad issues has caused the League to lose ground with some of its affiliates who are more resource-specific." Whether or not this was the case, the fact that the question was being raised at all showed that, once again, the League was struggling to pin down its identity.

The trouble was, the days were long gone when conservation meant simply the conser-vation of game and fish. By 1990, it was almost impossible to separate an exclusively hunting or fishing issue from the complex stew of *all* environmental issues: solid waste, hazardous waste, air quality, water quality, forest management and so on. Added to the mix, of course, were the tangential but time-consuming debates over budgets, programming and politics. Taken together, they made for a sprawling, complex agenda, one that no single organiza-tion should have been expected to address, least of all an organization so small you could count its staff on one hand.

The League was used to living without the support of mainstream "environmentalists." But now it seemed to be losing stature even among those whom it considered its "primary membership base," Tennessee's hunters and anglers. An unscientific survey of TWRA license holders (conducted by the League as a fund-raising tool in late 1989) revealed that many sportsmen had no idea who the League was, or what exactly it did. That revelation was bad enough. But even more disturbing was the loss of support among *existing* members. The same League that one time had counted well over one hundred active clubs now claimed barely fifty; and of these, fully half were in "serious arrears." Some local clubs had disbanded due to lack of interest; others, struggling to stay afloat, were hard pressed to come up with the $2.50 per member yearly dues assessment. The board could handle this: club dues never amounted to much of the budget anyway. What was considerably tougher to swallow was knowing that at least some of these delinquent clubs were dropping out deliberately. During its latest renewal cycle, for instance, the venerable Cherokee Rod and Gun Club, one of the League's largest affiliates with four hundred members, had renewed memberships for its board of directors only.

To the League, whose ultimate strength had always lain in the size and number of its local clubs, this trend was both mortifying and potentially lethal. On September 16, 1990, during a weekend board meeting in Sewanee, Tony Campbell wondered aloud why the League was bleeding affiliates, and what could be done to stanch the flow.

IS THE SPORTSMAN-CONSERVATIONIST A THREATENED SPECIES?

"All of us in here can remember the old sportsman/conservation clubs," Campbell said during that meeting, "all types of hunters and fishermen who loved the out-of-doors and enjoyed it. If you look across the state now there are not many of those clubs left."

Though some thought that the problem was a shortage of hunters and fishermen altogether, that was not likely. According to the 1991 national survey by the U.S. Fish and Wildlife Service and the Bureau of the Census, the number of resident sportsmen in Tennessee 16 years and older had risen roughly 11 percent between 1980 and 1990, to approximately 800,000. (Of these, 485,000 fished only, while 90,000 hunted only. Slightly more than 222,000 did both.) TWRA records seemed to confirm that trend. Sales of resident combination (hunting and fishing) licenses, the agency's most popular license category, had risen slowly but more or less steadily since World War II, finally breaking the half-million mark in 1981, and remaining there for most of the decade. Though sales of combination licenses began to dip below a half-million in 1990, that decline was more than offset by rising sales of the all-inclusive sportsman's licenses, at sixty dollars or more each.

Assuming the numbers of sportsmen were stable, puzzled observers had been struggling for several years to account for the downturn in sportsmen's clubs in general and the League's membership in particular.

Maybe we're all turning into couch potatoes, suggested Sam Venable, Jr., the popular *Knoxville News-Sentinel* outdoor writer in the '70s and early '80s. On the other hand, maybe we're workaholics. Or maybe we're just not as civic-minded as our fathers and grandfathers were.

In a 1996 article in *Tennessee Out-Of-Doors*, Criminal Court Judge Lee Asbury blamed the loss of support on the League's shift to "big-picture environmental issues" in the early '80s. The change of focus may have earned more grants and donations for the League, said Asbury, a member from East Tennessee since the early '60s, but in his opinion it "significantly altered [the League's] character," causing it "to grow far away from its roots." He was appalled when,

Sam Venable, Jr., entertains at the
Tennessee Valley Sportsmen's Club's
annual wild game banquet in 1996.
One of Tennessee's most popular
outdoor writers since the early 1970s,
Venable has seen the sportsmen's
movement go through many changes.
Courtesy of the Tennessee Valley
Sportsmen's Club.

at one recent meeting, someone suggested that "any major shift to hunting and fishing is-sues would amount to a step backward."

Bob Ford suspected there was an even more insidious cause for the change. "A few years ago," wrote Ford in 1990, "sportsmen gathered in 'conservation clubs' and supported land management for the benefit of all wildlife. Today, however, hunters gather in specialty groups that target deer, quail or turkey. [They] become so specialized they forget a wildlife popula-tion is a link in a complex chain of biological events, and not just the end result of a properly placed food plot."

Tony Campbell agreed with Ford. "What we are getting now more and more are very narrow special interest groups that are interested in one thing—killing something and show-ing it off. The whole philosophy behind what created TCL and a lot of our sportsmen clubs has disappeared. . . . They have lots of deer now, lots of turkey . . . [so] they don't care about water quality and these things."

So maybe *that* was the problem: the old battles—over water quality, forest fires and so on—had all been won, or nearly so, and some sportsmen felt there was nothing left to fight for. People respond to a crisis, said Venable. Remove the crisis and you remove the reason for organizing. Find a new crisis and you have a new group. Look at two of the state's young-est clubs, the Tennessee Sportsman's Association and the Tennessee Striped Bass Associa-tion. The TSA was formed to force striped bass out of Norris Lake; the striper group was formed to keep them there.

It's a cycle, said Venable. "Instead of [sportsmen] coming together Monday night to raise hell because there's no deer, they're going deer hunting. The accomplishments of the early [sportsmen's groups] may have negated the reason for their existence."

Not that there was any shortage of environmental crises in the 1990s. From overpopula-tion to toxic wastes to the destruction of the rainforests, a willing activist still had plenty of causes to choose from. In fact, said Campbell at the Sewanee meeting, these were the sort of broad-based environmental issues that many of the League's newest members wanted the club to address. They were also the sort of issues that the League had pledged to embrace when it accepted the terms of the Meeman grant back in 1972.

Unfortunately, however, they were also the sort of issues that seemed to hold little interest for the typical sportsman. "The reason they don't care about TCL anymore," said Mark Benko's father, Greeneville director John Benko, "is that there are no issues today for the sportsmen. You had sportsmen's clubs back then and every time you came to a TCL meeting you had an argument about something and it had to do with sport hunting or fishing. You don't have that today so you don't go to your club meeting because there is nothing there for you." That was why the Cherokee Rod and Gun Club dropped out, he said.

Depressing thought: had the League become obsolete?

"WE EITHER LEAD OR WE BECOME IRRELEVANT"

If nothing else, the League could at least take some comfort in knowing it was not alone. According to the National Wildlife Federation, just about every other state affiliate in the country was having similar problems.

In July 1992, NWF president Jay D. Hair and other conservation leaders gathered in Bozeman, Montana, to discuss the issue at a three-day conference called "North America's Hunting Heritage." The central message of the gathering was that hunters still played a vital role in the ongoing battle to protect natural resources, even if the terms of engagement had changed somewhat from the earlier days. If sportsmen allowed themselves to be distracted by the "entirely artificial" divisions between their interests and so-called "environmental interests," said Hair, then the battle would surely be lost.

"We either lead or we become irrelevant," he said bluntly. If hunters don't continue to fight to protect natural resources, whether those resources seem directly related to hunting or not, then the leadership will fall to others who will protect them.

As it happened, the timeliness of the Bozeman meeting was illustrated a few years afterwards. In 1996, an unlikely partnership formed between what one columnist called the "tree-huggers" and the "hook-and-bullet crowd." Galvanized by recent Republican attacks on the Clean Water Act and other environmental laws, some of the nation's largest environmental groups had formed an alliance with some of its largest conservation groups. Calling themselves the Natural Resource Summit of America, their stated mission was to "make [America's] natural resources a priority and to hold elected leaders and candidates accountable for their positions." The press made much of the novelty of such a marriage, but the most pointed comment came from a Department of Interior staffer, who asked, "Will [they] stick together when the attacks on the environment are on the way out?"

Tony Campbell believed the League would, and should, lead Tennessee's activists through the '90s and into the next century. But he also believed that some sportsmen would simply drop out if they felt the League was moving too far from its hunting and fishing origins.

Campbell had a suggestion. Perhaps, he began tentatively at the Sewanee board meeting, the board might consider forming a separate organization for "some of our folks who have real strong feelings about this sort of thing"—that is, who felt the League should continue to focus on hunting and fishing issues. This idea had been knocked around at the last meeting of the executive committee, he said. They even came up with a name, the Sportsman's Council of Tennessee. This Council would be an affiliate of the League, but it would have its own bylaws, membership and so on.

The board was skeptical. Some members noted sourly that sportsmen nowadays were just plain apathetic no matter what group they belonged to. Another doubted whether "we should spend a lot of time worrying about some of these clubs because they don't spend any time worrying about [us]." Another observed, with no little sarcasm, that the League seemed to be proposing "to segregate sportsmen out of the Tennessee Conservation League."

Campbell withdrew the suggestion, admitting that it had been made "in somewhat desperation." Still, there was a certain undeniable irony in what had just passed, especially to anyone who had been around in 1969 when the League formed the Tennessee Environmental Council. The move to form TEC had been successful precisely because it freed the sportsmen from dealing with issues that either intimidated or bored them. But to do the opposite—to give away the very issues that interested and inspired them most—surely that would be the death of the League?

Though the proposal was soon forgotten in the face of more pressing (and cheerful) topics, its implications were not so easily dismissed. It revealed not only that the League was indeed "in somewhat desperation" for an answer to its membership crisis. It also demonstrated something that its leaders had been struggling with for nearly fifty years: that maybe TCL *wasn't*, after all, for everyone. It was a topic that went to the very heart of TCL's existence, and it wasn't settled yet. They would return to it at least once more before the decade was over.

THE LEAGUE SHOWS ITS SOCIAL CONSCIENCE: NATURELINK

Besides, it wasn't as though TCL in the '90s was ignoring its core constituency.

On the contrary, it continued to juggle at least a half-dozen hunting-and-fishing-related issues, from repelling antihunting challenges to founding a new wildlife management area. And even though it did so with a decidedly modern twist, it even found a way to fill some of the void left by the departure of the youth camps and deer registries.

When TCL discontinued the youth conservation camps in 1992, many in the League had been sorry to see them go. The camps were the only extended social activity the League sponsored, and even though they were intended for teenagers, they had become a popular annual event for a lot of adult volunteers. In fact, the board was already looking for something to replace them with, perhaps teacher workshops. However, the fall of 1993 brought a better idea. Region III vice president Rosemary MacGregor had just spent a weekend with the Georgia Wildlife Federation, trying out a new NWF program called NatureLink. NatureLink was the youth camp of the '90s, a combination of social activism and environmental education.

Instead of targeting high school teenagers already interested in conservation (as fifteen years of youth camps had done), NatureLink targeted families who had very little notion of the outdoors at all, but who, in the words of the TCL brochure, "wish[ed] to explore the wonders of nature in a safe outdoor setting"—people from the inner city, the physically challenged,

Kim Lee practices casting into Old Hickory Lake during the first NatureLink weekend in 1994. Her mentor is Greer Tidwell, Jr., general counsel for the Department of Environment and Conservation. TCL file photo.

recent immigrants trying to overcome language barriers. The cost to host a NatureLink weekend was considerable, an estimated fifteen thousand dollars, but the League soon got sponsors: First Tennessee Bank, TVA, TWRA and Trout Unlimited. Participants paid forty dollars each, but scholarships were available.

The first NatureLink weekend was at Camp Easter Seal on Old Hickory Lake in October 1994. A total of sixteen families came, many of them single mothers and their kids, and almost as many "mentors," such as Greer Tidwell, Jr., who taught kids to cast, and Dick Urban, who demonstrated the cautious art of removing a hook. Others taught rappelling or led nature hikes or canoe rides; there were campfires at night, and a catfish dinner cooked by the Nashville Sportsman's Club.

As NatureLink became an annual event, the weekend began drawing a wider audience: fathers as well as mothers; two-car families from the suburbs In 1996, NatureLink director Rick Murphree got a TCL President's Award for his efforts.

HUNTERS FOR THE HUNGRY

Now that the League was no longer sponsoring deer registries, it was eager to find something else to offer deer hunters. In 1991, assisted by TWRA, it joined Hunters for the Hungry, a program started the year before in Texas. The idea was simple. The successful hunter took his deer to a participating meat processor, the processor ground the donated venison into two-pound freezer packages and a local food bank distributed the meat to homeless shelters and soup kitchens. While hunters usually paid some or all of the processing fee, they could declare the value of the meat a charitable donation.

The program had enormous potential. With a record deer kill of 121,596 in Tennessee in 1991, and an average yield per animal of 40 to 50 pounds of meat, Tennessee hunters could, conceivably, have given away at least 5 million pounds of venison. Most hunters, however, were not so charitable. Between them, they donated only about 4,500 pounds in 1991. The following year's donations were fewer still. By 1994 the total contribution was a mere two thousand pounds.

The problem may have been a lack of publicity, though posters were hung in every checkpoint and wildlife agency office in the state, and in the windows of participating processors. More likely the problem was simply that it was too much trouble. Since home-processed meat was not accepted, donations had to be channeled through approved meat processors, but in 1991, only twenty-four processors signed up. The following year was even worse, because participating processors were now required to take a training course, then be certified by a state meat inspector. It was a lot to ask. After four years, fewer than thirty processors were involved.

Still, Hunters for the Hungry attracted lots of media coverage that cast hunters in an uncommonly sympathetic light. Beleaguered for so long, sportsmen welcomed the chance to be seen as the good guys for a change. Twenty years after the antihunting challenges began, sportsmen found they were still underappreciated.

THE ANTIHUNTING CHALLENGE CONTINUES

For instance, in late 1990, a small coalition of Morgan County residents filed a challenge that, if successful, could have undermined TWRA's ability to control its wildlife management areas for hunting and fishing. In this incident, the local citizens objected to TWRA's clearcutting, timber sales and other forest management practices on the 89,000-acre Catoosa Wildlife Management Area. The Sierra Club backed them up, formally charging that Catoosa was not being managed for multiple uses.

It was true that Catoosa's forests were "intensively managed" by clear-cuts, prescribed burning and other methods designed to make the most of Catoosa's varied game populations. It was also true that Catoosa wasn't managed for multiple uses. But Catoosa wasn't intended for multiple use. It had been purchased for sportsmen's use, with sportsmen's funds, in the early 1940s. Through subsequent acquisitions, all financed by the Game and Fish Fund, the original 63,000 acres had been expanded by nearly a third. The League, of course, rose to the defense of TWRA, and the dispute was eventually resolved. However, it was soon followed by a much broader assault on hunting rights.

In that episode, several environmental groups sued the U.S. Fish and Wildlife Service, claiming that certain uses of the country's national wildlife refuges were not compatible with their stated purposes. Though it originally questioned such uses as livestock grazing, the suit quickly became a challenge to hunting and fishing. Either or both activities were allowed on about half the 504 refuges in the National Wildlife Refuge System, including all seven USFWS refuges in Tennessee.

In an unusual out-of-court settlement in 1993, the USFWS agreed to review every existing use of every refuge in the NWR system. The plaintiffs reserved the right to approve its findings. Any uses they found unacceptable were to be "expeditiously terminated."

The League and every other sportsmen's group were appalled by the terms of the settlement. *Tennessee Out-Of-Doors* followed the case closely as it moved through the courts. But they needn't have worried. In late 1994 the U.S. Fish and Wildlife Service released a seventy thousand-page report demonstrating, to the plaintiffs' satisfaction, that hunting and fishing *were* compatible with every refuge where they were currently allowed. In fact, of the more than five thousand recreational, commercial and other uses evaluated, fewer than one hundred were found to be inappropriate—and these were mainly things like jogging on beaches where piping plovers were nesting.

CORA, KOPPERS AND ROYAL BLUE

In 1990 the League also went to bat for the Campbell Outdoor Recreation Association (CORA) and their leader from Jacksboro, Lee Asbury. At issue was a 53,000-acre tract of land in Campbell and Scott Counties known variously as the Koppers tract (for the Koppers Coal Company, an early owner) and Royal Blue (presumably for the Blue Diamond Coal Company, an even earlier owner). The rugged, mountainous region had been much abused by shaft- and strip-mining in the earlier part of the century, as well as clear-cutting and the construction of Interstate 75 in the 1960s. Nevertheless, the Koppers tract was rich in wildlife, hiking trails and other recreational resources, and at least three parties were now vying for control of it.

CORA wanted TWRA to turn the entire tract into a wildlife management area. TWRA was willing, but the asking price of eighteen million dollars (including some other property TWRA did not want) was way too steep. TVA, which had owned the mineral rights since 1962, wanted the estimated seventy million tons of coal lying beneath the surface. The current owner, a Houston savings and loan association that had acquired the property in 1987, wanted to develop most of it and lease the rest to private clubs. That's when CORA formed, specifically to raise the funds so local sportsmen could lease the Koppers tract themselves, at about a dollar an acre. Asbury and a few of his friends spearheaded the $57,000 annual fund-raising effort. Hunters who couldn't afford a full share were told to pay what they could.

Meanwhile, in 1990, the savings and loan went into receivership. Fire sales are always a good time to go shopping, so Lee Asbury, Tony Campbell, Caryville State Representative Jerry Cross and TWRA assistant director Ron Fox began looking for some sort of creative financing. Meanwhile, U.S. Senator Jim Sasser worked with TVA to accept some restrictions on mining in the area. At length, the General Assembly agreed to let TWRA dip into the wetlands acquisition fund to buy the Koppers tract. In the fall of 1991, TWRA bought 43,000 acres of the Koppers for four million dollars, and renamed them the Royal Blue Wildlife Management Area. Judge Asbury was named Conservationist of the Year.

PICKING POCKETS AT THE STATE WILDLIFE AGENCY

At least one other issue of the early '90s was inherently interesting to the sportsmen— the debate over who should control the purse strings at the Wildlife Resources Agency.

Apart from a few special appropriations, the wildlife commission had been completely self-supporting from the day it was created, its expenses paid by the sportsmen either through their fishing and hunting licenses, fines and so on; or through the federal excise taxes they paid on hunting and fishing gear. Yet these revenues were so substantial (and obviously so conservatively managed) that every year there was some left over to put in the Game and Fish Fund. Even after paying off a $1.3 million building loan in 1983, the reserves by the end of the 1980s had reached $16 million.

Occasionally TWRA had asked for allocations from the state's general fund, but most of these were for the nongame program. The only other money that routinely passed between the agency and central government were standard payments by TWRA for its share of the state's administrative and operating costs, vehicle maintenance and other day-to-day overhead.

During the economic recession of the late 1980s, however, the state of Tennessee was having financial trouble, and one solution was to raise the rent, figuratively speaking, on the wildlife agency. (In fact, at one point the state did propose charging "rent" on the headquarters building that TWRA already owned.) Despite protests from both the agency and the sportsmen, TWRA's share of overhead charges nearly doubled. At the same time, more than $800,000 of TWRA money in the motor vehicle maintenance fund apparently had disappeared into the maw of central government. Meanwhile, the state's Finance and Administration Department decided, unilaterally, to take over building management at TWRA, charging roughly double what TWRA had been paying for things like janitorial services and pest control. According to Tony Campbell, total overbillings could amount to $1.8 million a year.

TWRA was vexed, but this was not simply a matter of turf control. In the agency's opinion, these excessive payments amounted to improper diversions of wildlife agency revenues. If they continued, the agency was in danger of losing its annual apportionments of Pittman-Robertson and Wallop-Breaux monies. With federal funds accounting for nearly a quarter of its budget, the agency could not well withstand such a loss. In the history of the agency the two programs had channeled tens of millions of dollars into Tennessee for wildlife and fisheries restoration. The allocations for 1989–90 alone were $2.4 million for P–R and $1.8 million for W–B.

At first the state refused to admit the charges. The League threatened to sue, and for several weeks the matter was debated in the newspapers. Finally, in January 1991, the state agreed to refund the motor pool surplus; it also agreed to assess "reasonable" charges for overhead and building management.

Still Fighting Over West Tennessee Tribs

And finally, if anybody really doubted the League's commitment to the sportsmen of Tennessee, he had only to consider the West Tennessee Tributaries Project, the most expensive, most exhausting, yet ultimately the most significant resource conservation issue in the League's history, perhaps in the state's.

The WTTP had now been in litigation for more than two decades. Although the Corps was finally preparing to hand over the first of the mitigation lands ordered by a federal court back in 1973, the case was more divided, more acrimonious and more deadlocked than ever.

The 1985 settlement, as it turned out, had settled almost nothing. As many had predicted, most landowners in the Obion-Forked Deer River Basin refused to grant the conservation easements required by the consent decree. Consequently, almost no new work (nor even routine channel maintenance) had gone forward in the last five years. In early 1990, a bill had been introduced in the state Legislature making it easier for landowners to channelize, but it was opposed by a second bill making channelization almost impossible. In the end, neither bill made it out of committee.

The landowners were growing mutinous. On October 2, 1990, more than a thousand of them gathered in Jackson for a "Landowners Awareness Day" sponsored by the Tennessee Farm Bureau Federation and the Tennessee Forestry Association. Their petition for fewer wetlands regulations was hand-delivered to President Bush's Interagency Wetlands Task Force in Washington a few weeks later.

Meanwhile, the rivers continued to flood. One angry landowner claimed to have lost $75,000 worth of timber because he wasn't allowed to remove blockages. Another ditched part of her property anyway, declaring that "[t]his nation was founded on private property rights." When EPA ordered the basin authority to restore her drained wetlands, the authority refused, saying that it had merely cleared an existing channel.

Chester McConnell, of course, had been wary of the consent decree from the first. Nor had it made him any happier when, in the late 1980s, the state gave the Corps authorization to channelize two particularly flood-prone stretches of channel, the so-called Fowlkes and Mengelwood items. (Under Section 401 of the 1972 Clean Water Act, all federal water projects "which may result in any discharge into the navigable waters" must be certified by the host state.) Larry Bowers was manager of the Natural Resources Section of the Division of Water Pollution Control at the time. As he later explained, neither of the two areas in question was judged to contain significant wetlands. Already heavily farmed, and already channelized at least once, both Fowlkes and Mengelwood "looked like a straight ditch through a cornfield."

The Sidonia item, on the other hand, though partly channelized in 1969-1970, "looked like a true riverine system," said Bowers, with natural meanders, bottomland hardwoods and forested wetlands on both sides. McConnell fought strenuously against 401 certification for Sidonia, even hiring a lawyer to make his case before the Water Quality Control Board. After extensive review, including a personal visit by Commissioner of Health and Environment James Word, the Division in 1990 agreed with McConnell, and denied 401 certification for the Sidonia item.

The Corps was furious, said Larry Bowers; one official even threatened to "turn him in" to the FBI. But the Corps must have known, deep down, that the state wasn't the problem. The problem was that the Corps was whipping a dead dinosaur. After all, there were the Fowlkes and Mengelwood items, both ready to move forward as soon as the necessary conservation easements were in place. But now it was the landowners holding things up. West Tennessee Tribs had become a colossal, immoveable log jam, and the Corps knew it. By the end of 1990, the Corps announced that it was "initiating shutdown" of the West Tennessee Tributaries Project.

WEST TENNESSEE TRIBS II: A SOLUTION AT LAST?

The Corps may have issued a death warrant on West Tennessee Tribs, but angry landowners refused to sign it. Led by M.V. Williams of the West Tennessee Tributaries Association, basin residents contacted Governor Ned McWherter, demanding something be done about the continued flooding. The governor was in a peculiar position. He was a West

Tennessee farmer and businessman himself, so he understood the landowners' position. He was also a duck hunter and sportsman, so he understood the plaintiffs' position. But above all he was a politician, and as such, he was "just begging them [all] to sit down with each other and strike a balance."

In 1992, McWherter contacted the Corps office in Memphis, asking the agency to resume the WTTP—only this time following an entirely new work plan based on the more benign Stream Obstruction Removal Guidelines. The Corps was polite but wary. The governor's proposal meant learning a whole new way of doing things. It also meant a whole new round of arguments with opposing interest groups. However, if the governor would put an unbiased middleman in charge of the reformulation, the Corps agreed to return to the table.

An unbiased middleman? The governor's office asked Tony Campbell if there was such a person. Campbell suggested Ben Smith, head of the Environmental Policy Group in the State Planning Office, former director of the old Safe Growth Team and winner of the League's 1985 Conservationist of the Year Award. If anybody could keep a cool head on such a hot topic, Campbell figured, it was Ben Smith.

The West Tennessee Tributaries Steering Committee, as the task force came to be called, was the most ambitious one yet. It eventually included twenty-two people, including Tony Campbell for the League, Richard Swaim for the basin authority, Gary Myers for TWRA, Chester McConnell for the Wildlife Management Institute, Clark Akers for the National Ecological Foundation and M. V. Williams for the West Tennessee Tributaries Association. The EPA was represented, as was the Farm Bureau, the Environmental Council, the U.S. Soil Conservation Service, the U.S. Fish and Wildlife Service, the Tennessee Department of Agriculture, the Department of Health and Environment (later the Department of Environment and Conservation), the Tennessee Forestry Association, the U.S. Geological Survey, the Tennessee Association of Conservation Districts and two more citizen groups, Basin Cities and Basin Counties. The Corps had a seat at the meetings, of course, but it had no vote.

There were also, fortunately, two mediators from the Federal Mediation and Conciliation Service.

The steering committee met almost monthly at first. At times, it seemed, members might as well have been deaf, so little did they seem to listen to one another. But under the firm guidance of Smith and the mediators, they grudgingly moved onto at least patches of common ground. By the following year they had reached enough consensus to draft a mission plan. They had also designed two restoration-demonstration projects (one large, one small) for sections of the Middle Fork of the Forked Deer. They had even secured an EPA grant to help fund the projects.

Basically, the new plan called for the Corps engineers to return the ditched waterways to something like their former paths. This meant removing levees, creating diversions and rerouting the streams to their natural meanders and oxbows, much as their colleagues in Florida had been forced to do on the Kissimmee River in the 1970s. The plan also called for them to implement new soil conservation practices, set aside at least ten thousand acres of public recreation land and restore nearly seven thousand acres of bottomland hardwoods.

In 1996, the Memphis District announced that the two projects were not only technically feasible, they also qualified for funds under the original West Tennessee Tributaries Project (though they would need up to twenty million dollars in new funding). The contract on Stokes Creek, the smaller of the two pilot projects, would probably be awarded by summer 1997. Governor Don Sundquist, who had reauthorized the West Tennessee Tributaries Steering Committee when he took office, now set a goal to have both projects finished by the year 2000.

Meanwhile, there had been another noteworthy development. In 1996 the General Assembly passed a bill changing the name, the makeup and the mandate of the Obion-Forked Deer Basin Authority. It was now the West Tennessee River Basin Authority, attached to the Department of Environment and Conservation. Its board was enlarged to include a forestry and an environmental professional. And now, its main job was "to preserve the natural flow and function" of the Obion, Forked Deer and Hatchie River Basin "through environmentally sensitive stream maintenance."

Where channels were already well established, or where restoration wasn't practical, the authority was authorized to "maintain or stabilize" the altered streams. But where it *was* practical, the authority was to restore, "in a self-sustaining manner, natural stream and floodplain dynamics and associated environmental and economic benefits (i.e., restore and conserve fisheries and wildlife habitat, wetlands, water quality, and naturally or economically productive bottom land hardwood systems)."

It would be hard to overstate the significance of these developments, said Dodd Galbreath, who succeeded Ben Smith as head of the Tennessee Environmental Policy Group, now called the Environmental Policy Office. True, the new WTTP restoration plan was neither complete nor foolproof. (The demonstrations could still "blow up," as another observer put it, over the question of easements, landowner rights and the several thousand acres of mitigation lands still outstanding.) But, said Galbreath, when both the Farm Bureau and M. V. Williams agree that channelization is probably not a good thing—when both a Republican and a Democratic governor agree that channelization is not a good thing—when the entire West Tennessee Tributaries Project has to be redesigned because it was *never* a good thing—well, if you can't call that history, you can at least call it progress.

HOME AT LAST

The Obion-Forked Deer controversy was not the only item on the League's agenda that had grown moldy with age.

In 1990 the idea of a Conservation Resource Center turned ten years old, but not so much as a spadeful of dirt had been turned. How could it? It didn't even have a building site. The last two proposals, one at Ellington Agricultural Center, another on the Grassmere property, had been ruled out. By May, Mitchell Parks, newly-elected president Mark Benko and the rest of the board had agreed to scrap the idea of new construction altogether. They were now talking about buying an existing structure, one that would "suit [their] needs with little renovation."

By the following spring, they had found it: an almost-new, two-story brick building just minutes from the White Bridge Road exit of Interstate 40 on the west side of Nashville. The building at 300 Orlando Avenue was plain but sturdy. Its 5,300 square feet were eminently serviceable, with front and rear parking, plenty of work and storage space, at least five offices, a conference room, a reception area, a kitchen and an unfinished second floor that might one day house the conservation center they still dreamed about. The price was $265,000.

Although barely thirty thousand dollars remained in the building fund (the League never could seem to keep its hands off earmarked funds), the board was able to put together a better-than-fifty-percent down payment, thanks in part to a generous gift from Lucius Burch, Jr., as well as a sizable chunk of the Meeman fund. (Because they were drawing on the corpus of the Meeman money, the building was to be held in the name of the Edward J. Meeman Conservation Foundation.) The sale closed in August 1991, and a short time later, staff and volunteers were carting boxes, hanging drapes and arranging furniture. A local garden club planted shrubs and trees; workers hung a large beige awning with *Tennessee Conservation League* in green letters. As a delighted and exhausted Sue Garner told board members, "For the first time in all these years, we don't have the appearance of just moving in or getting ready to move out."

By Christmas they were ready for the official housewarming. Some two hundred well-wishers ate, drank and toasted an ebullient Mitchell Parks. No one seemed to notice that 300 Orlando Avenue bore little resemblance to the grand architectural design sketched a decade earlier. That the League had finally made good on an eleven-year-old promise to itself seemed victory enough.

Perhaps it was the new surroundings, the smell of new paint or merely the panic of facing twenty thousand dollars a year in mortgage and operating expenses, but the move seemed to trigger a new vitality in the League. The mood at board meetings was noticeably less doleful; leaders announced an ambitious new corporate fund-raising campaign; the executive committee approved 10-percent salary hikes.

The League had also, a few months earlier, got a grant to hire a new staff member, a good-

The League signed the mortgage papers for its new home at 300 Orlando Avenue in August 1991. TCL file photo.

looking young sportsman named, improbably, Hardy Burch. With Alan Polk long gone, Burch had been hired to breathe life back into moribund affiliates. He began paying duty calls on clubs across the state, commending those whose dues were paid, rallying those who had fallen behind and beating the bushes for new ones. This direct appeal to the clubs' better selves seemed to work. By the end of the year, twenty-five of thirty-five delinquent clubs had paid up; five new affiliates had joined.

Burch also seemed to understand an important truth about member groups: they liked to support causes, but they also liked to have fun. That fall, Burch spearheaded the first annual Governor's Dove Hunt, the League's version of a celebrity fund-raiser. Some 75 hunters paid $150 each for the privilege of shooting doves and clay pigeons in a Dickson County farm field with Governor Ned McWherter. The one-day event—which included a steak dinner donated by the League's longtime friends at Jack Daniel Distillery—netted $5,073. Within two years the hunt would be charging less and making three times more.

HAPPY DAYS: CENTS GOES TO THE WHITE HOUSE

The energy that seemed to be released by the move to Orlando Avenue didn't stop with programming. For one thing, even though 1991 saw the last youth conservation camp, the League's education program was still active. For instance, West Tennessee director Kent Pettigrew, always keen on youth leadership programs, now established a conservation award for Future Farmers of America. (The award was quickly abandoned, however, when it proved awkward to make awards to another organization.) ReLeaf Tennessee, the tree-planting program for school kids, was already well on its way toward its goal of a million trees by the year 2000. Governor McWherter was the honorary chair.

Then there was Project CENTS. CENTS was now solidly established within the state Department of Education. (In fact, as proof of its bureaucratic status, in 1994 it was renamed the sensible and dull "Office of Conservation Education.") Though it had little actively to do with the program now, the League still sponsored CENTS, still lobbied for funding and still

On behalf of TCL and Project CENTS, Dr. Cindi Smith-Walters accepts a 1992 President's Environment and Conservation Award in a ceremony at the White House. Making the award is Michael R. Deland, chairman of the Council on Environmental Quality. Photo by Joseph H. Bailey. Copyright © 1992 National Geographic Society.

regarded it as one of its own great success stories. So it was happy to take some of the credit in June 1992 when the program, now almost ten years old, won a "certificate of environmental achievement" from the Washington-based Renew America.

It was even more proud when, a few months later, CENTS won an award from another Washington, D.C., address. In October 1992, President George Bush announced that the Tennessee Conservation League and its Project CENTS had won one of his new President's Environment and Conservation Challenge Awards.

The League was one of twenty-two recipients, along with such big-league names as IBM, Chrysler and Proctor & Gamble. Actually, the League was one of thirteen finalists receiving citations; the top nine entrants won medals. On December 2, 1992, Padgett Kelly (now teaching at Middle Tennessee State University) and Cindi Smith-Walters (who had replaced Kelly as CENTS director at the Department of Education) went to the award ceremony at the White House. Apparently neither knew until the last minute who would actually step forward to accept the citation; it was Smith-Walters, smiling and pregnant in a red suit.

MORE MONEY BLUES

Bobby Stanton, the League's development director, had nominated Project CENTS for the President's Award shortly before she left the League. Stanton was certainly the most ambitious development person the League had ever had, said Larry M. Richardson, one of the handful of board members with a knack for fund-raising, and he was sorry to see her go. But she had been offered a job as executive director of a Brentwood-based foundation, and the three-year development grant that had paid her salary had not been renewed.

This was unfortunate. More than ever, the League needed the kind of big money a development professional is supposed to deliver. By mid-1992, things were getting a bit dire. In June, president Bill Miller had been forced to take the unprecedented step of asking the board for emergency donations to get the League through the next payday.

Naturally, money problems led to morale problems. Staff knew they were underpaid, but the League had never been in a position to provide health insurance, pensions nor any other significant financial benefits beyond the periodic cost-of-living increase. The directors felt badly about this, of course (most of them knew better than to actually *work* for a nonprofit group). Once, in a rush of benevolence, they voted to pay a hefty 80 percent toward a group health insurance policy. On closer inspection, however, they realized the League simply could not afford this expense, and the offer, never really made, was withdrawn.

Several long-standing sources of income had been suddenly curtailed. Interest from the Meeman account had plummeted, of course, when the corpus was tapped to buy 300 Orlando Avenue. Meanwhile, after almost thirty years, the Sears, Roebuck Foundation announced that it was pulling out of the Conservation Achievement Awards program. Though the annual Sears grant—less than three thousand dollars—barely covered the cost of winners' meals and hotel rooms, it was money that now had to come from somewhere else. There was no question of canceling the awards program; it provided some of the best publicity the League had. Industries displayed their animal statuettes in corporate headquarters; legislators placed them on their desks; hometown newspapers ran stories on local winners.

The board viewed the ledger with dismay, but not hopelessness. There were always a few board members besides Larry Richardson who took an interest in budget matters. Mitchell Parks, for instance, found it preposterous that the League still charged just two hundred dollars for a lifetime membership, while most organizations got five or ten times that much. Parks proposed a new membership category, the "Conservation Heritage" lifetime memberships. The fee was one thousand dollars—but a donor could pay it in installments.

Then there was William R. Miller, III, an environmental manager with a master's degree in environmental science and engineering and a Ph.D. in aquatic ecology. Miller first encountered the League in 1986, when he and Tony Campbell served on the Citizens Environmental Committee at Saturn Corporation, the new General Motors subsidiary in Spring Hill. Determined to be a good neighbor, Saturn had invited a number of civic and conservation leaders to help guide its environmental policies during its formative years. (Miller was a consultant to Saturn at the time, but was later hired as manager of environmental affairs.)

Impressed by Miller's competence and common sense, the League began recruiting him for its own board. Miller became a director-at-large in 1987, then a vice president, and finally president from 1992 until 1995. (No one except four-term president Lou Williams held more consecutive terms.) It was Miller who hosted the corporate powwow at Saturn's Haynes Haven mansion in 1988, Miller who coauthored all four Environmental Quality Indexes and Miller who got Saturn to underwrite three of them.

Now, it was Bill Miller as much as anyone who tried to direct the League's new-found energy into useful action.

NO MORE BUSINESS AS USUAL

Perhaps it was because he worked for a Fortune 500 company, perhaps it was simply because he judged the League to be in need of a firm hand, but Miller approached his presidency with the rigor of a businessman and the engineer's passion for order. He had already begun compiling and cross-referencing every TCL resolution passed since 1972. Now, he designed a system for prioritizing and tracking "action items," a kind of rotating checklist of tasks, assignments and follow-throughs.

"I was tired of [watching as] commitments were made and then they would just evaporate," Miller said. "Sometimes we would talk about a thing for more than a year" before it happened, and sometimes it didn't happen at all. The tracking system was intended mainly as a way to keep staff (and board members) accountable and on task, said Miller. Unfortunately, it didn't work well. Commitments were still being broken or ignored; the chief difference now was that they had a record of it.

Under Miller's watch, the staff also started using detailed time-tracking sheets, special-event evaluation forms and written job descriptions. The old personnel manual from the 1983 reorganization was dusted off and updated. The executive committee passed a policy for "non-performing directors," a policy for approving press releases and a smoking policy. (Tony Campbell had to confine his cigarettes to his own office.)

For an organization as loosely supervised as TCL, such a barrage of regulations was a bit overwhelming, if not entirely futile. The management needs of a giant manufacturing plant

With his penchant for order and efficiency, president Bill Miller used bar graphs and statistical analyses to pinpoint the weaknesses at TCL. When he stepped down in 1995 after three consecutive terms as president, Miller said that being head of the League had been the hardest, as well as the most rewarding, job he'd ever held. TCL file photo.

simply didn't translate well to a nonprofit office with three or four employees who did everything from balancing the books to watering the plants. (As Miller would later concede, "There's a reason they call them *nonprofit*. They don't run at all like a business.") Though some of the staff dutifully filled out time sheets and kept lunch breaks to a strict forty-five minutes, the changes did not last, and things soon began slipping back toward their more familiar leniency.

But not entirely. Things were changing on the board, and Miller's brief administrative boot camp was only one proof of the changes. It was not a spirit of rebellion, exactly. More, it was a sort of new assertiveness, a realization among many directors, particularly those on the executive committee, that after all, *they* were the heads of the League. If their meetings had become boring and undirected, it was ultimately their faults, not the executive director's. If the League was poorly managed, well, according to the bylaws, they were responsible for hiring and firing the manager. If the League needed more accountability, more efficiency, more communication, more productivity, it was ultimately their job to see that it got them.

TAKING BACK THE LEAGUE

Bill Miller, Ed Thackston and Larry M. Richardson all agree that the movement to "take back the League" came primarily from the executive committee, that is, the president, the five immediate past presidents, the four regional vice presidents, the secretary and the treasurer. While the full board met only four times a year, the executive committee could meet as often as needed. During this "troubled time," as Richardson called it (roughly mid-1991 to early 1993), the executive committee met nearly every month.

They had plenty to keep them busy: lethargic affiliates, an aging leadership, a frustrated board, an undersized endowment, an overworked staff and an executive director who was showing signs of weariness over the constant struggles. Tony Campbell seemed tired, distracted and, to many, less effective. Some feared he might even have been "clinically depressed." But Campbell wasn't the only one whose energies appeared to be flagging. The board itself seemed listless. Despite all efforts, it remained increasingly hard to get a quorum. In one of his many statistical analyses, Bill Miller had found that barely one in three members routinely came to board meetings. Several had never been to a meeting at all.

Eventually Miller appointed a committee—Larry Richardson, Brad Weeks, Greer Tidwell, Jr., Don Byerly and himself—to look into the prospects for reformulating the League's leadership structure. Meanwhile, the entire executive committee got busy reviewing TCL's staff and director policies, editing the bylaws and weighing the League's operations against those of other nonprofits. In April 1992, they even invited the Ingram Group, a leading public relations firm, to attend a board meeting to "look at where we are, where we are going, ... set goals and determine how ... we get there."

Such an intense self-examination required a degree of candor, even bluntness, that many found distressing. Bill Miller, who succeeded Mark Benko as president part way through the reorganization period, described the meetings as "difficult." After one particularly gruesome session at the Cumberland Mountain Sand Company, Ed Thackston recalled feeling "physically ill" as he drove home to Nashville. "People were almost in tears," he said. "It was terrible."

They had been talking about Tony Campbell.

"BURNING GUTS ... AND A CERTAIN AMOUNT OF FOOLISHNESS"

By the summer of 1992, Tony Campbell had been with the League exactly twenty years, and he was feeling, as he put it, "worn out." He appreciated Bill Miller's efforts to slap the League into shape, of course; he was excited by the move to Orlando Avenue; and more than anything he still loved going down to the Legislature every January and locking horns with the politicians. The trouble was, when he got back to the office, the same old headaches were still there waiting for him.

Campbell was a likeable and talented man, deeply committed to conservation and deservedly proud of his many achievements in the field. But in recent years that pride had been tested. Constantly scrabbling for money, losing key legislative battles, watching longtime affiliates drop out, staying put while his associates moved on to bigger and better-paying jobs—these were tough blows for any man. To one who had given as much to the League as Campbell had, they were particularly bitter pills.

The board was reluctant to push him aside, as much out of loyalty as out of gratitude for all that he had done for TCL. Thankfully, they didn't have to. Campbell knew better than anyone that he was not performing to his own standards, let alone the board's. By September, Campbell had decided to make his move.

"As frank as I can be," he told the full board during a quarterly meeting in Townsend in September 1992, "I am tired of certain segments of this job." He had worried about the budget in 1972, he said; he was still worrying about the budget now—"and I'm tired of worrying about the budget." He did not want to leave TCL, he said; he just didn't want to be in charge of it anymore. "I don't think there is any doubt that this organization has grown to a point ... where we need to be looking at a transition and bringing someone else in." Otherwise, he finished bluntly, "I'm not so sure that I am doing the League justice or that I am doing myself justice."

In an earlier meeting with the executive committee, Campbell had proposed that the board create a new position for him, making him responsible for issues, lobbying and conservation policy—the things he had always done best and enjoyed the most. That way, he said, the board could "start looking for some young person who has the burning guts ... and a certain amount of foolishness that I had when I came on board twenty years ago."

The directors of the League respected their chief executive; some had known him since he first moved to Tennessee. Still, no one begged him to reconsider. The writing had been on the wall for some time, and most were inwardly grateful he had seen it for himself. Paying for two executive positions would not be easy, but it was worth a try. Certainly the League had more than enough work to keep them both busy.

In fact, this was precisely the sort of two-part structure that Bill Miller and his committee had been thinking of for the entire board. Rather than one large board dealing with conservation *and* administrative issues, the new system would create two boards. The first, called simply the board of directors, would continue as the League's principal governing body. The other, called the conservation policy board, would oversee issues, research and legislation. One advantage of the divided structure, obviously, was that members could be recruited for specific areas of expertise. Altogether there was room for about fifty members, the bulk of those on the conservation policy board.

By early 1993 the reorganization committee was drafting new bylaws to present to the 1994 annual meeting at Gatlinburg, along with an amended charter and revised constitution. Mitchell Parks was in charge of the logistics, including the daunting task of copying, collating and distributing eight thousand pages of reorganization materials. Tony Campbell had taken his place as vice president for conservation policy.

And, for the second time in its history, TCL began advertising for an executive director.

THE BOSS IS A WOMAN

The selection committee—Parks, Bill Miller, Mark Benko and Ed Thackston—knew what they wanted in a candidate: someone with a strong background in marketing and management. Experience in nonprofit development. Some understanding of conservation issues. Excellent communication skills, people skills and grant-writing abilities. But an articulate, business-minded administrator who also liked to hunt and fish? They dared not ask too much.

The response—156 resumes—was a far cry from the two dozen Bob Burns and M. L. Brickey had reviewed back in 1972. Three candidates were interviewed; one quickly rose to the top. On May 15, 1993, the board voted to make an offer to Ann P. Murray of Nashville.

Murray was apparently the dream candidate the board had dared not hope for. Vice president of marketing and development at the Cumberland Science Museum, she had earlier been director of development at the Tennessee office of The Nature Conservancy. Before that, she had been an options trader at J. C. Bradford, before that, a stock broker in New York City, and before that, a buyer at Bonwit Teller. She had a degree from the University of Alabama and extra training from the New York Institute of Finance. She was articulate, outgoing and authoritative. She had a gift for graphic design. She knew how to work within the system. She was kin to Lucius Burch. And she loved to hunt and fish.

And so it was that in 1993, three years shy of its fiftieth anniversary, the oldest, largest and strongest sportsmen's organization in Tennessee—the group that, for much of its lifetime, had been managed exclusively by men—was now to be run by a woman.

Murray quickly got down to business. After spending several months scrutinizing the League's operations, she announced that she was ready to make some changes. To begin with, she said, the League's accounting system was "chaotic." Checks were bring written without purchase orders; accounts weren't being tallied; there was no allowance for things like special or even routine building maintenance. Trying to pull together donor records in order to do a targeted fund-raising was, as she put it, "pathetic." Murray's tone was not harsh, but she hadn't worked on Wall Street for nothing.

Murray also decided it was probably time to drop Sherman Kelly, the membership management firm TCL had been using since 1986. Kelly had always reached his projections for new members; that was true. But the League's most important money came from renewals, and these, said Murray, seemed to "plateau out." The League should be able to make more money, and would certainly have greater control, if all membership operations—solicitations, renewals, even the database—were brought in house. This meant buying new computer software, probably even some new computers. But with the money saved from Kelly's commission, Murray was confident the League could do these things and hire a membership coordinator to oversee them.

(In fact, that was how Sue Garner finally got a promotion. In 1995, Garner moved into her own office as director of membership and special events.)

Governor Ned McWherter, Ann Murray, Congressman Bob Clement and Tony Campbell get out of the sun during the 1994 Governor's Dove Hunt. TCL file photo.

Sue Garner and Tony Campbell
share one last laugh during
Campbell's going-away party
before he leaves to join the
National Ecological Foundation.
Campbell had been with TCL for
twenty-three years. Sue Garner
had been his assistant for
nineteen of those. TCL file photo.

Meanwhile Murray had been putting together a marketing plan. The League needed a new image, she said, a lively look that people would recognize and respond to. She suggested they redesign the newsletter and produce a new membership brochure. She also wanted a new logo. Some folks were sentimental about the old deer-in-the-hand logo, she knew, but it had been around for twenty-five years now, and it was hopelessly dated. Besides, it put too much emphasis on hunting. In fact, the board had been thinking along the same lines. Mitchell Parks had even brought in a few sketches of his own, but they had been politely rejected (to his considerable chagrin).

Murray was inclined to hire a professional. She recommended Dan Brawner, a TCL member with his own Nashville studio, an impressive portfolio and a price well below the competition. Champion International gave five thousand dollars to develop a complete design package, and in 1994 Brawner presented several possibilities for the new logo. The one the board chose, a contemporary design in blue, green and black, seemed to suggest the natural world without being either too literal or too cute.

THE CHANGING OF THE GUARD

The entrance of a new director, and a woman at that, marked a turning point for TCL. Ann Murray had a head for fiscal management, she did not mind fund-raising, and she seemed actually to enjoy wrassling with budgets and spread sheets. At the same time, however, she also enjoyed lobbying, negotiating policy and shooting doves with the governor. For Tony Campbell, accustomed as he had been to running the shop, it was a major adjustment.

Yet they tried to respect each other's territory. Murray was grateful for Campbell's expertise and institutional history; Campbell was delighted to turn management duties over to a real manager. But the arrangement was not to be a permanent one.

In early 1995, Tony Campbell got a job offer from Clark Akers, his old comrade-in-arms from the Obion-Forked Deer days. Akers wanted Campbell to join the National Ecological

Foundation as executive director. Campbell would still be in Nashville; in fact, he would continue to serve on TCL's conservation policy board. Nevertheless, his last day at the League, March 31, 1995, felt like the end of an era. He had been there exactly twenty-three years.

But the changing of the guard had begun well before Campbell left. Not long after her arrival, Ann Murray, the professional shopper, had gone shopping for new board members. The board needed new blood, she thought. Whether the recruits were sportsmen or not—whether they were *men* or not—that didn't matter. What the League needed, on both the governing and conservation policy boards, was new vision, new ideas and new expertise.

The press had watched the changes at TCL with interest. When Murray was first hired, the *Johnson City Press* declared that the League was "steadily broadening its base." An approving editorial in *The Tennessean* called Murray's selection part of a trend at TCL "to break away from its traditional image as a special interest group of male hunters and fishermen." It was true. Though a handful of women had served on the board in the past (Carol Knauth, Shirley Patterson and Ruth Perruso in the early '70s, Ruth Neff and Josie Hope briefly in the early '80s), most of them served no more than a single term, and none ever held an executive role.

The shift had really begun with Rosemary MacGregor.

A League Of Their Own

A native of Tipton County, Rosie MacGregor had joined the TCL board in 1979 as a regional director for West Tennessee. At the time, she belonged to the West Tennessee Sportsman's Association (now defunct) because she loved the outdoors and she loved hunting. In fact, she got her first shotgun, a twelve-gauge, when she was nine years old. Her two brothers did not care about the sport, so MacGregor became her father's "third little boy," as she put it, joining him on trips to the Hatchie River for squirrel, rabbit or wild turkey. In those days, MacGregor told a reporter, girl hunters were almost as scarce as the gobblers.

When Rosemary MacGregor turned fifty, the League threw a birthday party. Among her gifts: salt-and-pepper shakers shaped like wild turkeys, reference to the sport she had come to love as a girl in West Tennessee. TCL file photo.

In 1986, MacGregor, then living in Nashville, was elected vice president for Region II, the first woman ever to serve on the executive committee. (She was replacing Mitchell Parks, who had just been named president of the League in another milestone: the League's first black president.)

MacGregor did a little of everything, organizing deer registries, manning the front desk at annual meetings, soliciting door prizes for sportsman's rallies. Evidently it didn't bother her that she was the only woman director at the board meetings, and almost certainly the only one at field events. But that was changing, too.

By the 1990s, women hunters were said to be the fastest-growing segment of the hunting population. In Atlanta, Carolyn Waldron took over as head of the Southeastern regional office of the National Wildlife Federation. In Chattanooga, MacGregor began organizing a chapter of Women Hunters in America. In Crossville, more than a hundred women from five states attended TWRA's first annual "Becoming An Outdoors Woman" weekend in 1994. And in 1995, Rosemary MacGregor was elected president of the Tennessee Conservation League, the first woman president in its history.

It was a significant moment. But after all, MacGregor *was* a hunter, the kind of person who made no weekend plans in early spring because they might interfere with turkey season. It took another woman to complete the passage. In 1989, a free spirit named Daryl Durham joined the board as an at-large director for Middle Tennessee. Durham, who has a master's degree in wildlife and fisheries management, was at that time the natural areas coordinator for the Department of Conservation. She favored sandals and cotton dresses, and she was no hunter. Though she had spent time in Africa, it was not on a big-game safari. Rather, she had been in the Peace Corps, researching habitat loss in the Gambia. If the League had been hoping to diversify its image, it could not have done better than Daryl Durham.

Durham stayed on the board for seven years. During that time, she co-wrote three of the four Environmental Quality Indexes, conceived the Tennessee Biodiversity Project and promoted it to a national audience. In 1993, with rigorous lobbying from her fellow board members, she even got elected to the National Wildlife Federation's board of directors. Bill Miller remembers driving with Don Porter and a truckload of party supplies all the way to NWF's 1993 annual meeting in Austin, Texas, purely to woo the votes of fellow delegates. Only once before in the League's history had a member been named to the NWF's governing board. Dr. Greer Ricketson had served as both a regional and at-large director for some twenty years, stepping down in 1985. (He and Clark Akers also served as trustees of the NWF Endowment.)

Though Durham had commented on the scarcity of other "baby boomers" at her first League convention, she did not seem uncomfortable. Besides, other women were coming onto the TCL boards in the 1990s. Mary Evelyn Jones, a businesswoman in Nashville's recycling industry, was elected to an at-large directorship in 1995; Patty Coffey and Shari Meghreblian joined the new conservation policy board at the same time. By 1996, the leadership of TCL was more than ten percent female. It wasn't exactly a stampede, of course. Averaged out over fifty years, the ratio of men directors to women has been something like forty to one. Still, the entrance of women into the League was no fluke. The face of the League was subtly, slowly shifting.

THE CHANGING—AND UNCHANGING—FACES OF TCL

Mike Pearigen was a good example of the change. Unmarried, barely forty years old, Pearigen was an environmental law specialist recently made partner in the Nashville law firm of Waller Lansden Dortch & Davis. As Tennessee's deputy attorney general for environment in the 1980s, Pearigen had been a key player in the litigation against Champion International and its pollution of the Pigeon River. He had also represented TWRA in its protracted litigations over Reelfoot Lake drawdowns. Though Pearigen occasionally fished, he didn't hunt at all. His tastes in outdoor recreation ran more to backpacking and whitewater rafting. But he was impressed by the League's record of accomplishments. So when Ann Murray invited him to join the board in 1994 as an at-large director, he accepted, and promptly immersed himself in its affairs. By the end of his first year he was in charge of planning the League's fiftieth anniversary celebration in 1996.

In fact, by the time the League turned fifty, its leadership had become, if not quite a melting pot, at least an interesting mixture of talents, genders, races, ethnicities and interests. On one hand, for instance, there was Diane Scher, an attractive young Jewish woman who managed hazardous waste for a living and considered herself "mostly vegetarian." On the other hand was W. S. "Babe" Howard, former chairman of the Game and Fish Commission and in many ways the epitome of the West Tennessee good ol' boy. Yet in 1995 Howard had risked three million of his own dollars to save the Beasley tract, four thousand acres of Wolf River headwaters, from logging and development.

The changing faces of TCL: W. S. "Babe" Howard, former Game and Fish commissioner, goes for a ride, while environmental lawyer Mike Pearigen dries out after a whitewater rafting trip in Utah. Courtesy of W. S. Howard and Mike Pearigen.

There was Leonard Bradley, former policy wonk in the Dunn and Sundquist administrations; Ben Smith, former director of Safe Growth Team; and David Jackson, former head of The Nature Conservancy, who like Pearigen had joined the board in answer to Ann Murray's call. Dick Urban, senior wetlands ecologist with TVA, was now chair of the conservation policy board, and Larry M. Richardson, another TVA veteran, had been elected to his fourth term as president. In fact, as the League embarked on its second half-century of resource protection, there was hardly a person on either board who did not feel comfortable dealing with what Lee Asbury had called the "big-picture" environmental issues.

Except, perhaps, Asbury himself.

The Jacksboro jurist was still not quite convinced that the League was heading in the right direction. "There are an awful lot of sportsmen who've lost confidence in the League," he said. "A lot of hunters and fishermen no longer feel TCL represents them." Whether or not that was so, hunters and fishermen *were* still the League's core constituency, still the bulk of its affiliate membership (approaching forty clubs by 1997). This was true not only of such longtime loyalists as the Greene County Fishing and Hunting Club, the Outdoorsmen, Inc. and the Unaka Rod and Gun Club. It was also true of the more recent arrivals, including Asbury's CORA, the American Fisheries Society and the rapidly multiplying chapters of Trout Unlimited, Ducks Unlimited and the National Wild Turkey Federation. Meanwhile, after fifty years of trying, the League still had not attracted a single backpacking club or paddling club or birding club (unless you call the Tennessee Bird Hunters Association a birding club).

Of course, it may have been that this larger constituency was only just beginning to arrive as more and more nonhunters joined TCL as individual members. Then again, maybe the League never would attract the "big-picture" environmental groups. And maybe that was okay, said Dick Urban, so long as the sportsmen themselves learned to see the big picture. The members of the Fayette County Rod and Gun Club, for instance, had taken time out from hunting in the mid-1990s to help save the same Wolf River wetlands that had so motivated Babe Howard. The effort earned one of its members, David Smith, the League's Conservationist of the Year Award for 1995.

Sportsmen really have no choice, said Urban, himself a member of the Waldens Ridge Sportsmen's Club. "There are growth demands occurring in Tennessee that aren't being focused, land-use decisions being made on an ad hoc basis. People come to Tennessee because they like [to enjoy] the scenery, the streams, the forested mountains [and] the hills," as well as the hunting and fishing. "What I'm afraid is that we are fast approaching the point where none of it's going to be possible. We are straining our infrastructure capabilities so badly that we're going to bankrupt ourselves."

THE LANDSCAPE VIEW OF CONSERVATION PLANNING

This was no revelation for the League, of course. It had been preaching land-use planning since at least the '70s, when it sponsored the symposium at Henry Horton. But Urban was right. By the 1990s, the need for comprehensive planning had become a crisis. There were more roads, more cars, more schools, more subdivisions, more manufacturing plants and more people than ever before. Dozens of Tennessee settlements that had not even qualified as towns thirty years ago were now listed in the latest *Columbia Atlas and Gazetteer of the World*. Many of these neo-cities were on the outskirts of existing urban centers, of course, such as Hendersonville, a feeder community for Nashville, whose population had jumped literally a thousandfold in just thirty years; or the Memphis suburb of Germantown, gone from a thousand residents in 1960 to thirty thousand in 1990. But a fair number of the growth towns, such as Spring Hill, were the result of new industry that chose, for perfectly understandable reasons, to locate in the middle of prime farmland or rural open space.

But even as the need for land-use restrictions was growing, the public's (and lawmakers') willingness to tolerate them seemed to be shrinking. The backlash was evident not only in the recent attacks on the Clean Water Act, the Endangered Species Act and so on, but also in the flurry of so-called "takings" bills, citizen-sponsored efforts to limit the government's ability to restrict land use, no matter how clearly in the public interest.

By 1995, it had become clear to the Clinton White House that it needed to counter these Republican-led assaults with some proactive lobbying of its own. In 1995, Interior Secretary Bruce Babbitt went on tour, hop-scotching among states with outstanding examples of citizen-supported conservation programs. Tennessee was one of the states Babbitt had in mind. The Great Smoky Mountains National Park had recently been enlarged by 4,700 acres of critical bear habitat, donated to the park by the Foothills Land Conservancy. The Conservancy had raised more than a million dollars to buy the property; TCL directors Rick Murphree and Randy Brown had been instrumental in forging the public-private partnership that eventually included the Department of Interior, the National Fish and Wildlife Foundation, the Lyndhurst

The directors of the Fayette County Rod and Gun Club review plans to save Wolf River wetlands, a project that won William David Smith (far right) the League's Conservationist of the Year Award for 1995. Others in the discussion are (left to right) club president Tom Morgan, Gary Rich, Milton Chambers and Bill Torkel. Courtesy of the Fayette County Rod and Gun Club.

Foundation, TWRA, the Shikar Safari International Foundation and many individuals. (The Foothills Conservancy was named TCL's Conservation Organization of the Year in 1996.)

Babbitt's staff had asked Ann Murray and the League to plan the Secretary's itinerary, which they did, said Mike Pearigen, "from start to finish." They arranged for Wilma Dykeman Stokely, Tennessee historian and conservationist, to serve as Babbitt's guide; they arranged a visit to the black bear habitat; they even arranged for a few hours of fly-fishing. They also, no doubt, put in a plug for some of the League's own public-private partnership, the Tennessee Biodiversity Project.

By 1996, the Biodiversity Project was looking for more ways to make itself useful. By now it had compiled dozens of surveys, maps, inventories and databases, representing ecosystems, plants, animals and geophysical features across the state. To help manage and apply this information, TCL had also tripled its technical staff, hiring biologists Mike Butler and Mike Roedel within the last eighteen months. The League was ready to do some land managing; all it needed now was a plot of land willing to be managed.

They found it in Tims Ford State Park, a smallish park on the Elk River in Franklin County. The state had recently acquired several thousand acres of land adjacent to the park, a perfect opportunity for the League to road-test its land-management theories. In early 1997, Ann Murray presented the League's plan to Justin Wilson, outgoing commissioner of the Department of Environment and Conservation (now deputy for policy to Governor Sundquist). Under the proposal, Tims Ford would be enlarged from its current four hundred acres to more than two thousand. There was provision for everything from protected caves and wetlands to a Jack Nicklaus golf course, all "without compromising the park's rustic nature," said Wilson. The idea was "mammoth," he effused, "a whole different way of doing things."

In fact, it may have been even bigger than that. The Tims Ford proposal was just one section of a larger plan that embraced all of Franklin County, a resource-rich area that includes Arnold Engineering Development Center, Woods Reservoir, Monteagle Mountain, Carter State Natural Area, Sinking Cove and numerous springs, caves and wetlands. So pleased had officials been with the Franklin County plan that by 1997, TCL was negotiating to draft similar plans for the counties of Fayette and Polk. Its ultimate objective was nothing less than an "ecological planning guide" for every county in the state.

AN EMBARRASSMENT OF LAND-USE RICHES

In fact, now that the League was in a position to do some serious land-use planning, opportunities seemed to be falling in its lap. The source of much of this unexpected largesse was the Tennessee Valley Authority. In recent years, TVA had been moving to divest itself of everything that was not part of its revenue-producing electric utility. In January 1997, TVA chairman Craven Crowell shocked Washington by announcing that after 1998, his agency would no longer seek taxpayer support for its nonpower programs. A few weeks later, President Bill Clinton's 1998 budget proposed to do the same thing: eliminate the annual federal subsidy to TVA. Though Congress's current appropriation to TVA—$106 million in 1997—was but a fraction of the agency's $5.7 billion budget, cutting it meant also cutting every recreational, environmental and economic development item in the TVA ledger.

Among the first to go was Land Between the Lakes, TVA's thirty-year-old recreation-demonstration area on the Kentucky border. When TVA decided to cut the cord to this huge park, it offered to turn the Tennessee section over to TWRA and the Department of Environment and Conservation to manage. New management, of course, meant a new management plan. To TCL, it was an opportunity for the taking. Throughout 1995, the League worked closely with TWRA, TDEC and other parties, drafting a proposed management plan that made room for hunting, fishing and forestry as well as less consumptive uses.

Another TVA project, the erstwhile Columbia Dam, was also drawing a new sort of land speculator. In 1996, having conceded that the dam would never be finished, the agency announced that it would unload the twelve thousand acres of land it had acquired along the Duck River in Maury County, including thirty-five miles of shoreline. The Duck River Development Agency wanted the land for industrial and commercial development; TWRA wanted it for a wildlife management area. By early 1997, the League was helping draft a proposal that would allow for both.

With so many new projects emerging, it was only a matter of time before the League would find its Nashville quarters too small. Remarkably, it didn't have to wait.

In 1996, the League received a $50,000 matching endowment from Lucius E. Burch, III, the nephew and namesake of one of the League's legendary members. In January 1997, the Lucius E. Burch Center for Conservation Planning opened on a campus of the University of Memphis. Bob Ford, who at one time had managed the Hatchie State Scenic River before coming to work at TCL, now moved back to West Tennessee to direct the League's new branch office. Though he would continue to work on the Tennessee Biodiversity Project, Ford's activities would now take on the flavor of the Mississippi flood plain: wetlands conservation, songbird habitat protection and management strategies for bottomland hardwood forests.

PRIVATE ACTS REVISITED: THE ROCKFISH CONTROVERSY

The transition years between executive directors—roughly 1992 to 1994—were so consumed by administrative matters that for a while conservation issues became almost secondary. The new conservation policy board didn't start meeting—didn't even officially exist—until the annual meeting of 1994, when the delegates approved the new constitution and bylaws and elected Don Porter as its first chairman. In the meantime, Tony Campbell, long accustomed to dominating board meetings with hours-long policy discussions, now found himself taking the floor only long enough to deliver a ten-minute summary of his legislative activities.

However, when the League finally did turn its attention back to the Legislature, it found an old antagonist waiting: private wildlife acts. The issue that had so aggravated Joseph Acklen in 1903, the issue that earned Prentice Cooper the first Z. Cartter Patten Award in 1944, the issue that TCL itself had tried to eliminate once and for all in 1985—the private act was still as strong and troublesome as ever, a reminder that, as much as some things might have changed, others just stayed the same.

Or got worse. Like Hydra heads, private acts seemed to multiply whenever they were cut off. In 1990, Mark Benko helped TCL overturn one private bear-dog act in Unicoi County, only to find themselves soon fighting two or three more. It was the same with private fishing acts. Local fishermen had overturned a trophy trout zone on the Caney Fork in 1990; three years later they tried to do the same on the Clinch. In 1994 the League and Trout Unlimited sued to have all private fishing acts in the state declared unconstitutional, but like the coon dog lawsuit of 1985, this one failed also.

None of these local bills, however, was as bitterly contested as a series of threatened acts to ban rockfish in Norris Reservoir.

Rockfish (or striped bass) is a large predator species, often growing to thirty pounds or more in the deep, cold waters it inhabits. Angling for rockfish trophies had become a popular specialty among many fishermen; the Tennessee Rockfish Association was one of the League's oldest affiliates. But there were others, crappie and bass fishermen in particular, who believed the growing striper populations in Norris Lake were destroying the smaller, native species. Some assumed they were simply being crowded out, but others believed they were actually being eaten.

As the agency responsible for stocking Norris and several other reservoirs in Tennessee, TWRA tried to explain that the species lives mainly on alewife and threadfin shad. If the numbers of game fish were declining at Norris, said the agency, it was probably because the reservoir itself was declining. Built in 1936, Norris was the oldest major impoundment in the state, and it was aging normally. Indeed, stripers appeared to be declining right along with

Herbert and Nell Odum, members of the Tennessee Rockfish Association, take third and fourth place in a rockfish "fish-off" on Percy Priest Reservoir in 1979. Their winning catches weighed in at 23.9 and 22.0 pounds. Courtesy of Herbert Odum and the Tennessee Rockfish Association.

all other game species.

By the mid-'90s, the issue had become volatile. In 1994, a coalition of Norris-area fisher-men organized as the Tennessee Sportsman's Association (TSA) to demand that TWRA stop stocking rockfish at Norris. In 1995, they persuaded the General Assembly to consider two rockfish bills, one imposing a five-year moratorium on stocking, the other removing daily limits. Strictly speaking, neither of these bills was a private act, since a private act must first be approved by a county commission, which then finds a legislator to introduce it as legisla-tion. However, they had much in common with private acts, and were met by the same sorts of arguments. "The Legislature has no business becoming involved in a fishing controversy," said the president of the Tims Ford Striper Club. "[Regulating wildlife] is the job of the Ten-nessee Wildlife Resources Agency. They are professionally trained to make such decisions."

The League came out in support of TWRA. In fact, TCL had supported the rockfish pro-gram from the beginning; a 1975 resolution called it "a very attractive program in its infancy." Though some members, including Dick Urban, doubted the wisdom of stocking any nonna-tive species, the League's official position was that TWRA should be allowed to make its own decisions, based on "sound scientific data and not emotions," as Ann Murray put it. In the end, neither bill made it out of the House Calendar Committee.

Unfazed, TSA members in four Norris Lake counties approached their county commis-sioners, asking them to introduce private acts banning the stocking and rearing of rockfish in their jurisdictions. In theory, such acts would eventually eliminate the species from Nor-ris Reservoir, since rockfish do not reproduce naturally there.

THE LIFE CYCLE OF ROCKFISH

In fact, rockfish are not native to Tennessee at all. They are naturally a saltwater species that enters fresh water only to spawn. The fact that they live in inland waters owes to an in-teresting accident. When South Carolina's Santee-Cooper Reservoir (now Marion and Moultrie Lakes) was impounded in the 1940s, spawning adults were trapped behind the dams. Fish-eries workers fully expected the hapless survivors to die off. So when baby rockfish began showing up throughout the lake several years later, the biologists were stunned. As TWRA fisheries manager Wayne Pollock would later recall, the discovery "touched off a wave of excitement" among inland wildlife workers who saw in the species a way to make use of their large shad populations. Soon most states, Tennessee among them, were sending trucks to the Atlantic coast to catch or buy mature rockfish to bring home.

Beginning in 1958, Tennessee stocked 1,298 adult rockfish in Kentucky Lake, then waited expectantly. Though the fish grew remarkably large, they did not reproduce. The disap-pointed biologists eventually realized that the problem was habitat. Rockfish need up to a hundred miles of moving water to spawn; otherwise their eggs sink and die. Eventually, sci-entists figured a way to produce more buoyant eggs, as well as a way to induce females to spawn in hatchery conditions. By the mid-1960s, Tennessee was setting up its first rockfish hatcheries at Morristown and Springfield, followed several years later by the "ultramodern" hatchery at Eagle Bend on the Clinch River, just south of Norris Dam. The program was run by Dave Bishop, who became something of a celebrity when he developed a hybrid rockfish by crossing striper with white bass.

By 1996, TWRA had placed more than twenty million rockfish in reservoirs around the state. The fishery was thriving, worth an estimated $18 million to the state annually. Norris Reservoir was said to account for nearly a third of that.

Given the history, popularity and economic value of Tennessee's rockfish industry, shutting down Norris would not be an easy matter for TWRA, even if Norris were the only lake in question. But apparently that was not the case. In an October 1995 letter to TWRC commissioner Earl Bentz (and copied to the rest of the wildlife resources commission and several legislators), TSA board chairman O. L. Dabney made it clear that TSA's private acts would also halt rockfish production at the Eagle Bend hatchery, where nearly all the state's rockfish were produced. "The question that remains," said Dabney a bit ominously, "is where beyond Norris Lake will the rockfish issue take us."

Earlier that month, TWRA commissioners asked for a meeting in Caryville in hopes of reaching a compromise. At first, TSA leaders had planned to be there. But when they learned that TCL was also on the guest list, they boycotted the meeting. As Dabney explained to Bentz, the fishermen found the League's presence "insulting." Everyone knew the League was TWRA's "indentured servant," he said bluntly. "[G]iven its partisanship on this and related issues, [its] self-promotion as an arbitrator and consensus builder is absurd."

Though the chief plaintiffs weren't there, the others met at Caryville anyway. At the next meeting of the Wildlife Resources Commission, they offered a compromise: a two-year moratorium on striper stocking at Norris while an independent research team—approved by the TSA, paid for by the agency—studied the conditions of all species in the lake, not just rockfish. All parties would agree beforehand to abide by the recommendations of the technical team—"[even if] it meant never stocking another striper" at Norris, as TWRA director Gary Myers put it.

The TSA rejected the proposal, earning the group no end of scorn from the outdoor press. But at length, cooler heads in the Legislature prevailed, relatively speaking, and TWRA implemented a three-year moratorium, including a two-year independent study. The low bid came from Mississippi State University, a team that included Steve Miranda, one of the most respected warm-water fisheries experts in the country. In 1996, the team began the most extensive "bioenergetics" study of its kind in the Southeast, one that considered not only numbers of fish and who eats what, but even things like the metabolic rate of an individual fish at various times of the year.

The Old Refrain: Keep Politics Out Of Game And Fish

The return of the private acts issue was a pointed reminder that in politics, almost nothing is ever really settled; it's just waiting for a new election cycle. And private acts are really just a subcategory of the much larger issue of politicians trying to run the wildlife agency. Political meddling had plagued the wildlife agency since its founding in 1949. Now, it was happening again.

What made this especially ironic was that in every important respect, the Game and Fish Commission (and its successor, TWRA) had been a resounding success. Wildlife was again abundant; habitat was improving; license sales were soaring; nongame species were thriving. No longer did anyone doubt the benefits of putting trained administrators in charge of a long-term wildlife program, free of political pressures and revolving-door commissioners.

Nonetheless, some politicians had never quite gotten used to the idea of home rule. Even Gordon Browning, though a hero to TCL leaders for supporting their model law back in 1949, had refused to endorse the Game and Fish Commission unless they gave him a seat on it. And while you're at it, he told them (in so many words), give one to my commissioner of Conservation, too. Both seats were nonvoting, however, so the sportsmen hadn't quarreled too much.

Then came the failed ambush of 1953, which, though averted, had ended with the commissioner of Conservation getting veto rights over all personnel decisions at the agency. (TCL fought that until it was repealed six years later.) Then came the skirmishes of the early '60s, including the bizarre Cludie Farley incident, followed by a period of relative calm.

But in 1971, the Game and Fish Commission was again under heavy attack. Though some lawmakers were for abolishing it altogether, they settled for elevating the Conservation commissioner from ex officio to full voting status. "That was all right," allowed *Tennessean* writer Bob Steber. Commissioner Bill Jenkins may have made a number of "politically-oriented gestures," but he also brought "a level head" to many of the commission's deliberations.

Steber was not so forgiving in 1972, however, when the General Assembly proposed adding three more citizen seats to what was now effectively a ten-man board. They also wanted to create a "legislative advisory board" to which the commissioners would have to answer. The term "advisory" was a sham, declared Steber. The legislators would have "the final say" on all programs, "[n]o matter how biologically sound."

Called to arms by president Charlie Rhea, TCL members in 1972 managed to squelch both proposals, and within eighteen months, the reorganization into TWRA and TWRC was underway. For a while, the lawmakers left the agency pretty much alone.

In 1986, however, they were back. The commissioner of Agriculture now became the third ex officio member of the commission, and the second with full voting powers. They also added a tenth citizen seat, bringing the number of voting commissioners to twelve. (When Ned McWherter took office in 1987 he gave the seat to liquor lobbyist Tom Hensley, a TCL board member from Jackson.)

The new seat had a term of eight years, rather than six. When those eight years were up, in 1995, the Legislature voted to abolish the seat. But only, apparently, to make room for two *more* seats, serving just two years each. (Hensley was named to one of them.) Unlike the original nine, these two new commissioners could be reappointed indefinitely, nor were there any restrictions as to geographical distribution. Both members could be from West Tennessee, if the lawmakers liked, because that's who got to name them. Not the governor, not the sportsmen, but the legislators themselves. The speaker of the House got to pick one, the speaker of the Senate picked the other.

To some, this sounded exactly like the old political patronage system that the League had fought so hard to overthrow back in the 1940s. Lou Williams and Herman Baggenstoss must have been turning over in their graves.

SOME THINGS END, SOME BEGIN

For they were both dead now, Herman and Lou. Herman Baggenstoss died shortly before Christmas in 1992 at age eighty-eight, scrappy till the end. Lou Williams had lived a longer life, though he died earlier: he was ninety-two when he died in 1984. Five years later the League erected a memorial to him on the North River, on a boulder beside the one bearing the plaque to Karl Steinmetz. Nat Winston's son played "Amazing Grace" on his bagpipes. Hubert Fry, who in 1968 had tried to get TWRA to name its new headquarters after Williams, now made good on another promise to honor his old friend. "Twenty-five years ago," he said, "Lou and I stood right here looking at old Steinmetz. I told him, 'Lou, if I live long enough we'll get a plaque for you, too, on this rock right here.'"

It was a bit sad, really, the end of an era. All the old soldiers were dying. John Bailey, the League's eternal secretary, was already long gone; so were Cartter Patten and Nat Winston, Mayland Muse and Nash Buckingham, "Peck" Peckinpaugh and Walter Amann. By the time the League held its half-century celebration in May 1996, Joe Halburnt alone of the League's original fifteen founders was known to still be alive, and he was in his nineties. Even Lucius Burch, Jr., who many hoped would be the guest of honor at the anniversary festivities, did not survive long enough to enjoy them. After a lifetime in the service of conservation in Tennessee, Burch died on March 10, 1996. He was eighty-four years old.

On the other hand, Lucius Burch's legacy now lives on in the conservation planning center named in his honor, and the forested natural area he helped establish. Karl Steinmetz has his bronze plaque on the North River, but his testimony is really the entire Cherokee Wildlife Management Area that he helped create. Herman Baggenstoss' legacies to Tennessee include Grundy Forest, a nature center named for him and the entire South Cumberland State Recreation Area. As for Lou Williams, his vast endowment includes the Wildlife Resources Agency and of course the Conservation League itself. Fifty years of protecting the environment leaves a long and fruitful legacy. The movement that started with these men certainly has not ended with their deaths.

Today, there is hardly a law, policy or environmental program in Tennessee that does not somehow bear the League's mark. The model game and fish law, the Tennessee Water Quality Act, the Nongame and Endangered Species Act, the West Tennessee Tributaries Mission Plan, the Office of Conservation Education, the Greenbelt Law, the Tennessee Forestry Association, the Wetlands Acquisition Fund, the Scenic Rivers and Scenic Trails acts, the Tennessee Biodiversity Project, the Hunter Education Act, the Tennessee Environmental Council, the Royal Blue Wildlife Management Area, the Solid Waste Management Act, the Natural Areas Acquisition Act, even the license plate with a bluebird on it—these are all part of the League's enduring legacy to Tennessee.

Postscript

Once More To The Read House

TCL Turns Fifty

The Tennessee Conservation League was officially organized on February 12, 1946, in an afternoon meeting at the Read House Hotel in Chattanooga. Fifty years (and eleven weeks) later, the League came back to celebrate its golden anniversary.

Though League conventions are typically held in February or March, this one was a bit later, May 2-4, because so many events were outdoors: a riverboat cruise along the Tennessee River Gorge, a tour of TVA's Raccoon Mountain and field trips to the Cherokee National Forest and the Olympic whitewater site on the Ocoee River. (Only one event, the dedication of a commemorative plaque, did not go as planned, but only because the plaque idea had fallen through. President Rosemary MacGregor gave her dedication speech without it.)

At eighty-five dollars for the weekend, the registration fee was almost as historic as the setting (though perhaps not quite as good a deal as the first Regional Wildlife Conference in 1937, when $2.50 bought three days' worth of events—including a banquet speech by Ding Darling himself—and field trips to "the new" Norris Dam and Pickett State Forest.)

Still, the folks in Chattanooga got their money's worth: all the field trips were included in the registration fee, all the receptions and meetings and pretty much every meal, including a breakfast courtesy of Chattanooga's Wheland Foundry, lunches courtesy of the field trip organizers and dinners courtesy of two longtime affiliates. Waldens Ridge Sportsmen's Club provided a fish fry on Thursday, and on Friday the Highland Sportsman Club hosted a steak dinner at its club house on Chickamauga Creek.

Here, between dinner and dancing, guests got a chance to bid on the TCL Fiftieth Anniversary Commemorative Quilt, squares of League history sewn together by the women (and one man) of the League. The bidding was active. Nonetheless, when the weekend was over the quilt returned to Nashville with the League. A bloc of anonymous buyers, reluctant to see this heirloom disappear into private hands, had commissioned Ann Murray to buy it back for TCL. (The plan now is to send it out on tour from time to time, like the treasures of King Tut.)

On Saturday evening, guests moved to the Tennessee Aquarium for the awards banquet. Ed Thackston was master of ceremonies for the umpteenth time, but no doubt he had never enjoyed the job so well. He began by turning the podium over to William Howard, president of the National Wildlife Federation, who presented the prestigious NWF Chair's Award to Gary Myers, director of the Tennessee Wildlife Resources Agency. It was a fitting tribute, considering that the history of the wildlife agency is practically synonymous with the history of the League.

There were also four special Fiftieth Anniversary Excellence Awards, handsome walnut plaques to the outstanding affiliate in each of the League's four regions: the Fayette County Rod and Gun Club, the Highland Sportsman Club, the Tennessee Valley Sportsmen's Club and—most appropriately—the Nashville Sportsman's Club, the all-black affiliate that wasn't even allowed to join the League during its first twenty-five years, but that had done so much for it in its second.

Finally, following the League's traditional round of Conservation Achievement Awards and assorted other recognitions, the evening closed with a special presentation: the Fiftieth Anniversary Lifetime Conservation Achievement Award. As Ed Thackston noted, it wasn't easy to single out a winner. The League is made up of high achievers and lifetime conservationists. But no one would quarrel with the award committee's choice. It was Bob Burns, the TVA engineer who had breathed life into a dying League twenty-five years ago, and had been the most loyal of friends to it ever since.

After a lifetime of achievement, Bob Burns relaxes at the barbecue. Groundhog, anyone?

APPENDIX A

TCL PRESIDENTS AND ANNUAL MEETINGS

Terms begin at the annual meeting.

1946-47	Louis J. "Lou" Williams	Chattanooga	Read House, Feb. 12, 1946
1947-48	Lou Williams	Johnson City	John Sevier Hotel, Feb. 21-22, 1947
1948-49	Lou Williams	Nashville	Hermitage Hotel, Feb. 27-28, 1948
1949-50	Lou Williams	Knoxville	Andrew Johnson Hotel, Apr. 22-23, 1949
1950-51	Lou Williams	Jackson	New Southern Hotel, Feb. 24-25, 1950
1951-52	C. J. Murphy	Nashville	Noel Hotel, Feb. 8-10, 1951
1952-53	B. H. Plunk	Chattanooga	Read House, Apr. 4-5, 1952
1953-54	Mayland H. Muse *	Jackson	New Southern Hotel, Apr. 2-4, 1953
1954-55	J. Earl Glover	Johnson City	John Sevier Hotel, Apr. 8-10, 1954
1955-56	Lucius E. Burch, Jr.	Nashville	Noel Hotel, Apr. 7-9, 1955
1956-57	Robert S. Hines	Memphis	Peabody Hotel, Mar. 30-31, 1956
1957-58	O. W. Stevens	Chattanooga	Hotel Patten, Mar. 15-16, 1957
1958-59	Gilbert B. Wilson	Jackson	New Southern Hotel, Mar. 20-22, 1958
1959-60	Carl O. Bolton	Nashville	Noel Hotel, Mar. 17-19, 1960
1960-61	Daniel Boone	Knoxville	Andrew Johnson Hotel, Mar. 17-19, 1960
1961-62	Roy M. Lanier	Cleveland	Cherokee Hotel, Mar. 17-18, 1961
1962-63	M. L. Brickey	Buchanan	Paris Landing Inn, Apr. 12-14, 1962
1963-64	Verland H. Jernigan	Chattanooga	Read House, Mar. 22-23, 1963
1964-65	Jack Ramsey	Nashville	Noel Hotel, Mar. 19-21, 1964
1965-66	A. T. Bayless	Memphis	Peabody Hotel, Mar. 18-20, 1965
1966-67	Cecil D. Branstetter	Oak Ridge	Holiday Inn, Mar. 16-19, 1966
1967-68	Will Roper	Nashville	Noel Hotel, Feb. 24-25, 1967
1968-69	Louis M. Doney	Jackson	New Southern Hotel, Mar. 15-17, 1968
1969-70	Lester R. Dudney	Chattanooga	Read House, Mar. 21-22, 1969
1970-71	Penn Foreman	Nashville	Noel Hotel, Mar. 7-8, 1970

1971-72	Charles Rhea	Memphis	Albert Pick Motel, Mar. 11-13, 1971
1972-73	Greer Ricketson	Gatlinburg	Mountain View Hotel, Apr. 6-8, 1972
1973-74	Travis McNatt	Nashville	Airport Hilton, May 10-12, 1973
1974-75	Robert Burns	Jackson	Civic Center, Mar. 21-23, 1974
1975-76	Al Ballinger	Chattanooga	Read House, Mar. 20-22, 1975
1976-77	J. Richard Swaim	Nashville	Airport Hilton, Apr. 2-3, 1976
1977-78	Loyd L. Ezell	Jackson	Holiday Inn, Mar. 18-19, 1977
1978-79	William H. Blackburn	Gatlinburg	Mountain View Hotel, Apr. 13-15, 1978
1979-80	Edward L. Thackston	Chattanooga	Sheraton Downtown, Mar. 1-3, 1979
1980-81	Edward L. Thackston	Nashville	Airport Hilton, Mar. 6-8, 1980
1981-82	James M. Whoric *	Memphis	Rivermont Holiday Inn, Mar. 13-14, 1981
1982-83	Larry M. Richardson	Gatlinburg	Glenstone Lodge, Mar. 26-28, 1982
1983-84	Larry M. Richardson	Nashville	Maxwell House, Mar. 11-13, 1983
1984-85	Tracey Simpson	Chattanooga	Read House, Mar. 2-4 , 1984
1985-86	Tracey Simpson	Nashville	Loew's Vanderbilt Plaza, Feb. 23-25, 1985
1986-87	Mitchell S. Parks	Memphis	Airport Hilton, Feb. 28-Mar. 1, 1986
1987-88	Mitchell S. Parks	Nashville	Maxwell House, Mar. 6-8, 1987
1988-89	Don Byerly	Gatlinburg	Holiday Inn, Mar. 4-5, 1988
1989-90	Larry M. Richardson	Clarksville	Riverview Ramada, Mar. 3-4, 1989
1990-91	Mark W. Benko	Johnson City	Sheraton Plaza, Mar. 9-11, 1990
1991-92	Mark W. Benko	Nashville	Loew's Vanderbilt Plaza, Mar.1-3, 1991
1992-93	William R. Miller, III	Chattanooga	Quality Inn, Feb. 27-29, 1992
1993-94	William R. Miller, III	Memphis	Ramada Convention Center, Mar. 5-7, 1993
1994-95	William R. Miller, III	Gatlinburg	Holiday Inn, Mar. 25-27, 1994
1995-96	Rosemary MacGregor	Nashville	Maxwell House, Mar. 10-12, 1995
1996-97	Larry M. Richardson	Chattanooga	Read House, May 2-4, 1996
1997-98		Savannah	Pickwick Landing Inn, May 16-18, 1997

* did not complete term

APPENDIX B

TCL BOARD MEMBERS

TCL has elected hundreds of board members in fifty years. Many served far longer than a single term. For practicality's sake, board members are listed here according to the decade in which they were first elected. Names may appear more than once, if the member returned to the board after an extended absence. Please note that some names may be missing. The list is as complete as surviving records allow.

ELECTED IN THE '40S

James Alexander
Walter Amann, Jr.
W. L. Anderson
E. T. Bales
A. T. Bayless
Frank Beck
Enoch Brown
Paul Bryant
Nash Buckingham
James Corn
E. Lee Cross
C. Clifford Curry
Virgil Davis
Lou DeQuine
C. B. Duke
John Flippen
J. Earl Glover
Frank Grant
Tom Greene
Frank Grout
Joe Halburnt
Major B. Harris
John Holladay
John Jared
Milburn Jolly

Bart Leiper
James Long
Ed Mangus
Bill Marrs
C. J. Murphy
Fred Ogle
Z. Cartter Patten, III
E. H. Peckinpaugh
B. H. Plunk
Dave Seaborn
Karl Steinmetz
Frank Vestal
Kyle Walker
Lou Williams
Sam Wilson
Nat Winston

ELECTED IN THE '50S

L. D. Adkins
J. B. Anthony
Sam Austin
John H. Bailey
E. R. Baker
Hal Baker
Carl Bolton
Daniel Boone

W. P. Bowes
Cecil Branstetter
M. L. Brickey
Robert A. Britton
W. C. Brooks
Bob Burch
Lucius Burch, Jr.
Chester Caldwell
L. L. Cook
H. F. Cooper
John DeArmond
Bill Dowdle
John Dyche
Paul Essary
Paul Fairleigh
Felix Grasty
William Gray
Charles Grisham
Tom Hardy
William Henson
Frank Herndon
R. S. Hines
Henry Hollingsworth
James Hooper
Al Hutchinson
V. H. "Doc" Jernigan

elected in the '50s ...

Oren Jones
B. C. Kilgore
Dale King
Joseph Krechniak
Frank Langford
J. E. Latture
Walter Lewis
George Lynch
Ralph Marshall
Raleigh Miller
Neil Mims
Howard Misner
William Mullins
Mayland Muse
Gurney Owens
Chambliss Pierce
Joe Pitts
Jack Ramsey
Will Roper
Phil Scudder
Harry Spier
Bob Steber
O. W. Stephens
William Taylor
Carl Tisdale
A. B. Townsend
J. B. Tyson
Ansell Usrey
Louis Wakefield
S. R. Ware
Jack White
R. M. Williams
Gilbert Wilson
J. H. Wilson

ELECTED IN THE '60S
J. R. Allen
James Asbury
Lee Asbury
W. Frank "Red" Aycock
Herman Baggenstoss
C. L. Barker
Bill Bellis
Charles Berry
Powell Bilyou
W. G. Blankenship
Harry Bryan
Jim Burch
Robert Burns

Frank Camp, Jr.
Phil Carmen
Herbert Clark
H. B. Conley
Henry Covington
Fritz Crane
Pete Day
Lou Doney
L. R. Dudney
Lynn Farrar
Penn Foreman
George Freeman
J. C. Gleason
J. A. Goforth
Carl Grazier
Paul Gustavson
Emmet Guy
William Hall
Jimmy Hancock, Jr.
Roy Hardison
Clay Hargis
James Hooper
Smith Howard
Travis Johnson
A. D. Jones
Leon Jones
Roy Lanier
W. H. Leitsinger
Hal Love
Robert "Bud" Martin
William Mashburn
James McKee
R. H. McNabb
Travis McNatt
Ned McWhorter
Evan Means
Shirley Mills
Jack Mitchell
Robert Orrin
Ike Peel
Bill Pendergrass
Clyde Pennington
Ralph Peters
Walter Powers
Henry Reynolds
Charles Rhea
Greer Ricketson
William Roberts
Robert Rodgers
Leroy Rymer
Edwin Schreiber
Harold Smartt

Clenton Smith
A. B. Stone
Vern Snowden
Bill Stagg
A. B. Stone
Ray Strong
William Taylor
Ernest Teasley
Gerald Trout
Elmer Walker
Jim Warren
Harold Webb
William Weeks
Julian Whitley
James Wilkes, Jr.
Curtis Williams
Bob Witt
Neely Wright
Reams Wyatt
W. D. Zugschwerdt

ELECTED IN THE '70S
J. Clark Akers, III
Tommy Akin
Logan Arnold
Al Ballinger
Ray Barger
Jack Barrett
John Benko
D. A. Berry
William Blackburn
Curtis Blane
Johnny Bone
William Brandes
Hillard Brown
Lucius Burch, III
Wayne Burton
W. C. Butler
Don Byerly
Robert Cannon
Herman Carrick
J. Robert Clark
B. W. Cobb
William Coleman
Charles Connor
Ramsey Cutshall
Bill Dance
Albert David
Bob Dean
Henry DeGolyer
Charlie Detchon
David Dudney

Elected in the '90s ...

Joe Bogle
Leonard Bradley
Sam Brocato
William Brooke
Mike Burgess
Wilson Burton, Jr.
Kim Allen Chamberlin
Val Chapman
C. B. Coburn
Patty Coffey
Greg Dale
Jonathan Evans
Leonard Ezell
Bill Guinn
W. S. "Babe" Howard
David Jackson
Greg Jernigan
Mary Evelyn Jones
J. Padgett Kelly
Les Kirk
Tommy Lovell
Scott May
Jesse Mayo
Shari Meghreblian
Rick Murphree
Marvin Nichols
Chris O'Bara
Mike Pearigen
Stu Phillips
Charles Price
Jimmy Reeves
Mark Reeves
Richard Rucker
Joe Savery
Diane Scher
Peter Schutt
Ben Smith
Reid Tatum
Greer Tidwell, Jr.
Dick Urban
Hugh Vice
Cheryl Ward
Jim Wilbanks
Clay Wilson

APPENDIX C

TCL AFFILIATED CLUBS

More than two hundred organizations affiliated with the League at one time or another. Though surviving records are not complete (and though most clubs no longer even exist), the following is a reasonably accurate accounting of TCL-affiliated clubs since 1946.

American Fisheries Society
Anderson County Sportsmen's Club
Appalachian Sportsman Club
Appalachian Valley Fox Hunters Association
Arnold Center Shooters Club
Atomic Hunters
Bald River Bear and Boar Club
Beechriver Watershed Development Authority
Bisanabi Bowhunters
Black Bear Society
Blount County Sportsmen's Club
Bradley County Sportsmen's League
Buck Buster Club
Bucks Club
Burbank Sportsmen's Club
Calderwood Sportsmen's Club
Calebs Creek Bowhunters
Camden Sportsmen's Club
Campbell County Sportsman's Association
Carter County Coon Hunters Club
Carter County Hunting and Fishing Club
Cedar City Bassmasters
Cedar Creek Club
Central Peninsula Gun Club
Central Tennessee Fox Hunters Association
Chattanooga Bass Club
Chattanooga Big Game Hunting Club
Chattanooga Rod and Gun Club
Chattanooga Trout Association
Chattanooga Yacht Club

Cheatham County Sportsmen's Club
Cherokee Archery Club
Cherokee Bassmasters
Cherokee Ramblers Holiday Club
Cherokee Rod and Gun Club
Cherokee Sportsmen Conservation Association
Chickamauga Bowmen
Chickamauga Fly and Bait Casting Club
Chilhowee Rod and Gun Club
Church Hill Rod and Gun Club
Clarkrange Hunting Preserve
Clarksville Bass Club
Clarksville Pointer and Setter Club
Cleveland Bear, Deer and Boar Hunters
Cleveland Hunting, Rifle and Pistol Club
Collins River Sportsmen's Club
Concerned Citizens Conservation Club
CORA (Campbell Outdoor Recreation Association)
Council Bend Bowmen
Cree Archers
Dale Hollow Sportsmen's Club
Davidson County Sportsmen's Club
Dickson Rod and Gun Club
Dickson Sportsmen's Club
Donelson Sportsmen's Club
Drakes Creek Rod and Gun Club
Ducks Unlimited, North Hamilton County Chapter
Dunlap Rod and Gun Club
East Tennessee Coon Hunters Association
East Tennessee/Southwest Virginia Fox Hunters

East Tennessee Sportsman's Federation
East Tennessee Wildlife Improvement Club
Fayette County Rod and Gun Club
Fiery Gizzard Sportsmen's Club
Fort Campbell Rod and Gun Club
Fountain City Sportsmen's Club
Fur, Fish & Feathers Club
Giles County Sportsmen's Club
Goldern Circle Bass Club
Great Smoky Mountain National Historical Assoc.
Greene County Bear Hunting Club
Greene County Bird Dog Club
Greene County Coon Hunters Club
Greene County Fox Hunters Club
Greene County Fishing and Hunting Club
Greene County Junior Sportsmen
Greeneville Archers
Guardians of North Chickamauga Creek
Hamilton County Pointer and Setter Club
Hamilton Sportsmen's Club
Happy Hollow Bowmen
Hardin County Sportsmen's Club
Harpeth River Fox Hunters Association
Harpeth River Sportsmen's Club
Hatawi Corporation
Haywood County Sportsmen's Club
Henderson County Sportsmen's Club
Henry Horton Archery Club
Hickman County Conservation Club
Highland Sportman Club
Holston Valley Sportsmen's Club
Hook and Bullet Club
Huntingdon Lions Club
Jackson B.A.S.S. Club
Jackson County Sportsmen's Club
Johnson City Garden Club
Karns Sportsmen's Club
Kentucky Lake Bass Anglers
Kentucky Lake Wood Duck Association
Kingsport Archers
Kingsport Rod and Reel Club
Knox County Coon Hunters Club
Knox County Humane Society
Knox County-Tennessee Valley Sportsmen's Club
Knoxville Boat Club
Knoxville Rod and Gun Club
Knoxville Tourist Bureau
Kyles Ford Rod and Gun Club
Lakatchka Archery Club
Lakeside Rod and Gun Club
Lakeside Sportsmen's Club
Lakeview Hills Saddle Club

Lawrence County Conservation Club
Lawrence County Wildlife Conservation League
Lewis County Bassmasters
Lincoln County Sportsmen's Club
Little Tennessee Sportsmen's Club
Lonesome Pine Conservation Club
Madisonville Sportsmen's Club
Magic Valley Hunters Association
Malesus Hunting and Fishing Club
Manchester Bear and Boar Club
Marion County Sportsmen's Club
Maury County Horseman's Association
McNairy County Sportsmen's Club
Medina Bow and Gun Club
Memphis Anglers Club
Memphis Bow Hunters
Memphis Rifle and Revolver Association
Middle Tennessee Fly Fishers
Middle Tennessee Nature Conservancy
Mid-South Serviceman's Rod and Gun Club
Mid-State Bird Hunters
Mid-State Sportsmen's Club
Millington Sportsmen's Club
Montgomery County Conservation Club
Moore County Sportsmen's Club
Morristown Rod and Gun Club
Mountaineer Hunting and Fishing Club
Municipal Archers of Memphis
Music City Beagle Club
Nashville Archers Club
Nashville Sportsman's Club
Nashville Tree Foundation
National Wild Turkey Federation,
    Cherokee Chapter
    Cumberland Chapter
    Middle Tenn. Chapter
    Tennessee Chapter
Necedah Bowhunters
Nimrod Hunting Club
Norris Lake Striper Club
North Hamilton County Improvement League
Oak Ridge Big Game Club
Oak Ridge Conservation Club
Oak Ridge Coon Hunters Association
Oak Ridge Sportsman's Association
Old Hickory Kennel Club
Old Hickory Lake Bowmen
Old Stone Fort Conservation Club
One Gallus Fox Hunters Association
Outdoor Sportsmen Club
Outdoorsman, Inc.
Paint Rock Hunting and Fishing Club

Paris Rod and Gun Club
Parkburg Sportsmen's Club
Pick-A-Poo Bowmen
Plateau Wildlife Conservation Club
Powell's Valley Conservation Club
Putnam County Rod and Gun Club
Quail Unlimited, Upper Cumberland Chapter
Rohm & Haas Fishing Club
Rosedale Sportsmen's Club
Rutherford County Sportsmen's Club
Scott County Conservation League
Sevier County Sportsmen's Club
Shelby Forest Council
Smith County Sportsmen's Club
Smoky Mountain Archers
Smoky Mountain Big Game Association
Smoky Mountain Fox Hunters Association
Smoky Mountain Game and Fish Club
South Knoxville Sportsmen's Club
Southern Field and Creel Club
Sportsman's Club of Chattanooga
Stones River Sportsmen's Club
Successful Deer Hunters
Sweetwater Valley Sportsmen's Club
Tellico Sportsmen's Club
Tennessee Archery Association
Tennessee B.A.S.S. Federation
Tennessee Beagle Club
Tennessee Bear and Boar Club
Tennessee Bird Hunters Association
Tennessee Commercial Fisherman's Association
Tennessee Conservation League Ladies Auxiliary
Tennessee Coon Hunters Association
Tennessee Fur Harvesters Association
Tennessee Long Hunters
Tennessee Park Rangers Association
Tennessee Rockfish Association
Tennessee State Fox Hunters Association
Tennessee State Rifle Association
Tennessee Taxidermist
Tennessee Valley Sportsmen's Club
Thomas Bridge Sportsmen's Club
Tipton County Wildlife Federation
Toothpick Club of Memphis
Tri-County Sportsmen's Club
Tri-County Sportsman's League
Tri-States Game and Fish Association of Memphis
Trout Unlimited,
    Appalachian Chapter
    Cherokee Chapter
    Cumberland Chapter
    Great Smoky Mountain Chapter

Trout Unlimited,
    Little River Chapter
    Overmountain Chapter
Unaka Rod and Gun Club
Unicoi County Rod and Gun Club
United Fox Hunters Association
Upper East Tennessee Archery Association
Upper Norris Conservation Club
Viking Rod and Gun Club
Volunteer Conservation Club
Volunteer Emergency Rescue Squad
Volunteer Sportsmen's Club
Volunteer State Amateur Field Trial Club
Waldens Ridge Sportsmen's Club
Warren County Conservation Club
Washington County Fox Hunters Association
Watauga Area Sportsman's Preservation Club
Watts Bar Sportsmen's Club
West Tennessee Archers
West Tennessee Beagle Club
West Tennessee Campers and Hikers Club
West Tennessee Fur Takers
West Tennessee Land Reclamation Company
West Tennessee Sportsman's Association
White Bluff Sportsmen's Club
White Pine Sportsmen's Club
Wingfoot Sportsmen's Club
Wolf River Conservancy
Wolf River Hunting Club
Wolf River Sportsmen's Club
Wolf River Watershed Association

APPENDIX D

THE Z. CARTTER PATTEN AWARD

Zeboim Cartter Patten, III, a Chattanooga philanthropist, outdoorsman and later a state senator, established the Z. Cartter Patten Award in 1943 to recognize outstanding contributions to conservation in Tennessee. The prize was administered by the Tennessee Outdoor Writers Association at first but was transferred to the League in 1947.

Governor Prentice Cooper won the first Z. Cartter Patten Award in 1944 for founding a state forest near Chattanooga and for banning private wildlife acts. (No award was made in 1945 because of the war.) In 1946, TVA fisheries biologist R. W. Eschmeyer won for opening TVA lakes to year-round fishing. In 1948, TCL president Lou Williams and vice president Nat Winston were honored jointly for their vision in founding the League. Fifty years later, Z. Cartter Patten's legacy remains the most coveted conservation honor in Tennessee.

Date indicates the year for which the award was given.

1943	Prentice Cooper	1968	Verland H. Jernigan
1945	Reuben W. Eschmeyer	1969	Lou M. Doney
1946	Nat T. Winston	1970	John Dyche
1947	Lou Williams	1971	Robert C. Burns
1948	Karl Steinmetz	1972	Paul Fink
1949	Gordon Browning	1973	Edwin Schreiber
1950	Lucius E. Burch, Jr.	1974	Henry Reynolds
1951	Walter Amann, Jr.	1975	S. Leary Jones
1952	Mayland H. Muse	1976	Travis McNatt
1953	John H. Bailey	1977	Bob Steber
1954	J. Earl Glover	1979	V. L. Childs
1955	Robert A. Britton	1980	Evan W. Means
1956	Carl O. Bolton	1981	Shirley C. Patterson
1957	Roy M. Lanier		B. L. Ridley
1958	Junius Crossett	1983	Edward L. Thackston
1959	Charles Rhea	1984	Carson Brewer
1960	Vern Snowden	1985	Henry Reynolds
1961	Herman E. Baggenstoss	1986	Mayland H. Muse
1962	James L. Bailey	1987	Hubert O. Fry
1963	M. L. Brickey	1988	James Word
1964	Charles Berry	1989	Ruth Neff
1965	J. B. Anthony	1991	Greer Ricketson
1966	Evan W. Means	1992	Tom Hensley
1967	Cecil D. Branstetter	1993	William D. Guinn, Jr.

APPENDIX E

EARLY CLUB AWARDS

TCL made assorted special awards in its early years. The first (besides the Z. Cartter Patten Award) was the Old Guide Award, honoring outstanding service by an affiliated club. Established by John Jared in 1954, the award was named for the late Paul K. Bryant, who played the character of the Old Guide on WSM's *Wildlife Club of the Air* in the 1930s and 1940s. The Old Guide Award was replaced in 1957 by the Britton Club Award, established by Robert A. Britton and Junius Crossett and called, at first, the Britton-Crossett Award. The Jack Ramsey Youth Award recognized service to conservation education, while the C. J. Murphy Legislative Award recognized unusual commitment to conservation by lawmakers. The John Dyche Professional Award went to an outstanding member of the Game and Fish Commission's field enforcement staff.

Not all awards were given regularly. A few, such as the Secretary's Award given by John Bailey, or the Ray Strong Award for clubs with fewer than three hundred members, seem to have faded away almost as soon as they were created. By 1972, all the early awards had been retired, replaced by the TCL Conservation Achievement Awards.

These lists are as complete as surviving records and newspaper accounts allow.

Date indicates the year for which the award was given.

	Old Guide Award		**Britton Club Award**
1953	West Tennessee Sportsmen's Association	1956	South Holston Conservation Club
		1957	Greene County Hunting and Fishing Club
1954	Greene County Hunting and Fishing Club	1958	West Tennessee Sportsmen's Association
		1959	West Tennessee Sportsmen's Association
1955	Greene County Hunting and Fishing Club	1960	Unaka Rod and Gun Club
		1961	Anderson County Sportsmen's Club
		1962	Oak Ridge Conservation Club
		1963	Dickson Rod and Gun Club
		1964	Chilhowee Rod and Gun Club
		1965	Morristown Rod and Gun Club
		1966	The Outdoorsmen, Inc.
		1967	Highland Sportsman Club
		1968	Middle Tennessee Conservancy Council
		1969	Montgomery County Conservation Club
		1970	Tennessee Valley Sportsmen's Club

C. J. Murphy Legislative Award

1961	Rep. Joan F. Strong
	Sen. Roy M. Lanier
1963	Sen. Lee Mathis
	Rep. M. T. Puckett
1964	Rep. Joan Strong
	Sen. Robert Taylor
1969	Sen. Fred O. Berry
1971	Judge Daniel R. Crum

Ray Strong Award

1960	Davidson County Sportsmen's Club

John Dyche Professional Award

1961	Price Wilkins
1962	Charles J. Chance
1963	Glenn Gentry
1964	George Tucker Brown
1965	Lou Boyd
1966	Sam Daniels
1967	Albert McCoy
1968	J. W. Rhodes
1969	Charles W. Harbison
1970	Bobby Bass
1971	Clyde Moore

Distinguished Service Citation

1962	C. J. Murphy
	W. D. Hastings
	J. B. Anthony
1963	Bob Witt
	Bob Steber
1970	Clark Akers, III
	William Dillon, III
	Sam Harwell
	John Tudor

Jack Ramsey Youth Award

1964	Chickamauga Fly and Bait Casting Club
1965	Tennessee-Arkansas-Mississippi Girl Scout Council
1966	William B. Stevenson
1968	William L. Smith, Jr.
1969	Jack Mitchell
1970	Chattanooga Big Game Club
1971	Tom Worden

Secretary's Award

1964	J. B. Anthony
1965	Evan W. Means

APPENDIX F

CONSERVATION ACHIEVEMENT AWARDS

The first TCL Conservation Achievement Awards—handsome animal statuettes signifying a variety of natural resources—were presented at the 1966 annual meeting in Oak Ridge. The National Wildlife Federation sponsored the program with funding from the Sears, Roebuck Foundation. The highest honor, the American bald eagle, was originally referred to as the Governor's Award because under NWF policy, the governor had to endorse the awards program. (Now, the award is simply Conservationist of the Year.) At first, TCL gave awards in ten categories. Several more have been added over the years.

Date indicates the year for which the award was given.

Conservationist of the Year		Forest Conservationist of the Year	
1965	Louis J. "Lou" Williams	1965	Thomas B. Swann
1966	Albert F. Ganier	1966	Hugh Faust
1967	John H. Bailey	1967	E. G. Weisehuegal
1968	Herman E. Baggenstoss	1968	Carl I. Peterson
1969	Z. Cartter Patten, III	1969	Douglas Boardman
1970	Lester R. Dudney	1970	John Barrett
1971	James L. Bailey	1971	Charlie Page
1972	Harold E. Warvel	1972	Evan M. Pitt
1973	Edgar W. Evins	1973	Tom Harshbarger
1974	Edward L. Thackston	1974	George R. Anderson
1975	Gedeon D. Petit	1975	W. Foster Cowan
1976	Harvey G. Bray	1977	Robert R. Lusk
1977	J. Clark Akers, III	1978	Max Young
1978	Zygmunt Plater	1979	Joe Simmons
1979	S. David Freeman	1981	Paul Somers
1981	James L. Byford	1982	Robert E. Drexler
1982	Willie Borchert	1983	David W. Wilson
1983	Al Hamilton	1984	Westvaco Corporation
1984	Lamar Alexander	1985	Washington County Soil Conservation District
1985	Ben Smith		
1987	Nelson Ross	1986	Will Skelton
1989	Gary T. Myers	1987	Roy Ashley
1991	Lee Asbury	1988	Mark W. Benko
1993	Ned Ray McWherter	1989	Jack A. Muncy
1994	Ruth Neff	1993	Champion International Corp.
1995	William David Smith	1995	Denise W. Ashworth

Water Conservationist of the Year

1965	S. Leary Jones
1966	John Jewell
1967	Fred W. Stanberry
1968	Lelyn Standnyk
1969	Christian C. Crossman
1970	David J. Wilson
1971	Kenneth Elrod
1972	Edward F. Williams, III
1973	Mayland H. Muse
1975	V. Wayne McCoy
1976	Roy E. Warren
1977	Eugene S. Cobb
1978	Anders I. Myhr
1980	Chester A. McConnell
1981	Ruth Neff
1982	Pat Patrick
1983	David McKinney
1984	Michael T. Bruner
1985	Ann Tidwell
1986	Raymond C. Norris
1987	Bevan Brown
1988	Richard D. Urban
1989	Barry W. Sulkin
1990	Robert H. Skinner
1991	Christopher D. Ungate
1992	Sidney R. Jumper
	Theodore H. Schmudde
1993	James Nance
1995	Michael L. Countess

Wildlife Conservationist of the Year

1965	Glenn Gentry
1966	James W. Warren
1967	W. B. Lockett, Jr.
1968	Frederick Emerson, Jr.
1969	Floyd F. Fesler
1970	Calvin J. Barstow
1971	Raleigh F. Lane
1972	Robert D. Bishop
1973	Chester A. McConnell
1974	Harvey G. Bray
1975	Gary T. Myers
1976	Edgar "Red" Anderson
1977	Elmore Price
1978	Joe Cathey
1979	Marsha L. Selecman
1980	Donald A. Hammer
1981	Jerry Parish
1982	Sam Brocato
1983	Quenton Henry
1984	James D. Carter
1985	Robert C. Burns
1986	Sam Williams
1988	Westvaco Corporation
1989	Wesley K. James
	Stephen D. Cottrell
1990	James S. Holcomb
1991	William G. Minser
1993	Ed Stiles
1994	Cherokee Chapter, National Wild Turkey Federation
1995	Daryl Durham

Conservation Organization of the Year

1965	Malesus Hunting and Fishing Club
1966	Tennessee Federation of Garden Clubs
1967	Hull-York Lakeland Association
1968	Reelfoot-Indian Creek Watershed Project
1969	Five Rivers Resource Conservation Development Association
1970	Nashville Children's Museum
1971	Manchester Jaycees
1972	Tennessee Valley Sportsmen's Club
1973	Radnor Lake Preservation Association
1974	Bowater Southern Paper Company
1975	Guardians of North Chickamauga Creek
1976	Tennessee Endangered Species Committee
1977	Tennessee Federation of Garden Clubs
1979	Youth Board, Washington County Soil Conservation District
1980	Lakeway Chapter, Izaak Walton League of America
1981	Tennessee Toxics Program
1982	Tennessee Valley Sportsmen's Club
1983	White County Wildlife Protectors Association
1984	The Nature Conservancy, Tennessee Chapter
1985	Lichterman Nature Center
1986	Gatlinburg Sportsman Club
1987	Black Bear Society
1988	Great Smoky Mountain Council, Boy Scouts of America
1989	Appalachian Chapter, Trout Unlimited
1990	Volunteer Chapter, Quail Unlimited
1991	Cherokee Chapter, Trout Unlimited
1992	Appalachian Sportsman's Club
1993	Tennessee Chapter, National Wild Turkey Federation
1995	Foothills Land Conservancy

Legislative Conservationist of the Year

1965	Rep. Joan F. Strong
1966	Sen. Lee Mathis
1967	Rep. J. William Pope, Jr.
1968	Sen. Dan Moore
1969	Rep. Victor H. Ashe
1970	Sen. John S. Wilder
1971	Sen. Fred O. Berry
1972	Sen. William R. Bruce
1973	Rep. Edward F. Williams, III
1974	Rep. Robert J. Bible
1980	Rep. Albert Gore, Jr.
1983	Rep. John M. Tanner
1984	Sen. Douglas Henry, Jr.
1985	Rep. Ed Jones
1986	Rep. U. A. Moore
1988	Sen. James R. Sasser
1989	Sen. J. Ronnie Greer
1991	Rep. Bill Purcell
1992	Sen. Ward Crutchfield
1993	Rep. Gary Odom
1995	Sen. Bud Gilbert

Land and Soil Conservationist of the Year

1965	Lester R. Dudney
1966	James H. Robinson
1967	Willis Huddleston
1968	Alfred K. McCalla
1969	John S. Wilder
1970	Glen S. Elkins
1971	Walter Reeser
1972	Dwight Treadway
1973	C. W. Clements
1974	Paul Howard
1975	Joe G. Wilson
1976	Richard Van Dyke
1977	Ronald G. Rains
1978	E. B. Dyer
1979	David Hinton
1980	Frank Clayton
1981	Steve Brunson
1982	James D. Hamilton
1983	Betsy Loyless
1984	Merrill T. Hitchcock
1985	Charles W. Cook, Jr.
1986	Charles Blackburn
1987	L. H. Burnett
1989	Washington College Ruritan Club
1990	Tennessee River Gorge Trust
1993	Tennessee Interagency Wetlands Committee
1994	Cameron Middle School
1995	W. S. "Babe" Howard Scott P. Ledbetter

Conservation Communicator of the Year

1965	E. "Bob" Burch
1966	Charles S. Roberts
1967	Bob Steber
1968	Coleman A. Harwell
1969	Jim Turner
1970	Carl O. Bolton
1971	Clarksville *Leaf-Chronicle*
1972	Wilma Dykeman Stokely
1973	B. Jack Brumit
1974	Keel Hunt
1975	Richard Knight
1976	Tom Rollins
1977	Sam Venable, Jr.
1978	*The Jackson Sun*
1979	Kingsport *Times-News*
1980	Marvin Bailey
1981	Clarence D. Coffey
1982	Ray Pradines
1983	Steve Eckert
1984	Carolyn Shoulders
1985	Tom Rogers
1986	Clark Schafer
1987	Marge McCormick
1988	Richard Simms
1990	WSMV-TV, Channel 4
1991	Lindy Turner
1992	L. Carol Ritchie
1994	*Heartland Series*, WBIR-TV
1995	Tom Charlier

Conservation Educator of the Year

1965	John H. Bailey
1966	Henry G. Hart
1967	James L. Bailey
1968	Harold N. Powers
1969	Sam H. Johnson
1970	Elizabeth Roller
1971	Paul Wishart
1972	Elsie Burrell
1973	John B. "Pat" Alderman
1974	Patrick J. Grimes
1975	Mack Prichard
1976	Edna Potter
1977	Barbara Wilbur
1978	Grace Riden
1979	Gladys Harris
1980	Johnny Lumpkin
1981	J. Padgett Kelly
1982	Marty Silver
1983	William D. Ratledge
1984	Marvin Hammond
1985	Ken Ripley
1986	Chattanooga Nature Center
1987	Pat Jordan
1988	Richard Davis
1989	Flavil Hatcher
1990	Cindi Smith-Walters
1991	Carolyn Edwards
1992	ReCycle Signal
1993	Dan Nieves
1994	Judy Butler
1995	Barbara Adams

Youth Conservationist of the Year

1965	Middle Tennessee Council, Boy Scouts of America
1966	Joe Lancaster
1967	Louise Davis
1968	Kyle J. Cherry
1969	John W. Cleveland
1970	William R. Alley
1971	J. Padgett Kelly
1972	James P. Bryant
1973	Tom Carter
1974	Tennessee 4-H Wildlife Program
1975	Neta Bilderback
1976	Kevin Edwards
1977	Youth Board, Pickett County Soil Conservation Service
1978	Sherry Koger
1979	Bobby Pace
1980	Kenneth Huddleston
1981	Trellis Marr
1982	Drew Buhler
1983	Youth Board, Montgomery County Soil Conservation District
1984	Kyle Edwards
1985	Kathy Renee Blackburn
1988	Jerry Martin
1990	Students Against Pollution
1991	Students Against Pollution, Boones Creek Middle School
1992	James R. Hall
1993	Drew Wilson
1994	Johnny Angel

Industrial Conservationist of the Year

1975	ALCOA
1977	Koppers Company
1978	Westvaco Corporation
1979	Jack Daniel Distillery
1981	Bowater Incorporated, Southern Division
1983	Dixie-Shamrock Oil and Gas
1984	Tennessee Eastman Division, Eastman Chemical Company
1985	Cumberland Mountain Sand Company
1986	Mead Paper
1987	Saturn Corporation
1990	Monsanto Company
1991	Siemens Industrial Automation and Texas Instruments Incorporated
1992	General Electric Appliances, Columbia plant
1993	Knoxville Utilities Board
1994	Savage Zinc Incorporated
1995	DuPont Company, New Johnsonville plant

Air Conservationist of the Year

1975	Harold E. Hodges
1976	C. N. Spencer
1977	L. Spires Whitaker
1978	Byron B. Winsett, Sr.
1979	Dean Hill Rivkin
1980	Mary M. Walker
1981	American Lung Association
1982	Mohamed T. El-Ashry
1983	Robert Foster
	Nile McCrary
1985	Paul J. Bontrager
1986	J. Wayne Cropp
1987	Jackie L. Waynick
1991	Quincy C. Styke
1993	Robert C. Burns

Hunter Education Award

1977	Robert Howard
1978	Ted Keirn
1979	George Scott
1980	John Hollingshead, Sr.
1981	Mayland H. Muse
1982	Mike Butler
1983	Thomas F. Sewell, Sr.
1984	Joe H. Ezell
1985	Jorene Turnage
1986	Calvin Parks
1987	Jerry McDaniel
1988	John Heirigs
1989	Charles M. Pardue
1990	Jim Cooper
1991	Joe P. Raines
1992	Joseph E. Smith
1993	Sondra M. Coffey
1994	Fay Hickerson
1995	Craig Chapman

Wildlife Conservation Officer of the Year

1976	Clarence D. Coffey
1978	J. W. Rhodes
	Quenton Henry
1979	Edgar Ray Jennings
1982	Wayne H. Schacher

FFA Student of the Year

1992	Mandy Denise King

Appendix G

Other Awards

National Wildlife Federation President's Award

1974	Hamilton County Sportsmen's Club
1977	Carter County Hunting and Fishing Club
1979	Nashville Sportsman's Club
1981	Tennessee Valley Sportsmen's Club
1995	Gary T. Myers

Awards of Merit/ Awards of Appreciation

1974	Volunteer Conservation Club
	Robert C. Burns
1976	Walter F. Moore
1979	Colonel Robert Tener
1981	U.S. Army Corps of Engineers' Natural Resources Management Staff, Dale Hollow Lake

National Wildlife Federation Service Citation

1975   Joe Criswell

Outstanding Affiliate Awards

1976	West Tennessee Sportsmen's Association
	Montgomery County Conservation Club
	The Outdoorsmen, Inc.
1977	Fayette County Sportsmen's Club
	Nashville Sportsman's Club
	Carter County Hunting and Fishing Club

Louis John "Lou" Williams Founders Award

1989	Robert C. Burns
1990	William H. Blackburn
	Loyd L. Ezell
1991	Mitchell S. Parks
1992	Larry M. Richardson
1994	Rosemary MacGregor

President's Award

1987	Bob Seaton
	Tom Hensley
1988	Donald L. Rollens
1989	Charles D. "Buzz" Buffington
1990	Carl W. Frazier
	Allen B. Townsend
1991	Johnny Lynch
	Clayton L. Wilson
1992	Douglas R. Clark
	Joe Kent Pettigrew
	Don L. Porter
1993	Curtis Blane
	Sue Garner
1994	Belle Austin
1995	William R. Miller, III
	Rick Murphree
	Michael D. Pearigen

Project WILD Facilitator

1987	Phil Neil
1988	Kenneth L. Ripley
1989	Brian Thompson
1990	Clarence D. Coffey
1991	Kenneth L. Ripley
1992	Mary V. Ball
	Allen E. Ricks
1993	Josephine Franklin
1994	David Whitehead
1995	Cecil "Bucky" Smith

TCL 50th Anniversary Excellence Awards (1996)

Region 1	Fayette County Rod and Gun Club
Region 2	Nashville Sportsman's Club
Region 3	Highland Sportsman Club
Region 4	Tennessee Valley Sportsmen's Club

Gedeon D. Petit TWRA Education Award

1992	Joe E. Busch
1993	Wayne Sanders
1994	Ken Ripley
1995	Tom Wood

50th Anniversary Lifetime Conservation Achievement Award

Robert C. Burns

Appendix H

Conservation Timeline

1641	The Massachusetts Bay Colony sets aside Great Ponds for public "fowling and fishing," in effect creating the first public game reserve.
1694	Massachusetts sets the nation's first closed season on deer.
1776	The first federal game law requires closed seasons on deer in all colonies except Georgia.
1782	The American bald eagle is named the national emblem.
1784	The State of Franklin is founded. It exists until 1789.
1802	The U.S. Army Corps of Engineers is created.
1818	Massachusetts passes the first state law protecting nongame birds.
1831	Tennessee hires a state geologist, Gerard Troost.
1832	Congress reserves Hot Springs, Ark., for public use.
1833	Tennessee prohibits killing fish by putting poisonous substances in rivers.
May 20, 1844	The New York Sportmen's Club becomes the first conservation club in the United States.
Mar. 3, 1849	The U.S. Department of Interior is established.
1850	Copper is discovered in Ducktown Basin, Tenn., soon renamed the Copper Basin.
1854	Tennessee creates a Bureau of Agriculture. The new Office of State Geologist and Minerologist is created in Agriculture. Gerard Troost heads the office.
1862	Congress creates a Department of Agriculture.
1864	George Perkins Marsh publishes *Man and Nature* .
1865	California's Yosemite becomes the first state park in the country. In 1872 it becomes the first national park.
1868	The Tennessee Horticultural Society is founded.
Mar. 26, 1870	The revised Tennessee Constitution authorizes the General Assembly to pass laws—general and local—for the protection and preservation of wildlife.
Jun. 6, 1870	The General Assembly passes the first private wildlife acts. Twelve Middle Tennessee counties ban fishing with seines and nets, Benton and Humpreys counties ban deer

hunting with dogs, and Shelby, Rutherford and Fayette counties set closed seasons on game birds, songbirds and deer.

1870	The American Fisheries Society is founded.
Oct. 19, 1871	Six of the twelve Tennessee counties named in the 1870 fish law exempt themselves.
1871	*American Sportsman*, the first national conservation magazine, debuts.
1871	The U.S. Fisheries Commission is created.
1871	The National Rifle Association is founded.
1871	The Bureau of Agriculture is renamed the Bureau of Agriculture, Statistics and Mines.
1872	Nebraska celebrates the nation's first Arbor Day. Tennessee follows in 1875.
Mar. 1, 1872	Congress creates Yellowstone National Park, the first true national park.
1873	Charles Halleck begins publishing *Forest and Stream*; in 1880, Dr. George Bird Grinnell takes over as editor.
1874	*Field and Stream* begins publication.
Mar. 5, 1875	Duck hunting for profit on Reelfoot Lake is banned.
Mar. 23, 1875	Tennessee's first general fish law bans seining and trapping at the mouths of streams; at least half the counties in the state claim exemption. Songbird hunting is banned statewide.
1875	The American Forestry Association is created (later American Forests).
1875	Arkansas establishes the first law prohibiting market hunting of waterfowl.
1876	Congress creates an Office of Forestry in the Department of Agriculture. It also allots $2,000 to study European forest preservation methods.
1877	Tennessee establishes a State Board of Health, but allocates no funding or executive powers.
1877	The 1875 law banning duck hunting for profit on Reelfoot is repealed, replaced by a law allowing market hunting for ducks by residents of Lake and Obion counties. Eight more counties opt out of the 1875 fish law.
1879	An epidemic of yellow fever, centered in Memphis, kills 20,000 people. The outbreak convinces the Legislature to give more funding and powers to the State Board of health.
1879	The U.S. Geological Survey is founded.
1881	The federal Office of Forestry becomes the U.S. Division of Forestry (renamed the U.S. Forest Service in 1905).
1881	Tennessee passes another general fish law and sets a penalty of $5–$25 for violators; fines go to the local schools.
1883	The American Ornithologists' Union is founded.
Mar. 3, 1885	Congress creates the Division of Economic Ornithology and Mammalogy in the Department of Agriculture. In 1896 it is renamed the Bureau of Biological Survey; in 1940 it is renamed the U.S. Fish and Wildlife Service.
1886	The first Audubon Society is founded in New York by George Bird Grinnell.

1887	The Boone and Crockett Club is founded by Theodore Roosevelt and his colleagues.
1887	Tennessee designates an Arbor Day in the public schools each November "to encourage tree planting in Tennessee."
1889	Tennessee bans quail netting and market hunting of deer and quail on property not one's own; 65 counties are exempt.
1891	The Forest Reserve Act authorizes the Forestry Division to buy lands for national forests.
1892	The Sierra Club is founded by John Muir.
1892	President Benjamin Harrison bans hunting and fishing on Alaska's Afognak Island, creating the first national wildlife reserve.
1893	The Tennessee Bureau of Agriculture, Statistics and Mines is renamed the Department of Agriculture.
1893	Tennessee creates the office of county commissioner of fish to study and improve the supply of fish; commissioners serve one-year terms.
May 7, 1894	The Yellowstone Park Protection Act bans the taking of wildlife and any other natural resources in the park.
1894	George Bird Grinnell in *Forest and Stream* warns of the dangers of lead shot.
1895	The New York Zoological Society is founded.
1895	Tennessee agrees to provide land for a federal fish hatchery near Erwin.
1896	The U.S. Supreme Court in *Geer v. Connecticut* affirms the concept of state ownership of game.
1897	The National Forest Organic Act restricts cutting of mature, deal or large-growth trees.
1897	The Camp Fire Club of America is founded in New York.
1897	Tennessee bans pheasant hunting for five years.
1898	The League of American Sportsmen is founded in New York.
1899	Congress passes the first River and Harbor Act defining and protecting navigable waterways.
1899	The Tennessee General Assembly passes 43 private wildlife acts, a record.
1899	Tennessee passes a municipal parks bill.
1900	The Lacey Act prohibits interstate transport of illegally killed game.
1900	President William McKinley directs the Secretaries of Agriculture and Interior to report on possible national forests in the Southern Appalachians.
1900	The Society of American Foresters is founded.
Apr. 23, 1901	Gov. Benton McMillan approves enabling legislation allowing the U.S. Forest Service to acquire lands in Tennessee for the Cherokee National Forest.
1901	The Tennessee Forest Association is founded.
1901	Sportsmen in Tennessee are required to have written permission to hunt on tillable or enclosed lands owned by another.

1901	Carter County prohibits dumping sawdust in streams.
1902	The National Association of Game and Fish Wardens and Commissioners is founded at a meeting in Yellowstone National Park. In 1917 it becomes the International Association of Game, Fish and Conservation Commissioners, in 1977, the International Association of Fish and Wildlife Agencies.
1903	The first official national wildlife refuge is established by Theodore Roosevelt at Pelican Island, Fla.
1903	Tennessee declares that all wild game within the state "belongs to the people in their collective capacity."
1903	Tennessee creates the office of state game warden and authorizes deputy wardens. All fines go to the officer making the arrest.
1903	Tennessee bans the hunting and selling of nongame birds and bird parts.
1903	Nonresident sportsmen are required to buy a license to hunt or fish in Tennessee. The fee is reciprocal; in 1905 it is set at $10.
1905	The U.S. Division of Forestry is renamed the U.S. Forest Service; Theodore Roosevelt names Gifford Pinchot as director.
1905	The National Association of Audubon Societies is founded.
1905	Tennessee creates a Department of Game, Fish and Forestry; it is headed by the state warden of Game, Fish and Forestry.
1905	Tennessee bans deer hunting for two years; the ban is not lifted until 1919.
1905	Tennessee sets a bag limit for ducks of 50 per day and establishes a commercial hunting/fishing license. The fee ranges from $5–$25, depending on the size of the applicant's hometown.
1905	The Tennessee Game and Fish Protective Association becomes the first statewide conservation group in Tennessee.
1906	The Antiquities Act authorizes the President to set aside significant historical, archeological or scenic areas.
1906	Judge Marshall Morgan premieres "Fins, Furs, Feathers and Other Comment" in the *Nashville Banner*. It is believed to be the first outdoor column in the country.
1907	W. J. McGee first uses the term *conservation* to describe the interrelationship between natural resources.
1907	Georgia sues to stop open-pit smelting in the Copper Basin.
Mar. 26, 1907	Gov. Malcolm Patterson signs a law repealing all "special or local laws for the protection of game" with the exception of open seasons on squirrels and doves. It is overturned by the 1915 reorganization.
Apr. 11, 1907	Tennessee passes its first general forestry law.
Apr. 12, 1907	Tennessee declares all fish within its borders to be the property of the state.
1907	Tennessee's first resident hunting license allows the holder to hunt on private property with verbal permission. It sells for $3 but purchase is optional.

May 1908	Theodore Roosevelt hosts a Governors' Conference on Conservation.
1908	Reelfoot Night Riders stage a brief reign of terror to protest the privatization of fishing and hunting at Reelfoot Lake.
Feb. 18, 1909	President Roosevelt convenes the first North American Conservation Conference.
1909	Tennessee provides for drainage districts, levees and dredge boats in West Tennessee.
1909	Tennessee creates its first mandatory hunting licenses, $5 statewide, $3 county-wide. There is no fee for game fishing.
1909	The Tennessee Geological Survey is created.
1909	The Reelfoot Lake Park and Fish and Game Preserve is created, the first state park in Tennessee. The Reelfoot Game and Fish Law establishes a $10 annual "tax" to sell Reelfoot fish or game.
1909	Tennessee's commissioner of Agriculture is named ex-officio commissioner of Game, Fish and Forestry.
1910	Tennessee creates a director of Rural Sanitation in the Tennessee Board of Health to deal with waterborne diseases.
1911	The Weeks Act authorizes the purchase of national forests in the eastern U.S.
1911	Firearms manufacturers form the American Game Protective Association, forerunner of the Wildlife Management Institute.
1911	The U.S. Forest Service acquires three forest units in East Tennessee for national forests.
1911	Tennessee bans the sale of robins and quail, including those "served under any fictitious name."
1912	European wild boars are introduced into the Southern Appalachians.
Mar. 14, 1913	The Weeks-McLean Migratory Bird Act establishes federal custody of migratory game and insectivorous birds.
1913	Dr. William Hornaday writes *Our Vanishing Wildlife*.
1913	The Garden Club of America is founded.
1913	Knoxville hosts the first National Conservation Exposition.
Sept. 1, 1914	Martha, the last passenger pigeon, dies in the Cincinnati Zoo.
1914	The position of state forester is created in the Tennessee Geological Survey.
May 13, 1915	Gov. Tom Rye's reorganization bill creates the Tennessee Department of Game and Fish, headed by the state Game and Fish warden, and the Game and Fish Protection Fund.
Oct. 7, 1915	The Tennessee Ornithological Society is founded in Nashville.
1915	The U.S. Army Corps of Engineers studies pollution in the Cumberland River.
1915	Tennessee requires all resident hunters to buy a "shooting license." It sells for $1 county-wide, $2 statewide. Fishing is still not licensed.
1915	Tennessee creates the State Highway Department.
Aug. 25, 1916	The National Park Service is created.

1916	The United States-Canada Migratory Bird Treaty regulates waterfowl hunting.
1918	The Migratory Bird Treaty Act authorizes Congress to comply with the 1916 Migratory Bird Treaty.
1919	The American Farm Bureau Federation is founded.
1919	The National Parks and Conservation Association is founded.
1919	Tennessee regulates insecticides and fungicides but only to protect the consumer from ineffective or mislabeled products.
June 14, 1920	Three National Forests are proclaimed in Tennessee: the Cherokee, Unaka and Pisgah.
1921	The first National Conference on State Parks meets in Washington.
1921	Benton MacKaye proposes a wilderness footpath from Maine to Georgia. The Appalacian Tirail is completed in 1937.
1921	Tennessee creates the Bureau of Forestry and the State Forestry Commission in the Department of Agriculture.
1921	Tennessee public schools are required to include "a study of forestry and plant life … which study shall include the names and varieties of trees grown in the state, their age of maturity, their value to the soil, to animals and birds … ." The law is repealed in 1963.
1922	The Izaak Walton League of America is founded in Chicago.
1923	Gov. Austin Peay's reorganization bill replaces the 1877 Board of Health with a Department of Public Health. It is responsible for matters of water supply, sewage control and rural sanitation. By 1927, these functions have been formalized as the Division of Sanitary Engineering and the Division of Rural Sanitation.
1923	Under Peay's reorganization, the 1915 Game and Fish Department is abolished, replaced by an Advisory Board for Game and Fish within the Agriculture Department. The Bureau of Forestry is also abolished, replaced by a Division of Forestry in Agriculture.
1923	Tennessee closes the season on wild turkey for five years.
1923	Tennessee allows private land holdings of at least 5,000 acres to be named State Game Preserves and closed to hunting for three years.
1923	Tennessee sets a fine of $50–$100 for polluting streams with sawdust or other debris.
1924	President Calvin Coolidge hosts the first National Conference on Outdoor Recreation.
1924	The Izaak Walton League lobbies to create the Upper Mississippi River Game and Fish Refuge, the first national wildlife refuge open to hunting.
1925	Tennessee forms a joint legislative committee to consider forming a state or national park in the Great Smoky Mountains.
1925	The Tennessee State Park and Forestry Commission is established.
1925	Tennessee's Arbor Day Law of 1887 is expanded to create "Bird, Flower and Arbor Day" on the first Friday in April. (In 1947 the date is changed to the first Friday in March.)
May 22, 1926	Congress authorizes the Great Smoky Mountains National Park.
1927	The Outdoor Writers Association of America is formed.

1927	Tennessee mandates that hunting and fishing revenues be "specifically appropriated to the use of" the Division of Game and Fish.
1927	Tennessee's first state forest is established when Madison County donates 38 acres of tax-delinquent lands to the state.
1928	The U.S. Supreme Court rules that federal law can override state law to protect federal lands.
1928	The Division of Sanitary Engineering initiates the first stream pollution studies in Tennessee.
1928	The Davy Crockett Chapter of the Izaak Walton League is founded in Nashville; Dr. S. John House is its first president. Chapters follow in Chattanooga, Knoxville and Memphis.
Feb. 18, 1929	The Migratory Bird Conservation Act establishes a Migratory Bird Conservation Commission and formally authorizes a National Wildlife Refuge system.
Feb. 20, 1929	Gov. Henry Horton signs a bill deploring the "lamentable condition" of the Big Pigeon River and appropriating $10,000 to correct it. The bill also authorizes "any necessary lawsuits."
1929	Tennessee builds its first fish hatchery at Springfield; Morristown hatchery opens in 1930.
1930	The National Park Service creates a Wildlife Division.
1930	The first major spillway in the state is built at Reelfoot Lake.
1931	The Great Smoky Mountains National Park opens.
1931	The Tennessee Game and Fish Act renames the Game and Fish Protective Fund. It is now simply the Game and Fish Fund. All Game and Fish revenues are still earmarked.
1931	The $2 hunting license is expanded to include fishing; the county-wide license is abolished. Women and children under 16 are exempt. The $2 rate remains unchanged until 1957.
1931, 1933	Tennessee sportsmen lobby unsuccessfully for an independent game and fish commission.
1932	Iowa State College establishes a game management school; it becomes the prototype for the Cooperative Wildlife Research Unit Program.
1933	The Tennessee Valley Authority is created.
1933	The Soil Erosion Service (the Soil Conservation Service after 1935) is created.
1933	FDR's New Deal creates the Civilian Conservation Corps.
1933	The More Game Birds Foundation is founded to preserve duck habitat; in 1938 it creates Ducks Unlimited, with which it soon merges.
1933	Game and Fish is removed from the Tennessee Department of Agriculture and made a freestanding department.
1933	Morgan, Bledsoe and Pickett State Forests are established by CCC crews.
1933	The Tennessee Valley Commission (the Tennessee State Planning Commission after 1935) is created.

Mar. 16, 1934   The Migratory Bird Hunting Stamp Act requires waterfowl hunters to display a $1 "Duck Stamp." Jay N. "Ding" Darling designs the first stamp.

Apr. 14, 1934   The Tennessee Federation of Sportsmen is founded at the King Hotel, Murfreesboro.

1934   Congress passes the Flood Control Act.

1934   The Coordination Act (a.k.a. the Fish and Wildlife Coordination Act) authorizes the U.S. Departments of Commerce and Agriculture to work with other agencies to restore wildlife, correct water pollution and minimize the impacts of new lakes and dams.

1934   The Taylor Grazing Act regulates overgrazing and soil erosion on public lands.

1934   President Roosevelt names Ding Darling chief of the Bureau of Biological Survey and appoints Darling, Aldo Leopold and Thomas Beck to a Wildlife Restoration Committee.

1934   The Robinson National Forest Refuge Act authorizes sanctuaries in national forests.

1934   A model administrative law for game and fish agencies is offered to states by the International Association of Game, Fish and Conservation Commissioners.

January 1935   The Tennessee Federation of Sportsmen introduces a modified version of the IAGFCC model law into the 68th General Assembly.

Feb. 8, 1935   Tennessee's first model game and fish law passes. It creates an autonomous Board of Conservation for Game, Fish and Wild Life and a new Department of Game and Fish Conservation. Damon Headden, Sr., is named director.

1935   The Works Progress Administration (later Works Projects Administration) is founded as one of Roosevelt's New Deal programs.

1935   The American Wildlife Institute is founded. In 1946 it becomes the Wildlife Management Institute.

1935   The Cooperative Wildlife Research Unit Program establishes programs at nine land-grant universities.

1935   The Wilderness Society is founded.

1935   The Reelfoot Lake Law bans hunting on all state-owned lands around the lake. It also creates a five-day trip license for $5.

1935   Grundy and Stewart State Forests are established by CCC crews; Herman Baggenstoss is supervisor of the Grundy Camp.

1935   Herman Baggenstoss starts publishing "Turkey Feathers, Boar Bristles and Fish Fins," the first publication of the Tennessee Federation of Sportsmen.

Feb. 3-7, 1936   President Roosevelt convenes the first North American Wildlife Conference in Washington.

Feb. 5, 1936   The General Wildlife Federation is approved by 1,500 delegates to the North American Wildlife Conference; Ding Darling is elected president. In 1938 the GWF is renamed the National Wildlife Federation.

1936   The United States and Mexico sign a Treaty for the Protection of Migratory Birds and Game Mammals.

1936   Tennessee's three National Forests are combined into one unit, the Cherokee. Tennessee and the U.S. Forest Service sign a cooperative management agreement creating the Tellico, Ocoee and other wildlife areas in the Cherokee.

1936	The first TVA dam creates Norris Reservoir.
1936	Tennessee issues 59,049 hunting and fishing licenses.
February 1937	Gov. Gordon Browning's reorganization bill creates the Tennessee Department of Conservation, makes Game and Fish a division of the TDOC and abolishes the independent game and fish commission created in 1935. It also creates the divisions of Forestry, Geology and State Parks and Recreation. Sam Brewster is appointed commissioner of the new department.
February 1937	The Tennessee Federation of Sportsmen begins publishing *Tennessee Wildlife*. Herman Baggenstoss is its editor.
March 1937	The Department of Conservation agrees to subsidize *Tennessee Wildlife*; in return, the magazine carries official news of the Department and its divisions.
July 1937	The Tennessee Federation of Sportsmen hosts first the first Regional Wildlife Conference of the General Wildlife Federation. Ding Darling is guest speaker.
Sept. 2, 1937	The Pittman-Robertson Federal Aid to Wildlife Restoration Act is signed by President Franklin Roosevelt. It imposes a 10% excise tax on sporting arms and ammunition, apportioned to the states for wildlife projects. During World War II the tax is raised to 11%.
1937	The Wildlife Society is founded.
1937	The Appalachian Trail is completed.
1937	An Education Service is established in the Department of Conservation; James L. Bailey is hired to direct it.
1937	The Tennessee Federation of Sportsmen becomes the Tennessee Wildlife Federation.
March 1938	President Roosevelt proclaims National Wildlife Restoration Week; Ding Darling creates the first series of wildlife stamps.
1938	Ducks Unlimited is founded by the More Game Birds Foundation to protect waterfowl breeding grounds in Canada and the U.S.
1938	The Division of Game and Fish begins a survey of Tennessee's major streams, beginning with the Big South Fork of the Cumberland.
1938	Tennessee creates the first official state park, Harrison Bay, when it leases Harrison Island Park, a 1,400-acre TVA demonstration area on Chickamauga Reservoir. Another 350 acres on Chickamauga are leased for Booker T. Washington State Park, the nation's first "Negro State Park," though it doesn't officially open unitl 1942.
1939	The Bureau of Biological Survey (in the U.S. Department of Agriculture) and the Bureau of Fisheries (in the Commerce Department) are transferred to the Department of Interior.
1939	Gov. Prentice Cooper repeals all private wildlife acts (his law is repealed in 1949). He also creates the first advisory Conservation Commission.
1939	Tennessee conducts its first outdoor recreation study.
1939	Tennessee's first Game and Fish lakes are completed: Bedford, Portland, Marrowbone, Carroll, Tullahoma and Whiteville. Laurel Lake follows in 1940.
1939	Tennessee gets its first Pittman-Robertson distribution, roughly $40,000.

1939	Herman Baggenstoss resigns as editor of *Tennessee Wildlife*; Edward J. Meeman takes over. The Federation goes into decline.
1940	The Bureau of Biological Survey and the Bureau of Fisheries combine to form the U.S. Fish and Wildlife Service.
1940	Franklin D. Roosevelt officially opens the Smokies in a ceremony at Newfound Gap.
1940	Tennessee's first Soil Conservation District is established in Sumner County.
1941	The USFWS leases a third of Reelfoot Lake for the Reelfoot National Wildlife Refuge; in return, it promises to spend a half-million dollars building erosion controls.
1941	The CCC begins a reforestation project in the Copper Basin.
1941-45	World War II suspends most conservation activity nationwide.
1941-46	Lou Williams writes the outdoor column for *The Chattanooga Times*.
Aug. 24, 1942	Catoosa WMA is dedicated.
Aug. 24, 1942	The Tennessee Outdoor Writers Association is founded.
1942	The CCC disbands.
1942	TVA proposes the Tellico Dam on the Little Tennessee River.
1943	Tennessee authorizes a Stream Pollution Study Board.
1943	Z. Cartter Patten establishes an annual conservation award with the Tennessee Outdoor Writers Association. In 1947 it is transferred to the Tennessee Conservation League.
1944	Pollution in the Cumberland River triggers a massive fish kill from Nashville to Clarksville.
1945	The Soil and Water Conservation Society is founded.
1945	The Tennessee Stream Pollution Control Law creates the Stream Pollution Control Board.
1945	The Tennessee Wildlife Federation revives briefly.
Jan. 30, 1946	The Tennessee Conservation League is chartered; 15 sportsmen sign the document.
Feb. 12, 1946	The Tennessee Conservation League holds its inaugural meeting at the Read House, Chattanooga; Lou Williams is elected president. Dues are $1, or 10¢ a head for clubs.
1946	Congress creates the Bureau of Land Management in the Interior Department.
1946	The new Fish and Wildlife Coordination Act requires federal water projects minimize harm to fish and wildlife.
1946	The American Wildlife Institute splits into the Wildlife Management Institute and the North American Wildlife Foundation.
1946	The chemical DDT goes into general use; toxic effects appear almost immediately.
1946	Sixteen states including Tennessee organize the Southeastern Association of Fish, Wildlife and Conservation Commissioners, a regional branch of the International Association.
1947	The USFWS creates four flyway regions: Atlantic, Mississippi, Central and Pacific.
1947	The Federal Insecticide, Fungicide and Rodenticide Act creates some controls but allows widespread use of DDT and other highly toxic chemicals.

1947	Defenders of Wildlife is founded.
1947	A No-Fence Law bans free-ranging cattle in Tennessee.
1947	TCL holds its first annual convention in Johnson City; Karl Steinmetz is appointed to draft a new model game and fish law for Tennessee.
1948	The federal Flood Control Act authorizes the Army Corps of Engineers' West Tennessee Tributaries Flood Control Project in the Obion and Forked Deer River Basin.
1948	The Federal Water Pollution Control Act authorizes federal appropriations for state sewage treatment programs.
Feb. 25, 1949	TCL's model game and fish law passes, three votes short of unanimous. It creates an independent, nine-member Game and Fish Commission, nominated by sportsmen and serving without pay. The governor and commissioner of Conservation are nonvoting, ex-officio members.
Apr. 7, 1949	The Tennessee Game and Fish Commission holds its first meeting; Lucius E. Burch, Jr., is elected chairman.
October 1949	Tracy City hosts Tennessee's first Forestry Fair.
1949	The USFWS holds its first annual Duck Stamp design contest.
1949	Up to a fourth of all National Wildlife Refuges are to be open to hunting.
1949	Aldo Leopold publishes *A Sand County Almanac*.
1949	Tennessee prohibits dumping trash in streams or on roads.
1949	Tennessee's Stream Pollution Control Board is temporarily suspended, replaced by a Stream Pollution Study Commission. A Pollution Control Law is due by 1956.
1949	TCL raises affiliate dues to 25¢ a member.
January 1950	A panel of visiting experts convenes to evaluate the Tennessee Game and Fish Commission's long-range program.
May 27, 1950	TCL hosts a forest-reclamation demonstration at Copper Basin.
Aug. 9, 1950	President Harry Truman signs the Dingell-Johnson Federal Aid to Sport Fish Restoration Act. It places a 10% tax on fishing tackle, distributed to the states for fisheries research and restoration projects.
1950	Congress authorizes TVA to build coal-fired steam plants.
1950	TCL begins a campaign to get sewage-treatment systems installed in every town in Tennessee.
Feb. 8, 1951	Keep Tennessee Green (the Tennessee Forestry Association after 1971) is founded; Lou Williams is elected president. Williams steps down as president of TCL.
June 1, 1951	Tennessee passes the game and fish code as revised by Karl Steinmetz; it is called the Wildlife Protection Act of 1951.
1951	Congress passes the Watershed Protection and Flood Prevention Act.
1951	The Nature Conservancy (national office) is founded.
1951	Tennessee's first annual Spring Wildflower Pilgrimage is held in the Smokies.

1951	Tennessee hosts its first managed wild turkey hunts in the Ocoee and Shelby Wildlife Management Areas. The success rate is 5%.
1952	Forest fires burn more than a million acres in Tennessee.
1952	TCL sponsors the first Science and Conservation Workshop for Teachers at East Tennessee Teachers College.
1953	Keep America Beautiful is founded.
1953	Woods Reservoir at Arnold Engineering Development Center opens.
1953	The Tennessee Game and Fish Commission narrowly survives an attack by the Legislature. The commissioner of Conservation is given veto power over personnel decisions at the agency.
1953	TCL is named Outstanding Affiliate of the Year by the National Wildlife Federation.
1954	The Game and Fish Commission signs a cooperative agreement with the U.S. Air Force to manage the wildlife area at Arnold Engineering Development Center near Tullahoma.
1954	TCL is again named NWF's Outstanding Affiliate of the Year.
1955	Duck Stamps, with die proofs, become part of the permanent collection in the Hall of Philately at the Smithsonian.
1955	Crossly, S-D Surveys, Inc. of New York conducts the first National Survey of Fishing and Hunting. The survey is repeated every five years.
1955	The USFWS divides into the Bureau of Commercial Fisheries and the Bureau of Sport Fisheries and Wildlife.
1955	Tennessee votes to ban commercial crappie fishing at Reelfoot Lake in an effort to reverse the decline in crappie sizes.
1955	Keep Tennessee Beautiful becomes the first state chapter of Keep America Beautiful.
1956	The Federal Water Pollution Control Act increases appropriations for municipal sewage plants and creates a Water Pollution Advisory Board.
1956	The federal Agriculture Act creates the first Conservation Reserve Program.
1956	The latest Fish and Wildlife Coordination Act requires federal water development projects to give equal consideration to wildlife values.
1956	The Stream Pollution Study Commission completes its five-year abatement plan. The Stream Pollution Control Board is reactivated.
1957	Tennessee's combined hunting and fishing license fee increases to $3.
1957	A Division of Water Resources is created in the Department of Conservation.
October 1958	The Reelfoot-Indian Creek Watershed District calls for 15 siltation retention dams for Reelfoot Lake.
1958	At President Dwight Eisenhower's urging, Congress establishes the Outdoor Recreation Resources Review Commission. Among its recommendations are a federal Bureau of Outdoor Recreation and a Land and Water Conservation Fund.
1958	The Fish and Wildlife Coordination Act of 1958 requires federal water projects give "equal consideration" to wildlife conservation.

1958	Tennessee state parks are formally declared wildlife preserves; hunting is allowed only in those managed as state forests.
Nov. 17, 1959	Karl Steinmetz dies.
1959	Trout Unlimited is founded.
1959	Tennessee repeals the power of the commissioner of Conservation to veto personnel decisions in Game and Fish.
1959	Herman Baggenstoss writes the first bill to regulate strip mining in Tennessee; it does not pass.
Jun. 12, 1960	Congress passes the Multiple-Use Sustained-Yield Act, requiring national forests be managed for a balanced range of uses.
1961	Congress passes the Wetlands Loan Act.
1961	The Association of Conservation Engineers is formed.
1961	The Ruffed Grouse Society is founded.
1961	The World Wildlife Fund is founded.
1961	Channelization begins in the Obion-Forked Deer River Basin in the first phase of the West Tennessee Tributaries Flood Control Project.
1961	The County Conservation Board Bill authorizes Tennessee counties to buy parks, forests and other public lands.
1961	TCL charges that pesticides around power lines kill small game.
1961	TCL dedicates a memorial to Karl Steinmetz on the Tellico's North River.
1961	TCL raises individual dues to $3; affiliate dues remain 25¢ per member.
1962	Rachel Carson publishes *Silent Spring*; NWF names her Conservationist of the Year.
1962	NWF begins publishing *National Wildlife* magazine.
1962	J. N. "Ding" Darling dies.
1962	President Kennedy hosts the Third White House Conference on Conservation.
1962	Congress appropriates funds for the Tellico Dam. It also appropriates funds to build a scenic mountain road from Tellico Plains to Robbinsville, N.C.
1962	Tennessee creates a Legislative Council Committee on Land and Water Resources.
1962	Gov. Buford Ellington ends the official racial segregation policy in state parks (except for restaurants and swimming pools), but no formal announcement is made.
1962	Tennessee wins the Beichler regional award for reducing forest fires. It wins again in 1963 and 1964.
1963	Congress passes the first Clean Air Act.
1963	The Bureau of Outdoor Recreation is established in the Interior Department.
1963	Congress passes gun controls.

1963	The Division of Water Resources in the Tennessee Department of Conservation introduces the state's first law to protect groundwater.
Sept. 3, 1964	The Land and Water Conservation Fund Act creates a user-fee system to finance outdoor recreation projects. States must submit a Comprehensive Outdoor Recreation Plan to the Bureau of Outdoor Recreation in order to be eligible for a share of the funds.
1964	TVA begins work on a recreation-demonstration project called Land Between the Lakes.
1964	The Public Land Law Review Commission is founded.
1964	The Wilderness Act creates the 9.1 million-acre National Wilderness Preservation System.
1964	The Game and Fish Commission reinstates commercial crappie fishing at Reelfoot; it also allows the use of nets.
1964	NWF gives TCL a regional award for "outstanding service to conservation."
1965	The Anadromous Fish Conservation Act protects salmon and other species that swim upstream to spawn.
1965	The Federal Water Quality Control Act creates the Federal Water Pollution Control Administration to provide research and development grants.
1965	The Federal Water Project Recreation Act requires federal water projects to consider recreation values during planning and implementation.
1965	Lady Bird Johnson hosts the White House Conference on Natural Beauty and helps pass the Highway Beautification Act. She receives one of the first NWF "Connie" awards.
1965	Congress passes the Solid Waste Disposal Act.
1965	Jacobs Creek Civilian Conservation Center opens in the Cherokee National Forest, the nation's first Job Corps project under the Economic Opportunity Act.
1965	The Tennessee Boating Safety Act creates a Boating Safety Advisory Board in the Game and Fish Commission.
1965	The NWF initiates a conservation awards program among its 49 state affiliates.
1966	Congress passes the Clean Water Restoration Act.
1966	The first Endangered Species Preservation Act authorizes the study and purchase of sensitive habitat but does not prohibit taking of designated species.
1966	The federal Transportation Act prohibits taking parklands, wildlife refuges or recreation areas for federal road projects unless "no feasible and prudent alternative exists."
1966	Congress passes the National Historic Preservation Act.
1966	Tennessee's combination license goes to $5.
1966	The Tennessee Scenic Rivers Association is founded.
1966	Tennessee Citizens for Wilderness Planning is founded.
1966	Edward J. Meeman dies at age 77.
1967	The Environmental Defense Fund is founded.
1967	The Fund for Animals is founded.

1967	The Tennessee Air Pollution Control Act creates an Air Pollution Control Board and a Division of Air Pollution Control in the Department of Public Health.
1967	The Tennessee Strip Mine Law of 1967 creates a Division of Strip Mining and Land Reclamation in the Department of Conservation.
July 31, 1968	A massive fish kill begins on the Cumberland River.
Oct. 2, 1968	The National Trails System Act designates the Appalachian and Pacific Crest National Scenic Trails and authorizes the study of 14 others.
1968	Congress passes the National Wild and Scenic Rivers Act.
1968	The National Water Commission is created.
1968	The Federal Gun Control Act sets age limits and requires some record-keeping.
1968	Tennessee hosts the U.S. Canoe Association's National Downriver Marathon at Devil's Jump on the South Fork of the Cumberland River.
1968	The Tennessee Scenic Rivers Act designates all or parts of eight streams, including the Hiwassee, the Harpeth, the Buffalo, the Collins, the French Broad, Blackburn Fork, Roaring River and Spring Creek. Tuckahoe Creek is added by amendment.
1968	The Game and Fish Commission moves into new headquarters at Ellington Agricultural Center. It rejects a request to name the building for TCL founder Lou Williams.
1968	The first of the siltation dams planned in 1958 is built at Reelfoot.
1968	The Tennessee Trails Association is founded at Cumberland Mountain State Park.
1968	The Game and Fish Commission hosts the first "Diana Hunt" at AEDC, the first women-only deer hunt in the nation. Women-only hunts are later banned as unconstitutional.
1969	The National Environmental Policy Act (NEPA) passes; it goes into effect Jan. 1, 1970. It creates a Council on Environmental Quality and mandates environmental impact statements for federal projects likely to affect environmental quality.
1969	The Endangered Species Conservation Act bans importation of listed species.
1969	The Environmental Law Institute is founded.
1969	NWF publishes its first annual National Environmental Quality Index.
1969	Oil spills off the California coast mobilize environmentalists nationwide.
1969	Residual mercury causes massive fish kills in a number of Tennessee reservoirs.
1969	The Tennessee Solid Waste Control Act creates the Division of Solid Waste in the Department of Public Health.
1969	Memphis citizens sue the U.S. Department of Transportation to stop the proposed route of Interstate 40 through Overton Park.
1969	The position of Game and Fish Planner is created in the Tennessee Game and Fish Commission to implement the wildlife phase of the State Comprehensive Outdoor Recreation Plan (SCORP).
1969	TCL proposes an umbrella organization, the Tennessee Environmental Council, to handle emerging environmental issues.

1969	TCL adopts a new logo, a hand holding a deer and a tree.
Apr. 22, 1970	The nation celebrates Earth Day.
Apr. 23, 1970	Four duck hunters sue the Army Corps of Engineers, charging that the West Tennessee Tributaries Flood Control Project is destroying waterfowl habitat in the Obion-Forked Deer River Basin. The project stops while the Corps prepares an environmental impact statement under NEPA.
Aug. 19, 1970	The Tennessee Valley Sportsmen's Club hosts a meeting at Norris Dam State Park to evaluate the future of TCL. The meeting leads to an extensive reorganization of the League.
December 1970	The Tennessee Environmental Council is chartered.
1970	The U.S. Environmental Protection Agency is founded.
1970	Congress passes the Resource Conservation and Recovery Act to regulate and reduce solid and hazardous wastes.
1970	The Dingell-Hart Act places a 10% excise tax on handguns, earmarked for wildlife restoration, hunter safety and shooting ranges. Proceeds are shared by states as part of their annual Pittman-Robertson distribution.
1970	The Environmental Education Act authorizes $45 million to fund pilot programs over the next three years.
1970	The Clean Air Act is upgraded.
1970	The Young Adult Conservation Corps is founded.
1970	Environmentalists block a proposed Corps of Engineers dam at Devil's Jump, urging a Big South Fork wilderness area instead.
1970	The Bureau of Commercial Fisheries moves from USFWS to the Commerce Department.
1970	NWF holds its first Camp Energy for youth at Land Between the Lakes.
1970	NWF hires a director of women's activities.
1970	Greenpeace is founded.
1970	The League of Conservation Voters is founded.
1970	The Natural Resources Defense Council is founded.
1970	A survey by the Game and Fish Commission finds 95% of license holders in Tennessee are white; 93% are male.
1970	The Tennessee Archeology Act creates a Division of Archeology in the Department of Conservation.
1970	Republican Winfield Dunn is elected governor of Tennessee on a strong environmental platform.
1970	Bowater Southern Paper Co. initiates a national system of Pocket Wilderness Areas with Angel Falls Pocket Wilderness Area on the Cumberland Plateau.
1970	Tennessee joins the Kentucky-based Cumberland Chapter of the Sierra Club; within a year or two it becomes the Tennessee Chapter.

1970	TCL raises club dues to 50¢ per member; individual dues are still $3.
January 1971	TCL appoints a special evaluation committee to guide the reorganization of the League; Lucius Burch, Jr., agrees to be chairman.
January 1971	TCL and the National Wildlife Federation join the National Ecological Foundation in its suit against the West Tennessee Tributaries Project.
March 1971	TCL celebrates its 25th anniversary in Memphis; a special issue of *The Tennessee Conservationist* is devoted to TCL history.
Fall 1971	TCL's evaluation committee submits its final report. A follow-up committee chaired by Bob Burns begins implementing its recommendations.
December 1971	The Edward J. Meeman Foundation offers TCL a matching grant of $100,000. It has five years to raise the match. TCL starts advertising for an executive director.
1971	The United States votes to ban whaling and whale product imports.
1971	The Environmental Defense Fund sues to stop work on the Tennessee-Tombigbee Waterway pending an environmental impact statement.
1971	Bowater's Laurel-Snow Trail is named one of 27 National Recreation Trails.
1971	The Tennessee Water Quality Control Act of 1971 creates a Water Quality Control Board. The Stream Pollution Control Board is renamed the Division of Water Quality Control.
1971	The Tennessee Trails System Act authorizes seven State Scenic Trails: Cumberland, John Muir, Lonesome Pine, Chickasaw Bluffs, Natchez Trace, the Trail of Tears and the Tennessee sections of the Appalachian Trail.
1971	The Tennessee Litter Control Law of 1971 imposes fines of $25-$50.
1971	Tennessee's Natural Areas Preservation Act creates a system to identify and preserve areas of outstanding natural value.
1971	The Tennessee Game and Fish Commission comes under widespread attack. The commissioner of Conservation gets full voting powers.
1971	Tennessee Citizens for Wilderness Planning hosts the first Intergroup Conference at Cumberland Mountain State Park.
1971	Lou Williams publishes *Tennessee's Conservation Revolution*.
Mar. 27, 1972	TCL votes to hire Tony Campbell of New Mexico as its first executive director.
May 1972	Judge Bailey Brown rejects the Corps' environmental impact statement for the West Tennessee Tributaries Project and orders a new one.
July 1972	TWRA begins a voluntary Hunter Education Training Program as an outgrowth of the National Rifle Association Firearms Safety Course.
July 1972	TCL opens an office at 2010 Church Street.
Sept. 23, 1972	President Nixon declares the first National Hunting and Fishing Day, saying that the sportsman "has always been in the forefront of today's environmental movement."
1972	Congress passes the Clean Water Act of 1972. Amendments include Section 401, requiring state certification of all federal actions discharging into the "navigable waters" of the U.S.; and Section 404, requiring a permit to discharge dredged or fill materials into those

waters. In 1975, a federal judge rules that "navigable waters" includes wetlands and tributaries.

1972   The Goodling-Moss Act places an 11% excise tax on archery equipment to be used for wildlife restoration. Monies are allocated to states as part of their annual share of Pittman-Robertson funds.

1972   The U.S. Forest Service begins a Roadless Area Review and Evaluation (RARE) to evaluate proposed National Wilderness Areas, mostly in the western U.S.

1972   Congress passes a series of marine protection acts, including the Marine Mammal Protection Act, the Coastal Zone Management Act and the Marine Protection, Research and Sanctuaries Act.

1972   The Federal Environmental Pesticide Control Act strengthens the 1947 Insecticide, Fungicide and Rodenticide Act; it bans DDT, chlordane and various other chemicals.

1972   The United Nations hosts the Conference on the Human Environment.

1972   The Convention on International Trade in Endangered Species of Wild Fauna and Flora begins circulating among likely member nations; the United States ratifies it in 1973. CITES goes into effect in 1975.

1972   The Alliance for Environmental Education is founded.

1972   The Trust for Public Land is founded.

1972   Energy conservation is the theme of National Wildlife Week.

1972   The National Wild Turkey Federation is founded.

1972   The Ohio Division of Wildlife introduces the nation's first nongame wildlife conservation stamp for $5.

1972   NWF holds its first national Wildlife Camp and Conservation Summit at Land Between the Lakes.

1972   Environmentalists sue under NEPA to stop TVA's Columbia Dam.

1972   The Tennessee Surface Mining Act regulates all mineral extraction, not just coal. It creates a Surface Mine Reclamation Fund and a Board of Reclamation Review.

1972   Tennessee creates the Obion-Forked Deer Basin Authority to serve as the local sponsoring agency in the West Tennessee Tribs project.

July 30, 1973   An independent panel of experts convenes to evaluate the Game and Fish Commission.

August 1973   TCL premieres its monthly newsletter, *Tennessee Out-Of-Doors*.

1973   The Endangered Species Act prohibits the hunting or taking of listed species and designates critical habitats for preservation.

1973   A number of state, federal and local agencies form the Tennessee Recreational Advisory and Data Exchange Council (the TRADE Council) to coordinate recreational policies and programs.

1973   University of Tennessee professor David Etnier discovers what appears to be a new species of darter in the Little Tennessee River.

1973	The Corps of Engineers agrees to give Tennessee 32,000 acres of mitigation wetlands in an attempt to settle the West Tennessee Tributaries lawsuit.
1973	TCL launches a $500,000 fund drive.
1973	The Nashville Sportsman's Club becomes the first (and only) all-black affiliate to join TCL.
Mar. 7, 1974	A reorganization bill restructures the Tennessee Game and Fish Commission as the Wildlife Resources Commission and the Wildlife Resources Agency. Four regional offices are created. The office of Game and Fish Planner becomes the Division of Planning and Environmental Resources (later the Division of Environmental Services).
Oct. 18, 1974	An anti-hunting coalition led by the Fund for Animals seeks an injunction on all waterfowl hunting; the request is denied.
1974	Congress passes the Water Resources Development Act.
1974	The Eastern Wilderness Areas Act creates three small wilderness areas in Tennessee.
1974	Congress passes the Safe Drinking Water Act.
1974	The U.S. Bureau of Outdoor Recreation releases a National Outdoor Recreation Plan.
1974	The Bureau of Sport Fisheries and Wildlife, created by the 1955 reorganization of the U.S. Fish and Wildlife Service, is again named the USFWS.
1974	The Worldwatch Institute is founded.
1974	Congress authorizes the Big South Fork National River and Recreation Area.
1974	TVA's first nuclear power plant at Browns Ferry goes on line.
1974	Tennessee passes a Nongame and Endangered or Threatened Wildlife Species Conservation Act.
1974	The Tennessee Outdoor Recreation Areas System (TORAS) is completed as a component of Tennessee's Comprehensive Outdoor Recreation Plan (SCORP).
1974	The gas shortage forces TCL to cancel its winter board meeting.
1974	TCL moves to 1205 Eighth Avenue, South.
1974	Individual TCL dues go to $5; club dues go to 75¢ per member.
Mar. 27, 1975	A U.S. District Court judge rules that Section 404 of the Clean Water Act of 1972 (requiring a permit to place material in "navigable waters" of the United States) applies to tributaries, feeder streams and adjacent wetlands.
Sept. 5, 1975	An anti-hunting documentary on CBS, *The Guns of Autumn*, sparks protest from sportsmen nationwide.
1975	Outdoor Women, the first national outdoor sports organization for women, is founded.
1975	Tennessee's Blaze Orange Law requires big game hunters (except turkey hunters) to wear fluorescent orange.
1975	TWRA starts publishing *Tennessee Wildlife*.
1975	Construction begins on the Tennessee-Tombigbee shipping canal from the Tennessee River at Pickwick Lake to the Gulf of Mexico at Mobile.

1975	Tennessee's combined license goes to $7.50. TWRA begins selling a $5 "nongame wildlife certificate."
1975	TWRA's Boating Safety Advisory Board is abolished.
1975	The Natural Heritage program is created in the Department of Conservation to inventory ecosystems, sensitive species and natural areas.
1975	TCL and TEC cosponsor a land-use planning symposium; TCL convenes a Resource Agency Coordinating Committee.
1975	TCL raises club dues to $1 a member.
Mar. 8, 1976	Joe Criswell leaves Dyersburg on a 185-mile "Conservation Walkathon" to the League's annual meeting in Nashville. He arrives April 4, having collected $3,225.
March 1976	The USFWS mandates nontoxic-shot hunting zones; the National Rifle Association sues, charging that steel shot causes firearms injuries. The suit is denied.
1976	UNESCO hosts the Man and the Biosphere conference in Paris.
1976	The Toxic Substances Control Act requires EPA to test for and regulate toxic substances such as PCBs.
1976	The amended Resource Conservation and Recovery Act creates the Office of Solid Waste within the EPA.
1976	The National Forest Management Act requires long-range plans for National Forests.
1976	The Federal Land Policy and Management Act mandates that public lands be managed for multiple use and sustained yield. Western states protest.
1976	The U.S. Supreme Court rules that Congress has jurisdiction over federal lands, including resident wildlife.
1976	The Wildlife Conservation Fund of America is founded.
1976	Congress designates parts of the Obed as a Wild and Scenic River.
1976	Gov. Blanton proposes merging TWRA and TDOC; the proposal is rejected.
1976	The Division of Sanitary Engineeering is absorbed into the Division of Water Quality Control.
1976	Tennessee's Agricultural, Forest and Open Space Land Act (the Greenbelt Law) gives tax breaks to developers who leave some commercial property undeveloped.
1976	The Environmental Action Fund, Tennessee's first environmental lobbying organization, is founded with seed money provided by actor Robert Redford.
1976	TCL raises individual dues to $10 and club dues to $1.25 per member.
June 3, 1977	TWRA and the U.S. Forest Service establish the Cherokee Wildlife Management Area, incorporating the entire 620,000-acre National Forest and absorbing the six existing wildlife management areas. A single Cherokee WMA permit is good for all species.
1977	The U.S. Forest Service begins its second Roadless Area Review and Evaluation (RARE II) to identify further wilderness areas in the eastern U.S.
1977	The federal Surface Mining Control and Reclamation Act establishes an Office of Surface Mining in the Department of Interior and creates an Abandoned Mine Reclamation Fund.

1977	Congress passes the Soil and Water Resources Conservation Act.
1977	Congress bans lead-based paint, CFCs in spray cans and the weed killer 2,4,5-T.
1977	The Department of Energy and Federal Energy Regulatory Commission are established.
1977	The Tennessee Environmental Council sues TVA over Clean Air Act violations; TCL declines to join the lawsuit.
1977	Tennessee passes the Water Quality Control Act of 1977. In December, the state signs an agreement with EPA, allowing the Division of Water Quality Control to issue National Pollutant Discharge Elimination System (NPDES) permits.
1977	The Tennessee Natural Areas Act is amended to allow some hunting.
1977	Tennessee's Hunter Educational Training Program is judged best in the nation.
1977	TCL creates four vice-presidential regions and 12 director districts. The constitution and bylaws are revised to reflect the changes.
1977	TCL holds its first Youth Conservation Camp at Montgomery Bell State Park.
1977	TCL meets the terms of the $100,000 Meeman challenge grant.
1977	Judge Bailey Brown rejects the Corps of Engineers' second environmental impact statement in the West Tennessee Tributaries lawsuit. He renews his earlier stop-work order.
1977	TCL votes to reject the USFWS ban on lead shot.
1977	TCL moves to 1720 West End Avenue.
February 1978	Gary Myers is promoted to director of TWRA.
Sept. 27, 1978	The National Ecological Foundation files a second lawsuit in the West Tennessee Tributaries case, charging that the Obion-Forked Deer Basin Authority is operating without permits. TCL votes to join the lawsuit the following month.
1978	The National Energy Policy Conservation Act sets efficiency standards for major appliances, authorizes solar demonstration projects and requires energy audits on all federal buildings. The Energy Tax Act offers tax credits for residential weatherization and taxes gas guzzlers.
1978	The National Parks and Recreation Act creates the Urban Recreation Recovery Program.
1978	The Endangered Species Committee ("God Squad") considers exempting the Tellico Dam from the Endangered Species Act. They rule unanimously against doing so.
1978	Colorado is the first state to offer a nongame checkoff on state income tax forms.
1978	Tennessee is authorized to administer the federal surface mine program.
1978	The Nature Conservancy establishes an office in Tennessee.
1978	The Tennessee Native Plant Society is founded.
1978	TenneScenic is founded to promote highway beautification and control billboards.
1978-80	TCL leads a coalition of groups lobbying for a bottle bill.
1978	TCL's affiliate dues increase to $1.50 per member.

1979	An accident at Three-Mile Island raises public fears of nuclear power.
1979	The Sagebrush Rebellion starts when Nevada declares public lands within its borders to be state property. Other western states follow suit.
1979	Congress authorizes the completion of Tellico Dam.
1979	The first lands are bought for the Big South Fork National River and Recreation Area.
1979	TCL contracts with TVA to evaluate its resource management plan for Land Between the Lakes.
March 1980	TCL receives NWF's Outstanding State Affiliate award for 1979.
1980	The Comprehensive Environmental Response, Compensation and Liability Act (the Superfund Act) mandates clean up of hazardous waste sites.
1980	The National Acid Precipitation Act mandates reductions in the emissions that cause acid rain.
1980	The Fish and Wildlife Coordination Act authorizes $20 million in federal matching grants to support nongame programs.
1980	The Alaska National Interest Lands Conservation Act passes.
1980	Congress passes the Conservation Easement Bill.
1980	TVA begins a five-year eagle hacking project at Land Between the Lakes.
1980	The latest Tennessee Surface Mining Act passes.
1980	Tennessee and the USFWS announce a $4.7 million restoration project for Reelfoot Lake.
1980	TVA agrees to cut by half its sulfur dioxide emissions over the next five years in a settlement of the 1977 environmentalists' lawsuit.
1980	TVA asks TCL and NWF to host a series of public meetings in all TVA districts in an attempt to upgrade TVA's public image.
1980	Mitchell Parks proposes TCL build a Conservation Resource Center.
1980	TCL urges Gov. Lamar Alexander to appoint an Obion-Forked Deer Task Force.
1980	Citizens file a lawsuit to stop TVA's Columbia Dam; TCL is one of the plaintiffs.
1980	TCL hosts its first sportsmen's rally at the National Guard Armory in Nashville.
1981	Quail Unlimited is founded.
1981	The Women's Environment and Development Organization is founded.
1981	Gov. Alexander announces a Safe Growth Plan for Tennessee and forms a Safe Growth Action Team.
1981	Tennessee enters a low-level radioactive waste compact with other Southeastern states.
1981	TCL receives 15 acres of land on Mill Creek at Murfreesboro Road as a possible building site for its Conservation Resource Center.
March 1982	Federal budget cuts force TVA to cancel its eagle hacking project; TCL takes over.
1982	Congress passes the Coastal Barrier Resources Act.

1982	The U.S. Department of Agriculture establishes a fish and wildlife policy.
1982	Pheasants Forever is founded.
1982	Tennessee's combined hunting and fishing license goes to $10.
1982	NWF establishes a Corporate Conservation Council; TCL sets up a similar council with Tennessee industries.
1982	NWF stops subsidizing affiliate newspapers; *Tennessee Out-of-Doors* begins publishing bi-monthly.
1982	TCL sponsors the first Tennessee conservation stamp and print.
1982	TCL affiliate dues go to $2 per member; individual dues remain at $10.
March 1983	The Legislature passes TCL's Mandatory Hunter Education bill.
Sept. 15, 1983	John Bailey dies.
1983	The Exxon Valdez runs aground in Alaska's Prince William Sound.
1983	Tennessee sues North Carolina over excessive pollution in the Pigeon River and demands a more stringent discharge permit for Champion International's paper mill in Canton.
1983	The Department of Public Health is renamed the Department of Health and Environment. The Division of Water Quality Control is renamed the Division of Water Management. The Water Resources Division in the Department of Conservation merges with the new Water Management Division of the new TDHE.
1983	Tennessee passes a Safe Drinking Water Act.
1983	The Tennessee Hazardous Waste Remedial Action Fund creates the Tennessee Superfund program in the Division of Solid Waste.
1983	TVA creates the West State Eight erosion control project.
1983	Tennessee sets regulations for underground injection of hazardous waste.
1983	The Tennessee Soil Erosion and Wetlands Protection Study Committee convenes.
1983	TCL launches Project CENTS (Conservation Now for Tennessee Students) with support from the Safe Growth Team and TWRA.
1983	TCL begins another major overhaul of policies and structure; the Presidents Award is created to honor top performers.
July 10, 1984	Lou Williams dies at age 92.
1984	Congress passes the Dingell-Johnson Expansion Bill, placing a 3% excise tax on fishing boats and motors. Called the Wallop-Breaux Federal Aid to Sport Fish Restoration Act, it formally replaces Dingell-Johnson.
1984	TCL and TWRA jointly launch the Tennessee Deer Registry.
1984	TCL cohosts the Tennessee Manufacturers' Environmental Symposium.
May 1985	A settlement in the West Tennessee Tributaries lawsuit requires less destructive stream renovation methods. It also requires that the state acquire conservation easements along all affected miles of stream.
Nov. 7, 1985	TCL sues to overturn private raccoon acts as unconstitutional.

1985	The 1985 Food Security Act (Farm Bill) creates Swampbuster and Sodbuster, conservation reserve programs that deny federal subsidies to farmers who plant in erosive soils or wetlands.
1985	President Reagan names Lamar Alexander to chair the President's Commission on Americans Outdoors; Alexander appoints a Governor's Commission on Tennesseans Outdoors.
1985	The Tennessee-Tombigbee Waterway opens.
1985	EPA won't approve North Carolina's proposed NPDES permit for Champion's Canton paper mill; EPA assumes authority for issuing the permit.
1985	A proposed National Guard training facility near Fall Creek Falls is blocked by environmentalists and federal budget cuts.
1985	The U.S. Department of Energy proposes a temporary storage facility for nuclear waste (MRS) at Oak Ridge; citizens, legislators and members of Congress object.
1985	The federal Office of Surface Mining takes over Tennessee's surface mine regulatory program, citing poor enforcement and other weaknesses.
1985	The Division of Water Management in the Department of Health and Environment splits into the Division of Water Pollution Control and the Division of Water Supply.
1985	TWRA proposes to draw down Reelfoot Lake to improve the fishery; residents sue for an EIS.
1985	The Tennessee Rare Plant Protection and Conservation Act passes.
1985	TCL votes to support the ban on lead shot.
January 1986	Lamar Alexander introduces a Cleaner Highways program to restrict billboards, promote scenic routes and reduce litter; it does not pass.
May 1986	The North American Waterfowl Management Plan is signed by the United States and Canada in an effort to restore migratory waterfowl and habitat.
Aug. 20, 1986	TCL's suit against private raccoon acts is rejected.
1986	The Superfund Amendments and Reauthorization Act (SARA) requires industries to monitor and report their hazardous wastes. Provisions include an Emergency Planning and Community Right-to-Know Act and an annual Toxics Release Inventory made available to the public.
1986	The national Rails-to-Trails Conservancy is founded.
1986	The Tennessee Department of Health and Environment issues advisories against PCB-contaminated fish in East Tennessee.
1986	TWRA begins a small game habitat program.
1986	Two new seats are added to the Wildlife Resources Commission: the commissioner of Agriculture and an at-large citizen appointee.
1986	The Cherokee National Forest releases its management plan; a coalition led by the Sierra Club appeals. TCL supports the Forest Service.
1986	Tennessee passes the Wetlands Acquisition Act to buy threatened wetlands in Tennessee. Funds come from an increase in the real estate transfer tax.

1986	The Tennessee River Gorge Trust is chartered.
1986	TCL cohosts a Teacher Conservation Summit.
1986	TCL raises affiliate dues to $2.50 per member; individual dues are still $10.
1987	A reactor explosion at the Chernobyl nuclear plant in the Soviet Union focuses attention on global resource issues.
Dec. 23, 1988	Gov. Ned McWherter rejects a proposed water quality variance in EPA's draft permit for Champion's Canton paper mill.
1988	Ned McWherter forms the second Governor's Interagency Wetlands Task Force.
1988	Tennessee completes a management plan for controlling nonpoint sources of water pollution.
1988	A State Trails Council forms.
1988	Tennessee passes a Hazardous Waste Planning and Reduction Act.
Sept. 25, 1989	EPA issues a more restrictive NPDES permit to Champion International.
Aug. 31, 1989	TCL dedicates a memorial to Lou Williams on the North River, next to the memorial to Karl Steinmetz. It also creates the Lou Williams award
1989	EPA releases the first Toxics Release Inventory under SARA; Tennessee ranks second in volume of releases nationwide.
1989	The North American Wetlands Conservation Act is passed, implementing the North American Waterfowl Management Plan. Gary Myers is named to the NAWC council.
1989	The nation observes the first National Public Lands Day.
1989	Tennessee prohibits blasting into bedrock to lay septic tanks and field lines.
1989	A Perry County mill owner proposes a wood chip mill on the Tennessee River. TCL and the Sierra Club call for an environmental impact statement.
1989	TCL and TWRA call for a mussel severance tax to address the declining mussel populations in the Tennessee River.
1989	Tennessee approves an $11 increase in the current $10.00 combined license fee, to be phased in over the next seven years.
1989	Grassmere Wildlife Park begins construction.
1989	The Tennessee Solid Waste Roundtable proposes a 60% reduction in solid waste.
1989	TCL moves to 11 Music Circle, South.
1989	TCL urges the state to remove the agriculture and forestry exemptions from state water pollution laws.
1989	TCL's individual dues go to $15; club dues remain at $2.50 per member.
April 1990	TCL releases a Tennessee Environmental Quality Index, the first of four annual reports.
1990	The nation celebrates Earth Day 1990.
1990	Congress approves an amended Clean Air Act.

1990	President Bush declares "No Net Loss for Wetlands"; landowners complain.
1990	The Sierra Club and others challenge hunting and fishing on Catoosa WMA.
1990	Tennessee passes the Hazardous Waste Reduction Act, requiring most industries to reduce hazardous wastes by 25% in five years.
1990	The State Parks administration announces plans to build a privately run golf course at Roan Mountain; citizens object.
1990	Gov. Ned McWherter is honorary chairman of ReLeaf Tennessee, an Arbor Day activity to plant a million trees by the year 2000. TCL is a cosponsor.
1990	TCL joins a citizens' lawsuit to force a decision regarding Reelfoot Lake water level management. The proposed drawdown is eventually abandoned.
1990	TCL contracts with the Department of Health and Environment to produce educational materials on nonpoint source water pollution.
1990	TCL cosponsors an Environmental Media Symposium.
1990	TCL joins Partners in Flight, an international birds-and-biodiversity program.
Jan. 4, 1991	Pigeon River residents file a $5-billion class-action lawsuit against Champion. The suit ends in a mistrial. Champion pays $6.5 million to settle.
June 1991	TCL holds its last Youth Conservation Camp.
August 1991	TCL buys 300 Orlando Avenue for its Conservation Resource Center and offices.
1991	Tennessee's Comprehensive Solid Waste Management Act creates a Solid Waste Planning Committee.
1991	Tennessee levies a mussel export fee; revenues allow TWRA to expand its mussel program.
1991	The Tennessee State and Local Parks and Recreation Partnership Act adds 4¢ per $100 of value to the real estate transfer tax; the funds will be used to buy parks and other natural areas. A portion is designated for nonpoint source water pollution programs.
1991	The Tennessee Rivers Assessment Program in the Department of Conservation begins an inventory of environmental, recreational, scenic and other values of the state's rivers.
1991	TWRA establishes the Royal Blue Wildlife Management Area, using money from the Wetlands Acquisition Fund.
1991	The Tennessee Environmental Protection Fund Act increases environmental regulatory fees in an effort to hire more regulatory staff and enhance state permitting programs.
1991	Ned McWherter's reorganization bill merges the Tennessee Department of Conservation with the environmental programs in the Department of Health and Environment to create the Department of Environment and Conservation. The Division of Forestry moves to the Department of Agriculture.
1991	TCL establishes Hunters for the Hungry with TWRA.
1991	The Birds and Biodiversity project, a three-year study of Neotropical migrant songbirds and their habitat, begins; TCL is a cosponsor.
June 1992	The United Nations Conference on Environment and Development (the Earth Summit) is held in Rio de Janeiro.

| Dec. 2, 1992 | TCL receives a President's Environment and Conservation Challenge Award for Project CENTS. |

Dec. 2, 1992 — TCL receives a President's Environment and Conservation Challenge Award for Project CENTS.

Dec. 13, 1992 — Herman Baggenstoss dies at 88.

1992 — A lawsuit challenging "incompatible uses" of National Wildlife Refuges threatens hunting and fishing on refuges.

1992 — Tennessee Senator Al Gore publishes *Earth in the Balance*.

1992 — Gov. Ned McWherter convenes a West Tennessee Tributaries Task Force in an effort to resolve the disputes in the channelization project.

1992 — TCL contracts with the Tennessee Department of Transportation to evaluate TDOT's environmental performance.

1992 — TCL cancels its founding membership in the Tennessee Environmental Council, citing a difference of philosophies.

1992 — At his request, TCL names Tony Campbell executive vice president for conservation policy and begins looking for a new executive director.

March 1993 — A Division of Pollution Prevention and Environmental Awareness is created in the Department of Environment and Conservation.The Tennessee 2000 Initiative is initiated to improve Tennessee's environment by the year 2000.

May 15, 1993 — Ann P. Murray becomes the new executive director of TCL.

1993 — The first International Migratory Bird Day calls further attention to global habitat issues.

1993 — EPA denies permits for three chip mills on the Tennessee River near Chattanooga.

1993 — The Tennessee Aquarium opens in Chattanooga.

1993 — Tennessee passes a used oil recycling bill.

1993 — The Birds and Biodiversity project is extended to include a pilot study with Kentucky and Alabama.

1993 — TCL completes a major reorganization, including a two-level board structure, one for administration and one for conservation policy.

1993 — TCL cohosts a Natural Resource Dialogue at Henry Horton SP, with various agencies.

1993 — Tennessee creates a Watchable Wildlife Fund.

Sept. 23, 1994 — James L. Bailey, first employee of the Department of Conservation, dies at age 87.

1994 — The Wetlands Task Force completes its Tennessee Wetlands Conservation Strategy.

1994 — TWRA hosts the first annual "Outdoors Woman" workshop.

1994 — Project CENTS is renamed the Office of Conservation Education. Recycling and solid waste issues are added to the curriculum.

1994 — The Tennessee Environmental Audit Bill proposes that manufacturers and industries self-monitor their environmental compliance; the bill is defeated.

1994 — The Tennessee State Parks Foundation incorporates. A "purple iris" license plate begins selling for $25 a year to benefit state parks.

1994	TWRA introduces an "Eastern bluebird" license plate to support "watchable" wildlife.
1994	TCL cohosts a series of Watchable Wildlife workshops.
1994	TCL and Trout Unlimited sue over private fishing acts; the suit is defeated.
1994	The first NatureLink weekend for families replaces TCL's youth camps.
Mar. 31, 1995	Tony Campbell leaves TCL for the National Ecological Foundation.
Apr. 27, 1995	Tennessee's Air Pollution Control Divison agrees to share industrial air emissions data with the Department of Interior in an effort to improve air quality in the Smokies.
April 1995	The nation celebrates the 25th Anniversary of Earth Day.
1995	TVA begins divesting itself of Land Between the Lakes and other recreation projects.
1995	A proposed Wildlife Diversity Funding Initiative would place an excise tax on recreational equipment to fund nongame programs.
1995	Gov. Don Sundquist abolishes the State Planning Office. The Environmental Policy Group moves into the Department of Environment and Conservation.
1995	Tennessee adds two seats to the Wildlife Resources Commission, to be appointed by the speakers of the House and Senate.
Mar. 10, 1996	Lucius E. Burch, Jr., dies at 84.
May 2-4, 1996	TCL holds its 50th Anniversary Convention at the Read House, Chattanooga.
July 1996	The 1996 Olympics kayaking events are held on the Ocoee River.
December 1996	North Carolina issues a new NPDES permit for Champion's paper mill. The Tennessee Wildlife Resources Commission and Gov. Don Sundquist issue separate statements calling for stricter regulations.
1996	Tennessee cancels the Smokies air-pollution agreement; Gov. Sundquist names an advisory board to find another way to protect Smokies air quality.
1996	The West Tennessee Tributaries Task Force completes its mission plan, including two pilot demonstration projects. Gov. Dundquist pledges to have them both completed by the year 2000.
1996	Tennessee's Environmental Boards Bill adds a TCL appointee to the Water Quality Control Board and a TEC appointee to the Air Quality Control Board.
1996	The final phase of the seven-year license increase brings the combined license to $21.
Jan. 13, 1997	Tennessee Attorney General Charles Burson files a petition in North Carolina, asking that Champion's new NPDES permit and color variance be overturned.
January 1997	TVA chairman Craven Crowell announces his agency will not seek federal funding for its nonpower programs after 1999.
January 1997	TCL opens the Lucius E. Burch Center for Conservation Planning.

SOURCES

"Acclaimed Defense Lawyer Presents Burch Lecture." *Vanderbilt Register*. Mar. 25-31, 1996: 3.

Akers, J. Clark, III. Telephone interview. Jan. 8, 1997.

Alderson, William T. "Legislative History of State's Game, Fish Set-Up." *The Tennessee Conservationist*. July 1955: 17-18.

Allison, Sue. "Governor Sidesteps Environmental Questions." *Elizabethton Star*. Apr. 20, 1990.

Amann, Walter, Jr. Editorial. *The Knoxville Journal*. Mar. 5, 1953: 6.

———. "House Group Refuses Hearings for Sportsmen." *The Knoxville Journal*. Mar.1, 1953: 5B.

———. "Outdoors Around Here." *The Knoxville Journal*. Mar. 1, 1953: A1-A2.

———. "Outdoors Around Here." *The Knoxville Journal*. Mar. 4, 1953: 3.

———. "Outdoors Around Here." *The Knoxville Journal*. Mar. 15, 1953: 5B.

———. "Outdoors Around Here." *The Knoxville Journal*. Mar. 20, 1953: 1.

———. "Outdoors Around Here." *The Knoxville Journal*. Mar. 23, 1953: 5B.

———. "Sportsmen Reach Compromise." *The Knoxville Journal*. Mar. 4, 1953: 3.

Anderson, Frederic R. *NEPA in the Courts: A Legal Analysis of the National Environmental Policy Act*. Washington, D.C.: Resources for the Future, 1973.

Anderson, Sam. "Tennessee Conservation League." *The Weakley County Press*. Oct. 4, 1990.

———. "Tennessee Conservation League." *The Weakley County Press*. Oct. 16, 1990.

———. "Tennessee Conservation League." *The Weakley County Press*. Nov. 20, 1990.

Asbury, Lee. "Where Do We Go From Here?" *Tennessee Out-Of-Doors*. Aug-Sept. 1996: 1, 3.

Baggenstoss, Herman. "Baggenstoss Resigns Post on Conservation Commission." News release. Apr. 2, 1953.

———. "Challenge to Conservationists." *Tennessee Wildlife*. Feb. 1937: 6.

———. "General Wild Life Federation." *Tennessee Wildlife*. Mar. 1937: 5.

———. "Governor Browning's Law Creating the Department of Conservation." *The Tennessee Conservationist*. Mar. 1937: 8.

———. "New Commission Is Well Balanced." *Tennessee Wildlife*. June 1939: 12.

———. "$100,000 Loss." *Tennessee Wildlife*. Apr. 1939: 2.

———. "Printed Annual Report by the Department of Conservation." News release. 25 Sept. 1939.

———. "Turkey Feathers, Boar Bristles and Fish Fins." Newsletter. Dec. 1936.

———. "Where to Now?" *Tennessee Wildlife*. Dec. 1938: 15.

Bailey, John H. "Conservation Workshop." *The Tennessee Conservationist*. Jan. 1955: 6.

———. Letter to V. H. Jernigan. June 10, 1963.

Baird, William. D. Letter to Thomas Kimball. July 16, 1973.

Ball, Marc W. Letter to Tony Campbell. May 28, 1975.

Bartlett, Richard A. *Troubled Waters: Champion International and the Pigeon River Controversy*. Knoxville: University of Tennessee Press, 1995.

Belanger, Dian Olson. *Managing America's Wildlife: A History of the International Association of Fish and Wildlife Agencies*. Amherst: University of Massachusetts Press, 1988.

Bender, Penny. "TVA Tries Forgoing Funding to Save Itself." *The Tennessean*. Jan. 26, 1997: 1B, 6B.

Bolton, Carl O. "Adios, Little T." *Tennessee Out-Of-Doors*. Sept. 1974: 12.

Bowditch, Deborah J. "Land and Water Conservation Fund Turns 25." *The Tennessee Conservationist*. July-Aug, 1990: 21-23.

Bowen, Brian. "Natural Areas Turn 25." *The Tennessee Conservationist*. May-June, 1996: 12-14.

Bowers, Larry. Telephone interview. Jan. 17, 1997.

Branham, Lowell. "Losing Raccoon Hunting Battle Won't Stop Conservation League." *The Knoxville News-Sentinel*. Aug. 22, 1986: 2C.

Branstetter, Cecil D. Telephone interview. Mar. 12, 1996.

Brewster, Sam. "Commissioner's Message." *Tennessee Wildlife*. Apr. 1937: 8-9.

Burch, Lucius, Jr. Letter to the Editor. *The Tennessee Conservationist*. Jan-Feb., 1985: 22.

———. Letter to Tony Campbell. Sept. 2, 1975.

———. Letter to Travis McNatt. Feb. 22, 1974.

Burns, Robert. Letters to Tony Campbell. 1972-1992.

———. Personal interview. Dec. 12, 1995.

Cadieux, Charles L. "Wilderness West-Wilderness East." *Better Camping*. Mar. 1974. Reprinted in *Tennessee Out-Of-Doors*. July 1974: 2-3.

Caldwell, John C. "Education and Publicity in Conservation." *Tennessee Wildlife*. Mar. 1937: 6.

———. "Public Stench Number One." *Tennessee Wildlife*. May 1937: 7, 15.

———. "Slants on the Deer Situation." *Tennessee Wildlife*. Jan 1938: 5,9.

———. "Taking Conservation to the Schools." *Tennessee Wildlife*. Dec. 1938: 5.

Campbell, Anthony J., William R. Miller, Ruth Neff, Larry R. Richardson and Edward L. Thackston. *Environmental Risk: How Are We Coping With It? 1993 Tennessee Environmental Quality Index*. Nashville, TN.: Tennessee Conservation League: 1993.

Campbell, Tony. Letter to M. L. Brickey. Mar. 14, 1972.

———. Letter to Lucius Burch. June 5, 1973.

———. Letter to Lucius Burch. Sept. 23, 1975.

———. Letter to Federal Communications Commission. Oct. 6, 1975.

———. Letter to Bill Jay. Oct. 29, 1975.

———. Letter to Bill Leonard. Sept. 15, 1975.

———. Letter to Arthur Owens. Nov. 7, 1975.

———. Letter to Paul Schmierbach, TVA. Aug. 18, 1992.

———. Personal interview. Jan. 15, 1996.

Carson, Rachel. *Silent Spring*. Boston: Houghton Mifflin, 1962.

Casey, K. Letter to Jacob M. Dickinson. Aug. 1, 1927. Jacob McGavock Dickinson Papers. Tennessee State Library and Archives.

Clapper, Louis S. "Wildlife Hardest Hit Resource, Climbs Back Toward Restoration." *The Tennessee Conservationist*. Feb.-Mar. 1950: 13-14.

———. "NWF's Influence on Congress: Outright Lobbying Was Illegal." *The Leader*. Feb. 1986: 19-20.

———. "Outdoors in Tennessee." *The Tennessee Conservationist*. Oct. 1955: 22.

Clement, Frank. "Governor Calls for Unified Program of All Conservation Divisions." *The Tennessee*

Conservationist. May 1953: 3, 22.

Cobb, Eugene. "Fishery Resources of West Tennessee." *The Tennessee Conservationist.* Nov. 1955: 8-9.

Cochran, John. "Chip Mills Raise Storm of Controversy." *The Jackson Sun.* Oct. 6, 1991.

Coleman, Bevley R. "A History of State Parks in Tennessee." Unpublished dissertation, George Peabody College for Teachers. August 1963. Reproduced by Education Service, Tennessee Department of Conservation. Nashville: 1968.

"Conservation Hall of Fame: Robert Adams Wilson." *Tennessee Wildlife.* Oct.-Nov. 1937: 7.

"Conservation League." *The Chattanooga Times.* 20 Feb. 1946.

"Conservationists Meet Here in 1952." *The Chattanooga Times.* 10 Feb. 1951.

Culberson, C. Ron. Telephone interview. Jan. 16, 1997.

Dabney, O. L. Letter to Earl Bentz. Copied to members of the Tennessee Wildlife Resources Commission. Oct. 16, 1995.

Darling, J. N. "Mr. Ding Goes to Town." *Tennessee Wildlife.* Mar. 1938: 8-9, 21.

Darnell, Denny. "Sportsmen, Blanton Fueding [sic] Over Water Control Board Appointment." *Kingsport News.* July 26, 1978: 3B.

Dickinson, Jacob M. Speech to the annual convention of the Izaak Walton League of America. June 28, 1927. Jacob McGavock Dickinson Papers. Tennessee State Library and Archives.

Donelson, John. *Donelson's Voyage.* Ed. Hugh Walker. Nashville, TN: *The Tennessean,* 1980.

Dow, Sumner. "Trophy Buck." *The Tennessee Conservationist.* Nov. 1960: 3-6.

Dudney, Lester R., ed. "Objectives and Membership Study for the Chairman of the Evaluation Committee, Tennessee Conservation League." Unpublished report. Spring 1971.

Dunn, Winfield. Letter to Thomas Kimball. May 18, 1973.

"Early Days." *North Dakota Outdoors.* Feb.-Nov. 1989.

East, Jim. "Big Business, Big Polluter." *The Tennessean.* Oct. 25, 1992. 6A.

——."Company Invests in Costly Cleanup." *The Tennessean.* Oct. 25, 1992. 6A.

Editorial. *The Chattanooga Times.* Feb. 20, 1946.

Editorial. *The Knoxville Journal.* Feb. 10, 1946.

Editorial. *Memphis Press-Scimitar.* Mar. 1, 1939: 1.

Fairleigh, Paul. "President Meeman Launches $500,000 Sustaining Membership Campaign." *Tennessee Wildlife.* June 1938: 15.

Farrell, R. P. "The Stream Pollution Problem in Tennessee. *Proceedings of the Fourth Annual Convention.* Tennessee Conservation League. Feb. 24-25, 1950: 21-24.

Ford, Bob. "Transformation of Sportsman Is Hurting Us." *Tennessee Out-of-Doors.* Nov.-Dec. 1990: 5.

Fox, David. "Water Panel Appointee May Be Challenged." *Nashville Banner.* July 10, 1978.

Fulcher, Bob. "Authors, Shepherds and Ramrods." *Tennessee Conservationist.* May-June, 1996. 9.

Galletta, Jan. "Where the Wild Things Are." *Chattanooga Free Press.* May 22, 1995: C1.

"Game and Fish Changes Urged in State." *The Tennessean.* May 26, 1971.

"Game and Fish Commission Has Short Period of Grace." Editorial. *The Tennessean.* May 27, 1971: 12.

Gooch, Bob. "The Voices of Wildlife." *Virginia Wildlife.* June 1992: 16.

Goodrich, David. Letter to Edgar Evins. Aug. 16, 1973.

Gottschalk, John S. "A Revolution in Fisheries Management." *The Leader.* Feb. 1986: 15-16.

Graber, Dean. "Proposed Mill Stirs Debate." *Nashville Banner.* Mar. 19, 1990: B1, B3.

Grant, John H., Jr. "An Exposition of Consequence." *Tennessee Conservationist.* Sept.-Oct. 1977: 22-24.

Gray, Gary G. *Wildlife and People: The Human Dimensions of Wildlife Ecology.* Urbana and Chicago: University of Illinois Press, 1993.

Grinnell, George Bird. Editorial. *Forest and Stream*. Feb. 3, 1894: 1.

———. Editorial. *Forest and Stream*. Feb. 11, 1886.

Griswold, Bill. Telephone interview. Dec. 13, 1996.

The Guide. Tennessee Game and Fish Commission newsletter. Aug. 1972.

Halburnt, Joseph. Personal interview. Jan. 17, 1977.

Hall, Hurat C. "Old Diary Described Reelfoot Lake 100 Years Ago." *The Tennessee Conservationist*. Mar. 1954: 8-9, 23.

Harris, Ed. "Paradise for Tennessee Sportsmen Envisioned." *The Knoxville Journal*. Apr. 24, 1949.

Harris, Harold. "Freeing Conservation Dept. From Political Influence Need Not Be Long-Term Project, Nash Buckingham Tells Newly Formed League." *The Knoxville News-Sentinel*. Feb. 17, 1946: B2.

Hatcher, Robert M. "Viewpoint: The Tellico Dam Project." *Tennessee Wildlife*. Mar.-Apr. 1979: 22-23.

Hay, W. M. "Tennessee's First Private Forest Preserve Is Established." *Tennessee Wildlife*. Feb. 1938: 11.

Hebestreet, Kristen. "NAR Ranked No. 2 on Tennessee List of Toxic Releases." *Johnson City Press*. Apr. 4, 1992: 1, 10.

———. "Power Bills May Rise With Lake." *Johnson City Press*. Feb. 13, 1990: 3.

———. "TCL Head Plans to Spread Word." *Johnson City Press*. July 18, 1993.

Hendrix, Charles. "Multiple Use of Wetlands." *The Tennessee Conservationist*. July 1959: 10-11.

Herndon, Paul. "This Wild Land Yesteryear." *The Tennessee Conservationist*. Dec. 1960: 12-14.

Hiles, Bill. "Basin Authority to Defy Order." *Dyersburg Gazette*. Oct. 10, 1990: 1.

Hines, Robert S. Letter to Tony Campbell. Sept. 24, 1975.

Hines, Tommy. "Tennessee's Foreign Game Bird Program." *The Tennessee Conservationist*. Nov. 1970: 5.

Hodge, Betsy and Jacquelyn Bonomo. "A Half Century of National Wildlife Federation History 1936–1986." *The Leader*. Feb. 1986: 6-10.

Hornaday, William T. *Our Vanishing Wild Life: Its Extermination and Preservation*. New York: Charles Scribner's Sons, 1931.

Horstik, Catherine K. "Michigan's Conservation Story: The Early Days." *Michigan Natural Resources Magazine*. May-June 1987: 48.

Houk, Dusty. "Mayland Muse." *Morristown Daily Gazzette-Mail*. Mar. 7, 1965.

House, S. John. "What Do You Think?" *Tennessee Wildlife*. Mar. 1937: 9.

"How to Form a Sportsman's Club." *Outdoor Life*. 1946.

Hurst, W. R. "New Lease for Reelfoot." *The Tennessee Conservationist*. Sept. 1969: 4-5.

Hutchison, Turner. "Legislature Passes Wetlands Acquisition Act." *Nashville Banner*. Apr. 10, 1986.

———. "Wildlife Project Makes CENTS." *The Tennessean*. Mar. 7, 1985.

International Association of Game, Fish and Conservation Commissioners. *Proceedings of the 16th Convention*. Unpublished proceedings. 1922.

———. *Proceedings of the 28th Convention*. Unpublished proceedings. 1934.

"Izaak Walton League Members With Truck of Young Trout for Middle Tennessee Streams." *Nashville Banner*. Mar. 25, 1932.

Izaak Walton League of America. *Expansion Program Bulletin #1*. June 9, 1927.

Jernigan, V. H. *History of the Tennessee Outdoor Writers Association 1942-1990*. Manchester, TN: Self-published.

———. "Hook, Line and Sinker." *Manchester Times*. Sept. 10, 1965: 4A.

———. "Hook, Line and Sinker." *Manchester Times*. Dec. 15, 1967: 6A.

———. "Outdoors." *Manchester Times*. Sept. 11, 1975.

———. Letter to E. W. Means. June 5, 1963.

Jiran, John. "A Program to Reclaim Orphan Mines." *The Tennessee Conservationist*. Oct. 1976: 14-15.

Johnson, Dennis A. "A Unification of Purpose." *The Leader*. Feb. 1986: 2.

Johnson, Ellen B., and Robert M. Conley. "Strip Mining in Tennessee." *The Tennessee Conservationist*. Nov.-Dec. 1977: 2-7.

Jones, Keith. "Mussels Have Been Important Resource for Centuries." *Tennessee Out-Of-Doors*. Jan-Feb., 1990: 9, 11.

Jones, S. Leary. "Stream Pollution Control Progress Report." *The Tennessee Conservationist*. Feb. 1958: 16.

Kaufmann, Betsy. "The Koppers: Diverse Interests Covet Scarred Acreage." *The Knoxville News Sentinel*. May 19, 1991: B1, B4.

Keller, Ernie. "Want More Industry? That Is Everybody's Joint Job." *The Tennessee Conservationist*. July 1961: 5, 19.

Kelly, Edwin R. Letter to Sen. Anna Belle Clement O'Brien. Oct. 17, 1983.

Kentucky Department of Fish and Wildlife Resources. "Kentucky's Department of Fish and Wildlife Resources History." Unpublished essay. n.d.

Killebrew, Joseph B. *Introduction to the Resources of Tennessee*. Nashville, 1874.

Kimball, Thomas L. "NWF During an Era of Change: The 1960s and 1970s Revisited." *The Leader*. Feb. 1986: 17-18.

Kirk, Don. "Outdoors Between the Lakes." *Citizen Tribune*. Nov. 17, 1985: 7B.

Knauth, Carol. Letter to Tony Campbell. Feb. 23, 1974 .

Knox, George C., Jr. Letter to Gordon P. Street, Jr. Dec. 18, 1973.

Kosack, Joe. *The Pennsylvania Game Commission 1895-1995: 100 Years of Wildlife Conservation*. Harrisburg: Pennsylvania Game Commission, 1995.

Kovalic, Joan M., and Alyson Hennelly, eds. *The Clean Water Act of 1987*. Alexandria, Va.: Water Pollution Control Federation, 1987.

Kuhne, Eugene R. "Your State, Your Streams, Your Sacrifice." *Tennessee Wildlife*. Jan. 1939: 7.

"Lands Unsuitable for Mining." *The Tennessee Conservationist*. July-Aug. 1979: iii.

Lendt, David L. "Ding Darling: The Extraordinary Apostle of a New Conservation Era." *The Leader*. Feb. 1986: 3-5.

"Local Farmers Prepare for Nashville Lawsuit." *The Dyersburg Mirror*. Aug. 6, 1970. 7A.

Locker, Mary, and Catherine Elick. "The Turbulent Past of Reelfoot Lake." *The Tennessee Conservationist*. May-June, 1987: 17-20.

Locker, Richard. "Channelization Becomes Major Issue in Tennessee." *The Commercial Appeal*. Feb. 28, 1990.

Loggins, Kirk. "Raccoon Population Called Thin." *The Tennessean*. June 4, 1986: 1B-2B.

———. "Raccoons Not Endangered, Two Wildlife Officials Testify." *The Tennessean*. June 5, 1986: 1B.

Luther, Ardi. "A Giant Green Band-Aid?" *The Tennessee Conservationist*. Apr. 1973: 2-4.

Maddux, Jared. Letter to Herman Baggenstoss. Feb. 8, 1963.

———. Letter to Herman Baggenstoss. Feb. 14, 1963.

Manning, Russ. "The Overton Park Controversy." *The Tennessee Conservationist*. Jan.-Feb. 1978: 15-17.

———. "Wilderness in the Cherokee: A Long But Successful Effort." *The Tennessee Conservationist*. Nov.-Dec. 1987: 15-19.

Mansur, Michael. "Draining Basins and Billboards." *The Commercial Appeal*. Mar. 4, 1984: 1H.

Marsh, Al. "Game-Fish Chiefs Rise and Fall." Letter to the Editor. *Nashville Banner*. Sept. 24, 1973.

Marsh, George Perkins. *Man and Nature*. 1864.

Mayfield, George. "Conservation Achievements." *The Tennessee Conservationist*. Nov.-Dec. 1948: 4-10.

McCormick, Marge. "The Conservation Teachings of Jim Bailey." *The Tennessee Conservationist*. May-June 1987: 2-5.

——. "Earth Day 1970: A 25th-Year Retrospective." *The Tennessee Conservationist*. Mar.-Apr. 1995: 20-27.

——. "Herman Baggenstoss: Man of Epic Proportions." *The Tennessee Conservationist*. Sept-Oct 1986: 3-5.

McCoy, Richard. "Deep Well Coverage Inadequate." *Waverly News-Democrat*. Oct. 30, 1992.

Means, E. W. "Banner's Fins, Furs, Feathers First Outdoor Column in U.S." *The Tennessee Conservationist*. Feb. 1964: 14-15.

——. "History of the Tennessee Conservation League." *The Tennessee Conservationist*. Mar. 1971: 1-5.

——. "The TTA and Tennessee Trails." *The Tennessee Conservationist*. Mar. 1972: 7-11.

Melton, Ted K. "Getting Turned on to Conservation." *The Tennessee Conservationist*. Mar 1975: 1921.

Michigan United Conservation Clubs. News release. Sept. 9, 1975.

Michigan's Conservation Story. *Michigan Natural Resources Magazine*. May-June 1987.

Mississippi River Commission. Public Hearing. Statements by James P. Smith, Richard Swaim, Travis McNatt and Willis E. Montgomery. May 12, 1970.

"More Air Pollution Data Needed From Industries, TCL Says." *Greeneville Sun*. Apr. 9, 1992: A10.

"Mr. Lucius Burch, Jr." Editorial. *The Tennessean*. Mar. 15, 1996: 16A.

Muir, John. *Our National Parks*. Boston: Houghton Mifflin, 1901.

Murray, Doug. Letter to the Editor. *The LaFollette Press*. Feb. 23, 1995.

Murray, William H, H. *Adventures in the Wilderness*. Boston: 1869.

Musick, Helen. "Fish and Game from the Beginning." *New Jersey Outdoors*. July-Aug 1974: 10-11.

Myers, Gary. Personal interview. Feb. 1, 1996.

Nashville Sportsman's Club. "50th Anniversary Celebration: The Nashville Sportsman's Club, Inc." Brochure. November 1995.

"NWF Embraced Bowlegged Girl 40 Years Ago: Now Nation's Biggest Conservation Group." *Tennessee Out-Of-Doors*. April 1976: 2.

Neff, Ruth. "An Approach to Land-use Planning." *The Tennessee Conservationist*. June 1976: 4-5.

——. "Land Use In Conflict." *The Tennessee Conservationist*. Mar. 1974: 18-19.

——. Personal interview. Nov. 18, 1996.

Norris, Ray. Telephone interview. Jan. 20, 1997.

"Obion-Forked Deer Basin Authority." *Tennessee Sportsman*. Feb. 1975: 19.

O'Bleness, Gene. "Legislators See Tough Time for Strip Mine Law Unless Citizens Support." *The Oak Ridger*. Feb. 10, 1967: 1, 9.

100 Years of Wildlife Law Enforcement. *South Dakota Conservation Digest*. July-Aug. 1993.

"110 Years of Fish and Game History." *Outdoor California*. July-Aug. 1990: 31-34.

"Organization News of the Tennessee Federation of Sportsmen." Nashville, TN: June 1936.

Our American Game Birds. Paintings by Lynn Bogue Hunt. Ed. Edward Howe Forbush. Wilmington, Del.: E. I. DuPont de Nemours, 1917.

Overall, Park. Letter to the Editor. *The LaFollette Press*. Mar. 2, 1995.

Owens, Geoff. "A Lesson to Be Learned." *The Tennessee Conservationist*. Nov-Dec 1979: 6-7.

Page, Charles R., Jr. "Herman E. Baggenstoss." *Forest Farmer*. Oct. 1960.

Patten, Cartter. *Signal Mountain and Walden's [sic] Ridge*. n.p.: 1972.

Paine, Anne. "Environmental Groups Fear Champion Plans to Clearcut." *The Tennessean*. June 2, 1994: 1B, 6B.

——. "Is Plateau's Beauty Suitable for Mining?" *The Tennessean.* Aug. 5, 1996: 1B-2B.

——. "State Hits Itself with $150,000 Fine." *The Tennessean.* Nov. 21, 1992: 1B-2B.

——. "TWRA Won't Have to Rent Own Facility; Due $600,000." *The Tennessean.* Jan. 6, 1991: 8B.

——. "Venison Program Helps With State's Food Banks." *The Tennessean.* May 5, 1991: 14C.

Peterson, Carl I. "Everybody's Responsibility." *The Tennessee Conservationist.* May 1953: 6-7.

——. "Skill and Equipment Saved Tennessee Woods from Destruction by Fire in 1953." *The Tennessee Conservationist.* Feb. 1954: 8-9, 22.

Petit, Ged. "Get the Lead Out." *Tennessee Wildlife.* Nov.-Dec. 1978: 15-18.

Pettijohn, Etta. "Striped Bass Wrapped in Controversy, Politics." *Clinton Courier-News.* Dec. 18, 1995: C1.

Pfeiffer, C. Boyd. "CBS Hunting Documentary An Exercise in Media Bias." *The Washington Post.* Sept. 9, 1975: D1.

Pollock, C. Wayne, and Gedeon D. Petit. Letter to John Bailey. Oct. 6, 1972.

Prichard, Mack. "Scenic Rivers, Worth Preserving." *The Tennessee Conservationist.* Mar 1975: 16-18.

——. Telephone interview. Dec. 11, 1996.

"Public Deserves Voice in Game and Fish. *The Nashville Tennessean.* Mar. 26, 1973.

Ramsey, J. G. M. *Annals of Tennessee.* Kingsport, TN: Kingsport Press, 1853.

Rea, Larry. "Hunters Give Meat to Help Feed Hungry." *The Commercial Appeal.* Oct. 18, 1994.

——. "New Regulations Hinder Flow of Deer Meat to the Hungry." *The Commercial Appeal.* Oct. 16, 1994.

Reed, Mary S. "Officials to Discuss Flap Over Funds." *The Jackson Sun.* Jan. 3, 1991.

Reed, Nathaniel P. and Dennis Drabelle. *The United States Fish and Wildlife Service.* Boulder, Colo.: Westview Press, 1984.

Reiger, John F. *American Sportsmen and the Origins of Conservation.* New York: Winchester Press, 1975.

Richardson, Larry M. Personal interview. Dec. 5, 1996.

Ricketson, Greer. Letter to Dr. Benjamin Carmichael. Dec. 12, 1972.

——. Telephone interview. May 15, 1996.

Ritchie, L. Carol. "Eco-Groups Politely Disagree." *Nashville Banner.* May 25, 1991: B1.

——. "Group Says 'Green Index' Flawed." *Nashville Banner.* Oct. 30, 1991: B3.

——. "State Pollution Agency To Attack 'Toxic' Image." *Nashville Banner.* Mar. 11, 1993.

Rogers, Joe. "Park Growth Plan A 'Dream Come True.'" *The Tennessean.* Jan. 4, 1997: 1A-2A.

Rogers, Tom. "Return of Eagle Verified." *The Tennessean.* July 26, 1984: 2E.

Roosevelt, Franklin D. Telegram to Jacob M. Dickinson. 28 June 1927. Jacob McGavock Dickinson Papers. Tennessee State Library and Archives.

"Salute to a Pioneer: Albert F. Ganier." *The Tennessee Conservationist.* Oct.-Nov. 1972: 6-7.

Schutt, Peter. "Lawsuits Fruitful for Tennessee Rivers." *The Daily News.* Nov. 1, 1995: 2.

Sherry, Dan. "Fish Kills: The Tip of an Iceberg." *The Tennessee Conservationist.* Apr. 1973: 12-14.

Simms, Robert. Letter to John Bailey. July 1972.

Smith, Gene and Joe Watkins. "Fish Dragged Into Politics." *The Tennessee Conservationist.* July-Aug. 1948: 3.

Smith, Lee. "Politics and Water Quality." *Kingsport Times.* July 24, 1978: 8B.

"State Opens Road To the Sky. *The Tennessean.* Oct. 11, 1996: 5B.

Steber, Bob. "Headwaters 'N Tailfeathers." *The Nashville Tennessean.* Mar. 17, 1969: 7E.

——. "Hikers vs. Hunters." *The Nashville Tennessean.* Jan. 23, 1973.

———. "Investigating Team Takes Look at Game and Fish." *The Nashville Tennessean.* July 31, 1973: 38.

———. "TCL Is Challenged." *The Nashville Tennessean.* Feb. 6, 1972.

"Steinmetz Given Patten Award; Browning Honored." *The Chattanooga Times.* Apr. 24, 1949.

Steinmetz, Karl. "Sport Talk." *The Knoxville News-Sentinel.* Feb. 16, 1936.

Stewart, Bob. "TSA Continues To Complain About Stripers." *Bristol Herald Courier.* Nov. 11, 1995: 1C.

"Story of Conservation." *The Tennessee Conservationist.* Jan.-Feb. 1950: 4-5.

Sullivan, Nick. "Conservation Called Reagan Hostage." *The Tennessean.* Mar. 28, 1982: 8C.

———. "Obion-Forked Deer Lawsuits Settled." *The Tennessean.* May 12, 1985: 15B.

———. "Society for Buckingham Forms." *The Tennessean.* Sept. 12, 1982: 10C.

Summerlin, Vernon. "Association Misleading About TWRA." *Ashland City Times.* Nov. 16, 1994.

"Surface Mining Act—1972." *The Tennessee Conservationist.* Apr. 1972: 10-16.

"Surface Mining Legislation Proposed." *The Tennessee Conservationist.* Sept.-Oct. 1979: vi.

"Surface Mining Regulations: The State-Federal Interface." *The Tennessee Conservationist.* Nov.-Dec. 1978: vi.

Survey of State Forestry Administration in Tennessee. Society of American Foresters and the Charles Lathrop Pack Forestry Foundation. 1947.

Swan, Susan. "A 50-Year Record of the Country's Major Environmental Legislation." *The Leader.* Feb. 1986: 20-22.

"TCL Breaking Tradition, Names Murray Director." *The Tennessean.* July 18, 1993.

"Tayloe Resigns; Seasons Set." *The Tennessee Conservationist.* July-Aug. 1949: 4.

Taylor, Mayo, ed. "Wilderness at Last: A Tennessee Time Line. *The Tennessee Conservationist.* July-Aug 1985: 16-17.

Tennessee. Comptroller of the Treasury. Department of Audit. Division of State Audit. *Program Evaluation on the Obion-Forked Deer Basin Authority.* William R. Snodgrass, ed. Sept. 1979.

———. Department of Conservation. *Natural Resources of Tennessee: A Report of the Department of Conservation for Fiscal Year Ending June 30, 1942.* Nashville: 1943.

———. Department of Conservation. Division of Forestry. *Biennial Report.* Nashville: 1952.

———. Department of Conservation. Division of Forestry. *Biennial Report.* Nashville: 1960.

———. Department of Conservation. Division of Water Resources. Surface Water Committee. "Tennessee Water Resources." Nashville, TN: April 1961. Reprinted as a series in *The Tennessee Conservationist.* Part. 1 (Climate). Sept 1961: 10-16. Part II (Surface Water). Oct. 1961: 22-27. Part III (Ground Water). Dec. 1961: 17-23.

———. Department of Environment and Conservation. *Tennessee's Environment: 25 Years of Progress.* Nashville: 1995.

———. Department of Environment and Conservation. Division of Water Quality Control. "History of the Division of Water Quality Control." Garland Wiggins, ed. Nashville: 1992.

———. Game and Fish Commission. (Tennessee Wildlife Resources Agency.) Annual Reports. 1949-1993.

———. Game and Fish Commission. *Progress Report 1949-1959. A Study of the Expansion of Services to Sportsmen in Relation to Budget and Need.* Nashville: 1959.

———. Game and Fish Commission. *Statewide Wildlife Survey of Tennessee: A Study of the Land, Wildlife, Farmer, Hunter and Trapper.* Ed. Vincent Schultz et al. Nashville: 1954.

———. Governor's Interagency Wetlands Committee and Technical Working Group. *Tennessee Wetlands Conservation Strategy.* Second Edition: *Current Progress and Continuing Goals.* Nashville: 1996.

———. State Planning Office. Natural Resources Section. *Critical Environmental Areas in Tennessee.* Vol. III:*Wetlands in West Tennessee.* Jan. 1978.

———. Wildlife Resources Agency. Region I. *Reelfoot Lake: An Assessment for Water Level Management.* Jackson: Apr. 1985.

———. Tennessee Wildlife Resources Commission. *Tennessee Wildlife,* various issues, 1975-.

Tennessee Conservation League. *Tennessee Out-Of-Doors.* All issues. Aug. 1973-Jan.-Feb., 1997.

———. Unpublished minutes of meetings. 1946–1996.

Tennessee Conservation League v. W. J. Michael Cody, et al. Tennessee Supreme Court document. Sept. 21, 1987.

"Tennessee Forest Fires of Last Fall Show Need for Additional Protection." *The Tennessee Conservationist.* Jan. 1953: 15-19.

"Tennessee Is Focus of National Spotlight for Biodiversity." *Wildlife Advocate.* Fall 1993.

"Tennessee Preparing for Second Annual Wildlife Restoration Week." *Tennessee Wildlife.* Feb. 1939: 4.

Tennessee Valley Sportsman. Ed. Joe Halburnt. June 1946.

"Tennessee Wild Rivers." *The Tennessee Conservationist.* July 1968: 16-17.

"Tennessee's Game Restoration Program." *Tennessee Wildlife.* Mar. 1938: 6.

Thackston, Edward L. Personal interviews. Nov. 17, 1996; Dec. 5, 1996.

Thackston, Edward L., and Gary Davis. *Gaps, Conflicts, Overlaps, and Inconsistencies in Tennessee's Environmental Laws and Regulations.* Tennessee Water Resources Research Center. Research Report No. 110. Knoxville: University of Tennessee. Sept. 1985.

Thackston, Edward L., William R. Miller and Daryl Durham. *Checking Our Progress: Tennessee Environmental Quality Index—1991.* Nashville, TN.: Tennessee Conservation League, 1991.

Thackston, Edward L., William R. Miller, Daryl Durham and Larry R. Richardson. *How Are We Doing? Tennessee Environmental Quality Index 1970-1990.* Nashville, TN.: Tennessee Conservation League, 1990.

Thackston, Edward L., William R. Miller, Daryl Durham and Robert P. Ford. *1992 Tennessee Environmental Quality Index.* Nashville, TN.: Tennessee Conservation League, 1992.

Thomas, Matt G. "Why, the Tennessee Federation of Sportsmen?" *Organization News of the Tennessee Federation of Sportsmen.* Newsletter. Nashville: June 1936: 1-3.

Thompson, Jerry. "Game and Fish Commission Practices Invite Criticism." *The Nashville Tennessean.* Mar. 14, 1971: 1B, 3B.

"Timanus Out—Now, Let's Have Real Representation." *The Jackson Sun.* Oct. 1978.

"Toxic List Includes Three Area industries." *The Daily Post-Athenian.* Aug. 11, 1989: 1-2.

Travis, Fred. "Raccoon Laws Challenged." *Johnson City Press.* June 5, 1986.

Trefethen, James B. *Crusade for Wildlife: Highlights in Conservation Progress.* Harrisburg, PA: Stackpole Co. and New York: Boone and Crockett Club, 1961.

Turner, Tom S. "Honor For Williams Ensures Friends Enjoy Favorite Spot." *Chattanooga News-Free Press.* Sept. 1, 1989: B3.

Udall, Stewart. *The Quiet Crisis.* New York: Holt, Rinehart and Winston, 1963.

Underwood, Evelyn. "Why the Huntress?" *The Tennessee Conservationist.* Dec. 1968: 4-7.

United States. Interagency Wetlands Task Force. *Our Nation's Wetlands.* Washington, D.C., 1978.

———. Department of Interior, Fish and Wildlife Service, and Department of Commerce, Bureau of the Census. *1991 National Survey of Fishing, Hunting and Wildlife-Associated Recreation—Tennessee.* Washington, D.C.: U.S. Government Printing Office, 1993.

———. Environmental Protection Agency. Office of Pollution Prevention and Toxics. *1994 Toxics Release Inventory.* Executive Summary. Washington, D.C., 1996.

———. Tennessee Valley Authority. *The First Fifty Years: Changed Lands, Changed Lives. State-of-the-Environment in the Tennessee Valley 1933-1983.* D. M. McCarthy, and C. W. Voigtlander. 1983.

Urban, Richard. Telephone interview. Jan. 25, 1997.

Vanderwood, Paul J. *Night Riders of Reelfoot Lake*. Memphis: Memphis State University Press, 1969.

Venable, Sam, Jr. "'Exotic' Wildlife Bill Opens Stream of Controversy." *The Knoxville News-Sentinel*. Feb. 21, 1974: 30.

———. Personal interview. Jan. 27, 1996.

———. "Poor Timing." *The Knoxville News-Sentinel*. Aug. 19, 1973: 30.

———. "State Game and Fish 'Survives' Public Test." *The Knoxville News-Sentinel*. Aug. 2, 1973. 30.

WPA Guide to Tennessee. 1939. Knoxville: University of Tennessee Press, 1986.

Walker, Buss. "Following the Sun." *The Chattanooga Times*. Oct. 3, 1962.

Walker, Hugh. *Donelson's Voyage*. Nashville: *The Nashville Tennessean*, 1980.

Washer, Gene. "Twister Hits Meeting, Smacks Game and Fish Heads." *Clarksville Leaf Chronicle*." May 1971.

Washington, Thomas L. Letter to Federal Communications Commission. Sept. 10, 1975.

"West Tennesseans Split on Conservation Issue at River Hearing." *Memphis Press-Scimitar*. Oct. 7, 1970.

Willard, J. Patrick. "State Ranked Near Bottom On Environment." *Nashville Banner*. Apr. 10, 1990: B1.

Williams, Louis V. Address to 1966 Annual Meeting. Unpublished speech. Oak Ridge, TN. Mar. 26, 1966.

———. "Attaining Objectives by Trial and Error (With Blood, Sweat and Tears)." Address to 1968 Annual Meeting. Unpublished speech. Jackson, TN. Mar 15, 1968.

———. "Conservation and Politics." *The Chattanooga Times*. Feb. 10, 1946: B1.

———. Letter to Herman Baggenstoss. Nov. 8, 1952.

———. *Tennessee's Conservation Revolution (And Some Reforms It Accomplished)*. Maryville, TN.: Brazos Press, 1971.

Williamson, Lonnie. "The Hunter As Conservationist." *The Leader*. Feb. 1986: 13-14.

Wilson, R. A. "Fins, Furs and Feathers for Rod and Gun Lovers." *Nashville Banner*. Dec. 4, 1913.

———. "Fins, Furs and Feathers for Rod and Gun Lovers." Apr. 2, 1922.

———. "Fins, Furs and Feathers." *Nashville Banner*. Dec. 2, 1934: 16.

———. "Fins, Furs and Feathers." *Nashville Banner*. Dec. 24, 1934: 12.

———. "Fins, Furs and Feathers." *Nashville Banner*. 29 Dec. 1935.

———. "Fins, Furs and Feathers." *Nashville Banner*. Mar. 18, 1938.

Winston, Nat, Sr. "The Romantic Possum Hunt. *Tennessee Valley Sportsman*. June 1946: 23 ff.

Winston, Nathaniel T., Jr. Telephone interview. Apr. 5, 1996.

Winfrey, Charles. "Lee Asbury Named Tennessee 'Conservationist of the Year.'" *Clinch Valley Chronicle*. Mar. 4, 1992.

Winter, Linda. "NWF's 50-Year Crusade to Save Wetlands Habitat." *The Leader*. Feb. 1986: 27-28.

Witt, Bob. "Ex-Chariman Roper Urges Less Meddling With G[ame] & F[ish]." *Nashville Banner*. Mar. 21, 1958: 18.

———. "League Voices Opposition to Game and Fish Change." *Nashville Banner*. Mar. 30, 1972.

Wright, Howard M. *Field and Laboratory Technic in Wildlife Management*. Ann Arbor: 1938.

"Wrong Way on Wetlands." *The Commercial Appeal*. Apr. 11, 1990.

Yarbrough, Willard. "Strip Mine Bills' Chances Dim." *The Knoxville News-Sentinel*. Feb. 10, 1967.

Younge, Gary. "'Tree Huggers,' 'Hook-and-Bullet Crows' Link to Halt GOP Policies." *The Commercial Appeal*. Aug. 18, 1996.

"Your Candidates' Stand on Conservation." *Tennessee Wildlife*. Aug. 1938: 8.

Zumbo, Jim. "Bringing Back Our Wild Game." *The Leader*. Feb. 1986: 11-12.

INDEX

Illustrations in **bold** type
Appendix entries in *italics*

Conserving Natural Resources

TENNESSEE
Conservation League

The Tennessee Conservation League relies on the support of people like you. If you are not already a member, why not become one, today?

YES! I want to help the Tennessee Conservation League protect the natural resources of Tennessee.

❑ Please enroll me as a member   **$100 $50 $25**

❑ My check is enclosed (payable to TCL)

❑ MasterCard   ❑ VISA   ❑ American Express

Account #_____ Exp. date _____

Name: _____

Address: _____

City: _____ State: _____ ZIP:_____

Telephone: (_____)_____

The Tennessee Conservation League is a 501(c)(3) nonprofit, tax-exempt organization. Your contribution is tax-deductible, excluding a $1.50 delivery charge for *Tennessee Out-Of-Doors*. Please return this form with your payment to:

Tennessee Conservation League
300 Orlando Avenue
Nashville, Tennessee 37209-3200

Questions? Call (615) 353-1133 or fax to (615) 353-0083.

Order Form

📭   Postal orders: Bench Top Books, 45 Burris Court, Mt. Juliet, Tennessee 37122-2001.

☎   Telephone orders: (615) 758-8647. Please have your VISA or MasterCard ready.

♣   Fax orders: (615) 754-0966. Fax orders must include VISA or MasterCard information.

Please send _____ copies of **Sportsmen United: The Story of the Tennessee Conservation League** to:

Name: _____

Address: _____

City: _____ State: _____ ZIP: _____

Telephone: (_____) _____

☐ This is a gift. Please enclose a gift card to read:

_____

_____ books @ $12.95 each: $ _____

+ 8.25% sales tax on TN orders ($1.07 per book): $ _____

+ $3 shipping per book: $ _____

Total due with order: $ _____

☐ Check enclosed for $ _____, payable to Bench Top Books.

☐ Please charge to my VISA   ☐ MasterCard

Account # _____ Exp. date _____

Name on card: _____

A portion of the proceeds from each sale goes to support the work and programs of the Tennessee Conservation League.

Please allow 2-3 weeks to receive your order. Thank you!

Order Form

Postal orders: Bench Top Books, 45 Burris Court, Mt. Juliet, Tennessee 37122-2001.

Telephone orders: (615) 758-8647. Please have your VISA or MasterCard ready.

Fax orders: (615) 754-0966. Fax orders must include VISA or MasterCard information.

Please send _____ copies of *Sportsmen United: The Story of the Tennessee Conservation League* to:

Name: _____

Address: _____

City: _____ State: _____ ZIP:_____

Telephone: (_____)_____

☐ This is a gift. Please enclose a gift card to read:

_____

_____ books @ $12.95 each: $_____

+ 8.25% sales tax on TN orders ($1.07 per book): $_____

+ $3 shipping per book: $_____

Total due with order: $_____

☐ Check enclosed for $_____, payable to Bench Top Books.

☐ Please charge to my VISA ☐ MasterCard

Account #_____ Exp. date _____

Name on card: _____

A portion of the proceeds from each sale goes to support the work and programs of the Tennessee Conservation League.

Please allow 2-3 weeks to receive your order. Thank you!